Information Technology in Developing Human Resources

INFORMATION TECHNOLOGY IN DEVELOPING HUMAN RESOURCES

DR. CH. SEETHA RAM
Ph.D.
Assistant Professor
Gitam Institute of Management
GITAM University
Visakhapatnam (A.P.)

DEEP & DEEP PUBLICATIONS PVT. LTD.
F-159, Rajouri Garden, New Delhi - 110 027

INFORMATION TECHNOLOGY IN
DEVELOPING HUMAN RESOURCES

ISBN 978-81-8450-265-7

Printed in India at MAYUR ENTERPRISES
WZ Plot No. 3, Gujjar Market, Tihar Village, New Delhi - 110 018

Published by DEEP & DEEP PUBLICATIONS PVT. LTD.
F-159, Rajouri Garden, New Delhi - 110 027 • Phone : 25435369, 25440916
E-mail : ddpbooks@yahoo.co.in · ddpubs@gmail.com
Showroom :
2/13, Ansari Road, Daryaganj, New Delhi - 110 002 • Telefax : 23245122

Contents

Preface

The world today is witnessing a new kind of revolution—the Information Revolution—ushered by technology. This revolution is in fact far more sweeping than any other revolution in history in its reach and influence, bringing fundamental changes in all aspects of our life. Information Technology is the engine used to drive useful information systems. This includes computer, software, internet, intranet and telecommunication systems. Information Technology provides the means for collection, storing, encoding, processing, analyzing, transmitting, receiving, and printing text, audio, or video information. This universal applicability of information systems has created unprecedented demand for qualified IT professionals. The projected demand for trained IT professionals is estimated at over 5,00,000 per year in India itself. All over the world information technology has become the most important part of all technological curricula. This book is written to meet the requirement of the modern curricula. The main objective is to teach IT concepts to people who will be the end-users and to those who need some insight on information technology. Our approach is to strike a balance between the why and the how of IT use. I wrote this book for business school students who wanted an in-depth look at how business firms use information technologies and systems to achieve corporate objectives. Information systems are one of the major tools available to business manager for achieving operational excellence, developing new products and services, improving decision-making, and achieving competitive advantage. When interviewing potential employees, business firms often look for new hires who know how to use information systems and technologies for achieving bottom line business results. Regardless of whether you are in accounting, finance, management, operations management, marketing or information systems major, the knowledge and information you find in this book will be valuable throughout your business career.

UNIQUE FEATURES

- Student-friendly, the book is written in a clear, concise, and lucid manner.
- Independent thinking and research n the subject imparts a practitioner perspective to it and makes the text thoroughly enjoyable.
- Emphasis is laid on practical application of theory, all ideas and concepts are presented with clear examples.
- Historical perspective describes components, systems, or events from the past.
- Text is well structured and well supported with suitable diagrams.
- Coverage of new and emerging topics in the field of information technology sector such as electronic data interchange, Blue tooth technology, and mobile communication.
- Describes major applications of information technology and their strategic implications for business and social activities.
- Inter-chapter dependencies are kept to a minimum.
- Chapter objectives, summary at the end of each chapter, and review questions.
- A comprehensive index at the end of the book for quick access to the topics.

TARGET AUDIENCE

- Primary usage as a textbook for students of BBM, BBA (H), PGDCA, BCA, BE, BIT, B.Sc. (IT), B.Tech., M.Sc. (IT), MCA and MBA courses offered by computer science, computer engineering, and management departments in colleges and universities.
- Also useful as a textual resource in vocational training courses offered by many colleges.
- As a self-study guide for non-computer science professionals.

This book serves the requirements of both students and professional. In fact it is aimed at all those people who desire to have knowledge of Information Systems.

Visakhapatnam DR. CH. SEETHA RAM

Abbreviations

ACARDCD : Advisory Council for Applied Research and Development Cabinet Office
ASP : Active Server Page
BARS : Behavioral Anchored Rating Scale
BAS : Business Analysis System
CAD : Computer Aided Design
CAI : Computer Assisted Instruction
CALC : Computer Assisted Learning Center
CAM : Computer Aided Manufacturing
CATS : Computerized Auxiliary Tomography Scans
CBM : Computer-based Multimedia
CBT : Computer-based Training
CCS : Computer and Communication System
CDTV : Compact Disk Tele Vision
CET : Center of Education Technology
CMI : Computer Managed Instruction
COLLIT : Common Wealth Learning Literacy
COM : Computer Output Medium
CPT : Computer Process Technology
CPU : Central Processing Unit
CRAES : Computerized Robotical Assisted Endoscopic Surgery
CRLP : Computer-based Rural Literacy Project
CST : Computer Storage Technology
CT : Communication Technology
DAE : Directorate of Adult Education
DBMS : Data Base Management System
DE : Distance Education
DECU : Development of Education, Communication Unit
DINK : Double Income No Kinds

DSL	:	Digital Subscriber Line
DSS	:	Decision Support System
ED	:	Executive Development
EDI	:	Electronic Data Interchange
EDUSAT	:	Education through Satellite
EFA	:	Education for All
EPR	:	Electronic Patient Records
ERP	:	Enterprise Resource Planning
ESS	:	Executive Support Systems
FTC	:	Farmer Training Centers
GIS	:	Geographic Information System
HAA	:	Human Asset Accounting
HD	:	Human Development
HDI	:	Human Development Index
HK	:	Human Knowledge
HR	:	Human Resource
HRD	:	Human Resource Development
HRIS	:	Human Resource Information System
HRM	:	Human Resource Management
IADP	:	Intensive Agricultural District Programme
ICBI	:	International Computer Driving License
ICDS	:	Integrated Child Development Scheme
ICT	:	Information Communication Technology
ICVT	:	Interactive Computer Video Technology
IGNOU	:	Indira Gandhi National Open University
IMM	:	India Millennium Mission
IPCL	:	Improved Pace and Contact of Learning
ISRO	:	Indian Space Research Organization
IT	:	Information Technology
ITP	:	Interactive Training Programme
JDCP	:	Jhabua Development Communication Project
JIT	:	Job Instructive Training
KM	:	Knowledge Management
KVK	:	Krushi Vigyan Kendra
LAN	:	Local Area Network
MBO	:	Management By Objective
MIS	:	Management Information System
NARP	:	National Agricultural Research Project
NCERT	:	National Council of Education Research and Training
NCMS	:	Network Communication Management System
NDDB	:	National Dairy Development Board

NIC	:	National Information Centre
NLM	:	National Literacy Mission
NTL	:	National Training Laboratory
OCLC	:	Online Computer Library Centre
OCTAPAC	:	Openness Confrontation Trust Authenticity Pro-action Autonomy and Collaboration
OD	:	Organizational Development
ODES	:	Open Distance Education System
OL	:	Open Learning
OLAP	:	Online Analytical Processing
PREAL	:	Project in Radio Education for Adult Literacy
PSP	:	Personal Software Process
QC	:	Quality Circles
RDCS	:	Rural Development Communication System
SAME	:	See Anywhere Map Everywhere
SITE	:	Satellite Instructional Television Experiment
SRC	:	State Resource Centres
TA	:	Transactional Analysis
TCLC	:	Technology-based Community Learning Centre
TLC	:	Total Literacy Campaigns
UK	:	United Kingdom
UNO	:	United Nations Organizations
USA	:	United States of America
USDLA	:	United States Distance Learning Association
VCM	:	Virtual Classroom Models
VSAT	:	Very Small Aperture Terminal
WTO	:	World Trade Organization
WWW	:	World Wide Web

Introduction

Information and Information Technology are the key drivers of the information age. The information age has ushered in a knowledge-based industrial revolution. The businesses in this era are networked and use it to service, grow and thrive in a highly competitive environment. Marketing executives experience, radical changes in advertising, real time promotion of new products, manufacturing and production executives face changes in EDI (Electronic Data Inter-channel) and in supply chain management and integrated logistics finance executive appreciate development in electronic currency, electronic payments, e-banking, buying and selling products and services in the electronic world, etc.[1] Now all business and Industrial organizations are dynamic. Infect economic liberalization, privatization and globalization made business firms further dynamic. In other words, they have been changing confusingly in terms of technology, type of business, products, services, organizational strength and the like. There charges invariably demand for the development of human resources.

With globalization and economic liberalization we are witnessing swift and often-unpredictable changes in business. We have to moot the challenges by innovations, technological advances, organizational restructuring and new ways of thinking to service and grow. A strategy to grow with high-tech is to use the computer in designing manufacturing, delivering managing and evaluating learning experiences. All proactive organizations use computer as training methodology for imparting new information and skills.[2]

Information Technology (IT) the latest industry buzz, is fast becoming an important part of the corporate arsenal and psyche use of hi-tech communication system is breaking the barriers of geographical distances and giving way to formation of global village. Evolution of computers and Internet has contributed a lot to speed up the entire business communication system. In such a digital scenario organizations that are trying to be global should ensure that they are competent enough to make use of IT for their excellence. They should prepare their employees also accordingly to adapt to the change. In the previous two decades many organizations across the globe realized the significance of Human Resource—IT amalgamation in growth of the organizations and invested in a big way to implement IT leveraged Human Resource systems.[3]

There is growing concern about widening disparities between information-rich and information-poor, countries. Widespread illiteracy and lack of basic education are among the key factors contributing to the digital divide. The task of making the vast population of illiterate adults literate is very daunting. However, there is hardly any serious debate and discussion on how to harness the benefits of Information Communication Technology's for providing literacy and basic education to the large population of unschooled youth and adults in the developing countries.[4]

It was unthinkable until few years ago that Internet and multimedia kind of thing will become an important medium in the education system adding new value in teaching and learning by covering wide spectrum of subjects, objects and locations.[5]

To put it in the cultural context in which it is occurring the Information Technology revolution is concomitant with the fundamental change in the way we organize our lives. The social scenario is no longer what it used to be. Higher mobility dissolution of national boundaries merging of cultural Identities has led to the emergence of the view of the world as a global village. A shift in gender roles has led to more women joining the work force. The emergence of DINK (Double Income No Kinds) families has made large amounts of disposable incomes available to households which are being spent on more "life style goods" companies are falling over each other to deliver better and faster products and services to the consumer who is finally living up to the capitalist description of 'king'.[6]

In the era of globalization, Indian agriculture gained a new look on business venture, which focused on developing profitable and sustainable agricultural enterprises to meet the increasing internal food demands and export. This approach calls for building farmers' capacity to absorb and integrate new scientific knowledge and practices with their indigenous wisdom to create and maintain sustainable enterprises (Swaminathan, 2000). In this context the extension system should reorient its roles and responsibilities and equip its human resources to meet emerging challenges. Training is crucial continuous input for any efficient and effective transfer of technology system. The Indian agricultural extension system, being the largest of its kind in the world is facing innumerable challenges in training its vast human resources base.[7]

Human being has evolved from agriculture age to industrial age to what is currently being termed as information age. It is technology that has made a marked contribution to this evolution technology itself can be said to be a direct consequences of education. Also technology affects the education delivered, there by resulting in a cyclic relationship where in education brings about technology and technology enhances education.

Information technology is the buzzword of the 21st century. With incredible finesse, it has changed the very nature of how we share, store and disseminate information. Two vital dimensions, that of increased volume and a speed, provided by Information Technology have captivated all human minds world over, irrespective of geographical boundaries keeping in view the growth of IT in the one hand and developments in teaching, learning and research. On the other, all concerned with higher education to day are attempting to grasp how IT could help in modernizing teaching research and learning.[8]

In every change in any of the components of a society a change occurs in the entire social fabric. Sometimes it is slow and sometimes it is fast. The rate depends on the vibration of the external components. However, small or big these changes ultimately affect every sphere of the total environment—natural or social. Now IT has emerged as a big stimulating force it is strongly influencing the human mind and its through process, the society and in the end the entire world IT has enhanced its capacity of accumulating and storing information. All the information of a library can now be stored in one's own Personal Computer and access to those information is matter of click of the mouse only. Thus information is matter of click of the mouse only. Thus information communication technology has a long recurring influence on the total education system.[9]

If the Shakespearean thought of transitory nature in true, i.e., "All this world is a stage where men and women are merely players, they have their entrance and exist. . . ." Then comes the question: What is permanent. The simple answer is thoughts; actions and deeds of mortal people may be permanent. Hence the documentation of human endeavors from time immemorial have taken shape in to various faculties viz, History, Arts, Science, Technology, Philosophy, etc. The accumulation of fact about material and men in various branches of human development leads to data, data properly organized become information. The rigorous training of gathering information and processing some purposeful and meaningful and product by developing some human faculty and understand in the accepted methods of information distribution leads to human knowledge.[10]

In the context of global economy and competitive markets, knowledge is a key factor contribution to economic development. Therefore, human resource development through education and training has become a key component within overall strategy for economic restructuring in developing countries. The future of global economy and democratic polity in the 21st century is likely to depend on skilled and educated workers and enlightened citizens. It was the world conference on Education For All (EFA) held in Jomtien (Thailand) in 1990 that high tightened critical importance of addressing the learning needs of all children, youth and adults who have been excluded and un reached by the existing system of formal and informal education, and contributed to building global consensus around the goals of EFA. In the context of globalization, basic learning skills and competences are necessary not only for children, but also for unschooled and illiterate youth and adults, who are valuable human resources of every society.[11]

Information Communication Technology (ICT) has become most widely used buzzword of the computer industry. It has affected all walks of life in one-way or another ICT is the modern science of gathering, storing, manipulation, processing and communicating desired types of information in a specific environment. Computer technology and communication technology are the two main supporting pillars of this technology and the impact of these two in the information storage and dissemination is vital. It is impossible to deny its importance in the educational, cultural, agricultural, scientific and technical disciplines of the world. Information needs are increasing day-by-day and in the present day society, every person is intending to be information-oriented.[12]

1.1 THE CONCEPT OF HRD

The concept of Human Resource Development (HRD) has been defined by economists, social scientists, industrialists, managers and other academicians from different perspectives. In a broad sense, HRD is the process of increasing knowledge skills and capabilities of all the people in a given society. In the national context, HRD is process by which the people in various groups are helped to acquire new competence continuously so as to make them more and more self-reliant and simultaneously develop a sense of pride in their country.[13] In economic terms, it means accumulation of human capital and its effective utilization for the development of economy. In political terms HRD prepares people for a active participation in the political process. From the social and cultural points of view, the development of human resources enriches life.[14] Several scholars have defined this concept. Some of them are as follows.

According to Nadler, HRD means an organizational learning experience, within a period of time with an objective of producing the possibility of performance change.[15]

"HRD is the process of increasing knowledge, skills, capabilities and positive work attitude and values of all people working at all levels in a business under taking."[16]

"HRD is development-oriented planning effort in the personal area which is basically concerned with the development of human resources in the organization for improving the existing capabilities of the corporate and individual goals".[17]

HRD is the advancement of knowledge, skills, discipline and will of the individuals For enabling them behave and perform in the manner in whom the in which the industries, organizations and sections prosper by fulfilling their objectives fully.

The definitions of HRD in terms of its components have ranged from the most comprehensive to the narrowest. The most comprehensive has been given by Myrdal who has enumerated eight components 1. Food and nutrition, 2. Clothing, 3. Housing and sanitation, 4. Health facilities, 5. Education, 6. Information media, 7. Energy consumption, and 8. Transport. The narrowest definition is given by the world bank which includes only three items—Health, Nutrition and Education. The latter definition has been used most widely. It has also been widely objected to for its narrow scope.

According to one of its recent reports: basic needs as understood in this report include two elements. First, they include certain minimum requirements of a family for private consumption, adequate food, shelter and clothing are obviously included as and even basic certain house holds equipment and furniture. Secondly, they include essentially services provided by and for the community such as safe drinking water, sanitation, public transport, health and education facilities, however even ILO was not able to integrate the two parts of the strategy.

HRD is a process in which the employees of an organization are continuously helped in a planned way to:

(a) Acquire and sharpen their capabilities to perform various obligations, tasks and functions associated with and related to their present or future expected roles,
(b) Develop their capabilities their individuals so that they may be able to discover their potentialities and exploit them fully for their own and organization not development purposes, and
(c) To develop an organizational culture when superior subordinate relationships team work and collaboration among different sub units are strong and contribute to the organizational wealth, dynamism and pride for the employees.[18]

Government culture is an area to which any government servant aware of Human Resource Development will have to pay particular attention. Over the years, systems might have been developed which discouraged creativity. The constant pressure of rules and fear of audit may encourage doing things correctly rather than doing the correct things.[19]

India signed the WTO treaty in 1996 along with 125 members of the UNO; consequently trade barriers were removed and there is a free flow of trade both ways. Now, India is at an advantage to export its agricultural goods and textiles to capture world markets. Liberalization in other countries also benefits India in the areas of software, construction, consultancy, medical services, manpower export, etc. While these are the avenues open to India, the country should adopt a HRD strategy and implement it effectively.[20]

International HRD experts have outlined a few trends, which will shape and effect the future of HRD. The computer revolution, adult education, increasing internationalization of business, transformation of the work force to the knowledge workers, the increasing sophistication of the buyers and sensitivity to the facts and the interdependence of the private and public sectors are all a part of the future that thinkers and futurists have visualized.[21]

The HRD is of recent origin. Though the functions have been carried out in various forms and ways for a long time, HRD became handy to the field of management only recently. Enabling capabilities in organizations is one of the hallmarks of HRD functions. For effective functioning of any organization human resource is considered is one of the key elements. When task, structure and technology are available, it is the human resource, which makes a complete circle of production. Human resource exploit the potential of all other available resources and are treated as highly critical and significant in contributions relating to effective organizational performance.[22]

Even at the national level governments are realizing the importance of HRD, and the government of India has shown the seriousness in attaching the importance to HRD by creating a separate ministry of HRD. In a sense HRD treats human as resource, which is instrumental in attaining organizational goals. The pivotal crux of the evolution of HRD is currently in the process of a radical change in farms of treating "Humans" as end rather than means to an end i.e., a resource. The basic change in focus has given birth to a new term Human Development. (HD).[23]

Human resource development is essentially an integral part of HRM. Its major focus is on extracting extra-ordinary performance from an ordinary employee by enhancing his/her physical, mental, social and spiritual well-being and enabling that individual to derive maximum level of life satisfaction. In this sense, the Human resource function is beginning to play a role much broader in scope much stronger in its impact and much more permanent in its effect.[24]

HRD is increasingly become necessary that human rights and developments considerations guide people related approaches at work. Many organizations have begun to respond positively to these societal developments, for the growing interest in HRD in India, namely, the changing industrial scenario. HRD might have started as an imported fad in some organizations in the eighties, it has now turned in to an essential condition for maintaining organizational effectiveness and competitiveness.[25]

1.2 CONCEPT OF INFORMATION TECHNOLOGY

The concept of Information Technology (IT) helps to increase knowledge, skills, capabilities, positive work attitude, and values at both organizational and societal levels. In India and abroad, most of the organizations have implemented recent trends in Training and Development through Information Technology to achieve the organization objectives. The worldwide organizations introduced several information technology measures to improve the efficiency of the employees and quality of customer satisfaction and there by enhance effectiveness of the organizations.

Information is the most valuable asset for any organization or institute. The growth of the Internet has greatly influenced the case and speed with which information is shared. Today's challenge is to make the information accessible. A typical information processing cycle consists of five steps namely input, processing, output, storage, retrieval, distribution and communication. Information Technology is the combination of different fields such as information science, computer technology, communication technology and management science.

Information Technology is the science and skills of all aspects of computing, data storage and communications. It is a new rapidly growing area that is radically changing the world by making possible new ways of doing business-making entertainment and creating art.[26]

The phrase Information Technology refers to the creation gathering processing storage and delivery of information and the process and devices that make all this possible information technology can do at least three things. Information Technology can process raw data in to useful information, information technology can recycle processed information and use it as data in another processing step and information technology can package information in a new form so its easier to understand, more attractive, or more useful.

Information technology stands firmly on two legs hardware and software. The term hardware is applied to any of the physical equipment in a system, usually containing electronic components and performing some kind of function in information processing. Hardware includes not only the computer and devices such as screens printers but also all the elements used to tie information systems together. Software is instructions that guide the hardware in the performance of its duties there is slogan button floating around that makes this distinction very clear. "Hardware: the part of the computer that you can kick. If you can only curse at it, its software".[27]

There is no single definition on Information Technology today that is universally accepted. Often the term is applied to computers and computer based systems. However, the roots of the word technology suggest that it is a "means to an ends".

Information Technology can be formally defined as it is the study design development implementation, support or management of computer-based information systems, particularly software applications and computer Hardware.

Another definition of Information Technology, "the technology which supports activities involving the creation storage, manipulation and communication of information together with their related methods, management of applications".

IT professionals have to integrate many of these techniques to satisfy the needs of society. Nowadays the IT entered almost all fields such as business, industry, science, engineering, home and entertainment, education and training, etc.[28]

1.3 IMPORTANCE OF INFORMATION TECHNOLOGY

Information is a valuable and costly asset that must be planned, protected, preserved and controlled as other valuable assets such as people, money, machines, facilities, etc. A major shift of the power of technologies is to focus on the power of information content. As we reach the threshold of 21st century, managing information involves professional approach to deal with the global dynamic interactive environment with the new policy of liberalization and globalization the professional in an information-based society. Information Technology is the technology portrayed as a major force for managerial and organizational changes.[29]

The world today is in transition from industrial age to information age. Computer and communication systems combined to be called as Information Technology are critical in the operation of every business today. The IT revolution is making a tremendous impact on the industry and trade by relentless technology innovation, massive growth in computer power world wide net works and ever-growing electronic factories. The convergence of telecom and computers in networks has further advanced the scope of communication equipment by bringing a wide range of improved products.[30]

The relationship between information and socio economic development was ignored until the 1970s in many developed countries and is still not recognized even today is some of the developing countries. Nonetheless information is one of the major yardsticks to measure socio-economic development of the country and hence its effective management using the latest technological tools in prerequisite for any nation. Information Technologies now the hold potential to change our working and learning patterns, our business, social relationships, academic research institutions and even our cultural spheres. As a part of IT telecommunication has become a major business and its hold the key for the growing and emerging service industries for all countries of the world.[31]

Efficient utilization of all resources is essential to maintain good academic quality with cost effectiveness. Truly collaborative knowledge management system using Internet in naturally suited for ensuring this in Open Distance Education System (ODES) due to its wide and low cost access without any geographic, distance time barrier. With Internet, ODES can easily ensure quality education for all, with cost effectiveness, at the doorsteps of learners.[32]

The use of Information Technology promises improved performance for organizations. The benefits of information technology can usually be measured in terms of enhanced processing speed, transmission rates and access time. The introduction of micro and minicomputers had enabled greater decentralization of information systems. Recent innovations such as Local Area Network (LAN) make possible the linking of task groups and managerial work processes. These capabilities likely to impact culture, structure and work practices.[33]

The regional dimensions of growth of the Indian economy are assuming increasing relevance in the context of the progressive diffusion of structural reforms at the sub-national level growth is getting increasingly assessed in terms of durable improvement in the regional growth profiles in which the interface between public policies for accelerating development and standards of living is the greatest. The information technology sector in India is important not just because of this performance and potential, but because these factors have influenced the policy environment in India. There are other issues raised in the context of Indian regional development, viz., fiscal, infrastructure and HRD.[34]

Several disabilities can be effectively dealt with using conventional devices, in the last few years scientists and IT engineers have developed special devices for the physically challenged that are much more sophisticated than traditional ones. Many of these devices are dependent on computers and computer technologies.[35]

Review of Research and Literature

P. Seeturaman and Siva Kumar[36] identified efficient needs to the training for human resource development in agricultural and rural areas through teleconferencing technology. This study indicated that, various countries like U.S.A, Ireland and India utilizing the teleconferencing facility by the urban and rural people Viz., audio conferencing, video conferencing, computer conferencing for developing human resources for agricultural and food development with technology. Nitin V. Patil and Damodar Suar[37] were conducted study on computer-based training. This type of training has been very influenced and effective by the quality of human computer interface, and studied on gestalt psychology of perception text and graphics combination, He stated that the computer based training created open learner culture in the organization.

T. Raju, Sangeetha Mohandas[38] were elaborated knowledge management through new technology seeds are right information to the right person, information technology store human intelligence and experience, and they also discussed on IT creativity and innovation for achievement of E-Business strategy goal. R.G. Desai[39] has studied major aspects of regional areas for economic growth of Indian culture with support of information technology. This study also represented raising issues in Indian rural development viz., fiscal, infrastructure and human resource development, penetration of IT in the state economies in the country, and also he has identified five parameters rated viz. network access, network learning, network society, network economy and e-governance.

P.N. Singh[40] recommended for the next millennium function of human resource development viz. talker, doer, plodder and controller. These all four are arranged as window for development of human resources. This study also presented powerful management tools for achieving objectives in the future millennium viz., people behaviour, follower, believeness, directing, responsibility and goal setting. D. Mukhopadhyaya[41] stated that, Information Communication Technology covers and controls some areas of the society and human live. This study represented components of quality education through information communication technology viz., easy communication, rapid access to information, easy access to library and databases, worldwide news, health forecast, weather forecast, health information and suggestions to the information society. He also described new issues and implications to the social and educational forecasting, these are education for all, training to teachers, accessing and processing knowledge.

Sheela Singh[42] has recommended the new directions for human resource development in public enterprises, viz. physical technology to information technology, capital centred economy to human centred economy, material growth to sustainable development, hierarchical to decentralized administration organizations and conflict to cooperative working relations. He also recommended flexible decision-making, effective changes, global perspective, consider time and hard work for developing human resources in enterprises. G.P. Pandey and Joya Chakraborthy[43] were stated that information technology has led to the various electronic-based innovations in the field of higher education viz., teletext and video text in the 21st century, identified close relationship between information technology and education. Education components are teaching, learning and researching, IT developing the education knowledge through electronically viz., www, Internet, research and development.

C. Ramachandra Prabhu[44] studied new challenges to the technical teacher in information technology environment. Impact of IT is bringing a threat to the identity of our unique Indian lifestyle, culture, values, and individuality. He also studied different roles played by the technical teacher in Indian and global perspective viz., to control, to harmonize, to remove, to accept and to decide. Dr. M.P. Gupta[45] stressed that electronic education is important device for developing human resources. He also described that training is potential to revolutionized business and executive education and it is develop the country economic growth.

Prof. V.D. Dudeja[46] elaborated need of information technology for industrial growth through optimum utilization and development of human resources. He also studied different aspects relating to HR challenges of IT, human resources aspects take easy route, actions required to achieve transformation along with enabling computing technology, and challenges are mentioned viz., purposeful direction, balance between credibility and conformity, growing technological and increasing competitive criticism. N. Upadyaya[47] studied benefits of computer-oriented system. This system helps in the organization efficiency for increasing interactions between top management and lower level management. He also studied efficiency of decision making through management information system, etc. The main objective of this study was eliminating the human element to computer element for more time for management objective decisions.

Dr. Neelu Rohmetra,[48] suggested four human resource development models for achieving organizational excellence, these models are stressed on individual development, team development, improving inter group relationships and integration of all the subsystems through planning and goal setting. This study suggested various aspects for development of organization excellence viz., developing organizational health, improving decision making skills, diagnostic skills and creating healthy open climate. Dr. P.L. Rao[49] focused on increasing the knowledge, skill, capabilities of human resources supporting with SWOT analysis. This study also focused on utilization of human resources as well as natural resources for developing the economic growth of the country in the new millennium.

Prof. Harish Kumar and Alpana Mishra[50] discussed on human resources leveraging through information technology. He stressed that, performance appraisal, effective training programmes; communication techniques are improving by the IT only in HR environment. P.J. Chatterjee[51] developing the human resources supporting with information technology in the new millennium. This study also identified some issues for achieving the potential knowledge in the information age viz., human resources information system, integrated computerized centralized employee database and work places. This study also given challenges for human resources professionals these are, skill development, working knowledge, dual career templates to suit the generalist have to modify with technology.

According to Ajay Kumar Singh,[52] human resources development basically depending on two aspects. One is formation of human capabilities and another is the use of acquired capabilities. This study also given recommendations to 21st century viz., most important perspectives is Indian Ethos for developing human wisdom, cooperation is powerful tool for team work, spirituality rises religion. According to A.K. Singh, Ethos is "the characteristic spirit and beliefs of community people". M.G.K. Murthy[53] described that global organization design framing and implementing organizational strategies. Human resources development is the integrated mechanism in the globalization. He also described global organizational levels viz., corporate, divisional and workplace initiated and achieved by HRD.

Dr. V.B. Dudeja[54] stated that information technology objectives improving operational efficiency, faster massage delivery, improving security and accelerating services to the customers/suppliers. This study mainly focused on challenges and opportunities of information technology in new millennium. He discussed different aspects that is i.e., caste society, and use of source resource and opportunity employment. Peter. F. Drucker[55] focused on the technology, people and organizations/firms through information. He stated that engulf education to the people and health care are essential powerful tools in the new information age.

Dr. R.P. Saxena[56] stated that information technology is being broadened through convergence of three technologies viz., computers, communication networks and consumer electronics. Modern view of management information system and decision support system are two combinations in the organizations for achieving global environment objectives. Saritha Singh and Jai B.P. Sinha[57] were stated that the human resources development involves in various aspects of the organization i.e., mission, developing vision, setting goals, concrete objectives, designing systems and procedures, and cultural settings provides an employee work habits and growth. They were identified in Indian perspective given more preference to the hierarchy type of organization enthusiastically implemented to the effective administration.

Dr. R.D. Pathak, S.K. Sripathi, Zafer Hussian and Dr. Sushil[58] were described about the information technology application in the business scenario viz., administrative tools, technical tools, integrated information systems, integrated manufacturing systems and convergence. These all are considered and coming under business applications. This study also has identified various information technology trends involving for rapid development. Reema Khurana[59] examined the two aspects for education delivery in the Information Technology. They are fixed education delivery and flexible education delivery. This study identified possibilities for education delivery through information technology. These possibilities make from instructive style of teaching to constructive style of teaching, among them computer-based training and television lecture is very convenient to the students as well as teacher.

According to Dr. Rajeswari Narendra and Dr. V. Narendra,[60] were stated Information Technology is deals with many aspects, i.e. socio-cultural, psychological, professional, economical, educational, health and medical. This study also described the relationship of information technology and human resource development. This relationship of the both playing vital and crucial role for organizational development to faster in various values. These both are participating in the organization for increase the various values viz., Openness, Confrontation, Trust, Authenticity, Pro-Action, Autonomy and Collaboration (OCTAPAC) for developing the organization culture.

Dr. Usha Mujoo-Munshi and Dr. Indervir Malhan[61] were studied the problems of administration through information technology in India. These problems are: human resource development, information literacy, telecommunications and power, adoption and absorption of technology. This study also presented, in Indian perspective to forecasting the connecting the rural village through information communication technology and to increase the country capital to this subject. This study also identified the reasons for lack of utilization of resources.

Ilapatel[62] stated that, technology, digitalization, convergence of radio, electronic convergence of radio, television and computer are increasing interest of the people on world wide distance education through information communication technology. This study also stated that, the using of information technology in education learning programmes for developing human resource of illiterate people through the National Literacy Mission, computer-based rural literacy project, common wealth of literacy project.

S.Y. Sree Kumar[63] evaluated that the development of human resources through distance education also helps to agriculture production and efficiency in using technology. The people are obtaining the education programmes through correspondence, satellite communication and radio for developing their human resources. The information technology shows good impact on HRD. Jack Fiorito and William Boss[64] discussed information technology has involved and used for potential improvements of the organizations. Information technology involves in administration, staffing, coordination and implementation of internal and external environment of the unions. The information technology had involved in organization function for improve the efficiency of the unions. This study also observed the different uses, which are obtaining through the information technology.

Rozhan Othman[65] stated that, information technology is participating in different activities for facilitating to effective communication in the organizations. This study also stated that information technology used for bridge the gap between inter-personal and intra-personal organizations for achieve the integration possibility. Ilapated[66] described that Information Technology is very most powerful tool for literacy programmes in India. Radio and televisions have been used for literacy programmes to development of human resources of the rural, and urban areas in the country. This study also observed that the audio-visual medium has been also used for distance education at higher levels. S.L. Mahajan[67] stated that, Information Technology has developed with the support of various factors, i.e. social, political, economic, unemployment and administration. He also stated that the Indians have been used satellite communication, radio, television and audio-visual programmes in distance education for development of human resources.

Dharam Kumar and Pardeep Rai[68] were viewed that an information technology play a key role in the delivery of distance education through, the computer for learning various courses like computer assisted instruction, computer managed instruction, computer mediated education, email, bulletin boards, Internet and w.w.w. etc. Manoj Killedar[69] has studied that, the information technology programmes are included in different aspects, i.e., business life, learning and teaching, E-learning. He has offered the excellent possibilities to transfer from the teacher centric education system to learner centric education system. This study also studied the generations of distance education system viz., external students, correspondence education, audio, video, radio, television and teleconferencing, web-enabled education, On-line education for developing knowledge and capabilities.

Rainer Ommerborn and Rudolf Schuemer[70] studied advantages and disadvantages of computers in disabled distance education programmes, computer is given valuable information to the disabled students through internet, e-mail, hear phone and web enabled education for developing the human resources. This study also identified the several problems in disabled distance education i.e., refer to cost, strain to eyes and wrists, lack of training, etc.

Teena Gomes[71] has evaluated the Indian IT companies have tried to improve the quality of education through information technology to the rural people in our country for development of human resources. This study also stated that the IT companies are established IT colleges for developing humans resources to the urban and rural people.

Deepak Kalan[72] evaluated, the information technology programmes are helpful to the disabled persons for development of human resources. He also stated that computer programmes and devices are available to allowed "Braille" text to the blind persons. This study also viewed that physically challenged persons, i.e., brain damage candidates using alternative communication system through computer Morse code, the deaf people using computer for hearing impaired in sign language, finger spelling, lip-reading through microphone, and selected word by the deaf person on computer it indicated correct pronunciation is displayed as a pattern on the screen.

Dr. O.P. Mishra and Dr. D. Ganguli[73] have described fastest methods in training i.e., case study, exercise, application project, in basket training, business games, sensitivity training, role playing, interactive lecture, simulation, games and programmed instruction. And this study also focused on current trends in training for development of human resources. These trends electronic technologies are i.e., computer, videotapes, Interactive Computer Video Technology (ICVT), broadcast television, cable television, capacitance Disc, computer-aided instruction, interactive system. Interactive video, tele-text and tele-conferencing, etc.

Manoj T. Thomas[74] has elaborated the lecture method was pedagogical tool for developing human resources. And he also discussed the comparison between lecture method and other methods, i.e. case method, programmed instruction, role-play, simulation. He was suggested that lecture method is best method than the other above indicated methods for human resource development.

Kirti Shiva Kumar and Vijai Caprihan,[75] have suggested In-Basket, is the excellent training technique for developing human resources in the present and they were also described the advantages and disadvantages about the technique of the basket training.

T. Venkateswarlu[76] analyzed, the success of business development with support of four aspects, i.e. supply chain, capital base, market presence and global mindset. The study also stated that information technology should also increasing the business consumption, production employment, and high gross of national income in developing countries for the achievement of global business targets.

Pravind Prashant[77] discussed that the quality education for management graduates delivery through technology, i.e. slide projectors overhead projectors, LCD projectors audio cassettes, Radios, video cassettes, video disc technology, cable TV, SINET, video conferencing, Floppy diskettes, CD-rom Internet, and Direct to home.

Seema Singh and Anil Kumar[78] were stated that an information technology is effective tool for sustainable agriculture in India and also they were identified few problems which are arise in the implementation of sustainable agriculture process through information technology.

According to F.L. Lobo[79] elaborated dimensions for training in electronic age, these are three zones viz., technical training in hardware and software, training in application of tools in the operations and the managerial aspects.

Mauli Halan[80] has suggested the success of development process through information technology i.e., satellites Geo-serve net, distributed spatial visualisation and streaming system. He also described the satellite mapping technology; geographical information system, remote sensing, positioning, and navigation systems are measuring the geographical encouragement situations. And also on the globe easy communication through SAME (See Anywhere Map Everywhere) is network centric, 3d spatial visualization, streaming system, listening with satellites viz., phone calls, fax, e-mail and telex messages sent anywhere for bridge the gap between the people in the world.

Garima Khanna[81] has elaborated, satellites to be used to connect remote areas for development of business activities, transition of communication through the radio, television and telephone and satellite can be used in estimation of wealth position. Ranjit Mettoth[82] identified learning of education process is still going on out of the classroom through the campus wide wireless local area network (LAN) for development of human resources to the students. This study also mentioned about the LAN has participated in the several aspects in education level for the students as well as teachers. The aspects are provide home page to the each student or teacher, creating board time table syllabus.

Preethi, J.[83] has described the solutions sees to be remote education programmes for development of human resources through various information technology concepts. This study also accounted the several methods for electronic teaching in learning process.

First, Education through Satellite (EDUSAT) will provides the information access to the excellent education at an affordable rate for both students and teachers in every institution in the country. Second, is DIRECWAY providing distance education programs for executives in global perspective. Third, is an I-Shiksha programme helps teacher for the maintenances of students in rural and underprivileged Government schools. Fourth is ENCORE is used to managing the student administration in institutes.

1.4 NEED FOR THE STUDY

As per the foregoing analysis of the review of literature on information technology in developing human resources, the work done by the researchers in the subject was scant in India. Most of the research studies are focused on human resources training and development, electronic education training, teleconferencing and computer based training, etc. The research in the area of role of IT in developing human resources has not been given much emphasis by the researchers in India. A comprehensive study on the "Role of Information Technology in Developing Human Resources" in the post liberalization, any researcher did not attempt globalization and information age so far.

The present study is intended to cover the research gap in the existing literature on information technology in developing human resources. The study helps for effective and efficient implementation of information technology concepts and the need for development of human competencies/resources viz., knowledge, skills, discipline and will through different Information Technology programmes.

1.5 OBJECTIVES OF THE STUDY

The study was carried out with the following main objectives:

1. To examine existing methods and techniques of human resource development in India.
2. To study the role of information technology in developing human resources in different sections of the society.
3. To assess the impact of information technology on different sections of the society.
4. To analyse perceptions of respondents regarding effectiveness of information technology on the development of human resources.

1.6 METHODOLOGY OF THE STUDY

The present study is confined to the selected respondents in the different sections of the society viz., students, employees, business people, professional people (like doctors, engineers, lawyers, teachers) and rural people, who are residing in Visakhapatnam which was popularly known as the City of Destiny, is jewel on the East Coast of India. A host of several large, medium and small enterprises, industries, business establishments, professional organizations, different educational institutions and sub-urban and rural villages.

The data was collected from both Primary and secondary sources. Primary data was collected with the help of a structured questionnaire. Secondary data was collected from different textbooks, journals, magazines, newspapers, records and reports available in different libraries and research centers located at important places in India (Bangalore, Chennai, Hyderabad, and Visakhapatnam) are the major sources.

Sampling

Quota sampling method was adopted to select a sample of selected eight sections of society these sections are students employees, business people, doctors, engineers, lawyers, teachers and rural people. On the basis of quota sampling method about 60 respondents from each section representing 480 in total are interviewed.

Notes and References

1. Dr. V.D. Dudeja, HR Challenges of IT, Indian Management, February 2001, pp. 20-27.
2. Nitin, V. Patil and Damodar Suar, Computer-Based Training Perspective, *Indian Journal of Training and Development*, October-December 2002, pp. 36-43.
3. Prof. Harish Kumar and Alpana Mishra, Role of IT in Leveraging HR, *Personnel Today*, July-September 2000, pp. 17-20.
4. Ilapatel, The Challenge of Illiteracy. Can Information Technology Help? *Indian Journal of Adult Education*, October-December 2003, pp. 5-11.
5. Dr. M.P. Gupta, Electronic Education and Training, Indian Management, September 1998, pp. 45-50.
6. P.K. Chatterjee, IT Revolution and Human Resource Development, Issues and Challenges, Personnel Today, January-March 2001, pp. 19-22.
7. T. Raju, Knowledge Management—Sowing the New Seeds of Technology for Extension Training in India, *Indian Journal of Training and Development*, October-December-2002, pp. 55-61.
8. G.P. Pandey and Joya Chakraborthy, Role of Information Technology in Higher Education in the 21st Century, *University News*, February 25 to March 13, 2002, pp. 11-14.
9. D. Mukhopadhyaya, Information Technology for Education of Learning Society, *University News*, November 4-10, 2002, pp. 11-16.
10. C. Rama Chandra Prabhu, Invasion of Information Technology on Technical Education, *University News*, May 28 to June 3, 2001, pp. 5-10.
11. Ilapatel, Information and Communication Technology and Distance Adult Literacy Education in India, *Indian Journal of Open Learning*, 2002, pp. 255-68.
12. S.L. Mahajan, Information Technology in Distance Education in India, A Challenge, *Indian Journal of Open Learning*, 2002, pp. 269-77.
13. Rawat Publications, Jaipur, 1988, p. 6.
14. Verma, M.M., Human Resource Development, Gitanjali Publishing House, New Delhi, 1988, p. 1.
15. Len Nadler, Defining the field—Is it HRD or O.D. or.... . . ..? *Training and Development Journal*.
16. Vardan, M.S.S., HRD for organizational effectiveness, University of Rajasthan, Jaipur on 8-4-89.
17. Sanker, C., SHRD in Banking Industry, *Indian Journal of Training and Development*, January-March 1984, p. 88.
18. Rao, T.V. and Pareira, D.F., Recent Experiences in Human Resource Development, Oxford and IBH Publishing Company, New Delhi, 1986, pp. 3-4.
19. Sheela Singh, HRD in Public Sector Undertakings: New Directions, Management and Labour Studies, February 2003, pp. 37-46.
20. Dr. P.L. Rao, National HRD Strategy for the New Millennium, *Personal Today*, January-March 2002, pp. 35-38.
21. Dr. P.N. Singh, HRD perspectives for the Next Millennium, *The Indian Journal of Commerce*, October-December 1998, pp. 213-15.

22. Prasanna Jackson, T. and R.Venkatapatty, Human Resource Development, Attitude and Climate an Empirical Verification with Reference to Various Types of Organizations, Small Enterprise Development Management Excellence, March, 2000, pp. 47-55.
23. Ajay Kumar Singh, HRD Perspectives in the 21st Century, *The Indian Journal of Commerce,* October-December 1998, pp. 167-77.
24. P.S. Yadapadithaya, Strategic Human Resource Development (SHRD): A Key to Competitive Advent, *The Indian Journal of Commerce,* October, December 1998, p. 195.
25. Dr. Saritha Singth and Dr. Jai B.P. Sinha, Human Resource Development: An Indian Cultural Perspective, Management and Labour Studies, July 1998, pp. 389-99.
26. P. Radha Krishna, Information Technology and Numerical Methods, The Hitch Publishers, 2002-03, pp. 4-7.
27. Dennis P. Curtin, Kim Foley, Kunal Sen and Cathleen Morin, Information Technology. The Breaking Wave, Tata McGraw Hill Publishing Company Limited, New Delhi, pp. 20-27.
28. P. Radha Krishna, Information Technology and Numerical Methods, the Hitch Publishing, Hyderabad 2002-03, pp. 4-5.
29. Dr. V.B. Dudeja, Infotech : Challenges and Opportunities in New Millennium, *Indian Management,* August 1999, pp. 21-24.
30. Dr. R.D. Pathak and Others, Harnessing Information Technology Trends, *Indian Management,* April 1998, pp. 32-43.
31. Dr. Usha Mujoo-Munshi and others, Information Technology Concerns and Issues in Developing Countries with Special Reference to India, *Library Herald,* July to September 1998, pp. 69-79.
32. Manoj Killedar, Distance Education through Internet-based E-learning, *Indian Journal of Open Learning,* 2001, pp. 68-79.
33. Rozhan Othman, Antecedents and outcome of IT use. Howdoes HRM fitin? *Asia Pacific Management Review,* 2001, pp. 91-103.
34. P.G. Pesai, Information Technology at Regional Level, Productivity, April-June 2003, pp. 55-62.
35. Deepak Halan, special Technology for Special People, Information Technology Electronic for you March 2004, pp. 42-44.
36. P. Seethuraman and Siva Kumar, Teleconferencing a New Technology for extension Training in India, *Indian Journal of Training and Development,* October-December 2002, pp. 55-61.
37. Nitin, V. Patil and Damodar Suar, Computer-based Training Perspective, *Indian Journal of Training and Development,* October-December 2002, pp. 36-43.
38. T. Raju and Sangeetha Mohandas T., Knowledge Management Sowing New Seeds of Technology, *Indian Journal of Training and Development,* Oct.-Dec. 2002, pp. 22-29.
39. R.G. Desai Information Technology at Regional Level, *Productivity,* April-June 2003, pp. 55-62.
40. P.N. Singh, HRD Perspectives for the Next Millennium, *The Indian Journal of Commerce,* October-December 1998, pp. 213-15.
41. D. Mukhopadhyaya, Information Technology for Quality Education of Learning Society, *University News,* November 04-10-2002, pp. 11-16.
42. Sheela Singh, HRD in Public Sector Undertakings: New Directions, Management and Labour Studies, February 2003, pp. 37-46.
43. G.P. Pandey and Joya Chakraborthy, Role of Information Technology in Higher Education in 21st Century, *University News,* February 25-March 3, 2002, pp. 11-14.
44. C. Rama Chandraprabhu, Invasion of Information Technology on Technical Education, *University News,* May 28-June 3, 2001, pp. 5-10.
45. Dr. M.P. Gupta, Electronic Education and Training, *Indian Management,* September 1998, pp. 45-50.
46. Prof. V.D. Dudeja, HR Challenges of IT, *Indian Management,* February 2001, pp. 20-27.
47. N. Upadhyaya, IT a Tool for decision-making, *Personnel Today,* January-March 1992, pp. 27-38.

48. Dr. Neelu Rohmetra, Achieving Excellence through HRD, *The Indian Journal of Commerce*, December 1995, pp. 60-66.
49. Dr. P.L. Rao, National HRD Strategy for the New Millennium, *Personnel Today*, January-March 2000, pp. 35-38.
50. Prof. Harish Kumar and Alpana Mishra, Role of IT in Leveraging HR, *Personnel Today*, July-September 2000, pp. 17-20.
51. P. Chatterjee, IT Revolution and Human Resources Development, Issues and Challenges, *Personnel Today*, January-March 2001, pp. 19-33.
52. Ajay Kumar Singh, HRD perspectives in the 21st Century, *The Indian Journal of Commerce*, October-December 1998, pp. 167-77.
53. M.G.K. Murth, Globalisation and HRD, *The Indian Journal of Commerce*, October-December 1998, pp. 179-86.
54. Dr. V.B. Dudeja, Infotech: Challenges and Opportunities in New Millennium, *Indian Management*, August 1999, pp. 21-24.
55. Peter, F. Drucker, Next Information Revolution, *Executive Capsule*, May-June 1999, pp. 5-8.
56. Dr. R.P. Jaxena, Studied Information Technology as a Strategic Tool for Attaining Success in Global Environment, *Paradigm*, July-December 1999, pp. 95-104.
57. Saritha Singh and Jai B.P. Sinha, Human Resources Development in an Indian cultural Perspective, *Management and Labour Studies*, July 1998, pp. 389-99.
58. Dr. R.D. Pathak, S.K. Sripathi, Zafer Hussian and Dr. Sushil, Harnessing Information Technology Trends, *Indian Management*, April 1998, pp. 32-43.
59. Reema Khurana, Information Technology and Education Delivery, *Paradigm*, July, 1999, pp. 75-80.
60. Dr. Rajeswari Narendra and Dr. V. Narendra, IT Revolution : Challenges for HRD, *Indian Journal of Training and Development*, April-June 2001, pp. 22-35.
61. Dr. Usha Mujoo Munshi and Dr. Inder Vir Malhan, Information Technology Concerns and issues in Developing Countries with Special Reference to India, *Library Herald*, July-September 1998, pp. 69-79.
62. Ilapatel, The challenge of illiteracy can Information Technology Help? *Indian Journal of Adult Education*, October-December 2003, pp. 5-13.
63. S.Y. Sree Kumar, Distance Education and Human Resource Development, *Indian Journal of Open Learning*, May-2000, pp. 169-78.
64. Jack Fiorito and William Boss, The Use of Information Technology by National Unions: An Exploratory Analysis, *Industrial Relations*, January 2002, pp. 34-47.
65. Rozhan Othman, Antecedents and Outcome of IT Use: How does HRM. Fit in, *Asia Pacific Management Review*, March, 2001, pp. 91-103.
66. Ilapatel, Information Communication Technology and Distance Adult Literacy Education in India, *Indian Journal of Open Learning*, May 2002, pp. 255-68.
67. S.L. Mahajan, Information Communication Technology in Distance Education in India: A Challenge, *Indian Journal of Open Learning*, May, 2002, pp. 269-77.
68. Dharam Kumar and Pardeep Rai, Distance Education, Use of Computers and Problem of Copyright, *Library Herald*, June 2002, pp. 119-29.
69. Manoj Killedar, Distance Education Through Internet-based E-learning, *Indian Journal of Open Learning*, January 2001, pp. 68-79.
70. Rainer Ommerborn and Rudolf Schuemer, Using computers in Distnae Study: Results of a survey amongst Disabled Distance Students, *Indian Journal of Open Learning*, January 2002, pp. 51-65.
71. Teena Gomes, IT Education for the Rich and the Poor, *Information Technology*, Electronic for you, February 2004, pp. 28-32.
72. Deepak Kalan, Special Technology for Special People, *Information Technology*, Electronic for you, March 2004, pp. 42-44.
73. Dr. O.P. Mishra and Dr. D. Gangali, Current Trends in Extension Training, *Indian Journal of Training and Development*, January-March, 2002, pp. 5-11.
74. Manoj, T. Thomas, Lecture as a Pedagogical Tool in Management Education and Training, *Indian Journal of Training and Development*, January-March, 2004, pp. 74-81.
75. Kirti Shiva Kumar and Vijay Caprihan, Using the In-Basket as Training Technique, *Indian Journal of Training and Development*, July-December 2003, pp. 28-35

76. Venkateswarlu, T., Globalisation of Business and Information Technology, *Labour Economics*, April 2004, pp. 639-50.
77. Pravin Prashant, Better Delivery, *Indian Management*, October 1997, pp. 54-58.
78. Seema Singh and Anil Kumar, Information Technology : An Effective tool for Managing Sustainable Agriculture, *Agricultural Situation in India*, February 2003, pp. 717-21.
79. F.L. Lobo, Training Dimensions of the Electric Age, *Indian Management*, October 2000, pp. 65-70.
80. Mauli Halan, Ground Control of Satellite Imagery, *Information Technology*, Electronic For You, New Delhi, May 2005, pp. 47-49.
81. Garima Khanna, Satellite Shrinking the World, *Information Technology*, Electronic For You, New Delhi, February 2005, 53-57.
82. Ranjit, Mettoth, Pathways sets kids Free, *Information Technology*, Electronic for You, New Delhi, October 2004, pp. 64-66.
83. Preethi, J., Technology Levels the Learning Field, *Information Technology*, Electronic for You, New Delhi, January 2005, pp. 47-49.

2

Methods of Human Resource Development

The greatest assets of every nation is it human resources. If the human resources of nation is not competent enough to achieve the desired target the nation will not be able to get the best out of its resources. HRD is the process of helping people to acquire competencies. The development of human resources now a day has become a special subject of economic enquiry is one of the main streams of analysis in the field of economic development. Recently some economists like T.W. Schultz and Simon Kuznets and others opened a new dimension of in economic thinking to enthrone man as a productive source of production. The result has been that HRD programme in many countries of the world has gained momentum and gradually dawned at the thought of economists, social scientists and policy-makers. In spite of the fact that rapid strides have been made in the industrialization of the country in the post-independence era, the decade 1950-60 more particularly being marked by industrial development in the country. Training and development hardly received any serious attention of the industry and business for some to come. It is about 1964 that the training and development under the gradual technological developments came about just emerging as separate function.

As time passed and more sophisticated technological developments in business and industry made their appearance, training and development gained popularity and came to be recognized as a very important function.

For instance, the Indian Government under this impact has restructured and renamed recently the Ministry of Education and Culture as the Ministry of Human Resource Development. In fact HRD is precondition for modern economic growth. The idea is that improvement in HRD can facilitates improvements and reinforce all other aspects of development. In short development of nation is identified with maximum possible utilization of human resource in productive activities and its fullest possible developments of skills, knowledge and capabilities.[1]

2.1 IMPORTANCE OF HRD

1. HRD improves the capabilities of the people by making them better aware of the skills required for job performance and by improving clarity about performance standards. The employees become innovative and enterprising ever ready to take risks and get ahead. It strengthens executive skills.
2. HRD improves teamwork employees become more open towards each other and they also trust each other. In this way the organizational climate also improves a lot.
3. HRD promotes organizational effectiveness. Appropriate employees centered policies help the organization achieve its goals more efficiently.
4. Performance-related rewards help employees realize the importance of utilizing their skills fully in the service of organizational goals. The organization health and self-renewing capabilities improve quite significantly.
5. HRD helps the organization in procuring the right people at the right time and in making their effective use.
6. HRD generates a lot of useful data, which facilitates human resource planning and control.

HRD ultimately leads to higher productivity lower costs and successful growth in the organization.[2]

2.2 OBJECTIVES OF HRD

- To maximize the utilization of human resources for the achievement of individual and organizational goal.
- To provide an opportunity and comprehensive framework for the development of human resources in an organization for full expression of their talent and manifest potentials.
- To locate ensure recognise and develop the enabling capabilities of the employees in the organization in relation to their present and potential roles.
- To develop the constructive mind and an overall personality of the employees.
- To develop the sense of team spirit, team work and inter-team collaborations.
- To develop the organizational health culture and effectiveness.

- To humanize the work in the organization.
- To develop dynamic human relationship.
- To generate systematic information about human resources.
- To develop and maintain a high motivation level of the employees.[3]

2.3 HRD METHODS/SUB-SYSTEMS

There are many instruments that can be used to facilitate HRD. These instruments may be called sub-systems or methods or mechanisms or techniques. Each of these sub-systems focuses on some particular aspect of HRD. To have a comprehensive HRD, many of these instruments may be needed to be use simultaneously. Any systematic or formal way of facilitating competency, motivation and climate development could be considered and HRD instrument. The most frequently used HRD instruments/methods are:

1. Performance Appraisal
2. Potential Appraisal
3. Employee Training
4. Career Planning and Development
5. Executive Development
6. Organizational Development
7. Quality Circles
8. Employee Counseling
9. Team Work
10. Communication Policies
11. Quality of Worklife

The greatest assets of every nation is it human resources. If the human resource of nation is not competent enough to achieve the desired target the nation will not be able to get the best out of its resources. HRD is the process of helping people to acquire competencies. The development of human resources now-a-days has become a special subject of economic enquiry is one of the main streams of analysis in the field of economic development. Recently some economists like T.W. Schultz and Simon Kuznets and others opened a new dimensions of in economic thinking to enthrone man as a productive source of production. The result has been that HRD programme in many countries of the world has gained momentum and gradually dawned at the thought of economists, social scientists and policy-makers. In spite of the fact that rapid strides have been made in the industrialization of the country in the post-independence era, the decade 1950-60 more particularly being marked by industrial development in the country Training and Development hardly received any serious attention of the industry and business for some to come. It is about 1964 that the Training and Development under the gradual technological developments came about just emerging as separate function.

As time passed and more sophisticated technological developments in business and industry made their appearance, training and development gained popularity and came to be recognized as a very important function.

For instance the Indian Government under this impact has restructured and renamed recently the Ministry of Education and Culture as the Ministry of Human Resource Development. In fact HRD is precondition for modern economic growth. The idea is that improvement in HRD can facilitates improvements and reinforce all other aspects of development. In short, development of nation is identified with maximum possible utilization of Human Resource in productive activities and its fullest possible developments of skills, knowledge and capabilities.[4]

Training is the creation of an environment where employees may acquire or learn specific job-related behaviors, skills, knowledge, abilities, and attitudes. If one wishes to make a distinction between training and development. It would be that training is directed at helping employees perform better on their current jobs, whereas development represents a future-oriented investment in employees. Development is based on the fact that an employee will need an evolving set of knowledge, skills, abilities (KSAs) to perform well in the succession of positions encountered during his or her career. The career—a long preparation of an employee for this series of positions is what is meant by employee development.

Education is considered a means by which the range of possible employee responses is increased rather than reduced. Education represents a broadening of the individual so that he or she may be prepared to assess a variety of situations and select for himself or herself most appropriate response. Although may unskilled, semi-skilled and skilled positions would primarily require training supervisory and management positions require elements of education. Recently there has been a blurring of the distinction between training and education. As more and more employees are called upon to exercise judgment and to choose among alternative solutions to job problems training programme have sought to broaden and develop the individual through education. For instance employees in enriched job and/ or employees in the service industries may be required to make independent decisions regarding their work and their relationships with clients. Hence organizations should consider elements of both education & training when planning their training programme.

2.3.1 Performance Appraisal

Once the employee has been selected, trained, and motivated he is then appraisal for his performance. Performance appraisal is the step where the management finds out how effective it has been at having and placing employees. Performance appraisal is the process of evaluating an employee performance of a job in terms of its requirements.

Performance Appraisal Methods

Managers usually conduct the appraisal using a predetermined and formal method like one or more of those described next. It is "predetermined" insofar as most firms do (or should) decide ahead of time what tools and processes they're going to use.

(a) Graphic Rating Scale Method

The graphic rating scale is the simplest and most popular technique for appraising performance. A graphic rating scale lists traits (such as quality and reliability) and a range of performance.

(b) Alternation Ranking Method

Ranking employees from best to worst on a trait or traits is another option. Since it is usually easier to distinguish between the worst and best employees, an alternation ranking method is most popular. First, list all subordinates to be rated, and then cross out the names of any not known well enough to rank indicate the employee who is the highest on the characteristic being measured and also the one who is the lowest. Then choose the next highest and the next lowest, alternating between highest and lowest until all employees have been ranked

(c) Paired Comparison Method

The paired comparison method helps make the ranking method more precise. For every trait (quantity of work, quality of work, and so on), you pair and compare every subordinate with every other subordinate.[5]

(d) Forced Distribution Method

The forced distribution method is similar to grading on a curve. With this method, you place predetermined percentages of ratees into performance categories.

(e) Behaviorally Anchored Rating Scales

A Behaviorally Anchored Rating Scale (BARS) combines the benefits of narratives, critical incidents, and quantified (graphic rating type) scales.

Developing BARS typically requires five steps:

1. Generate critical incidents: Ask persons who know the job (job holders and/or supervisors) to describe specific illustrations (critical incidents) of effective and ineffective performance.
2. Develop performance dimensions: Have these people cluster the incidents into a smaller set of (5 or 10) performance dimensions, and define each dimension, such as "conscientiousness."
3. Reallocate incidents: Another group of people who also know the job then reallocate the original critical incidents. They get the cluster definitions and the critical incidents, and must reassign each

incident to the cluster they think it fits best. Retain a critical incident if some percentage (usually 50% to 80%) of this second group assigns it to the same cluster, as did the first group.

4. Scale the incidents: This second group then rates the behavior described by the incident as to how effectively or ineffectively it represents performance on the dimension (7- to 9-point scales are typical).
5. Develop a final instrument: Choose about six or seven of the incidents as the dimension's behavioral anchors.[6]

(f) Straight Ranking Method

It is the oldest and simplest method of performance appraisal, by which the man and his performance are considered as an entity by the rater. No attempt is made to fractionalize the rater or his performance; the "Whole man" is compared with the "Whole man"; that is, the ranking of a man in a work group is done against that of another. The relative position of each man is tested in terms of his numerical rank. It may also be done by ranking a person on his job performance against that of another member of a competitive group by placing him as number one or two or three in total group, i.e. persons re-tested in order of merit and placed in a simple grouping.[7]

(g) Grading Method

Under this system, the rater considers certain features an marks them accordingly to a scale. Certain categories of worth are first established and carefully defined. The selected features may be analytical ability, co-operativeness, dependability, self-expression, job knowledge, judgement, leadership and organizing ability, etc. They may be: A—outstanding; B—very good; C—good or average; D—fair; E—poor; and B (or B) very poor or hopeless.

(h) Forced Choice Description Method

This method was evolved after a great deal of research conducted for the military services during World War II. It attempts to correct a rater's tendency to give consistently high or consistently low ratings to all the employees. The use of this method calls for objective reporting and minimum subjective judgment. Under this method, the rating elements are several sets of pair phrases or adjectives (usually sets of four phrases two of which are positive, two negative) relating to job proficiency or personal qualifications. The rater is asked to indicate which of the four phrases is most and least descriptive of the employee.

(i) Checklist

Under this method, the rater does not evaluate employee performance; he supplies reports about it and the final rating is done by the personnel department. A series of questions are presented concerning an employee to his behavior. The rater, then, checks to indicate if the answer to a question about an employee is positive or negative. The value of each question may be weighed equally or checklist is given below:[8]

(1)	Is the employee really interested in his job?	Yes/No
(2)	Is he regular on his job?	Yes/No
(3)	Is he respected by his subordinates?	Yes/No
(4)	Does he show uniform behaviour to all?	Yes/No
(5)	Does he keep his temper?	Yes/No
(6)	Is he always willing to help other employees?	Yes/No
(7)	Does he follow instructions properly?	Yes/No
(8)	Does he given recognition and praise to employees for work done well?	Yes/No
(9)	Is the equipment maintained in order?	Yes/No
(10)	Does he ever make mistakes?	Yes/No

(j) Free Essay Method

Under this method, the supervisor makes a free form, open-ended appraisal of an employee in his own words and puts down his impressions about the employee. He takes note of these factors:

(a) Relations with fellow supervisors and personnel assigned to him;
(b) General organization and planning ability;
(c) Job knowledge and potential;
(d) Employee characteristics and attitudes;
(e) Understanding and application of company policies and procedures;
(f) Production, quality and cost control;
(g) Physical conditions; and
(h) Development needs for future.

(k) Group Appraisal Method

Under this method, employee are rated by an appraisal group, consisting of their supervisor and three or four other supervisors who have some knowledge of their performance. The supervisor explains to the group the nature of his subordinates' duties. The group then discusses the standards of performance for that job, the actual performance of the job-holder, and the causes of their particular level of performance, and offers suggestions for future improvement, if any.

(l) Field Review Method

Under this method, a trainer employee from the personnel department interviews line supervisors to evaluate their respective subordinates. The appraiser is fully equipped with definite test questions, usually memorized in advance, which he puts to the supervisor. The supervisor is required to give his opinion about the progress of his subordinates, the level of the performance of each subordinate, his weaknesses, good points, outstanding ability, promotability, and the possible plans of action in cases requiring further consideration. The questions are asked and placed in the employee's personal folder. The success of this system depends upon the competence of the interviewer.

(m) Management By Objectives (MBO)

This method has been evolved by Peter Drucker. MBO is potentially a powerful philosophy of managing and an effective way for operational sing the evaluation process. Management by objectives can be described as "a process whereby the superior and subordinate managers of an organization jointly identify its common goals, define each individual's major areas of responsibility in terms of results expected of him and use these measures as guides for operating the unit and assessing the contributions of each of its members."

MBO Process

1. Set organization goals, i.e., establishment of an organization-wide strategy and goals. Such goals are expressed clearly and concisely and can be measured accurately. They have to be periodically revised. They should be challenging; high enough to provide motivation, but not so high that they are out of reach. Otherwise they might result in frustration among the employees and lead to defensive behavior. Clear attainable goals help channel energies in specific directions, and let the subordinate know the basis on which he will be rewarded.
2. Joint goal setting, i.e., establishment of short-term performance targets between the management and the subordinate in a conference between them. The individual manager must clarify in his own mind the responsibilities of their subordinates. Organization Charts and Job Descriptions may be sued. The manager may ask each subordinate to write down his personal goals, while in turn the manager writes out the goals he thinks subordinates should have. The manager and subordinate then discuss them reach an agreement about them, and put them in writing.
3. Performance reviews, i.e., frequent performance review meetings between the managers and the subordinate. During the initial stages of the MBO programme, monthly reviews may be used and then extended to quarterly reviews. For maximum effectiveness, reviews probably should be made more often than once each year.
4. Set check posts, i.e., establishment of major check posts to measure progress. The quirk of human nature demands that the manager be constantly alert and exercise sound judgment. However, as

subordinate learns to establish objectives and direct activities towards their goals, the rate of control and amount of checking gradually can be decreased.

5. *Feedback*: The employees who receive frequent feedback concerning their performance are more highly motivated than those who do not feedback that is specific, relevant, and timely helps satisfy the need most people fell about knowing where they stand.

Benefits of MBO Programme

1. MBO helps and increases employee motivation because it relates overall goals to the individual's goals; and helps to increase an employee's understanding of where the organization is and where it is heading.
2. Managers are more likely to compete with themselves than with other managers. This kind of evaluation can reduce internal conflicts that often arise when managers compete with each other to obtain scarce resources.
3. MBO results in a "means ends" chain. Management at succeeding lower levels in the organization established targets, which are integrated with those at the next higher level. Thus, it can help insure that everyone's activity is ultimately aimed toward organization's goals.
4. MBO reduces role conflict and ambiguity. Role conflict exists when a person is faced with conflicting demands from two or more supervisors; and role ambiguity exists when a person is uncertain as to how he will be evaluated, or what he has to achieve. Since MBO aims at providing clear targets and their order or priority, it reduces both these situations.
5. MBO provides more objective appraisal criteria. The targets that emerge from the MBO process provide a sound set of criteria for evaluating the manager's performance.
6. MBO forces and aids in planning. By forcing top management to establish a strategy and goals for the entire organization; and by requiring other managers to set their targets and plan so to reach them.
7. MBO identifies problems better and early. Frequent performance review sessions make this possible.
8. MBO identifies performance deficiencies and enables the management and the employees to set individualized self improvement goals and thus proves effective in training and development of people.
9. MBO helps the individual manager to develop personal leadership, especially the skills of listening, planning, counseling, motivating and evaluating. This approach to managing instills a personal

commitment to respond positively to the organisation's major concerns as well as to the development of human assets. Such a manager has a far greater change to move ahead within the management hierarchy than the non-MBO type.

Disadvantages of MBO

1. MBO programme takes a great deal of time, energy and form—completing on the part of managers. An individual becomes so enmeshed in performing assigned functions that he often loses sight of the goal, the reason for performance. It has been called "the activity trap". It requires a great deal of investment of the top management's time and effort before it arrives at realistic targets and reviews the performance.
2. MBO is far from panacea. Those executives who have been involved very often find it difficult to apply MBO concepts to their own work habits. They find it hard to think about the results of work rather than the work itself. They tend to over emphasize goals that are easy to quantify, sometimes forgetting that workers often behave almost like children at play—when the game no longer challenges, interest is soon lost.
3. In some areas, such as cutting costs or increasing sales, measuring performance is a straightforward and more or less objective matter. But in many other areas, such as subordinate development, appraising performance can be an acute problem.
4. Many times neither the managers know the rationale and value of MBO, nor the subordinates are clear about the goals. This unnecessarily becomes more exasperating.
5. There is sometimes a "tug of war" in which the subordinate tries to set the lowest targets possible and the supervisor the highest.[8]

(n) Assessment Center Method

The Assessment center concept was initially applied to military situations by Simoniet in the German army in the 1930s and the War Office Selection Board of the British Army in the 1960s. The purpose of this method was and is to test candidates in a social situation, using a number of assessors and a variety of procedures. The most important feature of the assessment center is job-related simulations.

The Assessment center programme commonly used follows. This procedure. First, a leadership group is established; each member supporting a predefined position, but the group must arrive at consensus. Then a task force is used with an appointed leader, who decides on a course of action. Simulation games and in-basket appointed leader, who decides on a course of action. Simulation games and in-basket exercises are used to test organizational and planning abilities. Oral report is made by the candidate, which tests his communication skills and straight into his present position. Personal interviews, and projective tests are used to assess work motivation, career orientation, and dependence on others. Paper and pencil tests measure intellectual ability.

(o) 360° Performance Appraisal

The appraisal may be any person who has through knowledge about the job done by contents to be appraised, standards of contents and who observes the employee while performing a job. The appraiser should be capable of determining what is more important and what is relatively less important. He should asses the performance without bias. The appraisers are supervisors, peers, subordinates employees themselves users of service and consultants. Performance appraisal by all these parties is called "360° appraisal".

(p) Human Asset Accounting Method

The human asset accounting method refers to activity devoted to attaching money estimates to the value of a firm's internal human organization and its external customer goodwill. If able, well-trained personnel leave a firm, the human organization is worthless; if they join it, its human assets are increased. If distrust and conflict prevail, the human enterprise is devalued. If teamwork and high morale prevail, the human organization is a very valuable asset.

2.3.2 Potential Appraisal

In making potential appraisal of managers, levels of talent and ambition have to be clearly identified. The objectives of potential appraisal are:

1. To assess an individual in terms of the highest level of work the individual will be able to handle comfortably and successfully in future without being over-stretched.
2. To assist the organization in discharging its responsibility of selecting and developing managers for the future to ensure its continuous growth.

Potential typically represents latent qualities in an individual which manifests in concrete terms while performing various tasks/jobs. Some characteristics representing potential are:

(a) Ability to foresee future opportunities and assess impact of any initiative/decision taken today.
(b) Has an institutionalized way of working to ensure continuity and consistency of approach.
(c) Ability to identify resource gaps by the use of basic intelligence/

subject knowledge/analytical and quantitative skills and further finds ways and means of overcoming these so as to ultimately create higher value.

(d) Personal quality to be levelheaded and to respond in an effective and measured manner even under conditions of severe stress.
(e) Ability to function in varied environments with confidence and deliver high performance.
(f) Ability to see the larger picture as well as recognize the need to get into micro-details.
(g) To display high degree of personal and intellectual integrity at all times.

During the assessment of these qualities the following factors should be considered:

(a) The relevance of problem and situation analyzed.
(b) The speed with which the analysis is undertaken.
(c) The weight and nature of problem and situations to be analyzed.

Creative Imagination

This quality elates to the ability of an individual to discern the various useful possibilities and alternatives, which are inherent in a problem area and are normally not obvious to less perspective observers.

Sense of Reality

This implies ability to interpret the reality of the situation. This can be viewed from a detached position:

- Speed of insight
- Approach to problems or situation
- Action
- Seeing the relative nature
- Judgment

Effective Leadership

This calls for the ability to energize and make positive impact on the team to facilitate the achievement of goal. Therefore, in order to lead people in the organization effectively, the leader should have the following qualities:

- Excellent job knowledge and compotence
- High level of energy and drive
- Excellent relationship skills

Conceptual Skills

To understand and visualize ones role in the larger context of the organization/industry economy and articulate the content and context of the future one should possess conceptual skills.

Technical Skills

These skills relate to the conceptual know how with regard to the subject is able to articulate future needs within a given context.

Commercial skills: One should be able to identify the opportunities in the business environment within socio-economic and legal framework. Also the individual has a higher order of analytical and numerical skills.

Communication Skills

These require the ability to articulate thoughts and ideas and situations in most appropriate manner so as to ensure complete understanding by the recipient.

Planning and Organizing Ability

This implies that one should have the ability, in the context of organizational objectives, to clearly define the requirement/course of action so as to achieve goals/targets.

Willingness to take Additional Responsibilities

This refers to the inherent quality in an individual of being self-motivated to be accountable for areas adjacent to ones own as well as at levels higher than where the individual is positioned.

Initiative

This means the display of an enterprising attitude towards pertaining the role/job assigned to the individual. Is a self-starter requires very little direction/advice in getting started.

Result orientations: For this, one should be extremely focused and single-minded in achieving the goal, and prioritize multiple tasks simultaneously to leverage resources, and should not adopt short cuts while adhering to time target, and should always abide by company policy and business ethics.

2.3.3 Employee Training

Training is the creation of an environment where employees may acquire or learn specific job-related behaviors, skills, knowledge, abilities, and attitudes. If one wishes to make a distinction between training and development. It would be that training is directed at helping employees perform better on their current jobs, whereas development represents a future-oriented investment in employees. Development is based on the fact that an employee will need an evolving set of knowledge, skills, abilities (KSAs) to perform well in the succession of positions encountered during his or her career. The career—a long preparation of an employee for this series of positions is what is meant by employee development.

2.3.3.1 On-the-Job Training (OJT)

The vast majority of all training carried on is of the job variety. A variety of training aids and techniques can be used in conjunction with on-the-Job training. Among these are procedure charts, picture manuals, sample problems demonstrations-oral and written explanations and tape recording.

This is the traditional method of skills learning, which is designed to maximize learning while allowing the employee to perform his job under the supervision and guidance of trained worker or instructor, practical application and making principles and concepts of learning meaningful and realistic. This is the most effective method of development applicable at all levels to a wide range of semi-skilled, skilled and technical job as well as supervisory and management development programme.

In the developing countries like India OJT is still favored and is most extensively used for training and development purposes in business and Industry.

Features

OJT is considered most appropriate for teaching knowledge and skills that can be learned in a relatively short time. It is useful for learning unskilled and semi-skilled manual type of jobs, clerical jobs and sales. Only one or at the most a very few employees be trained at the same time for the same job. This is designed to aid each employee to learn how best to perform his specific jobs. It is highly commanded method usefully deployed in managerial training and development.

Advantages

- OJT is the type of training which can be tailored to suit the specific requirement of each trainee, in terms of his back ground, attitudes, needs, expectations, goals and future assignments.
- The importance of learning by doing is well recognized in OJT.
- Since OJT does not necessitates moving out of the organization any managers their valuable time is saved.
- OJT strongly motivates the trainee, since it is not located in the artificial situation of a classroom. Rather with OJT a trainee while learning on the actual equipment with the real environment of his job, gets a feel of the actual production condition and requirements and thus can experience of feeling of accomplishment or achievement as a result of knowledge and skills gained at least east of improvement or progress in improvement in a relatively short period.
- In OJT standards of performance concerning quality and waste receiver added meaning.

- OJT is specific, practical and tangible,
- OJT is highly economical as its results in low out of pocket costs. Production is carried on the during training.
- The trainee learns the rules, regulations, and procedures by observing their day-to-day applications. He can therefore be easily sized up by the management.

Disadvantages

- In OJT there is tendency to neglect disregard and even to do away within some cases the essentials of principles and theory in favour of immediate production.
- Learner is essentially a producer. He is apt to err while learning on his job and there is every possibility of these errors creeping onto the performance resultant.
- Effect of which will be inferior quality production excessive waste and spoilage, which may cause trouble and thus post a problem to the management.
- The work place particularly a shop with environments surcharged with hustle and noise and the pace of skilled workers is most likely to affect the learning and may create a feeling of frustration in the mind of a trainee.
- With OJT production equipment may be lied up.
- OJT is time consuming and static as its tends to longer on with existing knowledge, skills and practices.
- On the OJT instruction is of ten haphazard and disorganized

OJT Uses

- OJT to be effective must be carefully planned, organized, staffed, supervised and controlled.
- While making selection of an instructor or a trainer it should be well judged that he is qualified trained, competent, adequately prepared to devote sufficient time, free from any interruption, for carrying on the training activities.
- It is of the essence of OJT that the trainee he provided with ample opportunity to practice what they learn.

A systematic feedback schedule need to be established to judge an evaluate the progress the learner has made during the course of his learning. Of which the trainee should also be well appraised.

2.3.3.2 Job Instructor Training Method

It suggested that before actual training begins the instructor must get ready to instruct four steps are recommended and these have applicability today in training programme for unskilled as well as skilled workers.

(i) *Prepare the worker*: Put the worker at ease find out what the person already knows about the job. Stimulate interest the learning job by explaining its relationship to other jobs and to the company product. Place the learner in the correct working position.

(ii) *Present the Operation*: Tell, show, illustrate, and question carefully and patiently stress the key points as listed on-the-job break down the sheet. Instruct clearly and completely taking up on one point at a time but no more than can easily be mastered.

(iii) *Try out performance*: Test the trainee through performance of the job. Have the learner tell and show what has been learned and also explain key points. Ask questions and correct errors continue until you're sure the trainees knows how to do the job.

(iv) *Follow-up* : Have the trainee work independently designating a source of help if questions arise. The learner should be checked frequently encouraged to ask further questions and to look for key points during learning. Be sure the trainee understood the reason for the job and its relationships to the other jobs in the departments or plants. As the learner acquires the skill and understanding taper-off the extra coaching and finally close your follow-up.[9]

2.3.3.3 Vestibule Method

This method of training is primarily when large number of employees must be trained quickly as needed, as a result of expansion of business activities by firms or industries though it is also helpful as a preliminary to on-the-job raining.

This method involves taking employees through a short planned course of instruction and practice, in sales, shop or office in a simulated real working situations and conditions in a school area. Such a course usually takes form a few days to a few weeks maximum. This type of training works best in case of newly appointed comptometer operators who acquire the "know how" of their work and are able to perform better and more efficiently on their jobs.

Advantages

- This is specialized superior method of instruction free from any pressure of getting out production.
- This has the fundamental advantage of training a number of people in a short period of time without causing any interruption of disturbance in the normal flow of work.
- This provides new employees an opportunity to adjust themselves to actual work conditions under guided direction and to graduate become accustomed to work routines and catch up the speed in

work as they gain confidence after recovery from their actual state of fear and nervousness before coming to them present jobs.

- This methods helpful in eliminating misfits or poor practices before actual production conditions are encountered and thus can prove to be a great savior of losses, due to wastage, spoilage as may actually occur when new employees without this training are placed on their jobs.
- This provides possibility of frequent lectures or discussing and greater personnel attention to individual trainees.

Disadvantage

- Since the working of the method requires the duplication of sales, shop office under the circumstances only such limited types of instructions by way of training this method can capable to render, in which the machinery needed is not too expensive to be installed in a school, used only occasionally may not entail excessive overhead costs.
- The method is limited, more or less to those jobs in which there is a high turnover, is continuously increasing demand for workers.[10]

2.3.3.4 Computer-based Training

As development of technologies proceeds at a rapid pace and the cost of computers continuous to decline high-technology training methods are finding increasing use in industry, academia, and the military.

Computer-based Training encompasses two distinct techniques computer assisted instruction (CAI) and computer managerial instruction (CMI). A Computer Assisted Instruction system delivers training material directly through a computer terminal in a interaction format computers make it possible to provide drill and practice problem-solving simulation gaming forms of instruction and certain very sophisticated forms of individualized tutorial instruction. A computer managerial Instruction is normally used in conjunction with CAI thereby providing an efficient means of managing the training function. Computer Managerial Instructions uses a computer to generate and score tests and to determine the level of trainee proficiency. CMI system can also track the performance of trainees and direct to them to appropriate study material to meet their specific needs with CMI the computer stakes on some of the routine aspects of training functioning the instructor to spend time on course development or individualized instruction.

Computer-based Training is being used more and more to train uses of Human Resources Information System (HRIS) trainers begins with relatively simple tasks such as entering a new employees records in the personnel life these proceed to more complex procedures as they master each task. The training dates are often simulated but the procedures are real.

Advantages of CBT

- Learning is self-paced.
- Training comes to the employee.
- All trainers get exactly the same training.
- New employees do not have to wait for a scheduled training session.
- Training can focus on specific needs as revealed by built-in tests.
- Trainees can be referred to on-line help or written material.
- It is easier to review a computer programme than to change classroom-training materials.
- Record keeping is facilitated.
- The computer programme can be linked to video presentation.[11]

2.3.3.5 Apprenticeship Training

The apprenticeship system is perhaps oldest and most commonly used method for training in industrial crafts, trades, and technical areas this was developed in the middle ages by then so called trade guilds. The ancient Greek and Roman state rewords go to show that this system of instruction was used to train doctors, dentists, lawyers, architects, teachers, as well as tradesmen. In the era that proceeded the industrial revolution there can about further developments in the practices of the system of apprenticeships, which have been made use of advantageously in the training of craftsmen.

Importance: The apprenticeship training essentially as it is combination of theory learning and of methods and techniques this proves to be extremely useful after a long period of classroom instructions and actual learning experiences as associated with the job. This training used to prepare the worker, who requires a wide range of job skills, knowledge, long period of practice and seasoned experience. Duration of training depends upon the extent and intensity of training.

Advantages

- It ensures the maintenance of a skilled work force.
- This training becomes productivity instantly.
- It greatly improves workmanship.
- It cuts down the employment cost as a resut or reduced turnover and lower production cost.
- This fosters a sense of belongingness and loyality in the minds of employees and opens up opportunities for their growth and development.[12]

2.3.3.6 Understudy Assignment or Attachment Method

An 'understudy' is a person who is under training to assume, at a future time, the full duties and responsibilities of the position currently held by his superior. In this way, it is ensured that a fully trained person is available to replace a manger during his long absence or illness, or on his retirement, transfer or promotion.

An understudy may be picked up by a manager from amongst a large number of subordinates, or several individuals. Such an understudy learns the complexities of the problems and how to solve them. Learns also the process of decision-making and investigation and making written recommendations to his superior. He is generally assigned a project, which is closely related to the work in his section. He is deputed to attend executive meetings as a representative of his superior, at which he makes a presentation and proposals. The essence is that the senior routes much of the departmental work through the junior; discusses problems with him and allows him to participate in the decision-making process as often as possible.

Merits

The understudy method enjoys certain advantages, viz.:

(i) It is practical and quick in training persons for greater responsibility for it lays emphasis on learning by doing.
(ii) The learners' interest and motivation are high and the superior is relieved of his heavy workload.
(iii) The trainee manager is also not overburdened with work and responsibility; at the same time he secures full participation in the running of the function and insight into the job-content.
(iv) The trainee is able continuously to obtain guidance of the senior. The work that passes through him opens up windows for him to appreciate different angles and viewpoints related to the job. He receives an opportunity to see the job in total.
(v) It ensures continuity of management facilities even when the superior leave his position.
(vi) The chances for costly mistakes or upsetting relationship within the group are eliminated.

Demerits

But the method suffers from some defects as well, such as:

(i) Since the understudy is picked up by the superior often on the basis of favoritism, he tends to perpetuate the existing practices of in-breeding.
(ii) The motivation of all the employees in the unit may decrease since the incentive to get ahead is partially destroyed when one particular subordinate is identified in advance as one who will be the next occupant of a higher-level managerial position.
(iii) Under a competent senior, the junior trainee might lose his

independence and his critical appraisal of the way of job is performed.

(iv) The subordinate employees might ignore him and withhold cooperation; they might tend to treat him as an intruding appendage to the function without authority and accountability.

(v) While there are opportunities for sizeable errors, this technique is used predominantly in situations where major or critical decisions can be delayed till the manager returns or can be made in close consultation with the manager next up in line.

2.3.3.7 Committee Assignments

Most large companies make use of committees for the training and development of their managerial. These are either regularly constituted or *adhoc* committees entrusted with some special objectives and responsibilities relating to the work of the organization strictly speaking they are not specifically, for training purposes. This membership of these committees is hold by very competent personnel.

Committee membership is essentially develops much needed understandings and brings in the fore the importance and value of the cooperative effort and provides good opportunity for group leadership.

Assignments on aspiring manager or potential worker to important committees can provide them with very broadening experience. They learn to view the company working in wider perspective. They also learn specific knowledge and skills related to the running of the business. The participation of the managerial and other personnel in the committees, which takes important decisions and make up plans, enables them to gain a firs hand knowledge of the personalities, issues, and processes governing the way the organization function. This also added to their knowledge of other functions, specially relating to coordination and integration.[13]

2.3.3.8 Audio-Visual Aids

There is nothing intrinsically new about a visual aids they have been used as a learning device ever since man has been able to draw. But the range variety and sophistication of such devices are increased rapidly over the past twenty years. So much so that there is now a danger of their misuse of relaying too heavily on them with drawing the human element from teaching almost entirely. Visual Aids are of great value in it improving effective communication. Between teacher and student but they should not replace the student-teacher relationship.

Learning aids range from such relatively simple devices as the black board, the felt board, charts, photographs and diagrams to the more expensive visual and audio-visual equipment such as films and slide projectors working models, overhead projectors tape recorders, and closed circuits televisions. Teaching machines may be classified as visual aids to instruction. The main reasons for the use of such devices include.

- The visual illustration of a verbal description that may be difficult to grasp in words only.
- The ability to attract and hold the attention of the students moving objects are found to do this more effectively to an static ones.
- The exercise of the theory of leaning by observing the learner protagonist method.

Research has shown that we acquire only 13 percent of our knowledge, via our aural senses, 75% via our visual senses and the balance through our other senses.[14]

2.3.3.9 Conference Leadership

This is the OJT technique though limited in its scope, but beneficial in personnel development. This method is extensively used in supervisory and executive development programmes. This method primarily aims at developing problem-solving and decision-making capabilities and learning about new and complex materials. Learning through this method is facilitated by building upon the viewpoints and ideas as contributed by the participants. This has also its objectives the inter-changing for information and fostering better communication and cooperation between different departments in an organization.

Advantages

- This is ideally suited for analyzing problems from different viewpoints.
- This is an excellent method for development of conceptual skills and knowledge
- With this method people learn from one another.
- This enables the trainee participants to improve their power of expression and deliberation.

Disadvantages

- This does not allow participation of larger groups but only limited ones.
- Discussions and deliberations generally within this method are slow, because of that fact that all the participants desiring to speak are allowed time and also some times irrelevant issues somehow get into discussions.
- Some times when the discussions are not directed or do not turn up to the felt needs of the participants, they do not take much interest and that way this method is not likely to meet with much success.
- There always lurks a danger that the group may not become over dependent on the leader, with the result that no useful purpose thus will be served for achieving the desired objectives.

2.3.4 Off-the-Job Training

Off-the-job training mostly commonly called the classroom training—the traditional way of education, places the trainee in a class room, off-the job training takes place either in side the organization or at some external selected sites may be institutes universities or professional associations which have no connection with the company.

Importance

- ❖ The ample provision of the ability to use the best instructor and the best-planned material.
- ❖ It seeks wider acceptance by people because of its popular usage, with which the people are very much familiar.
- ❖ This enables conveying information to a large number of people in a short time.

Objectives

To take the man away from his working environment to mix with men in a similar position to his own and as a result bring about change in his attitude and point of view, will widen his outlook so that he may be capable of looking at problem differently. This is the main objective off-the-job training. Off-the-job training has for its aims the imparting of knowledge or special type of information on the apprentice type of jobs or on clerical jobs and a part of some sales training.

Large companies can well afford to conduct classroom training within a company providing courses for business and industry. The classes are scheduled to be held either just before or just after the regular work shifts.

This results in a saving for the company so far as time compensation is concerned. However depending on the particular items of training the employees may be excused for one or two hours to attend classes.

Advantages

Classroom training can be rendered more effective and useful if there exists ample provision for questions from participants during or after the instructions or talk. This greatly helps in the better understanding of the trainees.

2.3.4.1 Lecture Method

The Lecture Method : The Lecture Method a conventional training technique and a traditional form of class room teaching still occupies though a very limited and specific place in the area of training and development because of the advent of a number of other new and improved methods and techniques.

This method of instruction and job training is very much concerned with talking to the lecture 'tells' you, this method permits the imparting of a substantial amount of material to a large group in a relatively short time. It is regarded as the most useful when philosophy, concepts, attitudes, theories, and problem-solving activities are to be learned.

A lecture is a formal organized talk by the instructor to a group of students a standard instructional method in colleges or universities.

Importance and Uses

- For rendering the lecture method most effective and useful, the uppermost consideration that should matter is that of the speaker or lecturer.
- A lecture should be well planned as to purpose main ideas, and organizations should be systematic and clear.
- Expert studies show that a lecture to be really its worth should not last less than 30 minutes or more than an one hour.
- A lecture to be really effective and purposeful participants are expected to make notes or better be provided with duplicated summaries these serve as a good aids to learning.

Objectives

- The lecture method aims at increasing intellectual thinking and understanding.
- The lecture serves as a good purpose when it is a question of imparting technical or special information of a complex nature.

Advantages

- This method can used for very large groups which are to be trained in a short time obviously the cost per trainee works out to be very low.
- This gives the trainer the greatest degree of control over the training situation. It enables him to present the material exactly in the manner as he wants to with little risk of any one's interruption or talking back.
- The lecture method serves as a good purpose for imparting technical and special information of a complex nature.
- A lecture one prepared has the advantage of being repeated on other occasions or given by a substitute lecturer.

Disadvantages

- This method essentially constitutes one way communication. Learners are passive and this violates the principle of learning by doing thus this has limited potential for use in skills training. Where hands on experience is essential.

- Lecturing needs and substantial speaking skills. An inexperience or untrained lecturer who may not be proficient enough to concentrate on the subject of talk may often go off the track and try to stuff up his lecture with unwanted material may lose the good will sympathy and attention of the listeners, who often fell bored and frustrated. Thus the utility of the lecture is undermined.
- The memorization of facts and figures as involved in a lecture hardly lay any stress on the application of knowledge.
- The presentation for material as often happiness is not geared to a common level of knowledge.[15]

2.3.4.2 Simulation Technique

It is a training technique which indicates the duplication of organizational situations in a learning environment. It is a mock-up of a real thing. This technique has been used for developing technical and inter-personal skills. The following procedure is usually adopted.

1. Essential characteristics of a real life organization or activity are abstracted and presented as a case not to be studied and analyzed as in the usual case study method but to be experienced by the trainee as a realistic life like circumstance.
2. Trainees are asked to assume various roles in the circumstance and to solve the problem facing them. They are asked to themselves not to act.
3. A simulation often involves a telescopic or compressing of time events; a single hour may be equated with a month or quarter of a year in real life, and many events are experienced in a relatively brief period of time.
4. Trainees are required to make decision that have a real effect in the simulation and about which they receive rapid feedback.
5. The simulation followed by a critique of what went on during the exercise.

- The advantages to simulation are the opportunities to attempt to create an environment similar to real situations the managers incur without high costs involved should the action prove undesirable. The disadvantages are that it is difficult to duplicate the pressures and realities of actual decision-making on-the-jobs, and individuals often act differently in real life situations when thy do in acting out a simulated exercise.[16]

2.3.4.3 Programmed Instruction Method

Programmed instruction involves a sequence of steps which are often set up through the central panel of an electronic computer as guides in the performance of a desired operation or series of operations. It incorporates a pre-arranged, proposed, or desired course of proceedings pertaining to the learning or acquisition of some specific skills or general knowledge. A programmed instruction involves breaking information down into meaningful units and then arranging these in a proper way to form a logical and sequential learning programme or package.

In such a programme, knowledge is imparted with the use of a textbook or a teaching machine. The programme involves: presenting question, facts or problems to the trainee to utilize the information given; and the trainee instantly receives feedback (and sometime rewards or penalties) on the basis of the accuracy of his answers.

The merits of the methods are: (1) Trainees learn at their own pace; (2) Instructors are not a key part in learning; (3) The materials to be learned are broken down into small units; (4) Immediate feedback is available; (5) Active learner participation takes place at each step in the programme; (6) Individual differences can be taken into account; (7) Training can be imparted at odd times and in odd places; and (8) There is a high level of learner motivation.

However, this method suffers from certain demerits too. These are: (1) The impersonality of instructional setting; (2) An advanced study is not possible until preliminary information has been acquired; (3) Only factual subject matters can be programmed; (4) Philosophical and attitudinal concepts and motor skills cannot be taught by this method; and (5) The cost of creating any such programme is very high.

This method is primarily used in teaching factual knowledge, such as mathematics, physics, a foreign language, etc.[17]

2.3.4.4 Case Study Method

The case study method pioneered by the Harvard Business School, Massachusetts, U.S.A., was first developed in the 1880's by Christopher Lang dell at Harvard law school. This is essentially a group-oriented technique, which has been steadly increasing popularity and wide use as a common form of training and a valuable training aid.

Objectives

This is an excellent means for integration the knowledge obtained from a number of basic disciplines cases are usually based upon real experiences and problem situations. Naturally, students interest tends to be high. Therefore, aims at making the learning process more experimental, carried out, as it is in an environment which encourage experiment with new ideas and alternation inter-personal behaviors.

- With the appropriate management of the learning situation by the instructor or the teacher case studies can have a powerful learning impact, but where the management is poor learning may be comparatively very low.

- The group of learners should be mature enough to have a good understanding of the different concepts of management.
- Distinguished studies lay much emphasis on the :

  (a) Content of the case as this is of significant importance in which skills of analytical thinking may be sharpened and power of perceptions and judgments may be enhanced.
  (b) The case should be a true or accurate representation of the issues involved, as objectively as possible without any observations from the case writer.
  (c) The case should be comprehensive in its description with a proper background history facts figures data thus enabling the group members to view the organization and the historical setting where the reported events took place in their true colors.
  (d) The case situation should be reproduced in full, though a part of it may be presented on a film or on television through role-playing.
  (e) It is emphasized that in case of managerial training it will serve quite a useful purpose if the company releases the written up case. This ensures authenticity of the date and represented the reality.
  (f) The case should be analyzed property. A preliminary analysis may be made either in general terms or in response to specific questions set by the instructor.

- The participants should have thoroughly assimilated the content of a case. This is best achieved by individual study.
- The discussion should be characterized by free informal and experiential atmosphere. Particularly there should be complete freedom to open up one's mind, also the same kind of freedom to cite first hand experiences.

Methodology generally adopted by the trainees for finding out the solution.

1. Problem Identification.
2. Analysis.
3. Development of Alternate solutions.
4. Selection of most appropriate solution.

Advantages

- Working through cases helps trainees develop or improve several skills.
- In encourage open mind ness and serve as a goods means of pooling the knowledge from different basic disciplines.
- It tends to motivate and heighten the interest of the students as cases usually relate to real problem situations.
- The real utility and strength of this method lies in the tangible evidence it offers to the value of collective decisions.
- This method attractive a mass appeal because it deals with detailed description of real life situation.
- This makes the trainees fully aware and lands them into a state of preparedness for obscurities and complexities they may have to encounter in their business careers.
- This enables students/trainees to have quick grasp of cases situations, which help them drawing out, there from the generalization and principles so easily.

Disadvantages

- The case becoming permanent precedents eking to the minds of the trainees thus may be used indiscriminately.
- If the case will overly artificial it will most likely be diminishing the learning experiences.
- The weakness of this method lies in its inability to do full justice to the feel of given situations.
- Cares play crucial role in the working of this method. Sometimes it so happens that cases are not made sufficiently realistic to be really useful.[18]

2.3.4.5 Role Playing Method

It was developed by J.L. Moreno, a Venetian psychiatrist. He coined the terms "role playing", "role-reversal", "sociodrama", "psychodrama" and a number of other specialized terms, originally it was developed for group therapy for mentally disturbed people.

Definition

"As an educational or therapeutic technique in which some problem-solving human interaction, real or imaginary is presented and then spontaneously acted out. The enactment casually followed by a discussion or analysis to determine what happened and why and if necessary, how the problem could be better handled in the future".

Role-playing essentially is one of the earliest forms of simulation technique in training. It has been increasingly accepted as a valuable training tool in recent years. The method being dramatic and a fun, is highly interesting and entertaining for participants. It is rather a very flexible training method. It is both corrective as well as instructive.

Importance

- The case should specifically relate to the trainees needs. The built-in problems as embodied in case should be such which concern most of the trainee either in his immediate job or some new job in the near future.
- The case should be written in a language as is easily understood and spoken by the trainees.
- The case should be very concisely and precisely written in simple style to well understandable by the trainees who have to act the roles.
- In plays which are a little complex and specially enacted with the objective of developing analytical and problem-solving skills. It may necessitate to supplement the role playing sheet by a page marked. General instruction or background information nature of the organization job duties of the role player, technical details of the work process, etc.
- The case should allow the actors to enlarge or develop their roles from the core facts, as provided then in their role description.
- In describing the behavior of the person in the role-play use of callous words like "jealous", "selfish", "greedy" should be avoided.

Utility Areas

- Role-playing is best used as a tool to develop implementation skills.
- Its most common uses for training supervisors in human relation skills.
- Training sales personnel in sales technique.
- It often used in the training programmes in the areas of interviewing performance reviews and conference leadership.

Methodology and Procedure: Role playing involves two or more persons depending upon the particular purpose for which the instructor uses the session. Instructor prepares the role of each actor and group describes the central theme of the role and as much background as required by the trainee to play it. He may also suggest crucial area for the study group to observe. Late he may use these areas as a framework for subsequent discussion. Role players are provided with either written or oral description of situations and are assigned to play before the rest of the class. The actors have to enlarge or develop their roles from the core facts as described in their role description. There are no lines to memorize and no rehearsals. The central idea of the role-playing is that the trainee understands the situation from a perspective different from his own.

After being allowed sufficient time to plan their actions and get ready they must then act out their roles implied in a given situation spontaneously before the group. They then switch role play the other roles out. The other members of the group observe and make notes of the presentation. The group then discussions criticize and evaluate actions of the players. The instructor summarizes all comments and conclusions pointing out lessons to be remembered.

Advantages

- It emphasizes learning by doing.
- It stimulates human sensitivity and interactions— students put into practice knowledge they have absorbed from text books, lecturer and discussions they become sensitive to the way their behavior affects others.
- It renders knowledge of results immediately, because the role players themselves as well as the study group participate in the discussion after the role-playing analyses, criticize and evaluate the performance and behavior of players.
- With role playing trainee interest and involvement tend to be high.
- In role-playing situation are so nicely maneuvered that the trainees would act out, as they would in real life.
- It develops skills and the ability to apply knowledge particularly in areas like human relations and leadership.
- It brings about desired changes in behaviors and attitudes.
- It helps trainees to appreciate other point of view.
- It encourages group members to act as well as it think.

Disadvantages

- It is time consuming and expensive.
- The number of persons that can be actively involved is limited.
- The problems formulated by the instructor may not be those that actually other the trainee. These may be unrealistic.[19]

2.3.5 Career Planning and Development

This method is mainly concerned with increasing the effectiveness of individuals and meeting the needs of an organization. An individual when he gets opportunity to participate in career. Orientation programmes— specific development assignments of educational activities, he gets varied experiences which help him in the upgrading of his skills, abilities and knowledge. These are designed to enable him to reach his highest potential in the shortest time.

This gives an individual a great satisfaction. He gets of belongingness in the organization he works where he finds that his interests are well looked after by the management. On the management side it can safely depend on such individuals of taking charge of challenging planned future posts career planning and guidance assumes still greater importance when there is scarcity in the availability of skilled and trained manpower particularly so in the case of managerial personnel. Career planning and guidance ensures its services of a loyal, experienced and dependable "work force". This further ensures the company the ready availability of trained personnel as when needed. No time is lost in search of trained manpower. Thus there remains a continuous production flow without any disruption. All these results in the welfare and profitability both the organization and its employees.[20]

2.3.6 Executive Development

2.3.6.1 Coaching

One of the most natural forms of OJT is coaching. On-the-job coaching it may be understood is the oldest on-the-job technique. This is continuous process involves daily instructions by the superior to his subordinate trainees. "Helping a man to help himself" is the essence of coaching. Here the superior may be supervisor, trainer or instructor, act as a tutor and starts with job instruction. He explains the job to the trainees and instructs them to perform the various tasks involved in their jobs and practice them well. He provides necessary assistance to facilitate them in the job learning process. He observes helps them with his constructive suggestions, in correcting their errors and provides them feedback in terms of the progress the trainees have made by way of improvement in the performance of their jobs.

People do learn by doing but the extent and speed of their learning to a greater degree depends on their immediate superior in most cases the supervisor who is the best possible position to help his subordinates to grow and develop. He is the singular person in the organization so well aware of the weaknesses and shortcomings of his subordinates and finding suitable opportunities, assigns such tasks individuals that will help make up the deficiencies in them. He, therefore, plays an active part in stimulating and guiding his subordinates in developing their skills.

Advantages

For coaching to be really effective there should exist sincere and healthy relationship built on mutual confidence between the immediate superior—the supervisor and the trainee. The supervisor must set-up person and business standards before his subordinates for them to follow. He should exercise best of his ability to communicate and stimulate the employees trainee and should have the patience to help and be readily available to render any assistance as and when the subordinate seeks or needs it.

It is emphasized that on-the-job coaching should cover all major phases of the job. On-the-job coaching work best, when used in conjunction with periodic formal classroom instruction and other types of training.

Disadvantages

- This mainly provides individual opportunities to grow only within the boundaries set by their jobs,
- This restricts a man from developing much beyond the limits of his own bass's abilities, and
- This coaching technique is authoritarian. Hence the loss tends to familiarize or to use at little stronger word, pressurize the subordinate with his own work habits, beliefs and frame of references even though some of these may be faulty.

2.3.6.2 The Multiple-Management Technique

It is a technique whereby juniors are assigned to Board or Committees, by the chief executive. They are asked to participate in deliberations of these Board and Committees. In these sessions, real life actual problems are discussed, different views are debated and decisions are taken. The juniors get an opportunity to share in managerial problems. When Committees are of *"ad hoc"* or temporary nature, they often take a task force activities designed to delve into a particular problem, ascertain alternative solutions, and make a recommendation for implementing a solution. These temporary assignments can be both interesting and rewarding to the employees' growth. On the other hand, appointment to permanent committees increases the employees' exposure to other members of the organization, broadens his understanding, and gives him an opportunity to grow and make recommendations under the scrutiny of other committee members.

Merits

This technique has several advantages:

(i) It gives Board members an opportunity to gain knowledge on various issues.
(ii) It helps identify those who have executive talent. Multiple judgments are obtained on each individual through the Board rating system.
(iii) The members gain practical experience of group decision-making and of team-work. As a result of the interaction process, they develop respect for the rights and view of their associates.
(iv) It is relatively inexpensive method of development.
(v) It permits a considerable number of managers to participate in certain activities within a reasonable period of time. Besides, the Boards do make important contributions to efficiency, productivity, and a better human relations climate. In fact, they assist in a better administration in the organization.

Demerits

The demerits or limitations of the method are:

(i) It is only suitable for middle and senior level managers.
(ii) It does not permit any specific attention to training needs of the manager.

The debates in these committees often tend to be discursive lacking purposiveness or authority. The deliberations often degenerate into academic discussion without the participants feeling committed to the conclusions.[21]

2.3.6.3 Job Rotation

The on the job training technique of Job rotation is designed to give the trainee knowledge and experience of operations in the various parts of the organization. The trainee while moving through various training positions receives instructions, gains knowledge and experiences in different situations, and is provided with feedback from his superior in each department.

Job rotation, which is also termed position Rotation, is a procedure or method for imparting diversified training to managers through their performance on a succession of different types of jobs. This provides an opportunity to young executives to familiarize themselves with the company in general and thus gain experience. Job rotation therefore essentially in the process of increasing the span of experience.

While considering job rotation extensive case made of replacement charts, schedules to take decisions, as to who is to be moved where and when on a coordinate company-wide basis. The transferring of their supervisors middle management, junior executive from job-to-job and from plant to plant on some planned basis for purposes of educational learning and training is widely practiced by many large companies and industrial undertakings.

Importance: In the executive training and development job rotation is most commonly used as a training device with the objective of broadening the outlook and background of the training by providing him knowledge of several or all major activities of the company in its wide perspective and thus helping him to gain on-the-job experience while shouldering greater responsibilities in a varied business situations and further gaining skillful higher level guidance and appraisal. Which all go a long way to develop his talents and help him discover his own special interest and performance.

Advantages

- Job Rotation helps developing generalists, instead of specialists initially most men are specialists and they will remain so, unless opportunities are provided to them for acquiring the broad.

Perspectives and diversified skills needed for widening the horizon of their experiences so essential for their growth and development.

- With the injection of new concepts, new ideas, fresh view points, job rotation bring about a change in the stereotyped working of the department, by eliminating routine practices or operations which have been carried an unnecessarily over a period of years and have been responsible for creating so to say a rut and boredom in the department. Thin undoubtedly results in the improvements and efficiency in the working of the department.
- Job rotation fosters development of better communication and inter-departmental cooperation between men within an organization.
- Job rotation will not only provide training but the health, efficiency and general well-being of the entire organization would benefit in so many ways.
- It promotes organizational flexibility through generating flexible human resources, which helps the organization build up management strength.
- It widens the trainees circle of acquaintance among company executives.
- With Job Rotation talents of an individual instead of remaining frozen and being wasted in a department, which does not hold any scope of further expansion, this affords the individual on opportunity to show his worth in the line of work for which he is better suited. This ultimately will result in the benefit of both the individual and the enterprises.
- It eliminates the assumption by an individual of any vested right in a particular job. The realities about men who have been holding jobs as a matter of favor, which may or may not have been justified thus come out in the open and thereby they are thrown out of jobs.
- Job rotation tests the individual executive ability and an all round capability and competency as demonstrated in progressive assignments that indicates individual's suitability for promotion to higher level positions and this then at their maximum effectiveness.
- It enables trainees to acquire all the advantages of on-the-job coaching in each situation as provided by their superiors.

Disadvantages

- Job rotation upsets the homely and family life of the rotates. It is particularly a great hardship for their children who must constantly readout themselves to new schools and new friends. There are also difficulties in adjustment to new surroundings.
- Job rotation discourages executives to go deep in their assignments.

- In job rotation most of the time of the new men is spent in familiarizing themselves with the environments of the department and learning new technology as involved in the new jobs.
- The rotation system is likely to be rendered over-centralized, inflexible, and closed.
- It is observed that job rotation often develops splits, internal friction, Jealously and non-cooperative attitudes and behaviors on the part of men working in different departments in an organization.
- Job rotation proves to be expensive for training and development purposes.
- With job rotation there may be risk of talented and deserving young persons being left out of availing of chance for their advancement.[22]

2.3.6.4 The Syndicate Method

This being association with the Administrative staff college at Honley-on-thames, U.K. with a group approach was developed and came in vague in 1948.

A syndicate is a form of small group organization, various small groups are often designated is syndicates. This method is used as a device not only for the study of specific problems but for other tasks also.

Features

- It is composed of members with different professionals expertise drawn from different functional areas and different types of enterprises.
- It focuses on task accomplishment in the sense that each study must produce a definite not product. The objective set in the study, be it a report, a summary, questions for conferences over action planning dealing with a particular situation, within the scheduled time.
- It is self-managing so to say, as it does not need any outside personnel to manage the study courses as chairman and secretary and members themselves.
- It provide self-assessment and evaluation which seeks to improve its effectiveness and utility.

Objectives

- To providing the managerial personnel practice in skills techniques and procedures so essential to a manager in his daily work routine, as he rises to occupy higher executive posts.
- To encourage members from various types of enterprises to share their experiences as and to learn from each other.

Importance

- It needs to be ensured that each group or syndicate represents as a wide range of experience as possible from different types of enterprises, different functional areas, and with different professional backgrounds.
- It is that of staring experience by participants in small groups or syndicates.
- The organization and participants have a clear understanding of the technique and mechanism of utilization of this method to avoid any waste of time and just keep off any possible frustration.

Advantages

- This considerably helps enhancing the knowledge of the managerial personnel.
- This helps in brining about a change in the attitude of managers.
- This helps upgrading the skills of the managers more particularly in the area of oral and written communications.
- This helps in creating a suitable committee behaviour.
- This helps broadening the outlook of the members and thus in their making effective group decisions.
- This stimulates each other thinking.
- This develops power of toleration, rather respect of views of others.

2.3.6.5 The Conference Method

In this method, the participating individuals 'confer' to discuss points of common interest to each other. A conference is basic to most participative group-centered methods of development. It is a formal meeting, conducted in accordance with an organized plan, in which the leader seeks to develop knowledge and understanding by obtaining a considerable amount of oral participation of the trainees. It lays emphasis on small group discussions, on organized subject matter, and on the active participation of the members involved. Learning is facilitated by building up on the ideas contributed by the conferees.

There are three types of conference. In the directed discussion, the trainer guider the discussion in such a way that the facts, principles or concepts are explained. In the raining conference, the instructor gets the group to pool its knowledge and past experience and brings different points of view to bear on the problem. In the seminar conference, answer is bound to a question or a solution to a problem. For this, the instructor defines the problem, encourages and ensures full participation in the discussion.

Merits

The conference is ideally sited for the purpose of analyzing problems and issues and examining them from different viewpoints. It is an excellent method for the development of conceptual knowledge and for reducing dogmatism and modifying attitudes because the participants develop solutions and reach conclusions, which they often willingly accept.

Demerits

However, the conference method suffers from certain limitations:

(i) It is limited to a small group of 15 to 20 persons, because larger groups often discourage the active participation of all the conferees; and

(ii) The progress is usually slow because all those desiring to speak on a point are generally allowed to do so. Consequently irrelevant issues easily creep in.

If the Method is to be Effective:

(a) The conferees should have some knowledge of the subject to be discussed at the conference.

(b) Good and stimulating leaders are needed, for it is they who summarize material at appropriate times during a discussion and think along with the group to help it analyze and reach decisions; adopt a permissive point of view which encourages members to express themselves without fear to censure or ridicule; control the more verbose members and bring out the more reserved; develop sensitivity to the thoughts and feelings of individuals and finally, ensure a general consensus on points without forcing agreement or side-stepping disagreement.

(c) The size of the group should be small enough to allow each individual to participate and become personally involved in the deliberations of the group.

(d) Training issue must involve a problem or need each individual is currently facing or interest in the conference results will wane.[23]

2.3.6.6 Critical Incidents

This method is associated with the name of Prof. Paul Pigors of Massachusetts Institute of Technology who developed it. A particular incident is the pivot around which the entire method revolves. Therefore, it becomes important to know how to get at these incidents.

It may be observed that an incident must relate to some real life work or business situation generally a superior keeps record of certain critical incidents may be good or bad. These incidents are brought in use for discussions with the employee trainee for purpose of determining the appropriate training. A superior may also sometimes well develop his own incidents and get at the relevant date-essential to be made use of in the process, through trail. The critical incidents method follows the five steps in the sequence in the process.

(i) *Studying the incident closely*: This essentially involves each member of the trainees group working alone for a couple of minutes and devoting his close attention to the study of the various aspects of the incident, just imagining to himself the situation in which the particular incident might have happened, which calls for prompt decisions.

(ii) *Getting organizing factual information*: The members of the group team while trying to place themselves into the real work situation, address questions to the instructor for obtaining more factual information about the case.

(iii) *Identifying and determining the key issues*: This step is mainly concerned with the highlighting of the key issue for decision-making. The trainee now assemble in like-mind small group examine analyze the incident in its entirely on the basis of the factual information and data, as already summarized is isolate the key issue will required decision-making. They identify determine the key issue.

(iv) *Making, crystallizing, presenting and testing decisions*: With the key issue having been determined the like minded group row busies itself to work out a possible solution for decision-making. They take about 20 to 25 minutes and ready with a possible solution and they choose a spokesman for their group. A spokesman of each group outline the position of his group. There is feeling in the groups that due to certain deficiencies left in their analysis of the case, the possible solution they have arrived at may not be right and correct one. In order to test its viability, each group approaches again the instructor for some additional facts about the case. This instructor provides them with more facts.

(v) *Looking back and reviewing the case* : This is the final phase in the process of case analysis for decision. Now the entire group gets together again to review the entire case situation. They look back over the whole sequence of events and behavior so to say in a realistic work situation. It is that this stage that the instructor now tells the trainees of the lacunae and shortcomings left in their as kings the might and pertinent questions which would have elicited from him the correct information helping the solutions of the case problem.

2.3.6.7 Seminar or Team Discussion

This is an established method for training. A seminar is conducted in many ways:

(a) It may be based on a paper prepared by one or more trainees on a subject selected in consultation with the person in charge of the seminar. It may be apart of a study or related to theoretical studies or practical problems. The trainees read their papers, and this is followed by a critical discussion. The chairman of the seminar summarizes the contents of the papers and the discussions which follow their reading.

(b) It may be based on the statement made by the person in-charge of the seminar or on a document prepared by an expert, who is invited to participate in the discussion.

(c) The person in-charge of the seminar distributes in advance the material to be analyzed in the form of required readings. The seminar compares the reactions of trainees, encourages discussion, defines the general trends and guides the participants to certain conclusions.

(d) Valuable working material may be provided to the trainees by actual files. The trainees may consult the files and bring these to the seminar where they may study in detail the various aspects, ramifications and complexities of a particular job or work or task.[24]

2.3.6.8 Business Game Method

Business games are also classroom simulation exercise in which teams of individual compete with one another or against an environment in order to achieve a given obedient. These games designed to be representative of real life situations, under these an atmosphere is created in which the participants play a dynamic role and enrich their skills through involvement and simulated experience manual games was developed in 1956 and described by Andlinger in 1958.

Importance

- Game should for the men who will play it.
- Game should complex enough to be of engaging interest but not so difficult that takes hours of advanced study to learn to play.
- The game should be easy to administer with the given facilities like staff space, computer, etc.
- The lesions that the game teachers should be fairly simple and pertinent to the contents of the rest of the programme.
- The players should respect the game it the game has local origin players may be more willing to accept the games rules and challenges.
- The real worth of this type of game may be seen in how the game is constructed, operated and evaluated.
- This method effective requires a well designed game that provides a focal point for thought and dissuasion and establishes a common basis for communication between student and teacher.

Objectives

- To provide learning for better management decision-making in an integrated manner and their implementation.
- To provide learning of woman organization or industry operate.
- To help identify interrelationships within the organization.
- To obtain a better idea and gain an appreciation as to how a decision in one organizational units affects other units.

Methodology

A typical business games involves taking a simulated business situation dividing the participants in to several teams, that organize into simulated competing companies. Each team consists of 2 to 6 members; the teams are expected to make typical management decisions concerning, production volume personal, prince, etc. related matters in the simulating environments. The game continues for 6 to 12 periods. The game may divided itself into three or four periods, a week representing two periods of six months each. For each period the teams work out the action in details taking into account also result of their past performance. The available games last from a few hours to a few days or weeks. Feedback is prompt so that they can learn the effects of their actions to improve their competitive business situations. At the end of particular period final results are worked out by each team and compared with those of others.

Advantages

- Business games can reflect real-life in organization and thus permit considerable transfer of training to the job.
- They are also essentially motivated and create substantial and active involvement and interests.
- This method helps developing the awareness of the numerous matters and that are affected by broad policy decisions.
- The trainee learn how to inter-act effectively with each other.
- The business games in addition to its being dynamic provide practice in using data about resource processes and often able to bring into play a number of potent factors like production schedules, etc.
- With this method several participants can be set to compete with one another.
- It provide a systematic method of exploring issues.
- In executive development this serve as a good tool for assessment.
- This forester team cooperation.
- Decisions are quick
- Management trainees get to have a wider perspective of the organization when they work with their senior colleagues in the game.

- The error of unsound decisions in a real business situation may be disastrous, but a management trainee in a business games learns from his mistakes and has a chance of making good his losses without any harmful consequences.

Disadvantages

- Business games being relatively new, efficacy of their use has not been adequately tested, proved and established, as training device. It is yet to be experienced whether the personnel who have been exposed to these games, actually improve give a better account of their behavior when they return back to their jobs.
- Business games by themselves alone, cannot serve as an effective training device. They need to be used in conjunction with organized theory which may be provided by reading, lectures or conference discussions.
- Business games are simple when compared with real life, these contain, many but not all the elements that are present in strength in every operating organization.
- This is time consuming and expensive
- This discourages any innovation, initiative and originally for teams have to strictly adapt themselves to rigid situations—fixed set of relationships programmed into the game.[25]

2.3.6.9 In Basket Method

In this method each team of trainees is given a file of correspondence bearing on a functional area of management. Each individual studies the file and makes his own recommendations on the situation. If further information is required by him, it is supplied by the members of the team. Later, the observations of each individual member are compared and conclusions on different functional areas reached, and these are put down in the form of a report. For this purpose such teaching methods as the incident process, role-playing, the syndicate method, and the conference method are used.

Merits

- Decisions are rapid, feedback is objective, and further decisions are based on the feedback of earlier decisions.
- The consequences of many possible alternatives in a situation can be evaluated over a period of time.
- The participants pay for the consequences of their decisions.
- Decision-making is by a group which consists of managers and specialists from different departments. Each member therefore gets an opportunity to participate in it.

- An abstract and complex situation is given the semblance of a real world situation, and this illusion facilitates the learning process.
- By mixing with managers from different functional areas manager get a better appreciation of other functional areas.
- The efficiency of planning and systematic approach can be demonstrate.
- Team cooperation can be fostered and departmental conflicts softened down or eliminated.
- The specified time limit imposes the time constraint on the trainees which stimulates reality.
- The method is inexpensive and can be organised easily.

Demerits

- It sometimes discourages originality for teams have to adopt themselves to rigid situations.
- The logical solutions suggested by the team to be abstracted from compulsions against which it had to be tackled in the actual situation.[26]

2.3.6.10 The T-Group or Sensitivity Training

The T-group training is variously termed as sensitivity, L-group (learning group) encounter group or laboratory training. This method is originally developed by kurthewin and later brought into prominence by the national training laboratories U.S.A. under T-group training is essentially concerned with real not simulated, problems or situations existing organizations or in some hypothetical settings.

Objectives

- The T-Group training is concerned most with the awareness of personal feelings, attitudes and needs and those of superiors subordinates and associates such awareness increased by training.
- The T-Group training developing both social sensitivity and behavioral flexibility.
- This training has so far been directed to improving speaking skills only, but now increasing use of this training has come to be made in other directions also.
- It aims at learning about group processes and to improve ones inter-personal and communication skills an intellectual understanding and thus change underlying attitudes and thereby behavior on the job. In the word of Leland Bradford "the goal of laboratory training", "as helping trainees to improve in quality and participation in human affairs".

Generally T-Group training programmes are arranged for three types of population, the first type are the stranger groups who do not know one another, are composed of trainees from different organizations, the second type are the family groups composed of people from the same department of the organization, representing different levels of hierarchy, the third type are called by the name of cousin groups composed of men from the same organization but from different departments.

Importance

The method comprises of a small group of trainees say ten to fifteen working under a trainer, the trainer simply raises questions and provides occasionally comments. The trainees begin to work together and develop as a group they might discuss topic that pertain to industrial problem and may relate to motives and impressions of other people. T-groups go through periods of shock, frustration and hostility but hopefully all such situations as they arise lead to understanding.

Advantages

- To be well aware and learn better about themselves especially their own weaknesses and emotions.
- To develop insights into how they react to others and how others react to them.
- To discover how groups work and how to make out human relations problems.
- To find out how to behave a more effectively in inter-personnel relationships and in particularly, how to manage people through means other than power.
- To develop more "Competent"—"Authentic" relations in which there is free and open expressions of feelings.
- To face interpersonal problems directly. So that they can be solved, rather than trying to avoid them.
- To learn how to get along with others, the superiors, the associates and subordinates.

Disadvantages

- This type of training exposes the trainees to considerable psychological stress situations, in fact mental breakdown and severe shocks have been recorded.
- There is always a risk involved that this type of training may lead to tearing people apart than of bringing them together.
- Such a training renders the management trainee so impulsive and sensitive to the feeling of others, that he is unwilling to take hard decisions.

- T-group ultimately works and to be expensive.
- It involves only a small number of trainees at one time.[27]

2.3.6.11 The Group Discussion Method

This is a popular technique under group centered approach and has proved in important means of training and development. It will perhaps be interesting to know how this group dynamics training come into being.

The national training laboratory in group development started functioning in Bethel Maine (USA) in 1947. This was sponsored by the research center for group dynamics at the university of Michigan and the National Education Association.

The Bethel group started offering training in group dynamics in many parts of U.S.A. In course of time it came to be recognized as an important technique for training far and wide, outside USA.

Definition

Group discussion as purposeful conversation about a topic of mutual interest among 6 to 20 participants under the guidance of trained participants called a leader.

Importance

- This offers maximum opportunity to individual participants to informally associate and share his ideas and experience with other members of the group with an open mind. This considerably helps in increasing his knowledge.
- With this method there also comes about display of an individual participants personality so helpful in his growth and development.
- This helps improving the power of expression and deliberation of the individual participant.
- This so freely allows to observe the reaction of others in situation introduced by the leader.
- The group inter-play proves to be of an immense value in forming learning situations in the minds of the participants as a result of the pooled experience and also weight of mass opinion rendered by group discussions.[28]

2.3.6.12 Laboratory Training

(i) Sensitivity Training

Sensitivity Training is an experimental approach to training. It provides participants an opportunity to actually experience some concepts of management just as a manager would experience them in his own organizational situation. Sensitivity Training is a group training method that uses intensive participation and give immediate feedback for self-analysis and change. This training has two advantages:

(a) Participants remain involved and enthusiastic.

(b) The responsibility for learning experience lies with the participants. He would make positive efforts to derive much benefits from the exercise. This training attempts to develop the diagnostic ability of the participants—the ability to perceive reality. At a group level, one learns about normative structures and authority relationships leading to better team work. It increases sensitivity and awareness how conflicts arise and are resolved. As the name suggests sensitivity training aims at developing sensitivity within people towards thoughts, feelings and behavior of other persons. Through this, improve upon one's human interactions. The effectiveness of sensitivity training depends upon the ability of the participant to apply concepts and awareness obtained in the laboratory or group to his job, the transfer of his knowledge to the organization is possible if the organization has an open discussion, encourage conflict resolution and promote mutual trust.

(ii) T-Groups

One of the methods of the sensitivity training is the T-Group. Bethel Maine of USA was the pioneer of the T-Group. It was considered necessary that to change behavior imparting necessary skills is required. A change in variety of skills and experiences like self-awareness, interpersonal relationships, team work, group, organizational process and inter-group conflict resolution. Sensitivity training has developed to the status of an intervention in organization development. T-Group training is process-oriented and not content-oriented where people operate a feeling level of communication, observing revealing, listening, unraveling messages.

Retraining

Retraining programmes are generally arranged for employees who have long been in the service of an organization. The retraining programme may be necessitated by the following facts:

(i) Some employees are engaged in a confined phase of a particular task and lose their all-round skills in a particular trade. Hence, to keep them active in all-round skills, such training is needed.

(ii) During prolonged lay-off periods, employees on certain highly skilled jobs are given retraining when they are called back to work.

(iii) Technological changes may make a particular job, on which an employee is working, unnecessary, and the company may desire to retrain him rater than discharge him.

(iv) An employee, because of illness, accident or incapacity due to age, may no longer be able to do his share of the work he performed when he was in normal health.

(v) Economic depression or cyclical variations in production create conditions in which employment stabilization may be achieved by having a versatile work-force capable of performing more than one job.[29]

2.3.6.13 The Sabbatical Method

Sabbatical is the institution or observance of a day of rest, a time of rest, peace, or quit. It is proving a very useful tool for development more particularly in the western industry. It have been quiet popular for many years in the academic world, where professors take a learn to upgrade their skills and advance their education or research.

Similar sort of plans have been adapted in business and industry some countries of the west, where some corporations give some of their employees six months or even more leave with pay to work on any socially desirable projects or on some special programme. These may be varied nature but having particular emphasis on the development of the individual availing of this type of leave.

Limitations

Paid sabbaticals can be expensive propositions.

The nature of the learning experience as an employee gains, is not within the control of the organization. The revise nature of the developmental experience is more or less left to chance.[30]

2.3.6.14 Transactional Analysis Method

It refers to a total system that includes many related branches and ideas. The understanding of behavior is fundamental to manager's success because his personal interactions have increased enormously.

This method developed by Eric Berne, commonly known as transactional theory of personality.

"Human being is striking hard to achieve goodness. Moses saw goodness as love, yet they all agreed that virtual however understood, was consistently undermined by something in human nature".

Eric Berne has defined "Transaction as the social intercourse of two or more people who encounter each other", studies have shown that there exist three types of egos is an individual.

- Child ego.
- Parent ego.
- Adult ego.

The first stages are recordings in the brain of actual experiences of internal and external events which occur during the first five years of life. The third stage is a data processing computer which grinds out decisions after assimilating information from three sources—parent, the child and the data which adult has gathered or in the continuous process of gathering and updating. This state is produced when the individual play back the recorded data of events involving real people, real time, real places and real feelings.

(i) *The parent* : The values and behavior of the parents are recorded and constitute the basic values of our personalities. Thus parental aspect is very important. If the child hears and gets the same kind of values from his or her mother—father as the information is recorded, then it becomes a source. But if on one hand the child is asked to value the truth and the other hand asked by his father sitting in the house to tell some one in the telephone that he is not there then the recording is confused. The examines normally have so much of confused recording that they are unable to divide. This leads to the formation of negative attitude towards life.

(ii) *The child* : The child may have reservoir of negative data about himself, like parent the child is a state into his current transactions. There can be many things that can happen to an individual which create the situation of childhood.

(iii) *The Adult* : The basic principle of Adult is to transform stimuli in to pieces of information and then process the information on the basis of previous experience. The adult starts testing parent data. If the parent directives are not grounded in reality the child through his own adult will give a sense of wholeness. Transactions types are :

(a) *Complementary transaction* : When communication continuous along parallel lines between individuals, the transactions are complementary.

(b) *Crossed Transactions* : In this type of communication the vectors cross and communication ceases at that point of time. Crossed transactions inhibit creativity, free thinking and social interactions.

(c) *Ulterior Transactions* : This communication has double meaning.

(d) *Gallows Transactions* : The inappropriate love or smile is the gallows transactions. A smile in response to a persons misfortune may serve as gallows transaction.

Importance and Advantages

- Transactional Analysis gives a new way of looking at management and leadership style can contribute to the development to appraisal and counseling skills.
- Transactional Analysis to be development of inter-personnel skills and goal planning abilities.
- Transactional Analysis has general contribution to make to the O.D.
- Transactional Analysis implicitly values autonomy and assertiveness.[31]

2.3.7 Organizational Development

O.D. refers to a long range effort to improve an organization problem-solving capabilities and its ability to cope with changes in its external environment with the help of external or internal behavioral scientists, consultants and change agents we called as O.D.

The interventions of organization development are the planned activities that are introduced into the system to accomplish the desired changes and improvements. Interventions are the methods and techniques that have been created by OD professionals and others to achieve improvements in the functioning of organizations.

Organizational Development Methods

1. Survey Feedback

The OD way of handling attitude surveys is to feedback the results to all the people who filled out the questionnaires. The data is first provided to the executive team. Then each executive holds a meeting with the people reporting directly to him to analyze and evaluate the survey results in a workshop setting. In these workshops plans are formulated to take actions to correct the problems identified by the survey. This workshop process proceeds downward throughout the entire hierarchy. Even rank and file workers are involved in discussing the survey results that apply to their own work unit. They can suggest solutions to problems. The workshop is conducted by the relevant manager or supervisor. Often the OD consultant participates in the workshops as a resource person.

2. The Managerial Grid

The managerial grid, created by Robert R. Blake and Jane S. Mouton, utilizes small face-to-face groups as the basic learning mechanism. The theoretical formulation underlying a grid seminar is the "managerial grid." This is a graphic way of expressing underlying assumptions and theories about ways of managing people in work organizations. Blake and Mouton have synthesized and summarized the salient features of current theory in organizational behavior. They postulate that managers may evidence a concern for production or a concern for people (or a combination of these) in their styles of management. The graphic representation in grid form displays concern for production along the abscissa or X-axis on a scale from 1 through 9. The ordinate or Y-axis expresses concern for people and is also on a scale of 1 through 9. A management theory that exhibits a maximum concern for production and a minimal interest in people (9, 1) is characterized by a high-pressure, authoritarian style. The converse of 9, 1 management is 1, 9 which shows a low concern for production and a high concern for people. This has been labeled "country-club" management. Leadership that evidences a high concern for both people and production is labeled 9, 9. This is held to be a most desirable pattern of management from the standpoint of conflict resolution, creativity, commitment, morale, and productivity. In addition to these three positions on the grid, there is the 1, 1 theory of management wherein management basically abdicates its responsibilities for both people and productivity and the 5, 5 theory wherein management compromises and adopts an "organization-man" strategy. These five basic theories of management can be supplemented by eight other positions or combinations on the grid to make a total of thirteen formulations.

There are six steps or phases in grid organization development. Phase I consists of studying the managerial grid as a theoretical framework for understanding human behavior in the organization. The participants are pointed toward a full comprehension of 9, 9 management as a basis of organizational excellence.

A grid seminar, typically of one week's duration, is composed of a number of study teams of five to nine members each. Participants come from various organizations. The objectives of the one-week seminar include helping each person to recognize his own grid style, developing team action skills, facilitating interpersonal communication within a team, strengthening the use of the critique for problem-solving and learning, and helping the members analyze their own corporate work culture.

The work of the seminar is focused upon various team problem-solving projects involving a time schedule, scoring, comparison with other teams' performance, and critiques. Toward the end of the week each team member will receive a written description of his own managerial style prepared by the other members of the team working jointly. This is based on their observations of this behavior throughout the week. Also each participant prepares a diagnosis of his own company's culture by characterizing it as 9, 1; 5, 5; 1, 9 and the like.

Phase 2, called teamwork development, is a seminar of one week's duration consisting of the members of the management of a single company grouped into family teams. Thus, a plant manager and his immediate subordinates could constitute one seminar team. Each member's perception of the team's culture is developed and discussed in the context of the actual problems faced on the job, whether they be financial, market strategy, quality control, union relations, or the like. The teams also work on objective-setting and problem-solving projects related to their area of corporate responsibilities. Participants learn the benefits of openness and directness in introducing problems and working them through to solutions.

Phase 3, designated inter-group development, focuses upon the relationships between different divisions, departments, and units. Frequently marketing, production, and engineering department exemplify contrasting orientations to the solutions of common problems. A major goal of phase 3 is to develop improved ways of resolving differences. In this phase, departments or groups that normally interrelate on the job are brought together, two at a time, to identify features of an idealized relationship and of their actual relationship. The participants then recommend measures for improving the inter-workings of their departments.

Phase 4, involves the creation of an ideal strategic model for the organization. The participants are primarily the chief executive and his immediate subordinates, although there is input from many other managers. These top executives study several books and articles written by successful business leaders who have described their corporate strategy problems and how they met them. When reading this resource literature the executives are provided with study guides that help them analyze the material according to six areas: financial objectives, nature of the business, nature of the markets, organization structure, policy, and development requirements. After completion of the above work, the team meets for essentially a full week of activity to relate the knowledge gained from the written sources to the formulation of an idealized corporate strategy plan. Although this seminar requires one full week, the actual creation of complete strategy model may take many months of on-the-job activity.

Phase 5 is implementation of the strategic model. This is carried out by working through the natural components of the corporation, whether they be divisions, profit centers, or product lines. For each component a planning team is established whose function is to examine all the essential elements of its operations, such as raw material procurement, manpower utilization, production processes and marketing channels, in order to insure that they are performed in the best possible way.

The sixth and last phase is a systematic critique of progress achieved using as a guide generalized criteria that Blake and Mouton have devised and presented under the designation Corporate Excellence Rubric.

3. Goal Setting and Planning

One method for accomplishing this is for top management to establish corporate and divisional goals for such items as return on investment, share of the market, new products, human resources, and community relations. Then each organizational unit working down through the structure sets its own goals, independently of top-management goals, but with knowledge of them. Next the statements of these unit goals are sent to the top management group. Analysis is made. If there are discrepancies top management may adjust its goals in the light of information from the various units. Also the discrepancies may be noted by top management and the unit goal statements sent back to them for modification. With successive interactions an agreed-upon set of organization-wide goals can emerge.

Confrontation Goal-Setting Meeting. Richard beck hard has created a one-day activity called the confrontation meeting. It can be used not only for goal setting but also for developing specific plans for change and solving operational problems. It can involve an entire management team of an organization of, say, 60 to 100 members. Following an introduction by the chief executive about the purpose of the meeting and the procedure to be followed, the people are divided into groups of five or six members each.

These people come from different departments. No boss is in the same group with a subordinate. These groups are given about an hour to prepare a list of changes that would improve their own situations and the organization generally. The items can deal with procedures, policies, facilities, attitudes, managerial behaviors, and the like.

Next, the lists are placed upon chart pads and explained to the entire assemblage of all groups. Then the total group helps the leader assign category headings to each item on the list. Following an intermission the participants reconvene into new groupings comprised of organizational units—such as engineering, personnel, and marketing—chaired by the heads of these units.

The organizational unit groups survey the entire list, choose three or four items that affect their group, arrive at a course of action for these items, and prepare a timetable for doing the work. In addition, these groups examine the total list for items they think are important for top-management action. Then they prepare a plan for communicating the results of the confrontation meeting to the rest of the people in their units who were not in attendance.

Following the above, the entire 60 to 100 members meeting is reconvened to hear each sub-group's report. At this meeting the top executive makes a response to each item presented. The final step consists of a follow-up meeting several weeks later at which each unit and the top executive report on progress.

4. Team building

The heart of team building is a series of off-site problem-solving sessions of two to five days' duration. These are usually for family groups, that is, a manager and all those reporting directly to him. Sometimes they are also conducted by a third party, either the external OD consultant or the internal staff consultant.

5. Interpersonal Peacemaking

Richard Walton describes the work that he has done in interpersonal peacemaking and presents and analytical framework for carrying out such third-party consultation. Walton's methodology is suitable for diagnosing and resolving conflict between two persons such as the managers of two interrelated departments, two members of the same department, or members of a standing committee.

At the outset it is important to identify the two basic (often interrelated) kinds of conflict. One concerns interpersonal disagreements over substantive issues such as policies, procedures, and the way a particular matter should be handled. The second concerns the personal and emotional conflicts arising between two interacting people. The techniques for handling these two issues are distinct. Conflict over substance requires bargaining and problem-solving measures between the individuals with the aid of meditative interventions by a third party. Emotional conflict requires a modification of a person's perceptions and the working through of feelings between the two people. The solving of substantive issues is more of a cognitive matter, while solving emotional controversies is more an affective matter.[32]

2.3.8 Quality Circles

The start of quality circles (C) in Japan is generally credited to the Union of Japanese Scientists and Engineers, along with Dr. Kaaru Ishikawa of Tokyo University. In the 1950s Dr. Edward W. Deming of the United States introduced the concept of statistical quality control in a series of lectures in Japan. A decade later, the idea of involving all employees, not just staff quality control experts and management, was introduced by the union with this total effort, Japan has moved from the little of "Junk Merchants of the World" to one of the world's leaders in quality products.

Objectives

Though the original initiation of the quality circles concept in Japan stemmed from a desire to improve quality, the fundamental objective has been stated as a desire to develop and enhance human resources. Japan viewed human being as its primary resource, and developed policies and practices that revolved around that attitude among specific policies followed were: 1. Lifetime employment for a substantial segment of the work force, 2. Considerable investment in training in as much as the employee will remain in the one organization, 3. Broad career paths with the employee working in various occupations within the firm, 4. Slow promotion, which reduces the need to cover up mistakes, and 5. Collective decision making which increases the speed of implementation once a decision has been reached.

Circle Processes

A quality circle typically consists of four to twelve volunteer members, the average in Japan being about nine per circle. At its first few meetings, instructions in problem-solving approaches are usually given by either the circle leader or a staff specialist. Among the specific techniques often given are:

1. Brain Storming

The purpose of this technique is to stimulate creativity through free association, unrestricted interaction with others, and the complete restraint of criticism. For a certain time period any idea that comes to mind is voiced. One idea suggests another. Ridiculous and unrealistic ideas are stimulated and not repressed. No criticism of any idea is permitted and all are recorded faithfully. Some have characterized this process as "cerebral popcorn" but it is a useful initial technique to develop an extended number of ideas.

2. *Cause-and-effect or Fish Bone Diagrams*

After a problem identified members are asked to suggest various pauses for the difficulty. It will be determined that some causes are the results of other causes, and their charting often resembles the bony structure of a fish.

3. *Sampling and Charting methods*

Members are taught how to make observations of events in the workplace and chart them in a manner that demonstrates significant relationships.

The first step in identifying workplace problems can come from listing suggestions from management or other employees, or in utilizing the brain storming techniques noted above. After discussion the QC members select a problem to work on. The analysis of the problem can involve any of a number of problem-solving techniques, as well as inviting functional specialists into the meeting to secure additional information. The behavior style of the circle leader promotes a maximum of discussion participation, and involvement by all group members. This is a major reason for keeping the circle size relatively small. At some point the group will settle upon a recommended solution to the problem.

The next step in the process can be rather unsetting for employees who have never been asked their opinion about any thing in the workplace. Selected members are asked to make a presentation to management discussing what has been found and explaining the nature of the recommended solution. Many managers have been both surprised greatly impressed with the comprehensiveness and lucidity of these presentations. After having the presentation management must decide whether or not to accept it or any part thereof. Reports indicate that on average 80 percent of all quality circles recommendations are accepted.

The final step in the process is the actual implementation of the decision. In as much as circle members had a lot to do with the suggested change, the enthusiasm for implementation tends to be high. Implementation often requires cooperation from those not involved in circle processes, and circle members can help here through providing background information to stimulate acceptance and cooperation.[33]

2.3.9 Counseling

A part from performance review interviews and discussions between Management and subordinates at the time of completion of employees' assessment reports counseling on a regular all-the-year round basis should be regarded as an impartment part of personnel development. Although in practice many managers put their subordinates on the mat from time to time for shortcomings and errors, it is unfortunately rare to find subordinates being counseled regularly and systematically on their strengths, progress and needs. At such interviews an opportunity should be given for employees to put their points of view openly and for them to discuss their career worries and ambitions fruity. Although no firm committements on promotion prospects should not be given, it is also useful to advise subordinates of the fact that near progress is good if this is the case. Generally people respond well as such comments and their work of ten improves even more. Furthermore an assurance that prospectus are good it work continues as such a standard many prevent employees from seeking jobs elsewhere. An unemotional discussion of performance problems at a time other than when a blunder has been committed may also be helpful to a subordinate development as far as possible it is usually found to be helpful for managers to encourage their subordinates to highlight their own problems and proposes remedies. Counseling is naturally a job for the appropriate line manager of supervisor. The personnel specialist's task is to encourage them to undertake such duties and advise them on the techniques of successful counseling.

2.3.10 Teamwork

This needs display of sensitivity toward personal behavior of the members/participants in a group. Making interventions with the objective to the value, adopting open communication on all matters related to group team and display of accountability to the other members in the group/team.

Subordinate Development

This requires understanding subordinates with respect to their personal and professional needs. The superior should be able to provide them with a role model and guide them, properly with the objective of enabling the subordinates to achieve higher order of job skills and competence.

Negotiation Skills

These are required to ensure a transaction which is mutually beneficial to the parties. Possessing clarity of purpose, practical creativity, and market orientation along with a high order of quantitative skills are essentials for successful negotiation.

Problem-solving and decision-making. Ability to evolve a solution on a difficult/complex issue/matter by adopting a resolution after due consideration all intervening factors in an objective manner is what one should possess to be a good decision-maker.

Process Orientation

To adhere to and abide by the norm and specifications provided such as standard operating procedure, one has to have a mindset to abide by the standards, protocol, work systems and procedures without being bureaucratic in his approach.

Based on these criteria employees need to be assessed during the annual performance appraisal. Basically, performance is the outcome of one's yearly input to the organization. Organization conducts yearly and half-yearly appraisal assessments of the employees to evaluate the performance of that particular year. The annual reward is based on the annual performance of an employee. During this process, it is essential to evaluate the potential of the employee to carry out his higher responsibility. This should be one of the important criteria along with the consistent performance of the employee for consideration for positional elevation.

Without assessing the potential of the employee, it is risky to promote the person to the next higher level.[34]

2.3.11 Communication Policies

Communication is one of the most basic functions of management, communication forms "a basis for management by objectives, long range strategic goal setting policy formulation, strategic planning, organizational development and organizational effectiveness, control decision-making and allied managerial activities aimed at effective achievement of organizational goals". Communication may be defined, it is a process of transmitting information, thoughts, opinions, facts, ideas or emotions and understanding from one person, place or thing to another person, place or thing, it is called as a communication. Communication need to (1) establish and disseminate goals of an enterprise, (2) develop plans for their achievement, (3) organize human and other resources in the most effective and efficient way, (4) select, develop and appraise members of the organization, (5) lead direct, motivate and create a climate in which people want to contribute, and (6) control performance.[35]

Process of Communication: The communication process model is made up of seven steps: i.e.:

- (i) *Information Source*: Under this step some idea or information has to be created.
- (ii) *Encoding*: The source initiates message by encoding a thought. The sender puts ideas and thoughts into some form of a logical and coded message which may be oral or written.
- (iii) *Message and its transmission*: A message is the actual physical product from the encoding source. The message is affected by the code or group of symbols used to transfer meaning, the content of the message itself, some channel or medium has to be selected. It may be sent directly or through proper channel.
- (iv) *Reception of the message*: When it is received, heard and read by the person for whom it was meant.
- (v) *Decoding of the message*: The burden of interpretation lies on the receiver. He takes the message and attempts to discover, it is meaning by analyzing the sender and his intent by booking at the sender's role, knowledge, experience and authority. Receivers predisposed attitudes and cultural background can be distort the message being transferred.
- (vi) *Action*: The receiver acts or reacts to the message he has interpreted.

(vii) *Feedback*: A feedback determines whether understanding has been achieved. It is the check on how much successful one has been in transferring his messages as originally intended.[36]

Organizational Communication

Basically the two most important media of communication—Formal and informal communication formal communication are those that are "official", that are part of the recognized communication system which is involved in operation of the organization. This communication may be oral or written. Informal communication grows out of the social interactions among people who work together. These are not bound by chart on the wall but are bound by conventions, customs and culture. Such communication provides useful information for events to come in the form of grapevine.

Downward Communication

It flows from people at higher levels to those at lower level in the organizational hierarchy. The kinds of media used for downward oral communication include instructions, speeches, meetings, the telephone, speakers, and even the grapevine. Unfortunately information is often lost or distorted as it comes down the chain of command.

Upward Communication

It travels from subordinates to superiors and continues up the organizational hierarchy. Unfortunately this flow is often hindered by managers in the communication chain who filter the messages do not transmit all the information especially unfavorable news to their bosses.

Cross-wise Communication

It the horizontal flow of information among people on the same or similar organizational level and the diagonal level flow among persons at different levels who have no direct reporting relationships. This kind of communication is used to speed information flow to improve understanding and to coordinate effort for the achievement of organizational objectives.

Written Communication

It is the advantage of providing records, references and legal defenses. The message can be carefully prepared and then directed to a large audience through mass mailings. Written communications can also remote uniformity in policy and procedure and can reduce lasts in some cases.

Oral Communication

A great deal of information is communicated orally. Oral communication can occur in a face-to-face meeting of two people or in a manager's presentation to a large audience, it can be formal or informal and it can be planned or accidental.

Non-verbal Communications

People can communicate in many different ways. Non-verbal communication is expected to support the verbal, but it does not always do so.[37]

2.3.12 Quality of Working Life

The most widely quoted definition of quality of working life is that formulated by Richard, E. Walton. Professor Walton explains it in terms of eight broad conditions of employment that constitute a good or desirable quality of working life. Walton's features or conditions are as follows:

1. Adequate and Fair Compensation.
2. Safe and Healthy Working Conditions.
3. Immediate Opportunity to Use and Develop Human Capacities: This includes autonomy, work requiring multiple skills, information and perspective, whole tasks, and involvement in planning.
4. Future Opportunity for Continued Growth and Security: This includes expanding of one's capabilities, opportunity to use new knowledge and skills, promotion opportunities, plus job and income security.
5. Social integration in the Work Organization. This includes freedom from prejudice, egalitarianism, supportive primary work groups, a sense of community, and interpersonal openness.
6. Constitutionalism in the Work Organization: This includes rights to privacy and free speech. It also includes equitable treatment of employees and "due process" procedures in handling employees and in appeal procedures.
7. Work and Total Life Space: Walton argues for a balanced relationship among work and no work and family aspects of life.
8. Social Relevance of Work: The employing organization should perform in a socially beneficial manner.

Self-managed Work Teams

Self-managed work teams are also called autonomous work groups or integrated work teams. In this method work groups of say, ten to twenty employees, plan, coordinate, and control their own activities. They have a team leader who is often a worker, not a member of management.

Groups of employees are given the authority not only to perform direct production operations but also to do certain activities that traditionally are done by service and staff group. Thus, an assembly group may take on the added tasks of planning work method, inspecting output, maintaining equipment, and even selecting employees for the team. These groups have authority to regulate their own work tempo. Key decisions are often made as group decisions.

The objective in setting up self-managed work teams is to create teams around whole units of work wherein the components of the work and the processes are interdependent. Generally several different skills and jobs are combined into each team. The team is accountable for performance of its whole unit of work (e.g. making sub-assemblies, processing customer claims) and given the personnel and resources necessary to complete the work properly. The reward system (pay, recognition, promotion) is related to both group and individual achievement.

Job Redesign and Enrichment

The content and structure of jobs can be changed in various ways. Whereas sometimes jobs have been enlarged horizontally to add more task variety and sometimes employees have been allowed to rotate from one limited job to another to introduce variety and interest, the principal thrust of those companies having quality of working life programs has been to enrich jobs that had previously been set-up on the basis of narrow division of labor.

Guidelines for designing enriched jobs are as follows:

1. Form natural work units so that the employee can experience a sense of ownership of the work and a feeling of responsibility. These tasks then become significant to the employee.
2. Combine tasks into larger units of accomplishment to enhance skills, variety and task identity.
3. Establish client relationships: The employee should have direct knowledge of and, if possible, direct contact with the person or group that receives his completed work. Examples of a client relationship are a secretary doing work for a supervisor and a draftsman preparing drawings for and engineer. In this way the employee can obtain feedback on how well his or her work meets the needs of those who use that work.
4. Load the job vertically: This means that "planning" and "controlling" tasks should be added to the job. In narrow fractionated jobs the planning and controlling is traditionally performed by the boss. In enriched jobs the employees make their own decisions on work methods, setting up of equipment and tools, work pace, and checking on quality of work produced. This process increases the person's sense of autonomy.
5. Provide direct information and feedback to the employee: This means that the individual must have full information necessary to do his job and that he should receive feedback on the quality and quantity of his performance. In traditional job designs the feedback is given to the employee by his boss and this is often viewed as an evaluation of one's character and is resented. The feedback should not be evaluative but rather should be objective.

Participative Management

By participative management we mean a system of management in which employees participate in making management decisions that affect them and their jobs. This process increases employees motivation, generates ideas that may not have occurred to management alone, and reduces resistance to new methods and processes. It helps meet the human needs for autonomy, achievement, and self-expression. Although participative management can be structured in a number of ways, typically it involves a departmental supervisor conducting meetings with his immediate subordinates to make plans and decisions regarding such matters as tooling, equipment, methods, safety, distribution of tasks, and working conditions. Generally the supervisor retains final decision-making authority but works closely with his people in getting ideas, testing their reactions, and shaping solutions.

Behaviour Modification

Proponents of behavioral modification are essentially interested in controlling and shaping behavior. They want to increase productivity, cut costs, or reduce absenteeism. They make no claims about improving job satisfaction and attitudes. They are not humanistic in their orientation.

The essential idea of behavioral modification is that behavior is determined by its consequences. The behavior desired by management is shaped by rewarding successive approximations of the desired behavior. Each small improvement is reinforced. Improper behavior is ignored rather than punished according to strict Skinnerian precepts, although some proponents do use punishment. Main ingredients of a behavior modification program are identification of key behaviors to be shaped, setting of new behavioral goals, providing feedback on performance to the individual, devising various forms of suitable reinforces and applying the reinforces.

Effective Leadership and Supervisory Behavior

Employees like to work for supervisors who show consideration for them, who are supportive, and who are fair and just in their treatment. The supervisor should create an atmosphere of approval in his relations with his subordinates. Employees' perception of their quality of working life is affected heavily by the treatment they receive from their supervisors.

The effective supervisor also must take actions to help get the work out. This dimension has been variously labeled "facilitation and goal emphasis," "initiating structure," and "production-centered" leadership. The supervisor must be able to organize and direct people who will produce work. He must possess technical knowledge in order to diagnose production difficulties. He must set challenging but attainable performance standards. In certain circumstances the employees themselves may participate in setting output standers. He must help his people solve work and equipment problems. He must also provide job instruction. In implementing this facilitation dimension of his job the supervisor should not be overbearing nor should he pressure his people around.

Another important dimension of effective leadership and supervision is the development of teamwork among employees. The supervisor should generate an appropriate degree of participation in day-to-day decisions on the part of his people. They should care about their work and about the department. They should be highly involved and not apathetic.[38]

Notes and References

1. A.S. Bhatia and Gurubachan K. Bhatia, Human Resource Development : India in Global context, Current Trends in HRD, Deep and Deep Publications, New Delhi, 1997, pp. 27-37.
2. Garry Dessler, Human Resource Management, Saurabh Printers Pvt. Ltd., New Delhi 2003, p. 244.
3. Garry Dessler, Human Resource Management, Saurabh Printers Pvt. Ltd., New Delhi, 2003, p. 250.
4. C.B. Mamoria and S.V. Gankar, Personnel Management, Himalaya Publishing House, Mumbai, 2003, pp. 369-70.
5. C.B. Mamoria and S.V. Gankar, Personnel Management, Himalaya a Publishing House, Mumbai, 2003, p. 375.
6. C.B. Mamoria and S.V. Gankar, Personnel Management, Himalaya Publishing House, Mumbai, 2003, pp. 381-85.
7. Pail Pigors and Charles A. Myers, Personnels Administrations, McGraw Hill International Book Company, New York, 1981, pp. 287-88.
8. C.B. Mamoria and S.V. Gankar, Personnel Management, Himalaya Publishing House, Mumbai, 2003, pp. 299-300.
9. Arthur Sherman, George Bohlander and Soott Snall, Managing Human Resources, South Western College Publishing, Cincinnati, Ohio, 1996, pp. 241-42.
10. D.V. Aggarwala, Manpower Planning: Selection, Training and Development, Deep and Deep Publication, New Delhi, 1997, pp. 275-76.
11. D.V. Agarwala, Training and Development, Deep and Publications, New Delhi, 1987, pp. 261-64.
12. A.K. Nayak, HRD Management : A Strategic Approach, Common Wealth Publishers, New Delhi, 1996, pp. 257-59.
13. D.V. Aggarwala, Manpower Planning : Selection Training and Development, Deep & Deep Publications, New Delhi, 1987, pp. 277-82.
14. C.B. Mamoria and S.V. Gankar, Personnel Management, Himalaya Publishing House, Mumbai, 2003, pp. 345-46.
15. C.B. Momoria and S.V. Gankar, Personnel Management, Himalaya Publishing House, Mumbai, 2003, p. 306.
16. D.V. Aggarval, Manpower Planning : Selection, Training and Development, Deep and Deep Publications, New Delhi, 1987, pp. 301-08.
17. D.V. Aggarwala, Training and Development, Deep and Deep Publications, New Delhi, 1987, pp. 308-14.
18. Dharam Veer, A., Manpower Planning : Selection, Training and Development, Deep and Deep Publications, New Delhi, pp. 259-61.
19. C.B. Monoria and S.V. Gankar, Personnel Management, Himalaya Publishing House, Mumbai, 2003, pp. 337-38.
20. Dharam Veer, A., Manpower Planning: Selection, Training and Development, Deep and Deep Publications, New Delhi, 1987, pp. 264-70.
21. C.B. Monoria and S.V. Gankar, Personnel Management, Himalaya Publishing House, Mumbai, 2003, p. 303.
22. C.B. Monoria and S.V. Gankar, Personnel Management, Himalaya Publishing House, Mumbai, 2003, p. 303.

23. D.V. Aggarval, Manpower Planning : Selection, Training and Development, Deep and Deep Publications, New Delhi, 1987, pp. 317-22.
24. C.B. Mamoria and S.V. Gankar, Personnel Management, Himalaya Publishing House, Mumbai, 2003, p. 341.
25. C.B. Mamoria and S.V. Gankar, Personnel Management, Himalaya Publishing House, Mumbai, 2003, pp. 342-45.
26. D.V. Aggarwala, Manpower Planning : Selection Training and Development, Deep and Deep Publications, 1987, pp. 285-87.
27. C.B. Monoria and S.V. Gankar, Personnel Management, Himalaya Publishing House, Mumbai, 2003, pp. 306-07.
28. Dharam Vira Aggarwal, Manpower Planning : Selection, Training and Development, Deep and Deep Publications, New Delhi, 1987, pp. 329-33.
29. K.K. Ahuja, Personnel Management, Kalyani Publishers, New Delhi, 1998, pp. 266-88.
30. Beard Well and Len Holden, Human Resource Management, Mc Millan Publishers, New Delhi, 1996, pp. 410-18.
31. Edwin Flippo, Personnel Management, McGraw Hill International Ltd., Singapore, 1984, pp. 416-18.
32. Biswajeet Pattanayak, Human Resource Management, Prentice Hall of India Pvt. Ltd., New Delhi, 2001, pp. 107-10.
33. Harold Koonz and Heinz Weihrich, Essentials of Management, Tata McGraw Hills Publishing, New Delhi, 2001, p. 367.
34. C.B. Mamorias, S.V. Gankar, Personnel Management, Himalaya Publishing House, New Delhi, 2001, pp. 658-59.
35. Harold Koontz and others, Essentials of Management, Tata McGraw Hill Publishing House, New Delhi, 2001, pp. 371-74.
36. Beard Well and Len Holden, Human Resource Management, Mc Millan Publishers, New Delhi, 1996, pp. 462-65.

Methods of Information Technology and its Role

Like all living things man also relies on information and its communication for survival. Cell reproduction, the senses, the thoughts, the control of vital processes and the defence of the organs and the organism, all require on (in-built) information system. On the other hand, the satisfaction of basic needs, such as food, clothing and social relations, demand the creation of a different system of information known as internal system of communication. In the past as well as today man dedicates large part of his lifetime to information and communication (written or oral). It has been estimated that man spends about seventy percent of his time in communication. Yet it is recently that a large section of people are being explicitly employed in information activities. Information and intelligent automation technologies offer us new and powerful instruments capable of intervening at all levels in all activities.

At present, Information technology plays a key role in developing human resources. This chapter intended to discuss various information technology aspects i.e., different types of technologies, methods and also discussed role of these methods in developing human resources.

THE CONCEPT

The term "Information Technology" in English, "informatique" in French and "informatika" in Russian encompasses the notion of information handling. In stricter sense information technology is the new science of collecting, storing, processing and transmitting information and connotes an assemble of technologies. They particularly cover the computer's capability to store and process information and communication technology, which is capable of transmitting information to distances. Basically, information technology is application of tools and methods that support through which or by means of which information is transferred, recorded, edited, stored, manipulated and disseminated. According to Advisory Council for Applied Research and Development of the Cabinet Office of U.K. there are three components of the new technology, i.e. new ways to store information compactly and cheaply; new mechanisms to manipulate, seam and search, such stores records; and new facilities for cheap and rapid transmission of information over long distance.

More recently the telephone, radio, television, satellite transmission, the computer and the microprocessor, represent distinct qualitative changes in the information technology, to the extent that we now have to accept the composite term information technology to include a whole range of new developments. These, the facilities required to capture, store, manipulate and distribute data and information, could broadly be called as Information Technology. Contrary to popular misconception, it is not just computers although they form a major part of it.

UNESCO defines information technology as "scientific, technological and engineering disciplines and the management techniques used in information handling, processing and their application, computers and their interaction with men and machines and associated social, economic and cultural matters".

At the moment the life cycle of IT is approximately three years. It is not known whether this life cycle will shorten, lengthen or remain the same in the future. But if past is any indication of the future, it will shorten. The life cycle is dependent on global economies; evaluate skilled technologists, the demand for improved technologies and social structures capable of integrating such technologies. The importance of information technology is that this is being applied to all such activities, which were previously directly mediated, by human knowledge perception, recall and reaction. In other words, information technology is being applied to (information-related aspects of) all sorts of work being carried out by human beings. It is a heartland technology, which changes the common sense of production and work organization.[1]

After decades of slowly expanding behind the scenes, Information Technology has suddenly exploded into public view and seems to be everywhere in the popular media. It is like a huge wave that has been building offshore, only to become noticeable as it crests and then breaks on the beach. At the moment we are all caught in the boiling surf of this breaking wave. It is almost impossible to avoid media stories on such topics as the information super highway, multimedia or the Internet. These aspects of information technology are just a few of the thousands of ways in which information technology will affect the way we work, live and play.[2]

The world today is in transition from industrial age to information age. "Computer and communication systems combined to be called as Information Technology", are critical in the operation of every business today. The IT revolution is making a tremendous impact on the industry and trade by relentless technology innovations, massive growth in computer power, world-wide networks and ever-growing electronic factories.[3]

"Information Technology refers to the creation, storage, and delivery of information and the processes and devices that make all this possible". Think of these processes and devices as tools that make your life and carrier better or more efficient. The tasks that are handled using information technology continue to increase almost on a daily basis. Information Technology can do at least three things—

- Information Technology can process raw data into useful information.
- Information Technology can recycle processed information and use it as data in another processing step.
- Information Technology can package information in a new form so it's easier to understand, more attractive, or more useful.[4]

Information Technology can be formally defined as : "It is the study, design, development, implementation, support of computer-based information management system particularly software and hardware".

Information Technology is "the technology which supports activities involving the creation, storage, manipulation, communication of information, together with their related methods, management of applications".[5]

Information Technology stands firmly on two legs—hardware and software. The term hardware applied to any of the physical equipment in a system, usually containing electronic components and performing some kind of function in information processing. Hardware includes not only the computer and devices such as screens and printers but also all the elements used to the information systems together. Software is instructions that guide the hardware in the performance of its duties. There is a slogan button floating around that makes this distinction very clear. Hardware the post of the computer that you can kick.

GROWTH AND DEVELOPMENT OF INFORMATION TECHNOLOGY

The start of modern science that we call Computer Science can be traced back to long ago when man still dwelled in caves or in forests, and lived in groups for protection and survival from the harsh elements on the Earth. Many of these groups possessed some primitive form of animistic religion; they worshipped the sun, the moon, the trees, or sacred animals. Within the tribal group was one individual who took the responsibility of the tribe's spiritual welfare. It was he or she who decided when to hold both the secret and public religious ceremonies, and interceded with the spirits on behalf of the tribe. In order to correctly conduct the ceremonies and thus ensure good harvest in the fall and fertility in the spring, the cavemen needed to count the days or to keep track of the seasons. From this tradition, man developed the first primitive counting mechanisms—counting notches on sticks or marks on walls.

The Antikythera mechanism used for registering and predicting the motion of stars and planets dates to the first century BC. It was discovered off the coast of Greece in 1901.

From the caves and forests, man slowly evolved and built structures such as Stonehenge. Stonehenge, which lies 13 km north of Salisbury, England, is believed to have been an ancient form of calendar designed to capture the light from the summer solstice in a specific fashion. The solstices have long been special days for various religious groups and cults. Archeologists and anthropologists today are not quite certain how the structure, believed to have been built erected since the technology required to join together the giant stones and raise the upright seems to be beyond the technological level of the Britons at that time. It widely believed that the enormous edifice of stones may have been erected by the Druids. Regardless of the identity of the builders, it remains today a monument man's intense desire to count and to track the occurrences of the physical world around him.

Meanwhile, in Asia, the Chinese becoming very much involved in commercial and bulls. Somehow, out of this need, the abacus was born. The abacus is the first true precursor to the adding machines and computers, which would follow. It worked somewhat like this.

Thus, the abacus works on the principle of place-value notation: the location of the bead determines its value. In this way, relatively few beads are required to depict large numbers. The beads are counted, or given numerical values, by shifting them in one direction. The values are erased (freeing the counters for reuse) by shifting the beads in the other direction. An abacus is really a memory aid for the user making mental calculations, as opposed to the true mechanical calculating machines, which were still to come.

John Napier (1550-1617) brought about the next great step towards step towards today's computers.

His Mirifici logarithmorum canonis descripto' (1614), was the first important work on mathematics produced in Great Britain, and one which inspired Briggs, the professor of Geometry at Gresham College, London, to develop the system of common logarithms with the decimal base.

William Oughtred (1575-1660), born in Edin, Buckinghamshire was an Anglican cleric and a schoolmaster. He is credited for two discoveries, both of which were forms of a slide rule. He invented the circular slide rule and the rectangular slide rule. Each of these instruments had a common accuracy of three digits. He wrote the 'Circles of proportion and Horizontal instruments' in 1632. In this book he describes both the slide rules and the various uses of the sundial.

Wilhelm Schickard, a professor at the University of Tubingen, Germany, built the first mechanical calculator in 1632. It could work with six digits, and carried digits across columns. It worked, but never made beyond the prototype stage.

Blaise Pascal (1623-62), born in Clermont (now Clermont-Forrand), Auvergne, France was a mathematician and the son of a mathematician and tax collector, Etienne Pascal.

He is most remembered among the Computer Scientists as the inventor of the calculator. In 1642 he presented this to his father to assist him. This calculator, called the Pascaline, resembled the mechanical calculators used in the 1940's. These were not his only contributions by far. He also invented the syringe, the hydraulic press, and Pascal's law of pressure. Pascal built Pascaline based on a design described by Hero of Alexandria (2AD) to add up the distance traveled by a carriage. The basic principle of his calculator is still used today in water meters and modern-day odometers.

Gottfried Wilhelm von Leibniz (1646-1716) was born in Liepzig, Saxony (now Germany). He is most associated with his contributions to integral Calculus. In 1694, he invented the Stepped Reckoner. This was another calculator similar in intent to that of the Pascaline, except that this device use stepped cylinders, like a music box, rather than gears. Based on the decimal system this device could multiply and divide as well as add and subtract. Unfortunately, both this and the Pascaline were simply too complicated for mass production and so they remained one-of-a-kind.

Joseph-Marie Jacquard (1752-1834) was born in Lyon, France. He was a stone mason and later a weaver. He created the Punched Card Loom in 1801. This device was a new type of loom for weaving cloth. Punched cards controlled its operation. Needles could pull threads through cards were there were holes and not where there were none. Thus patterns were stored on punched cards. This device never gained him the riches that he should have received as the labor union of the Silk Weavers was very strong at that time and they recognized the threat it posed from unemployment. They prevented its mass production with massive demonstrations and riots against the replacement of people with machines.

Thomas de Colmar (1785-1870), invented his first Arithmoneter in 1820. This was the first mass produced calculator. It did multiplication in much the same fashion as the Stepped Reckoner but at the size of about a desktop was much smaller and easier to produce. With some assistance from the user it could do division as well. This device was widely used, but the importance of it was the inspiration that it later caused.

While Thomas de Colmar was developing the first successful commercial calculator, Charles Babbage (1792-1871), realized as early as 1812 that many long computations consisted of operations that were regularly repeated.

In 1833, Babbage ceased working on the difference engine because he had a better idea. His new idea was to build an "analytical engine". The analytical engine was a real parallel decimal computer which would operate on words of 50 decimals and was able to store 1000 such numbers. The machine would include a number of built-in-operations such as conditional control, which allowed the instructions for the machine to be executed in a specific order rather than in numerical order. The instructions for the machine were to be stored on punched cards, similar to those used on a jacquard loom.

Ada Byron, Lady Lovelace (1815-52) was one of the more picturesque characters of the early history of computers. Ada met Babbage in 1833. She described the analytical engine as weaving "algebraic patterns just as the jacquard loom weaves flowers and leaves". Her published analysis of the analytical engine is our best record of its programming potential. In it, she outlines the fundamentals of computer programming, including data analysis, looping and memory addressing. Published in 1843, Ada's prescient might be used to compose complex music, to produce graphics, and would be used for both practical and scientific use. She was correct. When inspired, Ada could be very focused and a mathematical taskmaster. Ada suggested to Babbage writing a plan for how the engine might calculate Bernoulli numbers. This plan, is now regarded as the first "computer program". A software language developed by the US Department of Defense was named "Ada" in her honor in 1979.

Konrad Zuse, a German engineer, completed the first general-purpose programmable calculator in 1941. He pioneered the use of binary math and Boolean logic in electronic calculation.

Neumann in his paper demonstrated that a computer could have a simple, fixed structure, yet be able to execute any kind of computation given properly programmed control, without the need for hardware modification. He contributed a new understanding of how practical fast computers should be organized and built, these ideas, often referred to as the stored-program technique, became fundamental for future generations of high-speed digital computers and were universally adopted. The primary advance was the provision of a special type of machine instruction called conditional control transfer.

In 1947, William Shockley, John Bardeen, and Walter Brattain invented the "transfer resistance" device at Bell Laboratories which later came to be known as the transistor.

In 1950, Maurice V. Wilkes at Cambridge University first started using the assembler (symbolic assembly language) on the EDSAC.

In 1951, Eckert and Mauchley built the UNIVAC for the Census Bureau. This machine is certainly a fully functional computer.

Also in 1951, Grace Murray Hopper invented the notion of a compiler. She did that in a report entitled the education of a computer. In this report she described the techniques by which a computer could be used to select (or compile) pre-written code segments to be assembled into programs in correspondence with codes written in a high level language—thus describing the concept of a compiler, and the general concept of language translation.

1952 was another significant year for computer history. The first computer manual was written by Fred Gruenberger.

IBM introduced the 701 as its first electronic stored-program computer.

The Nixdorf Computer was founded in Germany. Remington–rand bought Engineering Research Associates.

RCA developed Bizmac with iron-core memory and a magnetic drum. This marked the very first database. It could store 12,000 digits in random access mercury-delay lines. EDVAC, for Electronic Discrete Variable Computer, was completed under contract for the ordinance department in 1952.

Harlan Herrick ran the first successful FORTRAN program in 1954. In the same year gene Amdahl developed the first operating system which ran on the IBM 704.

Kenneth Olsen founded the Digital Equipment Corporation in 1957. In 1958, at Texas instruments, Jack Kilby completed the building of the first integrated circuit, containing five components on a piece of germanium half an inch long and thinner than a toothpick.

Texas instruments and Fairchild Semiconductor (constructed by Robert Noyce) both announced the integrated circuit in 1959. In the same year, COBOL (Common Business Oriented Language) was invented which was defined by the Conference On Data System Languages (CODASYL). It was based on Grace Hopper's Flow –Matic. IBM developed the first automatic mass-production facility for transistors in New York in 1960.

In 1961, Fairchild Semiconductor released the first commercial integrated circuit. In 1963, Douglas Engelbart received a patent on mouse, the pointing device for computers.

Timesharing, the concept of linking a large number of users to a single computer via remote terminals, was developed at MIT in the late 50s and early 60s. in 1962, Paul Baran of RAND developed the idea of distributed, packet-switching networks.

In 1964, Gordon Moore suggested that integrated circuits would double in complexity every year. This later came to be known as the Moore's Law. Also, in the same year, John Kemeny and Thomas Kurtz developed the BASIC programming language at Dartmouth College.

The IBM 360 was introduced in April 1964 and quickly became the standard institutional mainframe computer. By the mid-80s, IBM 360 and its descendents had generated more than $100 billion in revenue for IBM.

In 1968, Douglas C. Engelbart, of the Stanford research institute demonstrated his system of keyboard, keyped, mouse, and windows at the joint computer conference in San Francisco's civic center. He demonstrated the use of a word processor, a hypertext system, and remote collaborative work with colleagues. Also, in the same year Robert Noyce and Gordon Moore founded the Intel Corporation.

Xerox created its Palo Alto Research Center—Xerox PARC in 1969. Also, in 1969, ARPANET went online. Its mission was to explore the "architecture of information". Fairchild semiconductor introduced a 256-bit RAM chip in 1970. In the late 170 Intel introduced a 1K RAM chip and the 4004, a 4-bit microprocessor. Two years later came the 8008, an 8-bit microprocessor.

Bill Gates and Paul Allen formed the Traf—O-Data in 1971 to sell their computer traffic-analysis system. Steve Jobs and Steve Wozniak were building and selling "blue boxes" in Southern Californai in 1971.

In 1972, Gary Kildall wrote PL/M, the first high-level programming language for the Intel microprocessor. In April 1972, Intel introduced the 8008, the first 8-bit microprocessor. Bob Kahn and Vint Cerf developed the basic ideas of the internet in 1973.

Jonathan A. Titus designed the Mark-8, "your personal minicomputer" according to the July, 1974 cover of Radio-Electronics. Also in 1974, Brian Kernighan and Dennis Ritchie developed the C programming language. BBN opened the first public packet-switched network-Telenet in the same year.

Popular electronic featured the MITS Altari 8800 on its cover, January 1975. It was hailed as the first "personal" computer. Thousands of orders for the 8800 rescued MITS from bankruptcy. Paul Allen and Bill Gates developed BASIC for the Altari 8800 and Microsoft was born.

1976: Steve Jobs and Steve Wozniak form the Apple Computer Company, on April Fool's Day. Also in the same year, Michael Shrayer completes writing electric pencil, the first popular word-processing program for microcomputers and Shugart announces its 5.25 inch "Minifloopy" disk drive for US $ 390.

1977: The Apple computer company is incorporated. Bill Gates and Paul Allen sign a partnership agreement to officially created the Microsoft company. Apple computer deliver its first Apple II system. Microsoft ships "Microsoft FORTRAN" for CP/M-based computers. Apple computer releases applesoft, a version of BASIC with floating-point capabilities. It is licensed from Microsotf. Dan Bricklin conceives the idea for the Visi Calc spreadsheet program.

1978: Intel introduces the 4.77-MHz 8086 microprocessor. Microsoft ships Microsoft COBOL. Apple computer introduces the disk II, a 5.25 floppy disk drive linked to the Apple II by cable. Epson announces the MX-80 dot matrix printer, which established a new standard in high performance with low price for printers. Taito develops the space invaders arcade game in Japan. Commodore introduces the CBM dot-matrix printer.

1979: Bob Metcalfe founds 3 Com corporation. CompuServe begins a service to computer hobbyists called MicroNET, offering boards, databases, and games. Microsoft releases its assembler language for 8080/Z80 microprocessors. Wayne Ratliff develops the Vulcan database program (Ashton-Tate later markets it as dBase II). Personal software releases VisiCalc for the Apple II, for US $ 100. The first Comdex show is held, in Las

Vegas. Approximately 150 companies show their products to some 4,000 visitors. Alan Shugart founds Seagate Technologies (hard disk maker), in Scotts Valley, California. Apple computer releases the word processing program Apple Writer 1.0. IBM introduces the IBM 3800 laser printer, capable of printing 20,000 lines per minute. A UUCP link between the University of North Carolina at Chapel Hill and Duke University establishes USENET. The first MUD is also developed at the university of Essex.

1981: MS-DOS runs for the first time on IBM's prototype microcomputer. Microsoft buys all rights to DOS from Seattle Computer Products, and the name MS-DOS is adopted. The first IBM PCs roll off the assembly lines. IBM announces the CGA graphics card for the PC, giving 940x200 resolution with 16 colors. Microsoft, incorporated becomes Microsoft Corporation. Hayes microcomputer products advertises the Smartmodem 300, which becomes the industry standard. Seagate Technologies begins shipping its 5 MB 5.25-inch hard drives, for US $ 1700. A college professor James Clark founds silicon Graphics, incorporated.

1982: Compaq Computer Corporation is founded by Rod Canion, Jim Harris, and Bill Murto, all former senior managers of Texas instruments. Sun Microsystems is founded. "SUN" originally stood for Stanford University network. Microsoft releases FORTRAN for MS-DOS. Mitch Kapor founds Lotus development corporation. Sun Microsystems begins shipping the Sun 1 workstation computer. Microsoft releases MS-DOS 1.1 to IBM, for the IBM PC. Sony Electronics demonstrates its 3.5-inch microfloppy disk system. Columbia Data products release the first IBM PC clone, the MPC. Lotus development announces the Lotus 1-2-3 spreadsheet program at Comdex in Las Vegas. Microsoft releases GW-BASIC, with advanced graphics capabilities. Microsoft releases Microsoft COBOL for MS-DOS. Andrew Fluegelman begins distributing his PC-Talk communications software, the first copyrighted program distributed as shareware. John Warnock founds adobe systems. Mouse systems introduces the first commercial mouse for the IBM PC. TCP/IP (Transmission control protocol and internet protocol) is established as the standard for ARPANET.

1983: AT&T announces Unix System V. Time magazine selects the microcomputer as its "Man" of the year. Lotus development ships Lotus 1-2-3 Release 1.0 for MS-DOS. Jonathan Sachs was the programmer, with Mitch Kapor as the software designer. Philippe Kahn founds Borland international. Microsoft introduces Multi-Tool word for DOS (later renamed Microsoft word) word processing program at Spring Comdex in Atlanta, Georgia. Microsoft introduces its first mouse, "The Microsoft Mouse." Borland international releases Turbo Pascal for CP/M and 8086-based computers. Microsoft officially releases Microsoft word 1.0, for US $ 375, or US $ 475 with the Microsoft mouse. IBM and Microsoft begin co-developing OS/2. Syquest introduces its SyQuest storage cartridge system to the PC market. Novell introduces the NetWare network operating system for the IBM PC. Wang announces the single in-line memory module (SIMM).

Philips and Sony develop the CD-ROM, as an extension of audio CD technology. Bjarn Stroustrup creates the C++ extension to the C programming language.

1984: Seiko instruments USA, Inc. Displays the first wristwatch computer, with a 10-character, 4-line LCD. Microsoft releases MS-DOS 2.11. It includes enhancements to better allow conversion into different languages and date formats. Silicon Graphics begins shipping its first 3-D graphics workstations. Apple Computer releases the color Apple Scribe printer, using a special waxed ribbon and thermal print head. Quarterdeck office systems officially launches DESQ, a text-based windowing environment for running DOS programs. Ashton-Tate ships dBase III. IBM announces its PC network local area network. IBM announces TopView, a DOS multitasking program. Intel introduce the 80186, 80188, and 80286 processors. Foxbase releases Foxbase for MS-DOS. The Massachusetts Institute of Technology (MIT) begins developing the X window system.

1985: Microsoft introduces Microsoft Excel for the Macintosh, in New York. Lotus development releases Lotus Jazz for the Macintosh. Aldus releases Aldus Page Maker for the apple Macintosh. IBM announces its token ring network. IBM announces the PC network software, its first networking software for PCs. US Robotics introduces the Courier 2400 modem.

1986: Microsoft releases MS-DOS 3.25 Intel ships the 80386. Adobe introduces Adobe Illustrator, a PostScript drawing tool, for the Macintosh. Software Publishing Corporation introduces Harvard presentation graphics for the PC. Gateway 2000 ships its first PC. The small computer system interface (SCSI-1) standard is finalized as ANSI X3.131-1986.

1987: Intel introduces the 20MHz 80386DX microprocessor. 3M introduces the 2-MB high density 3 ½-inch diskette. IBM introduces the IBM personal system/2 (PS/2) line, with IBM's forst 386 PC, and 3.5-inch floppy drives as standard. IBM unveils its Video graphics array (VGA) in its model 50 and higher of the PS/2 line. IBM and Microsoft announce operating system/2 (OS/2). Microsoft announces Microsoft windows 2.0. Microsoft ships Microsoft bookshelf, its first CD-ROM application. Lotus development announces lotus 1-2-3 for the Macintosh. Microsoft unveils the Microsoft releases Microsoft word 4.0 for the PC. Borland international ships the Quattro spreadsheet program. Hewlett-Packard releases the HP PaintJet color inkjet printer. The number of hosts on the internet breaks 10,000.

1988: Ashton-Tate releases dBase IV for MS-DOS. Microsoft releases Microsoft PowerPoint for the Macintosh. U.S. Robotics introduces the Courier Dual Standard modem, supporting both v.32 and HST protocols, and the courier v.32 modem. Hewlett-Packard introduces the HP DeskJet inkjet printer. NEC Technologies introduces the 4.2-pound NEC UltraLite laptop PC, the first "subnotebook." It features a stylus for input, and handwriting recognition. Caere ships the OmniPage OCR software for the Macintosh.

1989: Microsoft releases Quick Pascal, designed to compete with Borland international's Turbo Pascal. The VESA graphics standard emerges, providing a uniform method of accessing SuperVGA chipsets. Microsoft ships SQL Server. Borland international releases the Quattro Pro 2.0 spreadsheet program. Lotus development ships Lotus Notes. Microsoft ships word for windows 1.0. Creative Labs introduces the sound blaster, an 8-bit mono PC sound card. The number of hosts on the internet breaks 100,000.

1991: Microsoft releases Microsoft Excel for window 3.0 apple computer ships first TureType fonts for the famintosh. Microsoft announces the Microsoft BallPoint mouse, incorporating muse and trackball technology in a pointing device for laptop computers. Microsoft announces Microsoft visual BASIC for windows. Microsoft releases MS-DOS 5.0. It adds a full-screen editor, undelete and unformat utilities, and task seapping. GW-BASIC is replaced with Qbasic, 1.0. Hewlett-Packard introduces its first color image scanner, the HP Scanjet IIc. The 400 dpi 24-bit flatbed scanner is priced at about US $ 2000. Tim burners-Lee develops the world wide web. CERN releases the first web server.

1992: NEC introduces the first double-speed CD-ROM drive. The first version of the VESA VL-Bus standard for PCs is ratified. Borland international ships Quattro Pro for windows, release 1.0. Microsoft ships Microsoft windows for workgroups 3.1, which integrates networking and workgroup functionality. Quark ships QuarkXPress 3.1 for windows. Microsoft ships Microsoft access 1.0 database program for windows. WordPerfect releases WordPerfect for windows. Creative Labs introduces the sound blaster 16 with advanced signal processor, a 16-bit stereo PC sound card. Hewlett-Packard introduces the HP LaserJet 4 laser printer. The number of hosts on the internet breaks 1,000,000.

1993: Novell ships UnixWare. Intel releases the final specifications for the PCI standard, for card and socket connectors. Lou Gerstner replaces John Akers as chairman of IBM Intel introduces the Pentium processor. Microsoft introduces the MS-DOS 6.0. Microsoft ships Microsoft Encarta, the first multimedia encyclopedia for a computer. Microsoft releases the OLE 2.0 specification for windows development. Novell ships NetWare 4.0. Lotus development ships Lotus Notes Release 3.0. IBM releases OS/2 2.1, now including windows 3.1 support. Microsoft formally launches windows NT 3.1. Microsoft begins shipping windows NT workstation 3.1, and windows NT 3.1, Server 3.1. Sun Microsystems ships the 60-MHz Sun SuperSPARC processor. Gateway 2000 introduces the industry's first VESA VL-bus system. Cyrix begins shipping the Cx486DX microprocessor. Advanced Micro Devices introduces the 66-MHz Am486DX2. Microsoft ships windows for workgroups 3.11. IBM releases OS/2 2.1 for windows. Microsoft releases MS-DOS 6.2. Microsoft releases Microsoft word 6.0 for windows. Novell buys Unix System V. Lotus development releases Lotus Approach for windows, Release 2.1. Cyrix ships the Cx486DRx2 processor in 16/32, 20/40, and 25/50-MHz versions. The chips are designed to replace Intel 386DX processors, giving 486 compatibility and performance. Microsoft releases

FoxPro 2.5 for windows. The world wide web sports a growth rate of 341, 634% in Service traffic in its third year.

1994: NEC technologies ships its quad-speed CD-ROM. Microsoft releases Microsoft windows 3.11. It includes minor driver updates, but more importantly it gives Microsoft the opportunity to include a "certificate of authenticity" hologram sticker on the packaging, making illegal copying more difficult. Microsoft releases MS-DOS 6.21, removing DoubleSpace disk compression. Apple computer releases system 7.1, the OS for the Mac. Cyrix begins new shipments of the Cx486DX microprocessor, after fixing a flaw in the 32-bit floating-point code. Hewlett-Packard ships the HP DeskWriter 560C color inkjet printer. It features 600x300dpi, at a list price of US $ 720. Hewlett-Packard ships the HP DeskWriter 520 inkjet printer. IBM releases PC-DOS 6.3. Mosaic communications release Netscape Navigator 1.0, a world-wide web browser. Microsoft releases MS-DOS 6.22, bringing back disk compression under the name DriveSpace. U.S. Robotics ships the Sportster v.34 28.8bps modems. Microsoft ships Microsoft word 6.0 for the Macintosh. IBM formally launches OS/2 Warp version 3. Intel introduces the 75-MHz Pentium processor. Cyrix announces the M1 next-generation x86 processor. Novell ships PerfectOffice 3.0 for windows. Microsoft releases the FoxPro 2.6 for windows, UNIX and DOS. Iomega Corp. introduces its Zip drive and Zip disks, floppy disk sized removable storage in sizes of 25MB or 100MB. The SCSI-2 standard is finalized as ANSI X3.131-1994. NEC technologies ships the NEC MultiSpin 4xPro quad-speed CD-ROM drive. The main U.S. internet backbone traffic begins routing through commercial providers as NSFNET reverts to a research network.

1995: Apple computer announces the Newton MessagePad 120. Borland International ships Borland Delphi. IBM releases the ThinkPad 701C. It features an automatically expanding full-sized keyboard, dubbed the Butterfly. The laptop features a 10.4-inch thin-film-transistor display, 50-MHz Intel 486Dx2, 14.4K fax/modem, and weighs just 4.3 pounds. IBM releases PC DOS 7. Sun Microsystems, Inc., announces Java. Lotus Development renames Ami Pro to Word Pro. Intel releases the mobile version of the 90-MHz Pentium processor. Intel introduces the P6 processor. IBM buys Lotus Development for US $ 3.5 billion in cash. Intel announces the immediate availability of the 133-MHz Pentium processor. Iomega introduces the Jaz line of high-capacity removable cartridge drives. The cartridges hold 1 gigabyte, costing about US $ 100 each. Transfer rate of the drive is up to 5MBps. US Robotics begins shipping enhanced Courier V. Everything modems capable of transmitting data at up to 33.6Kbps. Cyrix announces the 100-MHz CX5x86 microprocessor. Lotus development ships SmartSuite 4.0 for windows 3.1. Intel demonstrates a system using a 150-MHz P6 CPU, running windows 95. Microsoft releases windows 95. Microsoft begins shipping windows NT Server 3.51. Compaq computer introduces nine new desktop models based on the 133-MHz Pentium processor. Microsoft introduces Microsoft office 95. Microsoft releases Microsoft internet Explorer 1.0. Intel announces the official name for the P6 chip: Pentium Pro. Cyrix announces the 100-MHz CX6x86 microprocessor. Intel announces the Pentium Pro microprocessor, at speeds of 150-, 180-, and 200 MHz. Intel destroys 1.5 million flawed Pentium chips, at a rough cost of US $ 475 million. Microsoft releases FoxPro 3.0 for windows, with OLE support. Sega introduces the 32-bit game system, Saturn. The first and only international conference on year 2000 problem tales place.

1996: The first world's Fair on internet—The internet 1996 world exposition—is held. Advanced Micro Devices and NexGen complete their merger, with AMD paying US $ 623 million for NexGen. Intel announces the immediate availability of the 60/150-MHz Pentium processor. Intel announces the immediate availability of the 66/166-MHz Pentium P55C processor. IBM releases OS/2 for the PowerPC. Compaq announces the Scanner Keyboard, which incorporates a color page scanner into an otherwise normal keyboard. Cyrix announces volume availability of the 110-MHz P133+ CX6x86 and 60/120-MHz P150+CX6x86 microprocessor. IBM ships OS/2 Warp Server. Apple computer licenses the MacOS to Motorola. Intel releases the 133-MHz Pentium processor for notebook computers. Advanced micro devices begins shipping the AMD5K86 microprocessor. Corel WordPerfect Suite 7, and Corel office professional Suite. Netscape communications releases Netscape navigator 2.02. Microsoft releases Microsoft internet explorer 2.0. Intel introduces the 200-MHz Pentium processor. Cyrix introduces the 6x86-P200+ processor. Advanced Micro Devices begins shipping the K5-PR100 microprocessor. It is a 100-MHz Pentium-compatible plug-in replacement. Intel begins shipping the 200-MHz Pentium Pro with a 512-KB cache. Microsoft releases windows NT 4.0. Microsoft releases OEM Service Release 2 for windows 95. Microsoft releases Microsoft internet Explorer 3.0. Intel releases the 150-MHz mobile Pentium processor, designed for use in portable computers. Microsoft unveils windows CE operating system for hand-held PCs. Codename of the project was Pegasus. "CE" stands for consumer electronics. IBM launches OS/2 warp 4, in san Francisco, California. Microsoft ships the Visual J++ Professional edition development kit. Hitachi home electronics ships the Hitachi handheld PC, running windows CE. Casio computer ships the Cassiopeia, a hand-held computer running windows CE. Microsoft unveils Microsoft office 97 at Fall Comdex. Intel begins shipping the 200-MHz Pentium Pro processor. At the microprocessor Forum, Cyrix announces the M2 processor, optimized for 16- and 32-bit code, supporting MMX, and including 64KB cache memory. The chip will plug into a standard Pentium socket. Panic hits as industry finally realizes the consequences of the Y2K problem, more than 50 international conferences on year 2000 problem takes place.

1997: Microsoft buys Web TV for US $ 425 million. Microsoft releases internet explorer 4.0. Lotus Corporation announces Lotus Domino 4.5. Compaq ships the 4000N NetPC. Oracle Corporation introduces the first commercial object-relational database-Oracle8. Y2K conversion efforts gain momentum as more and more companies joins the Y2K conversion efforts.

1998: Microsoft released windows 98. Compaq computer corporation acquired digital equipment corporation. Y2K conversion efforts gain are going ahead at full speed, yet experts predict full conversion will not be possible.

3.1. PROPERTIES OF INFORMATION TECHNOLOGY

It has three unique properties, they are:

- The growth of information and technology in irreversible. It is possible for us to forget something and ignore others. But once something becomes known, it is almost impossible to make it unknown. Similarly once something has been invented one can't uninvent it.
- The growth of information and technology is exponential the more is known and the more has been invented, the easier it is to know still more, and invent still more.
- There is no forceable upper limit to the growth of knowledge or inventions.[6]

3.2. DEVELOPMENT OF INFORMATION TECHNOLOGY

The post-industrial period has brought considerable advances and innovations in technology. As a result of this many new inter-disciplinary fields have emerged. Information Technology is one of them. Information technology is a recent and comprehension term, which describes the whole range of processes for the acquisition storage, transmission, retrieval and processing of vocal, pictorial textual and numeric information. Such processes may be mechanical in nature, chemical or biochemical, electronic and new microelectronic. They have been at work without human intervention throughout the process of organic evolution.

Development of new information technology can be grouped into following main areas: 1. Computer Processing Technology, 2. Computer Storage Technology, 3. Communication Technology, and 4. Document and Information Production and Retrieval Technologies. These are briefly explained as under:

3.2.1. Computer Processing Technology

The development of microelectronic components, which are small, compact, cheap and reliable make it possible to integrate computing power at much reduced cost. The central feature of microelectronic is the development of microprocessor, a special form of integrated circuit with functions of arithmetic logic and of control similar to these of central processing unit (CPU) of a computer and contained in a single chip. The microprocessor is the building block from which the modern computer systems are assembled. It uses very little energy and has few environmental requirements of older machinery. The advent of microprocessor led to the following four different trends in information processing design:

1. *Specialized High Performance Auxiliary Processors*: Bit slicing microprocessor architectures are being used to and specialized functions to the general-purpose computer.
2. *Processor Mimics*: Micros are being used as processors in mini-computer, which are compatible with large systems in performance in practical terms. The ability to mimic in a processor fairly easily, also means that if a family of computers is discontinued by a manufactured processor that can mimic the discontinued line can be manufactured at a much lower cost. This capability is utilized to introduce new hardware without rocking the boat.
3. *Multiprocessor Systems*: With the advent of inexpensive processors a tendency to construct system configurations with redundant processor to objectives of reliable, continuous operation has become a common feature. The Online Computer Library Center (OCLC) has made use of such a processor design. It is now a commonplace occurrence to have multi-processing systems with distributed responsibilities and a network of data sharing arrangements in a single system.
4. *Personal Computer Phenomenon*: The availability of microprocessor at lower costs has given rise to the advent of home computers; many manufacturers are assembling small and reliable devices. The availability of low cost computers with increasingly smaller dimension and with low power requirements is of great importance to scientific and technical communication. In house mini computers are used for more sophisticated data and text processing, database management and a variedly of their applications.

3.2.2. Computer Storage Technology

There have been notable developments in memory technology affecting three areas of performance spectrum: the high speed, high performance, the midrange and the low speed bulky memory systems.

High Speed and High Performance

It is now possible that even a small computer system may have cache memory. A small associative memory retaining most recently referenced information and in a readily available place.

The Midrange Memory

The development of change coupled devices and bubbled memories have filled the gap, which previously existed in the continuum of memory devices. These devices are faster than mechanical devices, such as fixed head magnetic disks, and slower than other semiconductor memories considered from the cost per bit, these memories occupy only the middle level. They have an advantage over the magnetic disks in that they contain no mechanical parts and could be used to store significant amount of information and can be treated like a structure file system.

The Low Performance Memory: There has been a continuous improvement in recording densities of magnetic media. Floppy disks and microfloppies provide a convenient media to store data. The development of videodisk has added a new dimension to the information storage the technology videodisks could be used to store large volumes of information in. digital form.

3.2.3. Communication Technology

The development of telecommunication technology is in a sense a symbol of man's effort to communicate rapidly over great distances. The computer lies at the heart of modern communication systems and a new technology called communication is emerging from the fusion of computer and communication technologies, which is found very useful for message transmission. Telematics is one of such new fields where computer is incorporated into satellite communication system. The new system provides computing and related services. The speed and capacity of data transmission are such that vast amount of data are capable of being transmitted across the world in seconds. Development of computer networks allows for collection, collation, integration, and dissemination of information on an unprecedented scale. Thus new office, factory, community and information exchange system.

Document and Information Production and Retrieval Technologies: Reprography as a method for providing documents has gained international recognition since 1963. Reprography includes photocopying, microcopying, duplicating, and implant printing and is characterized by the small scale of its operatives. Reprographic techniques include such processes as diffusion transfer quick stabilization diazo, thermography and electro statography for copying documents reprographic technology has been playing vital role in the dissemination of recorded information and has now come to stay as one of means to provide access to document resources geographically located in different plants.

Micrographic technology is an outgrowth of photographic technology. Since the technology is being increasingly used to supplement computer systems, strong electronic and photoelectronic influences make it multi-technology dependant. Micrographic technology finds its application not only as a publishing medium but also as a communication medium, computer output medium and storage medium. The production process for a micro-publication reflects a dual information flow. The content is either microfilmed or if it is available in machine readable form, converted directly into micro by a Computer Output Medium (COM) system.[7]

3.4. IMPORTANCE OF IT

- IT can process raw data into useful information.
- IT can recycled processed information and use it as data in another processing step.
- IT can package information in a new form so its easier to understand, more attractive, or more useful.
- Once information is created in any form, text, sound, pictures, animations and movies it can be instantly distributed to other forms and a variety of ways.
- Technology is advancing so rapidly that previously isolated fields such as television phone computer and radio are all converging into a single field.
- IT is the science and skills of all aspects of computing data storage communications.
- IT concerns development and deployment of applications and systems for business that cover the entire business enterprises.
- IT people solve technical, organizational and management problems involving information, collecting information, storing it, using it, retrieving it from storage.
- IT entered into almost all fields such as business, industry, science, engineering, home, entertainment, education and training, etc.[8]

3.5. NEW TECHNOLOGIES IN INFORMATION TECHNOLOGY

3.5.1 Hypermedia

The term hypermedia comprises of a set of ideas although it seems to be understood somewhat differently within different disciplines. The very first person to directly formulate the hypermedia concept was Vannevar Bush. American President Roosewelt appointed him manager of the organization, which coordinated technology research in the USA during world war II. In 1945 published the article "As we may think" in the magazine the Atlantic Monthly addressing some of the problems faced by modern science.

Hypermedia as a network containing several interlinked information units. The information units are called nodes, and the connections between the nodes are called links. Limited networks of nodes and links are called hyper documents. Inside the node there are links and information objects. Links connect nodes handling a natural transition from one node to another node or to other nodes. A link spot normally indicates links so that the user may see where the links go. Users may follow the link by clicking on this link spot. A mouse cursor may often be sensitive to link spots, changing its shape when on a link spot.

Accessing information basically different when using hypermedia than when using traditional database technology. Typical traditional database access is via direct inquiry using unique keys or queries in the information database. In hypermedia formation access is handled through structuring the information. Users access new information by following links from existing information to new information.

3.5.2. Data Warehouses and Data Mining

The primary concept of data warehousing is that the data stored for business analysis can most effectively accessed by separating it from the data in the operational systems. A data warehouse is a collection of computer-based information that is critical to successful execution of enterprise initiatives. A data warehouse is more than an achieve for corporate data and more than a new way of accessing corporate data. A data warehouse is a subject-oriented repository designed with enterprise-wide access in mind. It provides tools to satisfy the information needs of the employees at all organizational levels—not just complex data queries, but as a general facility for getting quick, accurate and often insightful information. A data warehouse is designed so that its users can organize the information they want and access that information using simple tools.

One of the principal reason for developing a data warehouse is to integrate data from various sources into a single and consistent architecture that supports analysis and decision-making within the enterprise. A data warehouse is typically a blending of technologies, including relational and multidimensional databases client/server architecture, extraction/ transformation programmes, graphical user interfaces and more.

Data Mining is the natural evolution of query and reporting tools, everyone, who creates queries and reports benefits from having data mining capabilities. Data mining techniques are the result of a long process of research and product development. This evolution began when business data was first stored on computers, continued with improvements in data access and more recently generated technologies that allow users to navigate through their data in real time. Data mining takes this evolutionary process beyond retrospective data access and navigation to prospective and proactive information delivery.[9]

Data mining techniques can yield the benefit of automation on existing software and hardware platforms and can be implemented on new systems an existing platform are upgraded and new products are developed. Faster processing means that users can automatically experiment with more models to understand complex data. High speed makes it practical for users to analyze huge quantities of data. Larger databases in farm yield improved predictions.

3.5.3. E-Commerce

Two Thousand years ago Roman roads brought trade and commerce to Europe in an unprecedented manner. At the dawn of the second millennium, the Internet is making fundamental changes to the lives of every one on the planet changing for ever the way business is conducted.

Generally there are three kinds of E-Commerce, business to business, business to customer and using digital middleman.

Business-to-Business E-Commerce

Since 1980s, organizations have been using EDI to conduct business transaction electronically. Some of these transactions include sending receiving of orders, invoices and shipping notices. EDI is a method of extending the organizations computing power beyond boundaries. But the high cost and maintenance of the networks made this method out of reach for small and medium sized businesses.

Business to Customer E-Commerce

The company first establishes a website on the Internet. On the website the company can put up information about products and services, allow customers to order these from the website and also provide customer support services. In order to get customers to the website the company must inform the public about its existence using traditional means of advertising like (commercials, advertise, brochures, etc.) and on-line advertising.

Digital Middleman E-commerce

The digital middleman in e-commerce could be a company that creates a virtual community on the Internet and then gathers several companies together into this community. The virtual community provides information of the products and services of each company to the visitors, allowing them to do comparisons and select the best deal. The middleman takes a fee from the companies for each Internet referral.[10]

3.5.4. On-Line Analytical Processing (OLAP)

The term OLAP was coined by E.F. Codd in 1993 to refer to a type of application that allows a user to interactively analyze data. An OLAP system is often contrasted to an OLTP (on-line transaction processing) system that focuses on transactions such as orders, invoice, general ledger transitions.

OLAP applications span a variety of organizational functions i.e., finance, marketing and production. The key indicator of a successful OLAP application is its ability to provide information, as needed, i.e., its ability to provide "Just in time" information for effective decision-making. This requires more than a base level of detailed data OLAP applications are found in widely divergent functional areas they all require the following key features:

1. *Multidimensional Views*: A Multidimensional view of data provides more than ability to "slice and dice", it provides the foundation for analytical processing through flexible access to information. Database design should not prejudice which operations can be performed on a dimension or how rapidly those operations are

performed. Managers must be able to analyze data across any dimension at any level of aggregation. With equal functionality and ease. OLAP software should support these views of data in a natural and responsive fashion, insulating users of the information from complex query syntax. After all managers should not have to understand complex tables layout. Elaborate table joins and summary tables.

2. *Complex Calculations*: The real test of an OLAP database is its ability to perform complex calculations, OLAP databases must be able to do more than simple aggregation OLAP software must provide a rich tool kit of powerful yet succinct Computational Methods to make developers more efficient and business users more self-sufficient, the vehicle for implementing computational methods should be clear and non-procedural. If the method for creating the desired calculations is not clear, development time and usage will suffer. If the calculations method proceeds then changes to the systems cannot be done in a timely manner which effectively eliminates the access to just in time information.
3. *Time Intelligence*: Time is an integral component of almost any analytical application. True OLAP systems understand the sequential nature of time. Business performance is almost always judged over time. The time hierarchy is not always used in the same manner as other hierarchies. In addition OLAP systems must understand the concept of balance overtime.

3.5.5. Geographic Information System (GIS)

A GIS is a computer-based tool for mapping and analyzing things that exists and events that happen on earth. GIS technologies integrate common database operations such as query and statistical analysis with the unique visualization and geographic analysis benefits offered by maps. These abilities distinguish GIS from other information systems and make it valuable to wide range of public and private enterprises for explaining events, predicting outcomes, and planning strategies. A working GIS integrates five key components hardware, software, data, people and methods.

A GIS stores information about the world as a collection of thematic layers that can be linked together by geography. This simple but extremely powerful and versatile concept has proven invaluable for solving many real world problems from tracking delivery vehicles, to recording details of planning applications, to modeling global atmospheric circulation. GIS work with two fundamentally different types of geographic models—the vector model and the raster model. In the vector model information about points, lines, and polygons is encoded and stored as a collection of x, y coordinates. The raster model has evolved to model such continuous features. A raster image comprises a collection of grid cells rather like a cannel map or picture. Both the vector and raster models for storing geographic data have unique advantages and disadvantages. Modern GIS are able to handle both models.

A GIS allows bringing all types of data together based on the geographic and location component of the data. GIS will given power to create maps, integrate information visualize scenarios, solve complicated problems, present powerful ideas and develop effective solutions like never before. GIS is a tool used by individuals and organizations, schools, governments, and businesses seeking innovative ways to solve their problems.[11]

3.6. HRD THROUGH INFORMATION TECHNOLOGY

Now Information Technology has emerged as a big stimulating force and it is strongly influencing the human mind and its thought process, the society and in the end the entire world. It has enhanced its capacity of accumulating and storing information. All the information of a library can now be stored in ones own PC and access to those information is a matter of click of the mouse only. Thus Information Communication Technology (ICT) has a long recurring influence on the total education system.

Internet, the second baby of ICT, is helping the society in different ways eg. offer information of health, education, entertainment, business, correspondence, tours and travels, etc. More and more parts of the world are entering into the field of net by the use of ICT and serving in many ways for different purposes at a time, e.g. provide consolation in the time of need, health advice when one is sick, etc., although these facilities are still not available to most of the people of the world. So equality in opportunities in every respect is very important for todays "Learning Society".

In the filed of education IT plays a strong and influencing role, though some are fearing some negative effects too. Today traditional systems, methods and methodologies have gone a distinct change. New technologies are entering into the field of education. Instead of only face-to-face education, one can now avail him of the opportunities of alternate types of education from distant and inaccessible places. Deprived people service-holders, housewives, and physically backward people can have the opportunity of access in education. The concepts like smart schooling, dischooling virtual university, virtual classroom, e-learning, e-library, etc. are not the imagination of the idle brains. IT is helping enormously in this process, educational institutions are now also in the middest of "Information Waves", today big schools or large universities are not essential for the learners. They can even learn sitting at their own homes and appear for the examinations too. The duties and responsibilities of the teachers are changing day-by-day. Today teachers are not only suppliers of knowledge, they also help to develop students to compute in the changing world, to adjust with the new society and the new environment.[12]

Today computers are slowly changing work pattern, lifestyle, business education, lecture time activities, etc. in such a dramatic way that the society is depending more and more on it. Today ICT covers and controls the following areas of the society and human lives.

3.6.1. IT Education for the Rich and the Poor

Even under IT education the initiatives taken by companies have been wide ranging. It has been observed that when it comes to primary education, most companies focus on rural areas. These companies through various programmes have tried to improve the quality of education in rural schools and have strived to make these students computer literate and technology savvy. On the other hand, when it comes to college education most initiatives have been taken in the areas of high-end research and particularly targeted at students of premium educational centers in India, like IITs and IIMs.

Infosys is playing a very active role in rural education. Under the Hon'ble chairmanship of Sudha Murthy, the infosys foundation has grown to be strong pillar in rural development. The foundation provides computers to rural schools and IT training to the teachers. Under the library for every school scheme, the foundation has donated several libraries to various schools in Karnataka; and each library is stacked with 200 to 2000 books. To simplify the standard of computer education for the students in rural areas a special book has been written and is being distributed under its library projects. This book has also been translated into Hindi, Tamil and Telugu to widen its reach. The infosys foundation has also been involved in related causes like reconstruction of old school buildings, construction of additional class rooms and donation for school and corpus funds.

The Reliance group undertakes its social welfare and humanitarian initiatives through various organizations, including trusts such as the Dhirubhai Ambani Foundation and Reliance Rural Development Trust. As part of its education initiative Reliance runs schools at its manufacturing locations providing quality education and computers to children living in nearby areas. In association with the Municipal Corporation of Greater Mumbai, Reliance launched the secondary schools computerization project to facilitate computer education for all 50 municipal secondary schools of Mumbai.

Wipro, through Azim Premji Foundation has introduced the concept of "Computer Assisted Learning Centres" in response to the needs of the people in rural Karnataka. The pilot project with 34 Computer Assisted Learning Centres (CALCs) was set-up in Bangalore and surrounding rural areas. It aimed at measuring the impact of computers in attracting out of school children to school and the improvement in learning levels among children in their regular academic work.

Microsoft, through its project Siksha aims to accelerate its literacy across Government schools in the country. Project Siksha aims at providing computer literacy to over 80,000 school teachers and 3.5 million students across schools in the next five years. It plans to deliver affordable software solutions, comprehensive training and curriculum leadership to enable students and teachers to realize their full potential Siksha is the largest most comprehensive IT education programme undertake by any private company in the world and it is the single largest education investment made by Microsoft to date.

IT the first phase of project Siksha Microsoft has signed a MOU with the State Government of Uttaranchal. The MOU being first in a series similar partnerships planned by Microsoft, underlines joint commitment by Microsoft and the Uttaranchal Government towards accelerating. The MOU will entail the setting up and running of a Microsoft IT academy centre in Dehradun to facilitate teacher training, formulation and implementation of a comprehensive teacher training programme creation of a localized IT curriculum for students, rolling out of teacher and students' scholarship programme and setting up a teacher's portal.[13]

3.6.2. Education for All

In many developing countries level of illiteracy is quite high. According to the latest census report—2001 (Government of India) 296 million people in the age group of seven years and above still remain outside the purview of the schools. On the other hand, we are still continuing traditional systems of education, which are unable to meet the growing demand of the merging society. Again there are debates between quality and quantity because a question of finance is involved here. So a compromise is also going on internally and externally regarding the question of quality *versus* quantity. For this reason education for all remains a proud declaration only in black and white. This is the scenario of most of the developing countries of the world. Again each and every country has its own cultural methods and the traditional systems are based on them on the question of sentiment and motivation is also involved in the process so setting of right goals, objectives and functions of education, structural readjustment at different levels of education, viz. lower, middle and tertiary level of education is very important. In each level education of women should be a priority area. This is important in view of the proven fact that fertility rate decreases with increasing levels of education of women and educated mothers can rear up their children more efficiently than their counterpart. IT can be used effectively in that case.

3.6.3. Training of Teachers and Other Work Forces

ICT has changed the role and concept of educational institutions. Now there are ample scopes to receive and update information from many other sources. Naturally the duties and responsibilities of the teachers should be considered on the basis of the emerging trends. In these days teachers have to accept the demands of the modern world and modify their old concepts, methods and instructional techniques according to the needs and they are to be trained as life long learners because now the rate of obsolescence of knowledge is tremendously high.

Now technology has created a host of new tools for use in the classrooms, laboratories at home on the move. Using these tools both students and teachers are equipped to become researchers. Teachers then coach their students to evaluate and use effectively the information they have generated for themselves. This is far closer to real life situation than the older styles of teacher transmission to students.

In the days of growing influences of ICT the new roles of educational institutions are not only to transfer information or merely prepare some literate pupil but also to mature them in such a way that they can face the competition in the new demanding situation should be prepared to take the responsibilities of training and retraining of the work force as and when required. Teacher training methods should be updated in such a way that they can bear the responsibilities of training the labour force update their knowledge and skills for the learning society.

Accessing and Processing Knowledge

Some are of the opinion that multidimensional information processing system would automatically change the entire society into a learning society. Sometimes the higher sections of the society convey this idea to accumulate and strengthen own control over information. Coming to the case education it is sure that quality education will not always be ready at hand. So development of good academic programmes with the help of IT, according to the need of the people, the society, economic of the country, cultural ethos of the society, etc., for different educational levels are important for a learning society.

IT and Languages of Communication

This is another vital and intriguing area when one wants to apply ICT in education. The Internet baby of ICT is language dependent most of the information received through the Net in English language. But a vast majority of the world population does not know the language. In the developing world the matter is more complex and trouble. A large number of the population is still illiterate. Language is the most important tool for communication, it helps creates and express cultural identity of the individual with the society.[14]

3.6.4. Satellite Communication India

India has been using satellite communication for educational purposes since 1975 when the first experiment called the Satellite Instructional Television Experiment (SITE) to broadcast educational programme to rural schools was conducted.

The University Grants Commission (UGC) National Council of Educational Research And Training (NCERT) and using satellite broadcasting on the national network for various educational programmes.

Indira Gandhi National Open University (IGNOU) has been transmit healing educational programmes over the national network to reach out to its learners. Now there is a talkback terminal available in satellite communication. The phone call or the audio channel from the classroom comeback to the teachers at studios who can interact with the students from any where in the country. Now the students can send a question through fax and e-mail through e-mail is not really online. IGNOU uses this studio to uplink. IGNOU uses earth station which sends signal to the satellite and then it is received back by something like 150 receiving terminals at the various regional and study centers.

This kind of network could be used by all the 9 State Open Universities also. All India Management Association uses this network for conducting diploma programmes. The NCERT use this technology for training 1,400,000 to 1,500,000 primary school teachers and that also in various regional languages. There is a programme called Integrated Child Development Scheme (ICDS) and almost every village has an ICDS worker who is a woman from the same village. This technology used for training 500,000 ICDS workers and functionaries of Panchayat Raj Institutions (local bodies). The UGC uses special training programme on new communication technologies orienting its staff at various EMRGs. This particular network namely the INSAT system covers not only India but also most of the adjoining countries namely Nepal, Bangladesh, Sri Lanka, Pakistan, and Maldives to some extent.

There are certain educational factors that influence the growth and adoption of the communication technology. Teachers play a crucial role in the adoption of a communication technology or an innovation. Besides there are some additional factors that influence decision maker to ignore or adopt technologies for educational purpose. Some of these are as follows:

- The teachers are usually not involved in planning and preparing the courseware.
- It is very difficult to cover the entire syllabus through one technology (medium), therefore other media are required to achieve the educational objectives in totality, but it is very difficult for many countries to adopt the multimedia approach to teaching learning.
- There is a dearth of variety in the courseware. The material borrowed from the developed countries may not be suitable for the students of developing countries.
- The students' dependency on book and the teachers' lecture discourage them to make use of the modern communication technology for learning.
- Educators prefer technology, which has the potential of solving educational problems, and consequently can improve the quality of instruction.[15]

3.6.5. Literacy through Radio

In India radio has been used extensively by the Government for disseminating information about various development issues. While meeting some of the information needs of rural communities, however, the potential of a non-visual medium of radio for imparting literacy instructions and training did not happen till the National Literacy Mission (NLM) conducted the Project in Radio Education for Adult Literacy (PREAL) in 1990.

PREAL was launched in 1990 as a collaborative project between the NLM and All India Radio (AIR) in which women were identified as the primary intended beneficiaries. It was partly funded by the UNICEF. The Directorate of Adult Education (DAE) conceptualized PREAL and implemented it in 17 technology.

Demonstration districts of four low-literacy Hindi-speaking states of Bihar, Madhya Pradesh, Rajasthan and Uttar Pradesh in collaboration with several government agencies and institutions. Radio-*cum*-cassette recorders (two-in-one) were provided to over 3600 adult education centers under the project. The primary objective of PREAL was to use radio to promote literacy skills (reading only) and facilitate teaching of literacy in adult education centers. PREAL was based on the premise that, the radio primer-based broadcast and the repetitive use of radio lessons in the non-broadcast mode would reinforce learning in adult education centers and supplement teaching of literacy skills by instructors.

Instructional content of the Radio lessons was prepared after a detailed linguistic analysis of the existing IPCL primers and local materials. The core content of the radio programmes focused on learning and teaching of reading skills. The overall pedagogy for production of the radio lesson was predetermined. It consisted of three parts. Listen and speak, listen and see, recognize and read aloud. To enhance appeal and comprehension of the radio broadcast, radio lessons waved in cultural specificity of different regions by the way of music, drama and local idiom. The AIR had the choice of selecting the story presentation style, language and programme format, however the hardcore literacy content was common to all radio programmes.

Twenty-six radio lessons on literacy were broadcast under the common title of Nai Pahel from seven local radio stations of AIR in the selected states on an experimental basis for six months to supplement teaching of literacy in the selected adult education centers. Language of the broadcast was both standard Hindi and Local dialect. To supplement radio broadcast, a radio reader known as Akashvani Pathmala, was specifically prepare in standard Hindi for all the districts except for two tribal districts and supplied to the selected adult literacy centers for all the learners. Each learner and instructor was expected to use Akashavani Pathmala during the broadcast. Each radio lesson of 15-20 minutes was broadcast once a week along with a repeat broadcast. At the end of the twenty-six radio lessons the adult learners were expected to recognize and read all the alphabets of Devnagari script along with the words from their active vocabulary.

3.6.6. Literacy through Television

Audio-visual medium of television has been used for distance education at higher levels. In adult education however no systematic efforts were made until 1990 to teach literacy through television. Three experiments/projects in imparting literacy through television show how television can be used for literacy and teaching. These projects are given under:

(a) Chauraha Project

A television serial of 40 episodes chauraha was the first experimental project that used television for teaching literacy. Doordarshan the public broadcasting system transmitted the serial for six months in 1992 for poor and illiterate women in Delhi slums and villages around Delhi. The Directorate of Adult Education in collaboration with the State Resource Centers (SRC), New Delhi conducted this UNICEF sponsored experiment.

Chauraha focused on imparting rudimentary literacy skills in Hindi while generating awareness among women learners to empower them through a powerful narrative situated in rural India. It used an innovative and absorbing approach to teach the viewers Hindi alphabets through devanagari script. Besides linking content of television programmes with the literacy primer used by the learners in adult education centers, television programmes were grounded in the day-to-day realities of learners. Chauraha entertaining format combined village soap opera with muppets and animation.

Doordarshan telecast chauraha more than once, but it neither telecast the serial at a suitable time for gave advance notice for the broadcast so that wide viewership could be ensured. The telecast of chauraha was also not supported by the adequate system on the ground. To reinforce teaching of the television programmes chauraha telecast was not linked with ongoing literacy teaching in adult education centers. Inadequate infrastructure facilities, lack of training of volunteer instructors in using television broadcast for literacy teaching and learning and lack of additional reading materials on chauraha were some of the problems with the reception of chauraha in adult education centers. Thus, educational potential of chauraha remained explored due to lack of support system for utilizing the telecast in adult education centers.

Nevertheless quick appraisal of chauraha by the SRC showed encouraging results in terms of literacy learning and social awareness. The study reported significant differences in literacy achievement (particularly in writing skills) among learners of adult literacy centers where chauraha was screened either through television or VCK as compared to learners from literacy centers where no screenings were held. SRC also explored the educational potential of chauraha by using it in adult literacy centers in the non-broadcast mode while supplementing literacy learning with a set of charts and books based on the sequence of alphabet and words taught through the television serial.

(b) The Jhabua Development Communication Project (JDCP)

The JDCP was introduced in November 1996 by the Development of Education Communication Unit (DECU) of the Indian Space Research Organization (ISRO) to use the dedicated satellite-based Rural Development Communication System (RDCS) for meeting communication needs of the predominantly tribal and under developed district of Jabhu in Madhya Pradesh. The Interactive Training Programme (ITP) using one-way video and two-way audio teleconferencing via satellite was an important component of JDCP for training development functionaries at block and village levels. In the light of effectiveness of the JDCP the project was extended till October 1999 and expanded to all 612 panchayats of the district by DECU/ISRO to focus on some of the thrust areas of development where television could be effectively used for a large population.

In JDCP evening television broadcasting for the general audience in the areas of health, agriculture, watershed management, education had built in component of adult education. However given the low level of literacy (1454 per cent in 1995) in Jhabu district. DECU/ISRO decided to give priority to promoting adult literacy through television. The district administration was also keen to revive literacy efforts for its post-literacy programme and use television to motivate learners and volunteers. The JDCP provided on opportunity to use satellite television broadcasting for support ongoing literacy programme in the district. Television was expected to supplement literacy teaching and learning in the existing adult literacy centers and motivate learners and volunteers for participation in district post-literacy campaign. The JDCP literacy project was implemented by DECU/ISRO as all lead agencies in collaboration with the state resource center (Madhya Pradesh) and district adult education administration of Jabhu. Interactive training program was also organized to orient the teachers and coordinators participating in the literacy project while face-to-face training was conducted by the SRC for volunteer instructors.

In the JDCP literacy experiment production of television programme was a mazor challenge. There was considerable debate and discussion on the style, format and language of television programs for supporting literacy teaching in adult education centers. First 20 television programs used to generate awareness about the literacy programme and motivating learners for learning. Then 58 television programmes loaded with the literacy content were broadcasting to support the existing IPCL primers for basic literacy. Programmes used simple Hindi along with some local words in drama and songs. In practice technology and systems management took priority over sustaining community participation in implementation of the project at the village level. Thus, literacy classes and television viewing of the lessons did not take place everywhere as envisaged by the project.

Limited success of the experiment was also attributed to lack of involvement of district and field staff in project implementation, lack of relevant and additional basic learning and teaching for literacy instructors and learners, and lack of basic infrastructural facilities in literacy centers. Thus, the JDCP experiment in promoting adult literacy through television remained "a top down technology and management driven project" with very limited benefits to adult learners for acquiring basic literacy skills.[16]

(c) Warna Wired Village Project

This project is jointly implemented by National Informatics Centre, Government of Maharashtra and Warna Vibhag Shikshan Mandal (a village cooperative society) covering 70 villages around Warnanager in Kolhapur and Sangi districts of Maharastra. The aim is to provide information to the villagers by establishing networked booths in the village institution. Each village has a "facilitation booth" with wire less LAN, CAI and INTERNET for high speed transmission of data to farmers on essential agricultural operations. The network is also being used to provide distance education for primary and high school. This initiatives has encouraged farm productivity increased the profits of the farmers and helped the areas cooperative societies to achieve an annual turnover of US $ 120 million.[17]

Computer aided instruction has been there in North American universities for a number of years without much changing the traditional methods. Virtual Universities are the new emerging concepts where high speed access will provide off campus students with two-way interactive classes at TV broadcast quality including video multimedia software access and on-line homework/question answer sessions/test/advising/intelligent tutors, etc.

These trends are gradually influencing the teaching methods of Indian institutions. Centre of Education Technology of IIT Delhi provides audio-visual equipments in classroom loaning projection and video hardware to faculty members as also designing and developing value added OHP transparencies 35 mm slider video programmes and computer software for teaching, seminars and project work. The centre maintains the state of the art studio classroom with all audio-visual resources with a 3 camera setup for on-line recording of courses, conducting cable extended classroom teaching preparing designed programmes and for Research and Development work with complete post production on high band U-matric and etacam machines.

The center also has a CAI laboratory with multimedia PC and range of software to design and prepare CAI packages plan and 3-dimensional animation E-mail, Internet facilities for world-wide networking and for teaching research and communications. The center has undertaken AT & T supported project for Global Distance learning initiative on video conferencing for faculty development and another project of AICTE on video teleconferencing and AICTE Nationally coordinated project on Education Technology.

3.6.7. Distance Learning

Distance learning is one dimension of education where experiment with new/information technology has benefited maximum. Distance learning has been a term used for years to describe any sort of education from Nursery/LKG to professional colleges/institution where the instruction occurs at one place and the education institution is somewhere else.

The issue here is computer mediated instruction which can be obtained from courses offered on the internet, computer and telecommunications allow for a more interactive integrated learning environment. Distance learning has been now redefined by United States Distance Learning Association (USDLA) as the delivery of education or training through electronically mediated instruction including satellite, video, autographic, computer and multimedia.

The new technologies of distance learning hold the potential to revolutionize business and executive education in India. Multinational have found it very useful, though its introduction in educational institutions is slow. IGNOU is the first open university having established one-way video, two-way audio conferencing facility supporting its distance learning programmes with two-way video or audio conferencing facility, this kind of system might facilitate an institution to open up courses and reach to student community in other locations take up in house training programme for industry and interact foreign collaborators in exchange of teaching and research resources.

IIT Delhi has been offered special fund from AICTE to develop conferencing facility in September 1997. The cabinet secretary (Govt. of India) inaugurated the full-fledged video conferencing facility of National Information Center (NIC). By linking various Central Government departments with state secretariats the video conferencing facility would improve government efficiency provide better service to citizens and bring in transparency. It will be especially useful in disaster management such as flood relief where several state and central agencies have to work together.

NIC had been asked to expedite the setting up of "VIDCON" studio's in the secretariat of all the 32 states/union territories in addition to the major government departments in Delhi within six months. The centre will bear the software and hardware costs. The system will cut down on travel and stay expenses associated with official meetings and interaction. The live interactive session though the multipoint video conferencing was boringly addressed by commerce secretary, chief economic advisor, Rajasthan chief secretary in addition to the cabinet secretary from their respective offices. NICs indigenous development of the software and hardware had brought down the costs for using the facility to Rs. 3000 per house less than the cost of a trunk call for point to point connection, the new facility has the potential of saving the government up to Rs. 1 lakh for each conference of about 10 people participating from different cities.[18]

3.6.8. E-Learning

E-learning consists of following components, which are created with the state of art Internet technologies for high quality case of use and effectiveness:

The Virtual Classroom

Virtual Classroom Modules (VCMs) are well prepared high quality lectures from the master trainers, with multimedia color presentations, VCM combines distance educational instructional pedagogy with latest interactive Multimedia Internet Technology. VCM helps the counselors to efficiently perform his basic job of providing information in less time without compromising the quality. Thus he can utilize his time for developing higher-level mental abilities like comprehension, application analysis etc., in students. Smaller time duration of each module (is about 15+15 minutes) ensures better concentration. Highly compressed formats about 200 VCMS which are enough for about 2-8 courses (subjects) or 16-32 credit points can be supplied on a single CD. Streaming media technology ensures simultaneous playing and downloading of a module from Internet, can be used as back up media for delivery of VCMs to provide a "Anywhere any time" learning. Use of video is kept to minimum possible level and normally restricted to imparting of skills. Easy and fast production of good quality VCMs is possible. Discussion and/or tutorial in real time with counselors and fellow students are expected to follow these lectures at each study centres. Thus, VCM ensures better learning through distance system in the following ways:

- *Better time utilization*: Through well-prepared lectures from master trainers.
- *Clear knowledge communication*: Through the latest multimedia and Internet technology.
- *Development of Better understanding*: Through discussion/tutorials in a group of fellow students with a counselor.
- *Repeatability and portability*: Student can repeat the module or its part on any multimedia computer can even dispatch it through internet/email.

The Discussion Forum

A discussion forum is an interactive website that let site. Visitors discuss topics by reading articles that have been posted replying to articles and posting new ones. Visitors can also use a search form to find articles of interest discussion forum offers asynchronous mode of communication, where messages can be prepared with editing and post or repaid devices without waiting for the receiver to be ready. But it allows only text-based interaction among students' counselors and the University any interaction on the discussion forum is visible to all. A discussion forum can have the following features:

- A table of contents that contains hyper-links to articles relevant fór the discussion topics. A search form that allows visitors to search the articles for a word. An entry from in which a visitors types on articles post.
- Threaded replies allow the visitors to choose weather the article they are posting is a new top-level topic for discussion. This feature creates well-classified and well-organized knowledge base on any academic or administrative topic in a short time. Frequently asked questions can be easily derived from this knowledge base.
- A conformation page, which conforms that, a visitors' article has been posted. A registration form that lets site visitors log into the website is the discussion web is protected. Discussion forums may be used in various situations.
- *Discussion forum for the University*: This forum will indicate perceptions and expectations of the society at large about the society. Also the following student services can be provided for all academic programmes.
- Per enrolment counseling. Information on dispatch and receipt of learning material. Feedback on counseling at each study centre. Information about any changes in the schedules. Counseling about various culmination related issues, etc.
- Discussion for each project of design and development of new academic programme here well classified and well organized record will be maintained on deliberations during the project among members of each team of academic experts. This will be valuable knowledge resource for taking decisions about any change in future, as it provides full historical context for it.
- *Discussion forum for each course (subject)*: Topics are classified for each unit (chapter), this forum is ideally suited for academic discussion among students and counselors at all study centers. This forum will indicate where the university needs to provide more academic support to the students of the course by indicating all difficult topics in a course.

Online Counseling

Online counselor is a well-qualified and experienced person who interacts with the students. Only through use of discussion forum, for clearing their doubts/difficulties, depending on the number of students, the university can appoint one or more "online counselors" for each course (subject). Once a week each online counselor will answer all the questions posted on the discussion forum of the respective course. He will also initiated academic interaction by posting 1. Home Assignments, 2. Quizzes, 3. Critical Thinking Questions, and 4. Any other academic information about the course online counseling will be a step forward towards "Learner Centric" education, as it provide anywhere any time counseling for those learners who cannot regularly attend counseling sessions at study centre due to various reasons. Online counseling cannot replace regular face to face counseling as study centre but can act like back up fort it and email discussion forums offer only text-based communication.

Features of E-learning: Web enabled fourth generation, "Open and Distance Education System (ODES)" at different stages of learning (Frame-work) are as follows:

1. *Information*: In E-learning the heavy emphasis on print media will be reduced but not totally eliminated in the delivery of learning material role for other media like audio, video, multimedia, etc. is substantially increased but is still only supportive. In E-learning academic information will be provided in three major forms, i.e., self-instructional texts, virtual classrooms and web resources.
2. *Self-study*: Self-study by the student using academic information provided by the university through various media will still be essential. But in the proposed system self-study of the student using print media is effectively supported by VCMs through web. It delayed for any reason; self-study at the right time is still possible as VCMs through web provide "Anywhere any time" back up for print media. Self-study will be much more enjoyable thanks to multimedia technology and the master trainers.
3. *Interaction and Counseling*: Academic help in the form of limited counseling will still be retained but quality and effectiveness of counseling sessions at each study centre will be greatly enhanced and enriched with the use of VCMs on the CD. With this approach University can easily ensure the same academic quality and standards at each study centers. Counselors and each study centre act as facilitators and guides. Utilization of counseling session will be much better.
4. *Formative Feedback about Learning*: Internet is a fast, easy and reliable communication media with a global presence. Active Server Page (ASP) technology offers excellent secured opportunities for interactive intelligent communication and on demand feedback about learning effectiveness on the Internet.
5. *Online Total Quality Management System*: It will allow any registered student or the recognized counselor to directly accesses all aspects of quality or retriever quality information about each of the following components, directly from online quality database. This will generate knowledge base for the quality of each important component. With this quality knowledge base, students can choose

better study centres or may insist for recognized counselor only. Thus, accesses study centres will have to offer better quality academic and administrative services.

6. *Online Examination Centre Allows any student to directly and immediate accesses*: His own knowledge level before studying any unit or VCM of the course by taking "pre-test" on any selected units or VCMs for the course.

- His own learning effectiveness after studying any course by taking self-test on any selected unit for the course. This provides valuable formative feedback about his learning effectiveness.
- His own learning effectiveness for the complete course by taking multiple-choice type of objective end examination on any course results of this type of end examination will be communicated immediately after its completion to the learner.[19]

Since 1988 the National Literacy Mission (NLM) as technological mission attempted to demonstrate the use of science, technology and management for tackling the enormous task of eradicating illiteracy through large scale, area-specific, volunteer-based and time-bound Total Literacy Campaigns (TLC). The NLM has introduced a new techno-pedagogic approach, known as the Improved Pace and Content of Learning (IPCL) to enhance the quality of learning materials while shortening the time span for achieving the NLM norms of functional literacy. The IPCL approach based on a number of linguistic methodologies was envisaged to enable learners to attain the expected level of literacy as per the NLM norms in about 200 hours are a period of six to eight months. NLM also initiated two experimental projects using radio, television for imparting literacy instructions i.e., computer-based rural literacy project and common wealth of learning literacy project. The details of these two projects are given as under:

3.6.9. Computer-based Rural Literacy Project

The Computer-based Rural Literacy Project (CRLP) innovative project was undertaken by the Tata Consultancy Services (TCS), Indian leading software services company as a part of its social sector initiative. It aims at eradicating illiteracy in a faster and cost effective way by using information technology along with printed literacy material. After initial experiments in Beeramguda village in Medak district (Andhra Pradesh) in 2000 the project was expanded to 80 villages across the state by April 2001. The salient aspects of the project are its technological configurations (hardware and software) for imparting literacy instructions in rural areas and the computer-based pedagogic approach for teaching literacy.

Access to communication infrastructures is a major hurdle in using information technology in rural areas. To overcome the obstacles of operating stand alone computers in remote areas the project used the wireless local loop technology. This technology used to effectively build the communication infrastructure for project without laying physical lines. It also helps in receiving regular feedback from volunteers engaged in teaching literacy to the villagers and in networking remote placed computers. The computers (48b PCs) with custom-made keyboard in the local language are installed in location such as "gram panchayat" (village level political counsel) office that is easily accessible to villagers. While keeping in mind the low-end computers the TCS has developed the beta version of the instructional software in the Telugu language for teaching and reading skills to illiterate adult learners to motivate adult learners and ensure increased attention. The project has developed multi-media software that incorporates some aspects of local culture in the design of the user interface. This software has demonstrated the possibility of enabling an illiterate adult to read a newspaper in the local language within 10 weeks.

The literacy module of the project consists of 18 computer-based literacy lessons. It uses the IPCL material produced by the NLM. However, the project has developed a new pedagogic approach for teaching literacy (language) to adults with the help of a computer. In this approach the basic unit of learning is not an alphabet but a syllable. It is based on the premise that reading skills are key to improving peoples' access to information and knowledge that is available in written form with the belief that adults process both pictorial and aural inputs in a contextual and holistic mode before breaking it down into smaller units of information the project uses the "word approach" instead of "alphabet-based" approach to teach literacy. The word approach enables learners to first build the vocabulary of 300-400 commonly used words. Literacy teaching starts with familiar words which are selected from commonly found themes and situations in a given community.

As Indian Languages are phonetic alphabets and scripts are introduced through the sounds that make up such words. Repeated flashing of symbols and icons in the local language on the computer screen induces learning. Word games are also used to reinforce recognition of these sounds and letters in different contexts and to construct new words with the composite letters. The pilot project claims that within 8-10 weeks learns can acquire reasonable reading skills to read a local newspaper in the local language.

Duration of each literacy class is flexible determine by the span of adult learners. Literacy classes in the project are not run by teachers or instructors but by the volunteers who teach the learners how to use computers. However given the limitations of visibility of the display on computer monitors per computer only about 15 students can be accommodated in a literacy class one teaching site of the project is expected to enable 300 adults to read functionally in a year.

With the encouraging results of the pilot project in Andhra Pradesh, the TCS is intends to expand the project in other states through interested NGOs. It has started the work on the Hindi and Tamil script. The pilot project also provided impetus to the TCS for developing an Indian Spice recognition engine that is capable of converting spoken words into written text and *vice versa*. This would further speed up the learning process.[20]

3.6.10. Common Wealth of Learning Literacy Project

The Common Wealth of Learning Literacy Project (COLLIT) founded by the British Department of International Development is a three year pilot project (1999-2002) undertaken in Zambia and India to explore the ways in which ICTs can be used in the local literacy programmes (Common Wealth of Learning, 2000). The primary objectives of the COLLIT is to demonstrate and evaluate the appropriateness and effectiveness to technology-based community learning centres (TCLCs) through which literacy instructors can provide literacy training to develop learner competencies in reading and numeracy and in the use and operation of ICT appliances. In India, the project aims at promoting literacy efforts of the NLM by enabling the learners to use ICT to generate their own literacy material and facilitate interactive learning.

The project implemented in India by Indira Gandhi National Open University (IGNOU) through its Centre for Extension Education since August, 1999 in collaboration with partners namely the State Resource Research Foundation (MSSRF) in Tamila Nadu that has joined the project since April, 2001. Through these partners eight TCLCs are established in rural areas, two by each SRC, and four by the MSSRF. Each TCLC is equipped with two computers (Pentium III/IV) a laser printer, television, VCR, audio cassette player and a still camera. Despite the problems related to communication infrastructure, the TLCCS have started functioning. Each centre is run by a team of male and female facilitators (sahyogi and sahyogini). Early findings on the basis of preliminary MIS and evaluation data and monthly reports from both the SRCs show encouraging trends in using ICTs for literacy work.

The COLLIT has contributed to augmenting the capability of SRCs and building their institutional potential for using ICTs in production of teaching-learning material. With the availability of ICT appliances at each SRC, and training of staff for using them each SRC has started modifying relevant printed literacy material into computer-based literacy material, and developing project specific materials (project brochures, posters training manual, DCs, etc.) for literacy instructor and learners. Access of the Internet in TCLC is constrained by inadequate communication infrastructure and electricity supply. However, some scanned information from Hindi web sites is stored in TCLC computers by the SRC indorse so that learners could have access to them. The TCLC facilitators are local people some of them had been actively involved in literacy work. The COLLIT project has contributed to building their capabilities for handling ICTs and using them for literacy teaching and community activities.

Availability of television VCR and audio cassette player at the TCLC have become useful tools to the facilitators to provide continuous education and generate awareness in the community about local developmental issues

(For example, productive health, HIV/AIDS, watershed development, etc.). Project activities at the TCLC level are shaped by the project goals of accessibility, interactivity, community mobilization and sustainability of various strategies have been used to harness the technology to respond to the divergent learning needs of the community. In the initial stage the project focused on 'demystifying' technology by rambling all learners to operate the computer. Young school going children and adolescent youth who acquired computer literacy voluntarily assist neo-literates in using computers and in reading sessions.

Neo-literate learners have started using the computer for reading the scanned material and practicing writing. They have also generated pictorial material with the help of MS-word, paintbrush and clip Art. They could operate television and radio and review existing audio-visual learning material and broadcast programmes. Other technologies such as digital camera, handy cam are also operated by the learners to take pictures and compose their own stories and materials. Access to ICTs has contributed to development of self-confidence among adult learners for literacy learning. Learner generated material has also enabled learners to practice literacy skills. Thus, acquisition of literacy skills is facilitated and reinforced and through the use of various technologies by learners themselves and by others in preparing teaching-learning material.[21]

3.6.11. Pathway Education Through WLAN

The WLAN was designed and implemented by IBM and CIESO in partnership. They conducted joint study wherein the analysed kind of applications that would be used, the band width requirement per user, the applications that students would need to access and the location to deploy the access points.

The solution is future proof as the wireless access points supplied are compatible with 802.11g. Presently, pathways is using the popular 802.11b Mbps. The options of upgrading to the faster 802.11g standard providing up to 54 Mbps connectivity on the same 2.4 GHZ frequency gives the school room to grow.

IBM, which provided the servers and the wireless enabled ThinkPads, implemented the projects, pathways has deployed two IBM X-235 servers. One is application server running on windows 2000 and the second is a Linux-based internet proxy (controlling the internet access of students and restricting specific sites).

The school server maintains a broadband connection, giving each student continuous access via the school intranet to external internet resources. Primus technologies is currently providing the Internet band width of 128 Kbps, which is expandable in the future. The school also has a radio must with an antenna that receives the signal from primus antenna that is connected to a router, from where it goes to the proxy server and into the WLAN. The two key applications that run on the WLAN are:

The Schools Intranet

This comprises the school management software. It also provides a homepage for each student and faculty member. This home page includes a bulletin board, time table, syllabus, assignments, lessons, the teacher or students' personal database and a link to library resources. Pathways intends to archive all workshops and lectures for students to access over the wireless network..

WLAN in Education

The WLAN initiative has helped pathways create a learning-based education system, wherein Wi-Fi acts as a facilitator to leverage conventional methods of learning. Teacher act, as a guides by assigning projects to students. This gives students an opportunity to learn by exploring books, CD-ROMs and the Internet.

Since pathways gives importance to project-based learning the school decided to adopt a modal without fixed seating patterns within a classroom resulting in the need to move around within the classroom. Pathways also wanted to introduce the concept of "any time, anywhere" learning. Students can sit anywhere in the campus (in parks, theatres, the dining room or their own rooms) and do their projects, submit assignments, send e-mails to teachers, access library resources over the intranet, research papers and access the Internet. This model therefore necessitated an environment with wireless connectivity. Towards this end, the pathways management created very interesting spaces within the campus and does not restrict students to sitting in one particular place to enjoy the Wi-Fi learning experience.

At pathways, Wi-Fi connectivity enhances the effectiveness of the conventional education system. While retaining certain values of the older education system like the face-to-face interaction between students and the staff wi-fi allows students to have better interactivity, mobility and 24 hour access to relevant resource banks. Education can never be restricted just to the classroom, and certainly not in those limited house. Wi-Fi also helps pathway to spread access more evenly to its students instead of making them crowd around the Internet-ready computers within the class room. Implementing a cutting edge education system was not easy but with the extensive effort put into planning and research. Pathways has not faced significant bottlenecks todate. The wireless network has today enabled the school to deliver on its promise of any time-anywhere education.[22]

3.6.12. EDUSAT

On the fourth of September, 2004 the Indian Space Research Organization (ISRO) launched the world's first satellite dedicated to education the EDUSAT. This was a long awaited solution to improve connectivity across the nation for the spread of distance learning. Tele-education is an important step towards improving education standards. And with a dedicated satellite many remote learning initiatives have suddenly sprung up.

ISRO's EDUSAT has six Ku-band transponders, out of which five are dedicated to specific regions of India, and six C-band transponders cover the entire country. An antenna with a 1.2 m reflect or is being used to direct the Ku-band beans towards the targeted regions. With this foot print, educational programmes can now be broadcast to the farthest, least accessible areas of the country. Virtual class rooms will now feature content relevant to primary education, adult literacy programmes as well as training modules for teachers, the content can be broadcast in 18 Indian languages and viewed on any television set throughout the nation.

ISRO has agreed to provide technical and managerial support to manufacturers and service providers for the EDUSAT ground systems.

Engineering colleges all over the Karnataka that come under the Visweswaraiah Technological University (VTU) will be networked through EDUSAT in the first phase, forming the TECHNET system. Each institution will have to set-up a minimum of six DVB-VSAT facilities. The TECHNET system will provide access to the best education at an affordable rate for both students and teachers in every institution in the country. Depending on its success the scheme will be extended to cover other disciplines in basic science, agriculture, arts and commerce.

TABLE 3.2

State-wise Band Width Available at STPI Center as on 2001

States	*Existing STPI centers no.*	*Proposed STPI centres*	*Bandwidth available (KbPS)*	*% of the total*
T.N.	2	4	7168	5.31
Maharashtra	2	3	15872	11.77
Karnataka	2	2	37184	27.57
A.P.	2	3	28544	21.16
U.P.	1	1	34496	25.58
Gujarat	1	1	10816	8.02
Kerala	1	1	768	0.56
W.B.	—	1	—	—

Sources: 1. Loksabha Unstarred Question No. 4609, dated 19-12-2001.
2. www.indiastat.com.
R.G. Desai-IT at Regional Level..., Productivity, April-June 2003, pp. 55-62

Virtual Renovation

The Indian Institute of Management, Bangalore (IIMB) has announced a partnership with Hughes Escorts Communication Ltd., together, they will offer distance education programmes for executives. While IIMB will be the content provider, the hardware will be managed by HECL through its DIRECWAY satellite-based broadband network. The project is called DIRECWAY global education.

3.6.13. i-Shiksha

Wipro and Intel partnered to launch i-Shiksha a programme that helps teachers in rural and underprivileged government schools manage students in a classroom or lab. The i-shiksha medal uses computers that are preloaded with multimedia interactive learning software (MILS), a learning software that encourages interactivity to better the classroom environment. MILS has features such as screen broadcasting, video/audio broadcast and much more. It also rebroadcast inputs from external peripherals, such as digital microscopes, cameras, or audio tape recorders that are connected to the teachers PC.

3.6.14. e-NCORE

e-NCORE is software released by NIIT that is used to manage student administration in institutes. It manages communication across remote centers ensures student registrations and even manages transfers.

A touch screen could also help many uneducated child or adult access vital information. A touch screen interface is most user friendly, so overall training time for computer novices and therefore training expenses can be reduced. Touch screens can also be used in assertive technology and for student registration systems. Similar to kiosks placed in cities, screens are being provided at villages.

Word processing and e-mail improve a students' communication skills while database and spreadsheet programmes promote organizational skills, and modeling software enhances the understanding of science and math concepts. This opportunity to grasp, use and understand technology right from their childhood will give students the boost they need to stay ahead in this age of computers and networking.[23]

3.6.15. Electronics in Training and Development

Electronics can counter the lack of interest in learning by bringing excitement and experiences into the learning process—sights, sounds, games, experiments, simulation anything that can create interest for an individual can be designed into the learning experience. With the aid of electronic device one can learn at one's own pace in one's time. Computers have been found to be very effective in getting school dropouts to go back to studying and learn at their own pace.

Training packages can be designed that will allow for interaction with the computer as well as networking with knowledgeable persons in the field to answer queries, solve problems, give direction, provide motivation by narrating their own experiences and explain with examples and cases, pre-tests can be conducted to assess the students' level of knowledge and ability and bridge knowledge gaps with linkages to other sources of information if required. Learning will be in incremental steps and the learning experience will ensure that each step is mastered with multiple ways of explaining the concepts, theories, techniques, procedures, etc. if it is sensed that these are not being followed or understand.

But learning need not be restricted to structured knowledge, which has been accumulated, classified and validated. It can also be used to create and discover new knowledge, conduct tests, experiments, create scenarios, etc. Experiences can be provided of writing novels, producing movies, creating functional characters, redesigning the world or making predictions of what could happen with information now available, the possibilities are infinite. What is required is an understanding of the importance of education, training and development for the future of mankind, of how electronics can help in this process and having the will to make the investments in this field.[24]

There are four main fields where electronics is being applied and where the training of the users is required, these are: Automation, Computation, Networking, Teleworking. The brief description of these four are given as under:

1. Automation

The drudgery from repetitive manual work can be eliminated by automation. This requires skills in designing, fabricating, testing, installing and maintaining automated devices, while the advanced countries are even using robots to do routine assembly and hazardous jobs, unfortunately, the skill to automate even simple tasks is not well developed in India. Low cost automation, which would greatly improve productivity, has not taken off. Instead companies have gone in for high cost automation in most cases has resulted in a drop in total factor productivity when one considers both the productivity of labour as well as of the capital employed. If productivity is to be improved, engineering skills must be given more importance.

2. Computational

The computational power of the computer can be exploited in designing buildings, machinery structures, etc., using CAD/CAM and other software. This requires that the uses are trained to effectively use this software, be they architects, engineers or draughts men. Through automated process control, process can be improved, material and energy consumption reduced, quality of the product enhanced, safety and health ensured and a host of other benefits. Here training is required in the use of the equipment, in the interpretation of the results in the design and application of mathematical and statistical models to optimize the operations, in the maintenance of the equipment and the systems.

3. Networking

Networking gives the power of obtaining knowledge and information over a very wide range of subjects from a global information base a global encyclopedia. As of now there are 40 million websites from which information can be obtained. The Internet has also created a level playing field where the small business can compete with the large business. The cost of communications via the Internet are a fraction of what they are if one is to advertise on the TV new ways of doing business are being created like e-commerce, g-com, m-com with e-mail one can communicate daily with hundreds around the globe. To take full advantage of the power of networking one need to be only aware of the potential and have access to the facilities of a computer screen linked to the Internet applications are user-friendly and no formal training is required.

4. Teleworking

Teleworking or distance working is the term used when one does work without going to an office. It is work down on the road, from home or from work site. Electronic facilitates working, reporting and control by e-mail, wireless and mobile phones. Journalists and salesman's can send in their reports and keep in touch with headquarters, housewives can do software accounts and office works from their homes, doctors in USA can send their reports on interviews with patients and meet the statutory requirements of having these transcribed by some one sitting in India.

Electronics as a technology has advanced to such a level that it can drive other disciplines. In education text books and teachers can be replaced with the interactive electronic systems through which one can learn at one's own pace and in one's own time. In medicine electronic equipment conduct tests and diagnosis which were not possible earlier like scans and EMI. It is note that existing procedures were automated but completely new procedures were invented which have become subjects of study in the media profession.

In entertainment scenes and experiences can be created which were an imaginable earlier. In manufacturing new techniques have emerged which have brought about radical changes in the ways of doing things like electrostatic deposition of materials, microwave for heating CNC machines for metal removal.

In building construction intelligent building are being constructed which can sense earth quiches the movements of individual within the building temperature and lighting changes adoption required to personal likes and tastes, etc. Electronics have revolutionized office work making the traditional concept of the office obsolete introducing time shifts making flexible working a reality, creating teleworking, new ways of buying and selling of shares, products and services, keeping and retrieval of records and million other innovations.[25]

3.6.16. Teleconferencing as Training Medium

Basically teleconferencing is the interactive exchange of information between individuals or groups in two or more locations through an electronic medium. It can bring people who are geographically isolated together to express their view points and share their experiences. In the 1960's the American Telephone and Telegraph company first introduced the teleconferencing system "Picture Phone" in USA. It has been a common mode of communication in the USA and European countries for many years. The following three basic types commonly available for use:

1. *Audio Conferencing*: Verbal communication through a telephone with additional capacity for telewriting or telecopying.
2. *Video Conferencing*: Exchange of video information and pictures between individuals or groups through specialized equipments.
3. *Computer Conferencing*: Computer-based meeting involving exchange of voice and pictures between two individuals or groups using special software in a networked environment e.g. bulletin boards, e-groups, discussion forums, mailing lists, real time chat and e-mail.

The advanced teleconferencing technologies offer integration of text, graphics, audio and video that can be transmitted over distance at a faster rate. Using a judicious mix of information, teleconferencing is capable of evolving a unique instructional strategy for each educational task. As a training medium at offers interactive experiences in real time as in a face-to-face conversation. The trainer can provide instructions, ask questions, seek responses and provide feedback on the responses. Besides this the training can be delivered individually to a large group of people. This flexibility helps the trainers to deliver a uniform training to the learners who are geographically isolated and have different learning styles. Hence, it is important for a user to choose the configuration according to their needs and conditions. Teleconferencing is a common medium for extension training programs in developed countries. Some of the experiences juried in application of teleconferencing in USA and Ireland are described below:

USA

The Missouri Cooperatives Extension Service successfully used audio conferencing to conduct meetings with its staff for information exchange, periodical assessment and training. Moreover, it is created a statewide network of communication through the educational teleconferencing system to facilitate administration of the extension agents. The Clemson University imparted 3-week Internet training on Soil Acidity and liming to 150-country extension Agents of 6 states. The training was organized through Internet discussions (5 hours/day through Bulletin Boards/List Servers) on-line survey revealed that the internet-based multimedia could be effective in teaching theoretical and applied aspect on soil management. A majority of respondents (55%) opined that the Internet-based multimedia training was as effective as face-to-face training. They also accepted the style of learning providing by the training.

Ireland

The Tesgac Agricultural and Food Development Authority used video conferencing for training the extension agents and farmers on grassland management soil testing analysis and use of computers in farm management.[26]

3.6.17. Information Technology Empowers Farmers

Information Technology can be used to deliver real time information and custom aside knowledge to improve farmers' decision-making abilities. Such knowledge would help them respond with speed to market demand, enhance quality and productivity and recover a fair price. IT can also enable setting up a direct marketing channel that is virtually connected to the Mandy system. This would help in obtaining knowledge of current price, cutting out the role of the middleman, and hence lowering transactions costs. In this scenario, the farmer rather than the middleman or trader would get the benefit of improved price realization have to some extent addressed the needs of the Indian Agricultural sector. The following I.T. programmes are very useful to formers and villagers:

(a) e-Procurement

The National Dairy Development Board (NDDB) launched the milk cooperative movement which led to an appreciable increase in milk production in India. The Dairy sector uses thousands of computers in rural locations to buy milk from the farmers efficiently and transparently. Each farmer is given a smart card.

Once the card is swiped it is electronically read and farmers identification number is transmitted to a PC. The milk is to be sold is then collected in a container kept over a weighbridge. The weight of the milk is simultaneously displayed to the farmer and communicated to a PC. An electronic fat testing machine displays the fat content of that milk sample to the farmers and records the same on the PC. The computer calculates the amount to be paid to the farmer according to a rate chart that lists the price for milk with different levels of fat content. The total value of the milk is then printed out on a payment slip and given to the farmer who can relieve his payment at a nearby counter. In most cases, the whole transaction takes less than half a minute. Millions of farmers have benefited from this application of IT.

(b) Gyandoot

The Gyandoot project pertains to community owned-rural Internet kiosks that enable farmers to access information with little investment. It was initiated in the Dhar district in Madya Pradesh, where nearly two-third of the population lived below the poverty line in the year 2000. The Internet kiosks offer services like:

- Informing farmers about the current rates of major crops at the local and other recognized auction centres around in India.
- Making copies of land records available. Online registration and

down loading of application forms for obtaining income/caste/domicile certificates.

- Online filing of public grievances. Auction facilities for farmers and villagers for land, agricultural machinery, equipment and other durable commodities.
- Other functions include online matrimonial advertisements, information regarding government programs, a forum for school children to ask questions and e-mail.

(c) Client-centered Networking Project in Rural India

The M.S. Swaminaathan Research Foundation (MSSRF) info village project connects 10 villages through a wired-*cum*-wireless network consisting of PCs Very High Frequency (VHF) duplex radio devices and related equipment to facilitate both voice and data transfer. The project creates content relevant for villagers, to access and use to make improvements in their living conditions. It was established with a commitment to harnessing science and technology for environmentally sustainable, social development. Since agriculture is the major industry in the villages, the focus was on the farmer. It was discovered that the most important information source for farmers was other farmers. Based on this in sight, information shops were set-up in a few villages.

The information shops main function is to collect and distribute information. It involves local volunteers who gather information organize it into a database, convert into the local language and upload on to the internet to be viewed and down loaded via the various wireless nodes across the villages.

(d) Remote Sensing

Agricultural management has greatly-benefited from remote sensing. However its usage is dependant on the availability of images with fine spatial resolution and accurate real-time data, with the vast progress in IT, today there are companies that provide images taken from aircraft. These meet the resolution and temporal requirements for accurate agricultural management. High-resolution satellite imagery also is an additional source of remote-sensed and accurate data. Advances in precision farming technology such as Geographic Information System (GIS), Global Positioning Systems, and variable rate equipment provide the tools needed to solve management problems using multi-spectral images. Some of the ways in which remote sensing serves the demand for information in precision agriculture are, i.e. Soil properties analysis, Pest Detection and Water Stress.

(e) ITCs e-Choupal

ITC's e-choupal initiative is the single-largest information technology-based project by a corporate entity in rural India. It transforms the Indian farmer into a progressive, knowledge-seeking citizen, which increases the value of his produce in the global market. ITCs e-choupal movement commenced in the year 2000 and covers 21,000 villages across six states, has 4100 installations and 2-4 million empowered e-farmers. A farmer is selected from a village based on his standing within the local farming community and his ability and willingness to get net savvy. This individual facilitates the physical interface between the computer terminal and the farmers. e-choupal delivers real-time information and customized knowledge to improve the farmers' decision-making ability, thereby better aligning farm output to market demands, improving the quality of the produce, improving productivity and also enhancing the ability to judge prices. The model helps in facilitating access to higher quality farm inputs at lower costs for the farmer. Most crucially, e-choupal initiative has cut farmers loose from the clutches of middleman.

The project uses a Mithi connect server as the e-mail engine of choice. The Mithi connect server is an out-of-the-box, e-mail server and messaging solution built on the open source components platform. It supports standard e-mail clients like outlook, Eudora, etc. and also offers Mithi web mail, a web client and collaboration application.

(f) The Simputer

The Simputer (Simple Inexpensive Multilingual Computer) is a cheap pocket sized computing device for rural India. The prototype was first announced two years ago by research at the Indian Institute of Science in Bangalore. The simputer has been used in pilot projects in the states of Karnataka and Chhattisgarh with good results.

The simputer is a hand held computing device with a touch sensitive screen that can execute several basic PC functions. It can work in several Indian languages and a single device can be easily shared by a number of users in the small village. However, it is different from a palm pilot. Along with the usual functions like e-mail, audio files and Internet access, future plans are in place for the simputer to provide text to speech systems in several Indian languages which would be a blessing for the 35 percent of Indians who can not read. Other applications such as telemedicine, services, micro-banking, information access for farmers and distance education for remote schools, are being developed to meet rural needs.

The simputer uses the open source, Linux operating system, promoting a growing movement that seeks to treat knowledge as the property of the public, rather than the monopoly of multinationals. Hence, users do not need to pay large sums for software. Efforts are on to encourage software developers to add their own improvements to its design. Even the simputer's hardware specifications and design are available on the Internet and can be down loaded for manufacturing under the SGPL licence.[27]

(g) Video in Farmers' Training

The emphasis on farmers' training continued with the launching of new agricultural strategies during 1960s, beginning with the Intensive

Agricultural District Programme (IADP), Farmers' Training Centers (FTCs) Block Level Training Programs and later farmers' training by the State Agricultural Universities (SAUs), were involved in disseminating messages on new agricultural technologies. A new turn was given to farmers' training with the launching of Krishi Vignan Kendras (KVKs) with emphasis on need based skill training. Today, there exists a network of FTCs, KVKs outreach stations of SAUs and National Agricultural Research Project (NARP) centers, non-governmental organizations and private input agencies involved in farmers' training it has been realized that the existing farmers' training infrastructures inadequate. This situation calls for more qualitative changes in transferring improved farming skills and also learning of new skills, new communication technologies can play an important role in imparting need-based skill-oriented training of farmers.

Video with its unique features of simultaneous recording and play back system is quite suitable for skill-based training. This has also found support in the world bank's efforts in strengthening Training and Visit (T&V) system in India. Extension personnel were trained in video production skills and also oriented in the methodology of producing need-based programmes. Despite the provision of sufficient funds for purchase of equipment and training of staff in video production, it has not been possible for various state departments of agriculture, to make systematic use in farmers'

TABLE 3.3

Region-wise Exports of Software and Hardware in India (2001-02)

($ million)

Region	Software	% to total	Hardware	% to total
South Region	4087	48.15	379	31.16
Karnataka	2201	25.90	—	—
T.N.	1231	14.50	—	—
A.P.	613	07.20	—	—
Kerala	42	00.28	—	—
North Region	2316	27.28	334	27.46
U.P.	943	11.10	—	—
Delhi	839	09.88	—	—
Haryana	157	01.84	—	—
Other states	377	04.44	—	—
Western Region	1869	22.01	488	40.13
Eastern Region	216	02.55	15	01.25
All India	8488	100	1216	100

Source : UNI data Published in *Deccan Herald,* dated 1-1-2003.
R.G. Desai, IT at Regional Level, *Productivity*, April-June 2003, pp. 55-62.

training. Thus farmers' training continued to suffer due to weak subject matter support, methods of training, academic approaches and absence of facilities for practical training and stress on quantity rather than quality. This situation signals the need to improve upon various dimensions of farmers' training including human input. Human input needs to be improved in terms of change in knowledge, attitude and skill.

Video is seen as a potential medium for human resource development. Video enhances training by visualizing verbal messages with motion, color and standardized information. Video adds another dimension of training sessions, by providing farmers with a visual picture of new techniques. Farmers' training using video has been tried in several countries. The brief description of this methodology is given as under:

Video-Based Training Methodology

The proposed methodology suggests modular approach to video-based farmers' training. Modular approach means breaking down of basic training program into specific components. Each unit is described in terms of its objectives and instructional materials are designed to match this sequence. A training module on a given subject is comprised of a unit split into smaller teachable units of shorter duration. There are certain design considerations to be kept in mind, while producing video-based training modules.

1. *Decide rationale*: The justification for producing the module should be decided first. The designer should have in mind an overview of the contents of the module and explanation of why adult learner should study it.
2. *Finalize objectives*: Objectives should be clearly defined in terms of what the learner is expected to gain from studying the module. This needs to be studied in performance terms.
3. *Determine entry point*: Determine existing level of adult learner in terms of previous knowledge and skills.
4. *Select appropriate formats*: The format selected should be able to generate interest among the learners and utilize maximum number of senses.
5. *Ensure learners active involvement*: Designer should allow for maximum involvement of the learner while designing video-based training models.
6. *Self-test*: A mechanism should be worked out to review and check if the designer is moving on the right direction in terms of producing need-based material for the learner.
7. *Post-test*: This is an examination to test whether the objectives module have been met.[28]

3.6.18 Bridging the Digital Divided Through Internet

The Kiosk was constructed in such a way that the monitor was visible through a glass plate built into the wall. A touch pad was also built into it. The PC driving the monitor was on the other side of the wall, in a brick enclosure. The PC used was a Pentium 266 MH_Z system with 64 MB of RAM, a hard disk, a true colour display and an Ethernet card. The kiosk had access to the Internet through a dedicated 2 Mbps connection to a service provider. The activity of the PC users was monitored by a remote computer and video camera mounted on a nearby tree. Key observations are:

- The regular users were very young children (age 6 to 12 year) who lived in the slum right next to the kiosk. The majority were at elementary school level. They all went to either government-run school or welfare school located nearby.
- Browsing the web was fun. The Disney website was a hit. Some of them were able to read the news, horoscopes and short stories. The Hindi news sites were very popular as were some Bollywood sites.
- Point was popular almost everyone used it draw pictures or write their names. Seeing their name on the computer screen was a big attraction.
- The children develop their own terms to describe the objects and events that they encountered while working at the kiosks. While the applications and websites were referred to by their names, the arrow cursor was called sui (needle in Hindi) the cross hair was called a kaanta, daabna for clicking (the Hindi equivalent of pressing *sabse rangeena button for the start button on the task bar, damroo* for the hourglass icon, *kaam kar raha hai* when the hourglass rotated, and *machcharki dawai* (insecticide spray) for the spray tool in paint.
- The kids also became familiar with some English words because of association.
- The children became very exited to see that the PC could work like a radio or TV. After a week the children discovered a free MP3 player from the Internet all by themselves and played their favorite songs.
- The kids did not know how to pronounce 'File' but they knew that within it are the options of saving/opening files.

The result of the experiment were very surprising showing new ways of bridging the digital divide. It revealed that it is important to realize that computer terminology is not crucial as compared to functional knowledge. In most computer classes students are taught terminology, but this seemed irrelevant to these children. They got a good idea of how to use the Internet all by themselves. This also shows how, given the opportunity to slum kids who often do not have teachers can use the Internet to do their homework and prepare notes.

This also helped remove a number of misconceptions. Critics say that since the Internet is in English this is a hurdle, which limits its popularity. But these children showed that even though they did not know the dictionary meanings of English words, they did have an operational understanding of them.

This opens up a new path to making India computer literate. If we are able to set-up some 100,000 such kiosks in India, we will be able to make 500 million children computer literate. This would cost approximately Rs. 100 billion. But if we had to pay to educate the same children using traditional methods it would cost twice as much. Minimally invasive education through public Internet kiosks for children should form an integral part of primary education in the 21st century.

3.6.19 Information Technology for Learners

Learning is understanding of concepts as against memorization alone for examinations. It is problem-solving learning requires active involvement of the learner in the learning process as against passively observing the information. Elements of learning cover reading, thinking, analysis deducing, mediating, writing work, discussion, etc. Learning requires discovery of relevant information through navigational techniques out of various sources-print and non-print material. Now, IT and multimedia have changed and pattern of learning where the teachers use technology through critical thinking to manipulate a quarry data in newer ways, instead of just attending lectures are reading activity. In this IT era we have moved from the old practice of memorizing facts to discovering data and information and synthesizing them for problem-solving. Hypertext and Hypermedia assist in linking the sources of learning if proper navigation is done. It has enabled the learner to encounter a large volume of data from which to sort out the relevant information.[29]

3.6.20 Information Technology for Researchers

In modern day research parlance the definition of information has broadened covering non-print material. Technology makes research more convenient and efficient. IT connects and helps synthesizing disparate bits of the information. For research it is essential to use information in print as well as electronic information. IT has made them both available, crossing the boundaries of specific libraries. For conduct in research, a research has to cover or touch various inter-related disciplines. This calls for collection and analysis of a large quantity of data, which at times can be quite unmanageable given the vastness of the information repository of the World Wide Web (WWW) of the internet. Modern day research thus requires a fitting of information electronically. To assist the researcher in this, the Internet is equipped with various navigational tools, software's and search engines. Research contributes towards enriching the entire body of knowledge and as such we should promote objective research and employ whatever technological and that available at hand.[30]

3.6.21 Infrastructure Management

Every device needs to be serviced and maintained, and big organizations some times find themselves unable to keep track of infrastructure-related issues. This is when firms come in and save the day with their package of solutions, consulting technical support and other offers.

All access devices, such as laptops, workstations, desktops, handled, printers, scanners, MFDs and even mobiles, should be clubbed under a single umbrella in an office and treated in the same life cycle. Planning for installation, MultiFinder support and even movement of such equipment is necessary and most times external help is taken. Life cycle stages such as trade in technology-refresh and asset recovery are taken care of if a customer chooses infrastructure management from a third party. For worldwide consistency is financing terms and conditions, pricing and employment of a service called Global Edge is being offered by Hewlett-Packard. This also provides a single global methodology for lease pricing, no matter where the lease originated from. The following components are coming under infrastructure management, these are as follows:

(a) *Networking and Monitoring*

From installation and commissioning to operating and trouble shooting network elements, PBXs, CTI/IVR set-up, servers and optical fiber networks, there are many factors that you need to take care of so that the company runs without any interruptions. Before you expand change the networking to suit your growing business the company to send officials to understand your current and future networking needs, and to formulate a network strategy with a suitable solution design.

(b) *Image and Document Management*

Imaging and printing can get really costly for any organization pay per use is a good service that makes managing peripherals much less complex while another company takes care of your entire physical installation, networking, maintenance, and technical support, employees will no longer have a reason to run aggressive if paper gets stuck.

Whether you are seeking an enterprise-wide approach that offers value for your entire organization or addressing a single aspect of your printing requirements, work place solutions are the answer. Organizing documents is result in effective access by work teams, and document-driven process like review, approval, assembly, publishing and archiving can be automated using software manager/Document manager. It manages documents efficiently throughout their life cycle, with features like version control, collaborative document creation, document inducing, access, rendering, retention and archiving. Thus it builds the foundation for the entire content management process.

(c) Security with Asset Tagging

Companies that wish to protect their systems and components can demand a service called "asset tagging" under this each PC will be assigned an electronic or physical asset tag with a unique number with asset tags customers will not run out of labels, and can avoid the hassle, time and expense associated with tagging systems once they are removed from the box with this service in place reporting on request and permanent identification is possible. CXOs can have better control over their inventory, and by standardizing the service can track down every resource.

(d) Customisation Services

Production orientation and training can be quite exhaustive even for a good team. What is needed bottom to top approach that will ensure that each employee is confident about every IT related issue and can work on the software without hiccups. For the work place to function like a well-oiled machine with all the gears moving without a break, employees need to know their function and if they will feel the problem is beyond their capabilities, they need to know whom to contact. Most times people give up because of a lack of responses from the IT department—very often, the limit to what they can handle is quite evident. This is when the choice of outsourcing infrastructure management seems to be the answer. With a helpdesk for any problem faced by employees, the company IT team can look at other issues and even turn their talents towards optimizing and customizing.

(e) Project Management

With the popularity of the Internet and mobile devices, accessibility and connectivity have become common to most employees has now expanded from just the office to the home, roads, malls and any other building that was, up to the last century, considered unreachable for work. Even your identity and career are related closely to the amount of data you deal with, and consequently what connectivity you choose, which solutions and technology you use and what kind of devices you keep close to you. In such scenario CXOs worldwide are facing the same a question of how to manage all the technology and train people effectively. The number of skilled employees that a company needs is directly related to its productivity and hence training and certification are essential. Educating and certifying innumerable employees in a particular domain is generally the burden of the IT department. Instead with special courses and definite timings allotted by a third party management becomes trouble free. Incident management has to be combined with effective project management to ensure an always-on infrastructure.[31]

3.6.22 Business Through Satellite

While five years ago the talk was about the future effects of technologies such as broadband, end-to-end connectivity and new developments in the video area, today there is traction in the satellite industry. Satellite operators are taking advantage of existing space and terrestrial capacity, and new technology to make available flexible solutions that increase network access for customers without requiring significant capital expenditures. Business through satellite elements are given under:

(a) Broadband as Driver

The driver with the most overall potential appears to be broadband, with its "always on" Internet access and multimedia content transport capabilities. High speed ISP customers account for about 13 percent of all residential subscriptions in the USA, up from five percent in the year 2000, according to JD power and associates. Some analysis are projecting that it will replace the dial-up modern as the standard means of Internet connection within the next five to ten years.

(b) Media and Entertainment as Driver

The current phase of communications via satellite involves the media and entertainment sector. This market has changed significantly over the years. Customers now demand integrated, end-to-end solutions that are delivered immediately and reliably and that are cost-efficient.

DTH (Direct To Home) is industry also experiencing an expansion of regional or niche (multi cultural) programming for additionally use of the Television is also considered to be an industry driver, with significant increases in demand causing the need for new, more flexible and tailor-made-applications.

(c) One-Stop Shopping

Perhaps the primary satellite communications driver today is the hybrid, space/terrestrial, end-to-and delivery system. This system provides customers with a variety of options for giving end users in both developed and developing countries a complete, global communications experiences at competitive prices. There is little future in strictly selling raw capacity. The future of this industry is in the integrated network of satellites, points-of-presence (POP) and earth stations situated in strategic locations allowing satellite operators to move further into the value chain and giving customers opportunities for one-stop shopping.

Satellite service is no longer a repeat business. It is now a repeat and deliver business with improved point-to-multipoint applications, more competitive price points, increased quality of service and programmes offering solutions of choice across a much wider range of communications requirements. It is the transport to assure delivery of bundled applications over flexible platforms that can talk to one another.[32]

3.6.23 Enterprise Mobility

Enterprise mobility is mobile computing and wireless communication systems accompanied with critical input/output technologies, which support real time distributed transaction processing throughout an enterprise-be it a retail store, a manufacturing plant, a distribution facility, a hospital or a public sector installation. The transaction processed could be the purchased of an item, the calibration of a machine tool, the sorting of urgent packages a submission of a prescription. Wireless technology, e-mail, capability and remote meetings are all becoming more important than ever. This transition from a desk top-based work force to note-book based work force can enhance an employees ability to balance her professional and personal life, and so increase productivity. Enterprise mobility is based on several steps, these are:

1. *Awareness Workshop (Envisioning)*: It deals with providing the management with information about the opportunities and benefits of existing mobile technologies and potential business values. While implementing solutions, the scope of end-to-end capabilities is taken into consideration along with the real time experience of the organization.
2. *Strategy and implementation roadmap (Planning)*: The strategy involves trying the mobility with business objectivity. It also identifies the key business processes that will benefit by mobilization. The return on investment are quantified for process investments. Organizational impact and support requirements are assessed. Thus, an enterprise chalked out for the business, which includes benefits realization and calculation of ROIs.
3. *Enterprise Mobility Design (Designing)*: This phase of the life cycle determines business and technical requirements. There is an emphasis on business process reengineering and change management. Business process improvements are finalized keeping in mind existing mobile devices, technologies and service delivery architecture middleware.
4. *Enterprise mobility implementation (Building)*: This phase deals with delivering resources, including architecture and system integration. The implementation may include thin or thick applications based on NET, JAVA, and the like.
5. *Enterprise mobility managed services (Maintaining)*: The maintenance phase includes helpdesk services, device management and configuration, training programmes and the support of post-development operations for both end user adoption and total cost of ownership.

3.6.24 Mobile Phones

Members of sales and marketing teams are the bread-earners of every organization. They are also the eyes and ears for most firms. Though mobile phones are common with those in the profession the models being used of then do not support key features that can be helpful in their work. Generally associated with personal entertainment an inbuilt camera can be very useful for those in the field. The camera allows them to trap information in the form of a visual which is very hard to explain other wise. A key benefit is best expressed by on often repeated Television advertisement of a leading mobile-phone vendor. Yes, we are taking about the ability to speak without having to bend on his neck. Typically, people tend to bend while talking over a mobile phone, and the situation is worse for marketing people as they are generally noting down something or the other. Hence, the bond of the neck needs to be even more acute to balance the phone. Ouch. A mobile phone that can rid your staff of the proverbial pain in the neck can prove to be very helpful.

But here is more to it than just health discussions, feedback inputs from multiple sources are a common phenomenon for marketing staff. A speaker phone allows them to capture the opinions of all those seated with them at the same time. Already many negotiations is being conducted using this feature-the entire decision making chain can communicate at a go with the client and bag the deal.

3.6.25 E-mail Access

Many orders can be saved if your team can access their crucial emails that generally bunch up as deadlines start looming large. While on the move to close one deal, three are lost because those clients had sought last minute clarifications through e-mail which marketing head was unable to access. A mobile with the email facility will route all e-mails to the mobiles of the marketing team members while they are on the move. They can also reply to those emails, if needed, or just give a call and close that deal.

Contacts are important resources for marketing team and keeping in touch with these contacts is the key to the teams survival. Hence it is a good idea to ensure that the mobile phones being chosen for them can store a minimum of 500 contacts. Of course, the rule of the thumb is the more the merrier.[33]

3.6.26 Information Technology Promotes Advertising

The advertising world is filled by human creativity. It is an environment where people go without sleep and bang their fists until the perfect idea pops up in their heads. Client servicing is the first step of the business operations at publics. A brief from the client is received explaining what they wish to communicate to their customer. These inputs are then passed on to the concerned departments using Job tracking software. For facilitating the task of ad design, designers use applications such as Free hand, Corel Draw, and Illustrator. Adobe photoshop is often used for image cleanup and manipulation. Creative pursuits fulfilled, the next task is to decide on the medium newspaper, TV channel, Radio show, etc. A media planning exercise helps to determine the best medium to use. Media planners have to work with a lot of data to make a decision. The data such as, viewer ratings, circulation and readership figures, ad rates, etc-is generally compiled from media-data-collection agencies. These agencies have developed software tools, like choices 3, Media Express, MAP, IRS, etc. for recording data and producing reports based on parameters specified by the planner. Planning comes the tracking of company operations. These, IT assists in the analytical process of media planning. Post-media-planning comes the tracking of company operations.

These operations entail creating estimates, releasing orders, handling bills, etc. The data generated here is managed through and industry standard software called Media Ware. With reams of financial and creative data created everyday, storage is major issue. For public keeping their operations connected across there locations is very important for business. Publicist has a reason to invest in leased lines rather than the cheaper DSL (Digital Subscriber Line) DSL is in consistent and downtimes are higher. DSL is also difficult to monitor it is a trade-off between higher quality of Internet connectivity and lower price. The company implementing web and video conferencing to enhance employee productivity. IT has enabled the agency to automate nearly all its processes. This has in turn, increased profitability, improved efficiency, and reduced over heads.[34]

3.6.27 Internet—the new Marketing Medium

Firms use various media to communicate with their current and potential customers. Marketing communications perform three functions-to inform, to remind and to persuade. The traditional one-to-many marketing communications model has corporations provide contend through a medium, to a mass market of consumers. The first two functions of marketing communications are performed by a traditional communication model. However, the persuasion function necessary to differentiate one brand from another is limited by the unidirectional nature of traditional mass media.

The Internet offers an alternative to mass media communication. From a business and marketing perspective, the most existing developments are accruing on the subset of the Internet, known as the World Wide Web. As a marketing and advertising medium the web can revolutionize the way firms do business by enabling the convergence of publishing, real-time communication broadcast and narrowcast.

Websites are available on demand to consumer 24 hours a day. A firm can gain a number of benefits from the use of the web as a distribution channel. First the web offers marketers to opportunity to participate in a market where distribution costs become negligible. Second, business transaction on the web transfer a lot of sales teams functions to the customer, though on line ordering and the use of fill-out forms. This not only helps to bring transactions to a conclusion but also a permit a third benefit by enabling the capture of customer information. The technology helps together market intelligence on the customers preferences for the navigational and purchasing options on the web.

Corporate Weblogs: A Weblog (blog) is one of the most significant on line trends. There are hundreds of thousands of there online journals most of them maintained by individuals. They could be linked to an online personal diary in that many contain a regular series of posting from individuals about a particular topic life in general or day to day events that impact them. A weblog might contain short notes with links to other sites that contain relevant news or information often with a bit of commentary. But increasingly weblog are becoming the new customer relationship tools for companies. Macromedia, the developer of Flash, shock wave. Dream waver and other digital creative tools has several weblogs pertaining to its products. Besides the corporate sponsored company weblog, customers are also using weblogs to report on a company products.

Online Advertising: online advertisements have a totally a different approach as compared to running a print advertisement. They combine straight advertising, product placement and direct response. All the major MNCs of the world advertise online e-be it Microsoft.

Webinars: A webinar is a multimedia presentation that allows participants to hear the instructor through a telephone conference call while following the presentation element via webpage. The web element also offers the added ability to ask questions via a messaging tool and allows instant polls on topics discussed in the webinar. Webinars allow delegates from any where in the world to be together at the same time with the instructor.

Webportals: A Webportal is a website that provides a starting point or a gateway to other resources on the internet or intranet. Portals are also known as enterprise information portals. Portals provide personalized capabilities to their users. They are disgned to use distributed applications, as well as different types of middle ware and hardware to provide services from a number of different sources. Business portals are designed to allow collaboration in work places. A further business driven requirement of portals is that the content is accessible on multiple platforms such as personal computers, personal digital assistants or cell phones.[34]

3.6.28 Information Technology in Medical

The internal environment, the most important part is the care of the patient in the hospital. Information Technology makes all the inputs or information required for patient care available at the point of care. This means, when doctors are examining patients, they can get not only their blood tests, but also their X-rays, MRIs, CT scans, etc., all together is one file all the information that goes into decision making is present at one point. This adds greatly to the ability of the physician to give precise treatment. Previously, a physician had to run around the hospital to access reports of various tests; this was tiring and distracting for him. Information Technology has made simpler by putting all the files together electronically to form EPRs (Electronic Patient Records).

Information Technology has made patient records available on the net for the referring doctor to review them any time, any where. This adds a huge strength in favor of the patient by way of the ability of the physicians-local physicians, referring physician, treating physician-to be able to access all the information at one point on the net.

About robotic or remote surgery, this is called "da Vinci", but we refer to it as "da Vinci" for "Robotically Assisted Endoscopic Surgery". In this the surgery sits on a console to which is attached a robotic arm. The surgeon operates on the console and the command is executed inside the body by the robotic arm. This is not science fiction-it is happening here every day. We have had it here since December 2002. This technology increases the multiplier effect immediately for a surgeon. You could have robots in ten locations and you could operate similarly, sitting in one place.

Another expertise-multiplier effect is achieved through video conferencing. Doctor sit here and look at angiograms or operating rooms-surgeons operating-across cities. Doctor can give them advice, on a better technique of operation. We are connected to all our satellite centres. We do live consultations.

We are now teaching connected to them through satellite you have here facilities of holding live conferences; live surgeries can be transmitted for teaching purpose. These are all incremental benefits of Information Technology.[35]

3.6.29 Telemedicine

Telemedicine attempts to virtually transport the specialist doctor to a remote patient. Normally doctors rely on all their five senses when treating a patient. In the case of a patient at a remote location, the specialist doctor cannot use his sense of touch. The MBBS doctor present at the telemedicine centre in a remote village will examine the patient, according to the instruction of the specialist and provide feedback related to symptoms. The specialist, in any case, has the patient entire case study before him. Through video conferencing, specialists can see, talk and examine the patient virtually, and all this helps them in a making a correct diagnosis. Telemedicine is video conferencing solutions, polycoms reputation for good sales services, which is critical, especially in remote areas, was the deciding factor.

About four years ago doctors were apprehensive about this new technology. Practicing doctors hardly have the time to experiment and the IT professionals in those days also found it difficult to understand what the doctors wanted. Telemedicine equipment varies—it could be a small desktop or a large screen. There are several packages that polycom offers and banks offer loans to doctors who want to set-up these facilities. The costs of installation are recovered in a very short time. The local doctors thrive as more and more patients come to them, and the patients benefit from the treatment prescribed by an otherwise unavailable specialist.

Telemedicine can help in combating tropical diseases, more so in a country like India with poor public health facilities and geographically isolated rural populations. For countries with limited medical expertise and resource, telecommunications has the potential to provide a solution to some of these problems. Telemedicine services have the potential to improve both the quality of and access to healthcare, regardless of geography.[36]

While often there is a concentration of medical specialists in the major cities, the suburban and rural areas can also be provided with medical diagnosis using IT. Through telemedicine patients can be examined investigated, monitored and treated, even when the patient and doctor are separated by a considerable distance. Tele is a Greek word means "distance". In telemedicine what travels is the expertise not the patient. A key objective of telemedicine is to do away with the unnecessary travelling of patients and their attendants. A PC, a scanner, a digital camera, suitable software and telecommunications can enable transfer of clinical data from any one part of the globe to the other. Image acquisition, image storage, image display and processing and image transfer are the basis of the telemedicine.

In the past telemedicine primarily implied tele-radiology, i.e., the transfer of high resolution medical images, X-ray pictures, ultra sound, CT and MRI pictures, live transmission of ECGs and echocardiograms. Today even a comprehensive clinical examination can be carried out remotely.

Currently, this practice of telemedicine is a common feature in many parts of the word. It has become an integral part of health care services in several countries including the UK, USA, Japan, Greece and even India, apart from others. Many studies have indicated telemedicine to be practical, safe and cost effective. In a major telemedicine project in the US it found that more than so percent of patients who would otherwise have been sent to an urban hospital, managed to remain in their community bring down their total medical bill by at least 40 to 50 percent.

Telemedicine in India: the distribution of medical specialists in India is highly irregular. For example, there are more neurologists and neurosurgeons in Chennai, than in all the states of North-Eastern India put together. More over tertiary care hospitals are concentrated in big cities, leaving huge chunk of population without access to them. The increasing availability of excellent telecommunication infrastructure and video conferencing equipments will help provide a physicians expertise where there was none before. While the medical facilities scenario is not very encouraging, computer literacy is fast developing. The prices of IT hardware and software are dropping and new medical software is being developed in India. Further, Internet and telephone penetration are rapidly increasing across the country.

Health care service providers are now looking at telemedicine as the new way of making specialists medical expertise available across the country. Theoretically it is simpler to set-up telecommunication infrastructure in sub-urban and rural India than to implant the hundreds of medical specialists required in this places. Satellite based technology is being developed and fiber optic cables are being laid. Doctors in India are licensed to practice all over the country and telemedicine could serve as a major motivational factor for computer literacy among doctors. Telemedicine can also ensure optimal utilization of sub-urban hospitals. The general practitioner in the rural areas will loss less patients to the city consultant, as specialist medical advise will be available via telemedicine.

India could be developed into a hub for offering global telemedicine services at reduced international rates. The country is already a center for suburban and rural India is heavily subsidized from agencies like WHO, the World Bank, Asian Development Bank, Government of India, etc. However a lot more needs to be done. Pilot studies need to be carried out to assess acceptance among patients, general practitioners, hardware, software and telecom service providers and the state Governments. Medical disciplines that lend themselves to treatment using telemedicine need to be identified. Relevant cost-effective and need based modules need to be developed and technical and medical personnel need to be trained. Medical coordinators for each specialty need to lay down ground rules. While technical coordinators are required to identify the most effective mode of data acquisition, compression, transfer and manipulation at the tele-doctors PC.

Apollo hospitals have led the way in terms of setting up the first modern secondary care rural hospital in India, using telemedicine. As a pilot project a secondary level hospital was set-up in a village with a population of about 5000, near Chennai. This village hospital had web cams ISDN telephone lines, a state-of-the-art video conferencing system and a VSAT (Very Small Aperture Terminal) satellite installed by ISRO (Indian Space Research Organisation).

About 200 tele-consultations, carried out by specialist and super specialists, were assigned to this village. Specially designed software called Mediscope was used. Images of X-rays and ultrasound were scanned, compressed and sent via ISDN lines. CT images, being DICOM compatible, were electronically transferred to the telemedicine computer for onward transmission to Chennai. Most of the tele consultations were initially offline and worked on a store-forward basis. After interacting directly with the primary physician via a "net meeting", the tele consultants opinion was then sent back to the primary physician. Later with the availability of better infrastructure, interaction between the rural physician and the tele consultant was enabled using state-of-the-art video conferencing equipment. All such online interactions were recorded and stored.[37]

3.6.30 Video Conferencing Technology

This technology involving two-way interactive television comes into play when a face-to-face consultation is required. Today it is the second most widely used technology (after store and forward which is used for transferring digital images from one location to another). It involves the patients, along with their health care provider (a doctor or a nursing practitioner) and a telemedicine coordinator (or a combination of three) at the rural site, interacting with the tele-consultant at a metropolitan centre. Video conferencing equipment is placed at both locations allowing for a consultation to take place in "real-time".

The good news is that video conferencing technology has become cheaper over the past few years, and computer programmes much simpler than before, enabling healthcare professionals to use nothing more than a simple desktop video conferencing systems. Almost areas of medicine have been able to benefit from video conferencing, including psychiatry, internal medicine, rehabilitation, cardiology, pediatrics, obstetrics, gynecology and neurology. Also, many different peripheral devices, like otoscopes (which help doctors look inside the ear) and stethoscopes (which enable a doctor to listen to a person's heart beat) can be attached to computers, aiding within interactive examination.

Video conferencing technology is also playing a large role in physician training and the dissemination of advanced practices. One of he more existing video conferencing applications in healthcare involve programmes that enable expert physicians to share advanced knowledge and techniques with counterparts around the country and across the globe.

Tele In Vivo device: The Tele In Vivo a transportable telemedicine work station, was developed for use in inaccessible areas, such as islands, rural areas and regions isolated by floods, earthquakes or other calamities. It combines a portable PC, which has telecommunication capabilities with alight, portable 3D ultrasound station.

The Tele in Vivo device is not expensive, has a low weight is easily transportable and is non-radiating. This integrated work station uses advanced software techniques that can collect the 3D ultrasound data of a patient. Ultrasound supports a wide range of applications, ranging from gynecology to cardio logical examinations, and is presently the only economically and practically, affordable imaging modality. The doctor in the field scans the patient and transmits the acquired 3D dataset using Internet, ISDN the phone line or GSM, to the distant expert.

The data transmission could be online, i.e., two doctors being connected, or offline (e.g. overnight or through narrowband channels). In the former case, the remote expert can request additional scans during the tele consultation for fine-tuning the diagnosis. The innovative idea of the system lies in the fact that after the transfer of the 3D ultrasound data and during the online communication, only control signals (e.g. position of the mouse, activation of buttons, etc.) are the transmitted the over the network. The actions of just one user are transferred to the remote location, while the second workstation locally calculates the corresponding image. Hence, no heavy image data needs to be transferred over the network, except for a few kilobytes of control signals. Ultimately the two doctors see the same image on their screens. The delay between two locations depends on the only latency of the intermediate network, which can be as low as that of a normal telephone line or even a GSM mobile phone. The device currently comes in to two versions-one fully portable, self-contained devices, and a work station version (PC attached to an ultrasound scanner for internal hospital use).[38]

3.6.31 Personnel Software Process

Software engineering often develops their personal practices they first learn to write programs. And most engineers start-off with exceedingly poor personal practices. Also reaching certain level of maturity in their skill is often time consuming. There is a needed for a sound method that is sure to deliver results quickly and easily. Personal Software Process promises (PSP) just that. PSP provides engineers with a disciplined personal frame work for executing quality software work. (PSP concentrated on the work practices of the individual engineers. This practice shows engineers how to manage quality from the beginning of the job how to analyse the results of the each job and how to use the results to improve the process for the next project).

PSP is an individual level model that helps individual engineers to plan their work, estimate the size, defects, effort and schedule to plan their work and track these while working. According to SEY early experience with the PSP have shown that average test defects rates improve by ten times, and average productivity goes up by 25 percent or more.

The conceptual structure of the personal software process is a "requirements statement" the first step in the PSP process is planning. There is a planning script that guides this work and a plan summary for recording the planning data. The engineers record their time and defect data on the logs. At the end of the job, during the post-mortem phase, the summaries the time and defect data from the logs, measure the program size, and enter this data in the plan summary form.

The rigorous PSP training process consists of a set of methods, forms and scripts that show software engineers how to plan, measure and manage their work. These methods are introduced in a series of seven process versions that are labeled PSPO through PSP3, the engineers have to write a defined set of 10 programming exercises and five data analysis reports with each exercise they are gradually introduced to various advanced software engineering methods. By measuring their own performance the engineers can see the effect of these methods on their work.

PSPO—the baseline process: The initial step in the PSP is to establish a baseline that includes some measurements and a reporting format. This provides consistent basis for measuring progress and a defined foundation on which to improve. PSPO is enhanced to PSPO 1 by adding a coding standard, size measurement and the Process Improvement Proposal (PIP).

PSP1—The Personal Planning Process: PSP1 adds planning steps to PSPO. The initial step to PSP1 adds size and resource estimation. In PSP1.1 schedule planning and status tracking are also introduced.

PSP2—Personal Quality Management: PSP2 adds personal design and code reviews to PSP1. These help the engineers to find defects earlier in their processes, which they analyse. The design process is addressed in

PSP2.1. The internet is not to tell engineers how to design but to address the criteria for design completion. Design completeness criteria are established and various design verification and consistency techniques are examined.

PSP3—A Cyclic Personal Process: To this point the PSP has concentrated on a linear process for building small programmes. In the sealing the PSP2 up to larger projects the approach is to sub-divided larger programmes into PSP2 sized pieces in PSP3. These large programmes are designed to be developed in incremental steps. The first build is a base module or kernel that is enhanced in interactive cycles. In each interaction a complete PSP2. It is used including design, code, compile and test. The PSP3 process is suitable for programmes of up to several thousand lines of code.

Implementing PSP: Engineers start planning by defining the work that needs to be done in as much detail as possible. If all they have is a one-sentence requirement statements, then that statement must be the basis for the plan. To make an estimate and a plan, engineers first define how the product is to be designed and built. However since the planning phase is too early to produce a complete product design engineers produce what is called a conceptual design. Later during the design phase they examine design alternatives and produce a complete product design. The PSP starts with engineers estimate the time required to do the work. In the PSP the size and resource estimates are made with the probe method.[39]

3.6.32 Computer Aided Design (CAD)

Not long ago all products went through an initial phase in which rough engineering drawings were taken to the drafting departments to be hand drawn in ink on vellum. Returned to the designer or engineer any changes required their going back to the drafting department again. There was not any thing at all interactive about the process. With the introduction of computer-aided design software not only are drawing easier to create and store they are much easier to revise, no small advantage since revisions are the main activity in product design. One of the latest innovations is to automatically convert drawings into VRML files so the designer can fly through the product seeing how the components fit together inside the model.

3.6.33 Computer-Aided-Manufacturing (CAM)

It refers to industries automation using computer controlled machines and processes. Some CAM software can take a CAD drawing and create the code for programming a Computer Numerical Control (CNC) machine such as a laser or lathe. Drawing can be used to programme robots the much more versatile machines that are used to assemble. Weld and paint products. Not all uses of robots are in heavy industry. Igor cronies of living design uses robot assisted manufacturing (RAM) for the industrial production of decorative fabrics and leather. The input is a combination of design ideas and special programming functions that merge during manufacturing to create output with continuous variation. The goal is to eliminate the mass produced look which keeping the products affordable.

3.6.34 Electronic Catalogs

Companies web pages that educate the public about their products and services are beginning to replace printed product catalogs that are expensive to produce and distribute and are soon out of date. Business to business electronic catalogs are rapidly growing a business. One electronic parts manufactures AMP that spends up to $ 10 million to publish 400 catalogs a year expects to save enormous amounts of money once electronic catalogs replace the printed ones. Customers benefit because printed catalogs are hard to file and search through for the right product. Search engines built into electronic catalogs allow potential buyers to search an entire product line using various key words or other characteristics.

3.6.35 Web Advertising

As you brows the web you find many pages adorned with companies names, medallions, and icons. These companies have paid the websites to put these elements on their pages and the hope is that some one visiting the page will chick one of the ornaments to visit the advertisers web site. To help advertisers measure the effectiveness of their ads and to develop leads to flows, software has been created that lets the companies know who is clicking and what they are viewing. This raises some serious privacy issues and a lot of people object to this capturing of information about their behavior the wonderful thing about the world of computers is that creative minds are also developing software that conceals your identity from these advertisers. These programs will become popular defenses as web users start getting phone calls around dinnertime that began.

3.6.36 Secure Transactions

One the early struggles with the Internet was finding a way to safely buy and sell goods transfer funds over it. But eventually this has been achieved. Since messages go through so many computers between a buyer and seller no transaction was secure. Credit card numbers and other sensitive information could easily be captured. The goal was to enable electronic commerce by providing a safe convenient, and immediate payment system on the Internet for transactions between consumer merchants and their banks as well as between individuals by processing them in real time and passing authorization codes back to merchants. Here is how one of these secure payment systems works:

- ❖ You visit the merchants website and select items to be purchased and enter shipping instructions. The merchants server then returns to you a summary of the item, price, and transaction ID.

- You click the pay button which launches the cyber cash wallet. You choose a credit card from your wallet and click ok to forward the order and encrypted payment information to the merchant.
- The merchant receives the packed strips-off the order and forwards the encrypted payment information digitally signed and encrypted with his private key to the cyber cash server. The merchant cannot see the consumers credit card information.
- The cyber cash server receives the packer, takes the transaction behind its firewall and off the Internet unwraps data within a hardware based crypto box reformats the transaction and forwards it to the merchants bank over dedicated lines.
- The merchants bank forwards the authorization request to the issuing bank via the card associations or directly to American express or discover for instance. The approval or denial code is sent back to cyber cash.
- Cyber cash returns the approval or denial code to the merchant who passes it on to you. From step 1 to step 6 to takes 15 or 20 seconds.

3.6.37 Micro Payments

Until recently very small charges on the order of fractions of a cent could not be handled economically. It was like trying to pay for a gumball with a credit card. Very inexpensive micro commerce transactions are important to on line publishers that want to sell news papers by the article, cartoons by the strip, or music by the song. Micro payment systems such as Digital Millicent TM systems are making this possible. Using this system, you sign up for a wallet and then buy a few dollars worth of script using a credit card or other form of payment. When you visit a site offering the service you can look at detailed information that would normally be available only to subscribers for only pennies per page. By visiting those sites where advertisers give you script to visit their site you can probably keeper your browsing free with the offsetting payments.[40]

3.6.38 Office Automation

Office automation is defined as using computer and communications technology to help people better use and manage information. Office automation technology includes all types of computers, telephones, electronic mail and office machines that use microprocessors or other high technology computers.

There are five primary technologies used in managing information in office automation: These are: 1. Text or written words, 2. Data as in numbers or other non text forms 3. Graphics-drawings charts and photographs 4. Audio as in telephone, voicemail or voice recognition systems and 5. Video such as captured images video tapes or teleconferencing.

In the past these forms of information was created using different technologies. Text was create using conventional type writers or more recently, word processing, data such as sales reports, was provided by the central computer. Charts and graphs were either hand drawn or created using 35 mm slide photography and video tape were used for training. Audio was limited to the phone or tape recording. It was not possible to combine these various forms of information.

Office automation uses computer based system to provide information to help knowledge workers make decisions that benefit the business. Office automation systems are comprised of many distinct subsystems; text management systems network and communication systems.

3.6.39. Text Management System

A text management system is a computer system designed to work with the written or typewritten word. It includes all kinds of typewriters, word processing systems, PCs with word processing desktop publishing and text editing systems and even computerized typesetting equipment. Text management systems are used for tasks like writing memos notes, letters and other short documents printing envelops and labels, repairing pre-printed forms such as invoices, composing complex documents such as proposals and reports, retrieving and editing documents such as contracts, creating display documents like newsletters, etc.

3.6.40 Business Analysis Systems

Managers need solid data from which to extract the information necessary to make good decisions for the business. In the past, these knowledge workers had to relay on their experience and other personal factors to make decisions. A business analysis system provides data that when used with the proper software helps its users better understand the business environment and make more effective decisions. Corporate users routinely use spreadsheets for analyzing cost and benefits and for creating budgets.

Other software tools for performing analysis that are commonly used in large companies are Decision Support Systems (DSS), expert systems and Executive Support Systems (ESS). A decision support system helps the knowledge worker to extract information from the various MIS database and reporting systems, analyze it, and then formulate a decision or a strategy for business planning. An expert system is a computer system that can store and retrieve data with special problem-solving expertise. An executive support system is an information system that consolidates and summarizes ongoing transactions within the organization. It provides the management with all the information it requires at all times from internal as well as external sources.

3.6.41 Document Management Systems

Document management systems aid in filing, tracking and managing documents, whether they are paper, computer-based, micrographic or purely electronic. Office automation demands that data be immediately accessible and instantaneously retrievable. For that reason we are slowly moving away from paper and toward document forms that can be stored on the computer.

3.6.42 Network and Communication Management Systems

Today, knowledge workers have many ways to communicate with one another primarily by voice, fax and email. They can communicate in real time, via phone or computer. They can also communicate using computer controlled PBX telephone systems to record a digital message and leave it in the recipient electronic mailbox. These systems are called network and communication management systems.[41]

3.6.43 Electronic Data Interchange (EDI)

Electronic Data Interchange is the computer to computer exchange of business documents in a standard format. These formats look much like standard forms and are highly structured. One widely used format is for purchase orders and consist of an outer digital "Envelop" both the addresses of sender and receivers. Inside the digital envelop on series of standard codes define the part number, cost, tax information, shipment methods, bill-to location, ship to location, and contexts to call. This EDI purchase orders can be automatically generated by the buyer when inventory falls below a certain point and sent via networks to the supplier. At that end it is automatically processed and creates a list of the products to be shipped even before the normal work day begins.

3.6.44 Teaching through Computer

Distance education covers the various farms in study at all levels which are not bound to continuation and giving lectures in classrooms. This denotes the activity of the student. Thus the distance study can be described as learning supported by those teaching methods in which, because of the physical separateness of learners and teachers, the interactive, as well as the proactive phase of teaching is conducted through print, non-print or electronic devices. Wide ranges of technological options are available to the distance educator. They fall into following four major categories, i.e. voice, video, data and print.

Voice: Instructional audio tools include the interactive technologies of telephone, audio conferencing and short wave radio; passive audio tools include tapes and radio.

Video: Instructional video tools include still image such as slides, pre-produced moving images and real time moving images combined with audio conferencing.

Data: Computer send and receive information electronically computer applications for distance education are varied and include:

Computer-Assisted Instruction (CAI): Uses the computer as a self-contained teaching machine to present individual lessons.

Computer-Managed Instruction: Uses the computer to organize instruction to track student records and progress. The instruction itself need not be delivered via computer, although CAI is often combined with CMI.

Computer-Mediated Education: Describes computer application that facilitates the delivery of instruction. For example E-mail, fax, real time computer conferencing and www applications.

Print: This is a foundation element of distance education programmes and basic from which all over delivery systems have evolved various print formats are available including text books, study guides, work books, course syllabus and carestudies.[42]

3.6.45 New Insights to Hi-Tech Teaching

A part from traditional role as knowledge creator, the teaching should also be a pathfinder for knowledge utility. Learner centered teaching and learning methods to update the swiftly changing knowledge, need based curriculum design and industry oriented learning methods. Adopt new methods of memory management configured in the lines of human brains information processing and learners cognitive styles. Making the student to slowly accustom and interact with computer aided instruction and simulation materials. Selection of students through their interest, ability and aptitude. Teachers role will be more as a director, coach and a facilitator producing persons who can create advanced technology because human resources in industry in the present days of IT revolution are defined not by what it does but by what it delivers. Understanding that perceptions acquisition and learning are media dependent and learners sense reception ability through different media, the teacher should create multi-media instruction. Teacher should become a software developer for media instruction. Teacher should taught interaction, feedback and control are achieved through mediated interaction using Tele-video and computer conferencing by virtual Tele presence of a teacher. Integrating their faculty with other faculties.

Literature survey to active research in dynamically assimilating the fast explosion of knowledge into teaching methodology using internet, media ET and Tele proactive strategic planning to be in tune with the global revolution of IT to produce well-rounded persons with over all developments who can be assets to an organized society. Evaluation-oriented towards testing the knowledge, competence and preparation of the candidate for a holistic development to achieve large social objectives. Finding methods to move from providing equality not only for access but also towards equality for success to every body to attract international students by making them to understand that quality technical education can be obtained in India at an affordable cost in comparison with other developed countries where by the fee burden on Indian students can be reduced. Exposing the learner to navigational tools and filtering of vastly growing information electronically and professionally with emphasis or regency and primacy of information. To act as a co-coordinator for resource sharing between institution, R&D organizations and industries converting professionals to entrepreneurs. Since global technical scenario requires world class people, exposure of learner to multi-critical and multi cultural aspects along with quality and productivity linked global competence and work culture should be developed.[43]

3.6.46 Sustainable Agriculture through IT

Information Technology can be a very effective aid in managing sustainable agriculture. In recent years, Government of India has realized the importance of IT in rural development and efforts have been made in this direction to facilitate marketing of products from rural area. IT has much more potential than just to facilitate marketing. However, to realize the full potential systematic initiative will have to be taken. The following elements are consider for sustainable agriculture development through Information Technology as given under:

(i) *Establish Partnership and develop a vision*: In place of command and control programme a community-based approach should be developed. It has largely been realized that the community does not require provider but enabler. Any development programme may be conceived at the grass root level with small group of people sharing common interest will be binding factor within the group. Government needs to facilitate open interactions of this group to develop a feasible development programme.

(ii) *Assess the quality of Land Water:* Depletion in the quality of land and water all over the country is a hard reality. However extent of depletion is not same through out the country. It is differentiated which needs to be analyzed before any programme for development of agriculture sustainable and food security is initiated. Accurate and reliable data should be gathered on following aspects for optimal land use and thus formulating policies for food security. Mapping of soil resources, land capability and irritability, Soil moisture estimation, Crop acreage and Land-use pattern.

Information thus received should be analyzed through Geographic Information System (GIS). GIS is capable of analyzing data in different layers. Final analysis should be made available to agricultural universities and farmers or production estimation (horticulture, multiple and mono-cropping).

(iii) *Development of Strategy*: Information thus received regarding quality availability of natural resources may be utilized by the local community can develop strategy based on their traditional knowledge about natural resources as well as social infrastructure at the village level. Indian Council of Agriculture Research and State Agricultural universities have also been working on management of sustainable agriculture. However, there is time lag in dissemination of information and timely intervention, if required. IT application in this regard will be very effective. Universities may help by analyzing feasibility of the development strategy thus developed suggestions improvement as well as information about various success stories can be sent back to the village.

(iv) Development of Relevant websites: Websites can be informative as well as instructive. The two websites are discussed as under:

Informative website: These websites may be designed to inform the farmers about:

- World trade organization (WTO) conditional ties.
- Traditional wisdom for sustainable agriculture and restoration of depleted land and water.
- Development programs of the government to enhance the productivity of the agricultural sector.
- Appropriate technology which is another important ingredient for any program of sustainable agriculture work in this direction is also being done by many organizations.

However, dissemination of information at ground level is far from satisfactory. Websites can also be developed to disseminate information, discuss efficient use of agricultural inputs as drip/sprinkler irrigation in place of bore wells, bio-fertilizers in place of chemical fertilizers, precisions farming, etc.

Instructive website: These websites may be designed to instruct the farmers:

- To proceed for registering grievances if any.
- To communicate with the experts through internet for solving problems related to their livelihood.
- Regarding existing market opportunity and variation in price rate for their products through Internet. Even if they do not go to the market, information will enable them to demand for better prices from the middle man. Information about market conditions is known to have helped price realization at the village level.[44]

3.6.47 e-Governance

One area where governments are interested is in indirect support for the IT sector by boosting the domestic market though its own purchases, of course, purchases sophisticated equipment and software that its unused in high level bureaucrat offices will have little positive impact. However there are reasons to be more optimistic about the use of IT for improved government functioning. First, back-office procedures can be made more efficient so that internal record keeping, flows of information and tracking of decisions and performance can be improved. Second, when some basic information is stored in digital form it provides the opportunity for easier access to that information by citizens. The simplest examples would be e-mailing requests or complaints, checking regulations on a web page, or printing out forms from the web so that a trip to pickup the forms from a physical office can be avoided. More complicated possibilities are checking actual records. Such as land ownership or transactions. Still more complicated are cases information is submitted electronically by the citizen. The successful pilot e-governance programmes that have made some of the above actions possible.

- ❖ The Bhoomi project of Karnataka an e-governance project which computerized 20 million rural land records belonging to over 6.7 million farmers and delivering them through 177 government kiosks. It is a trendsetter for better governance and helped to eliminate red tapism and corruption in civic services.
- ❖ Computer-aided registration of land deeds and stamp duties in Andhra Pradesh reducing reliance on brokers and possibilities for corruption.
- ❖ Computerization of rural local government offices in Andhra Pradesh or delivery of statutory certificates of identify and land holdings substantially reducing delays.
- ❖ Computerized check points for local entry taxes in Gujarat with data automatically sent to a central databases, reducing opportunities for local corruption.
- ❖ Consolidated bill payment sites in kerala allowing citizens to pay bills under 17 different categories in one place, from electricity to university fees.

E-mail requests for repairs to basic rural infrastructure such as hand pumps reducing reliance on erratic visits of government functionaries.[45]

3.6.48 Multimedia

Multimedia is, woven combinations of text, graphic art, sound, animation, and video elements.

Multimedia elements are typically sewn together into a project using authoring tools. These software tools are designed to manage individual multimedia elements and provide user interaction. In addition to providing a method for users to interact with the project most authoring tools also offer facilities for creating and editing text and images, and they have extensions to drive video disc players, video tape players, and other relevant hardware peripherals. Sounds and movies are usually created with editing tools dedicated to these media, and than the elements are imported into the authoring system for playback.[46]

3.6.49 Management Information System

Management Information System (MIS) may be described as an information system that provides information in the form of standardized reports and displays to managers. MIS is a broad class of information systems that are designed to provide information needed for effective decision making by managers. MIS emphasizes the management orientation of information processing in business. A major goal of computer-based information systems should be the support of management decision-making, not merely the processing of data generated by business operations. MIS emphasizes that a systems framework should be used for organizing information system applications. Business application of information systems should be viewed as interrelated and integrated computer-based information systems and not as independent data processing.jobs.[47]

3.6.50 E-Contracts

The proposed contract should be conspicuously displayed and available on the website of the seller company. The seller or distribute goods or services through their websites. Should include draft e-contract to which potential customers must give their unconditional assent. The proposed contract needs to be carefully drafted to protect the interests of the company.[48]

Notes and References

1. N.R. Satyanarayana, Information Technology : An Introduction, Information Technology Applications in Libraries : A text book for beginners, 2004, p. 1.
2. Dennis P. Curtan, Kim Foley, Kunal Sen and Cathleen Morin, Inforamtion Technology, Tata McGraw Hills Edition, New Delhi, 1999, p. 18.
3. Dr. R.D. Pathak and others, Harnessing Information Technology Trends, Indian Management, April 1998, p. 32.
4. Curtin and Others, Information Technology, Tata McGraw Hill, New Delhi, 1999, p. 20.
5. P. Radha Krishna, Information Technology and Numerical Methods, The Hi-Tech Publishers, Hyderabad, 2002-03, p. 4.
6. N.R. Satyanarayana, Information Technology : An Introduction, Information Technology Applications in Libraries: A Text book for Biginners, 2004, p. 2.
7. N.R. Satyanarayana, Information Technology : An Introduction, Information Technology Applications in Libraries : A text book for Beginners, 2004, pp. 2-8.
8. P. Radha Krishna, Information Technology and Numerical Methods, Hitech Publishing, Hyderabad, 2000, pp. 5-9.
9. Alex and Mathew Leons, Fundamentals of Information Technology, Leon Publications, 1999, pp. 32.1-33.1.
10. Dr. V. Chandra Sekhar Rao, Ex-Commerce, An Emerging Business Opportunity through Internet, *SBI Monthly Review*, May 1999, pp. 910-12.
11. Alexis and Mathews, Fundamentals of Information Technology, Leon Publications, 1999, pp. 344-51.

12. D. Mukhopadhyaya, Information Technology for Quality Education of Learning Society, *University News*, November 4.10, 2002, pp. 11-13.
13. Teena Gomes, IT Education for the Rich and the Poor, Information Technology, EFY publishers, New Delhi, February, 2004, pp. 28-30.
14. D. Mukhopadhyaya, Information Technology for Quality Education of Learning Society, *University News*, November, 04-10-2002, pp. 14-16.
15. S.L. Mahajan, Information Communication Technology in Distance Education in India, *Indian Journal of Open Learning*, 11(2) 2002, pp. 269-77.
16. Ilapatel, Information Communication Technology and Distance adult literacy Education in India, *Indian Journal of Open Learning*, II (2) 2002, pp. 255-68.
17. P. Seetharaman Siva Kumar, Teleconferencing : A New technology for Extension Training in India; *Indian Journal of Training and Development*, October-December 2002, pp. 55-61.
18. Dr. M.P. Gupta, Electronic Education and Training, Indian Management, September 1998, pp. 45-50.
19. Manoj Killedar, Distance Education Through Internet Based E-learning, *Indian Journal of Open Learning*, 2001, 10(1) pp. 68-79.
20. Ilapatel, The Challenging of Illiteracy : Can Information Technology help? *Indian Journal of Adult Education*, October-December, 2003, pp. 8-9.
21. I Lapalel, The Challenge of Illiteracy : Can Information Technology help? *Indian Journal of Adult Education*, October-December, 2003, pp. 5-13.
22. Renjith Mettoth, Pathways Sets Kids Free, Information Technology Published by EFY, New Delhi, October, 2004, pp. 64-66.
23. Preethi, J., Technology Levels the Learning Field, Information Technology, EFY Publishers, New Delhi, January, 2005, pp. 47-49.
24. F.L. Lobo, Training Dimensions of the Electronic Age, Indian Management, October 2000, pp. 65-70.
25. F.L. Lobo, Training Dimensions of the Electronic Age, Indian Management, October 2000, pp. 65-67.
26. P. Seethuraman Sivakumar, Teleconferencing: A New Technology for Extension Training in India, *Indian Journal of Training and Development*, October-December, 2002, pp. 55-61.
27. Mouli Halan, IT Empowers Farmers, Information Technology Magazine, Published by EFY, New Delhi, October 2004, pp. 50-52.
28. Prof. Parteek Bhatia, The Hole in the Wall-Bridging the Digital devide, Information Technology, Published by Electronic for You, May 2004, pp. 26-27.
29. G.P. Pandey and Joya Chakraborty, Role of Information Technology in Higher Education in the 21st Century, *University News*, February 25-March 3, 2002, p. 12.
30. G.P. Pandey and Joya Chakraborty, Role of Information Technology in Higher Education in the 21st Century, *University News*, February 25-March 3, 2002, pp. 12-13.
31. Preethi, J., Outsourcing Infrastructure Management, Information Technology, EFY Enterprises Pvt. Ltd., New Delhi, August 2005, pp. 69-71.
32. Conny Kullman, the Business of Delivery via Satellite, Information Technology, February, 2004, pp. 16-17.
33. Rishi Verma, Enterprise Mobility Business on the move, Information Technology, Published by Electronic for You, New Delhi, July 2004, pp. 28-31.
34. Benefit Bureau, ERP Systems, Information Technology, EFY Publishers, New Delhi, October 2004, pp. 10-11.
35. Akansha Pradhan, Mobile Phones for More Sales, EFY Enterprises Pvt. Ltd., New Delhi, October 2004, pp. 12-14.
36. Akansha Pradhan, IT-Forming the Backbone in Ad Biz., Information Technology, EFY Enterprises Pvt. Ltd., October 2004, pp. 36-38.
37. Garima Khanna, The Rise of the Digital Media, Information Technology EFY Enterprises Pvt. Ltd., New Delhi, January 2005, pp. 54-58.
38. Anjali Sen, Riding the IT wave, Information Technology Benefit, EFY Enterprises Pvt. Ltd., New Delhi, October 2004, pp. 22-23.
39. IT, Bureau, Appolo's Telemedicine Solution. Distance Healing, Information Technology, EFY Enterprises Pvt. Ltd., New Delhi, March 2005, pp. 34-35.

40. Mauli Halan, The World of Distant Healing, Information Technology, EFY Enterprises Pvt. Ltd., New Delhi, August 2005, pp. 48-50.
41. S.V. Malovika, Personal Software Process Improving Software Practices, Information Technology, EFY Enterprises Pvt. Ltd., New Delhi, May-2005, pp. 25-27.
42. Dennis, P. Curtin, Kim Foley, Kunalsen and Cathleen Morin, Information Technology (Breaking Wave), Tata McGraw Hill Publishing Company Limited, New Delhi, 1999, pp. 240-51.
43. Alexis Leon and Mathews Leon, Fundamentals of Information Technology, Leon Publications, 1999, pp. 33.1-33.4
44. Prof. Harish Suryavanshi, The Impact of IT on Legal Practice, Information Technology, Published by Electronic for You, New Delhi, April 2004, pp. 84-85.
45. Dharam Kumar and Pardeep Rai, Distance Education, Uses of Computers and Problem of Copyright, *Library Herald*, June 2002 pp. 120-21.
46. C. Ramachandra Prabhu, Invasion of Information Technology on Technical Education, *University News*, May 28-June 3, 2001, p. 8.
47. Seema Singh and Anil Kumar, Information Technology, An Effective Tool for Managing Sustainable Agriculture, Agricultural Situation in India, February, 2003, pp. 717-21.
48. R.G. Desai, Information Technology at Regional Level, Productivity, April-June 2003, pp. 55-60.

4

Impact of Information Technology on Society

Having missed the full impact of the Industrial Resolution due to more than two centuries of colonization, India is overtaken by the Information Revolution. The industrial resolution took centuries to spread to different areas of the world. But it has created super imposed impact on human society in a much shorter time than any thing ever. The rapid acceleration of change is further fuelled by concepts like-globalization, liberalization, economic and political reforms. In "Future shock" Alvin Toffler has shown his concern for the possible effects of on exponential growth of technological advance on a society ill-equipped and ill-prepared to deal with. He further mentions in his book "Third wave" about three waves of changes due to progress in science and technology, viz., agricultural civilization, industrial civilization and technological revolution. Out of which the third wave has tremendously altered forever the way in which we live work and play. In our opinion the third wave itself has created a much more forceful evolution which can aptly be called "Forth wave", i.e. emergence of Information Technology (IT).

When the rhythm of drumbeat changes the corresponding dancing steps also change. The advent of IT has spurt up drastic transformation process. Which has process, which has suddenly created a totally new wave in India. This has further brought an innovative boost and new definition to the developmental process with an open vision in preparation of welcoming the new millennium.

In the report submitted by the national task force of information technology, (Appendix II) emphasis has been given on Human Resource

Development (HRD) extensively. Based on this, we can say that the time is right to realize the importance of HRD in develop IT industry base as well as in harnessing IT for better governance.

This chapter attempts to assess the advantages, disadvantages and impact of Information Technology methods programmes on various sections of society, i.e., Students, Employees, Business people, Professional people like, Doctors, Engineers, Lawyers, Teachers, and Rural people.

4.1 E-LEARNING

E-Learning is the delivery of content via all electronic media, including the Internet, intranets, extranets, satellite broadcast, audiotape, video tape, interactive T.V. and CD-ROM the advantages and disadvantages of E-learning programmes are given as under:

Advantages

- E-learning is an important tool to improve academic quality, effectiveness and efficiency of open and distance education system.
- E-learning is a system that can empower both students and teachers. Teachers can clearly communicate more in less time using rich multimedia.
- It also creates a knowledge resource for the nation and any module can be easily shared by anyone, anywhere.
- E-learning provides much freedom to students regarding place and time of learning. This flexibility makes learning an attractive activity particularly for housewives and employed students.
- E-learning provides a new medium which significantly reduces the problems of education at a distance and increases the opportunities for interactive communication.
- It offers excellent possibilities to transform the present teacher centric education system in to highly responsive and dynamic learner-centric personalized education system.
- E-learning will be a giant step forward towards ensuring quality education for all with cost effectiveness, at the doorstep of learners.
- Knowledge is expanding at lightening speed. Students need to learn more, better and faster. No limit in the number of students. Location of students is irrelevant. It is self-paced learning. It provides up-to-date content and testing, timely information.
- It improves customer service, student performance and employee moral. It supports intellectual wealth creation. E-learning creates augment employee productivity and empowers citizens. It is lighten administrative load.
- It finds immediate feedback on students progress with on line testing. E-learning provides vast knowledge available on numerous

topics—something for everyone and Increase competitiveness, transparency, efficiency and increase access.

Disadvantages

- ❖ E-learning is a complex process. Teachers must use innovative methods for teaching so that learning becomes an enjoyable experience that sustains the interest and concentration of students
- ❖ E-learning is an access limited based on availability of hardware, software and internet connection. It is not usually associated with formal accreditation and E-learning is need self discipline.
- ❖ It needs lack of real human interaction, E-learning is may be intimidating to students with low computer skills.

4.2 E-MAIL

E-mail is an electronic message sent from one computer to another. Many orders can be saved if your team can access their crucial emails that generally bunch up as deadlines start looming large. While on the move to close one deal, three are lost because those clients had sought last minute clarifications through email, which your marketing head was unable to access. A mobile with the email facility will route all emails to the mobiles of the marketing-team members while they are on the move. They can also reply to those emails, if needed, or just give a call and close that deal. The advantages and disadvantages of e-mail are described as under:

Advantages

- ❖ E-mail is instantaneous with no limitation of timing or location and enables one to stay globally connected no matter where you may be. E-mail is estimated that the data traffic through the internet would outstrip the voice traffic in not-too-distant a future.
- ❖ E-mail provides access the information from any where in the world and Global communication is easier. It opened the door for more types of professionals to work at home, because they can still tap in to corporate information.
- ❖ E-mail has proved a big blessing for senior citizens and retired persons. E-mail ranges from just curious with no computer background to well experienced who have a computer at home and a laptop in their travel bag.
- ❖ E-mail can also enable to stand out in customer service, competitions, and sell products.

Disadvantages

- ❖ E-mail has created an information overload. E-mail is that it can become a distraction and can prevent people from doing any productive work. It is the very existence of electronic communication has perpetuated the myth that it will lead to better communication. But that not true, if you are not a good communicator without electronic technology you wont become a good communicator just because you use the technology.

- Technology improves our ability to communicate extends the reach of our communication and reduce long distance communications timelines, but it is the individual using the technology that makes the communications better or worst.

4.3. INTERNET

The Internet is a worldwide, self-governed network connecting thousands of smaller networks, and millions of computers and people, to mega sources of information. This is a technology that sinks vast distances, that blur political, ethnic, and national boundaries, and that is accelerating the pace of business change and revolution the way companies are managed. The advantages and disadvantages are:

Advantages

- Internet is an ideal marketing medium for companies in the industries. It is foundation pillar for education or learning, it covers the globe and includes large international networks as well as many smaller, local area networks.
- It offers access to data, graphics, sound, software, text and people through a variety of services and tools for communication and data exchange, i.e., remote login, file transfer, Hypertext and e-mail. It is the cheapest and fastest means to get information, provide information and compile information.
- It facilitate for visit websites, send and receive electronic mail. Read and post articles in news groups, download files to your PC, chat with other users on-line, and play games with others on-line, Access online multimedia including radio and video broad casts. Searching for information.
- It is facilitates to join in contests, contribute articles, other materials and also facilitate to do on-line shopping. Post your resumes on the Internet, Create your own websites, Create an e-mail ID and account for you Use the email remainder service and it is visually more appealing to children
- It can be effectively used to supplement textbook learning. It can expose children to a plethora of information and teaches them how to call relevant data. It is an early beginning assures that they are computer savvy at a later age.

Disadvantages

- Literacy is necessary for operation to Internet, Telephone line is must, perhaps no telephone connection not getting Internet facility. Children get used to ready made study material without having to search for it, it is possible through Internet.
- Discourages the habit of reading effect by the Internet, It is a time consuming device. Internet can leads to isolationist tendencies, Internet can affect leadership qualities, and Internet gives easy access to adult web sites. It will be badly effects on the students and younger people.

4.4 MOBILE PHONE

The mobile phone is truly a very powerful homing device, as well as obtaining location-related information. Location-based services are an application of mobile networking that use the awareness of your exact location in a city to issue information related to that area. The advantages and disadvantages are:

Advantages

- Mobile phone provides easy communication with mobile phones to anywhere to anywhere; SMS are very useful to the people with mobile phones.
- Mobile phones helping in the mathematical concepts, it provides stored the messages, provides camera facility and video facility, inexpensive and sufficient to the people, Avoid the communication gap with mobile phone
- Mobile phones creating interaction with known persons. Mobile phones help to people as convenient. Mobile phone provides caller identity facility to the users.

Disadvantages

- Communication barriers are involved. Signal problems are rising. Misuse of students in educational contents. Health problems, Misuse of camera phones, Use in office working hours.

4.5 GEOGRAPHIC INFORMATION SYSTEM

A Geographic Information System (GIS) is a computer-based tool for mapping and analyzing things that exist and events that happen on earth. GIS technology integrates common database operations such as query and statistical analysis with the unique visualization and geographic analysis benefits offered by maps. The advantages and disadvantages as under:

Advantages

- GIS helped reduce costs in streamlining customer service. It helped in the land acquisition costs through better analysis. It helped in reducing fleet maintenance costs through better logistics and It helped in analyzing data quickly.
- It can be improve organizational integration, It can be increases communication among individuals and departments, It can be used to help reach a decision about the location of a new housing development that has minimal environmental impact, is located in a low risk area, and close to a population center.
- GIS can be presented sufficiently and clearly in the form of a map and accompanying report, allowing decision makers to focus on the real issues rather than trying to understand the data, Because GIS products can be produced quickly, multiple scenario can be evaluated efficiently and effectively.
- It provides database creation. It making maps on basis of places.

Disadvantages

- Is more costly procedure and It is not possible to access by the more people.

4.6 VIDEO CONFERENCING

Exchange of video information and pictures between individuals or groups through specialized equipments. The advantages and disadvantages of video conferencing as under:

Advantages

- It is the most widely used technology. It is used for transferring digital images from one location to another location.
- Video conferencing technology has become cheaper over the past few years, and computer programmes much simpler than before.
- Videoconferencing technology is playing large role in the medicine, It provides excellent communication to the people.

Disadvantages

- Lack of facilities in the urban and rural areas. It is very expensive process. It requires big size screen
- Danger of over utilization and under utilization, Lack of availability of said programme.

4.7 TELECONFERENCING

Basically tele conferencing is the interactive exchange of information between individuals or groups in two or more locations through an electronic medium. It can bring people who are geographically isolated together to express their viewpoints and share their experiences. The advantages and disadvantages of tele conferencing are:

Advantages

- It reduced the resources requirement. It saves trainers time. There is less needed for a centralized training facility. It reduce and eliminate travel-trainees can be trained in the work place. It provides specialized management systems for tracking trainees progress and location.
- It helps to identify specific needs. It provides consistency of training in terms of quality and quantity of information presented. It provides standardization of training when training occurs in several locations simultaneously.
- It provides training can be administered instantly and simultaneously. It improves the training people in specific skills for specific performance.
- Train people in general skills that broadly effect general performance, it increases access to information tools for decision-making. Learning transfers well to the real conditions.

Disadvantages

- High cost of establishments, production, evaluation and distribution of educational multimedia packages
- Deficiency of technical expertise to maintain the system-poorly maintained teleconferencing systems frequently show ghost images, echo effects and voice errors which effect the quality of transmission and reception.
- Greater time needed for preparation of courseware—development of instructional packages requires considerably more time and expertise than an equivalent package required for traditional training.
- Skill requirement for producing using courseware. The design of multimedia package requires skilled persons with sound knowledge in instructional and educational design as well as computer operations which is always a constrain in India.
- Constantly changing technology and confusions over standards have added to the techno fobia created by lack of awareness about the potentials of state-of-art teleconferencing technologies and fears over the technology-based learning.

- Lack of familiarity of the users with the medium and equipments it requires additional time and resources for training users in understanding the medium and using the equipment and Danger of over utilization and under utilization of the equipments.

4.8 COMPUTER CONFERENCING

Computer-based meeting involving exchange of voice and pictures between two individuals or groups using special software in a networked environment. The advantages and disadvantages of computer conferencing as under:

Advantages

- Reduce time and resource requirements. Trainers increased control over the training. It is improve the job performance, It is important for a user to choose the configuration according to their needs and conditions.
- It is capable of evolving unique instructional strategy for each educational tasks, It participating in the various programmes, i.e. bulletin boards e-groups, mailing lists, real time chat and e-mail.

Disadvantages

- It needs cost of production and investment more. Danger of over utilization and under utilization of the equipments.

4.9 COMPUTER-BASED TRAINING (CBT)

As development of technologies proceeds at a rapid pace and the cost of computers continuous to decline high-technology training methods are finding increasing use in industry, academia, and the military. Computer-based Training encompasses two distinct techniques computer assisted instruction (CAI) and computer managerial instruction (CMI). The advantages and disadvantages of computer-based training as under:

Advantages

- Computer-based training enables learners to study at a time of their own choice. It enables learners to study at their own pace. It can offer a high level of interaction with immediate feedback.
- It provides opportunity for learners to check their understanding. It can be made available at different locations and offer privacy. It is versatile when it comes to on-screen display of information. It can keep student records automatically. It can be cost-effective, depending on the circumstances.

- It is a valuable vehicle for learning technical skills, particularly where large number of persons is to be trained. It is user choice of control and routing through the programme. That makes the medium sophisticated training tool.

Disadvantages

- It is relatively inflexible, depending on a pre-produced programme, It requires a grater self-discipline and commitment by the learner, since there is no trainer or peer group present to ensure participation.
- It may induce a sense of isolation, as individuals work on their own, it does not permit direct personal reinforcement, and hence the motivational effects of training are forgone. It can prove costly, as expensive hardware and software are required.

4.10 COMPUTER-BASED MULTIMEDIA (CBM)

Computer-based Multimedia is one of the fastest growing and most exciting areas in the information technology field. In addition to providing a method for users to interact with the project most authoring tools also offer facilities for creating and editing text and images, and they have extensions to drive video disc players, video tape players, and other relevant hard ware peripherals. The advantages and disadvantages of computer-based multimedia are:

Advantages

- It is widely used in the entertainment and education fields. It efforts range from simple slide shows to dazzling, breathtaking awe-inspiring and interactive presentation. It is easier to make a presentation on the computer and it does not need any special skills.
- It provides very quickly presentation The CBM integrates voice, video and computer technologies in to single delivery system. It referred to a room having slide projectors, tape decks and movie projectors.
- It presentations are more effective than an ordinary presentation using charts and white boards. Multimedia is being used in movie making very extensively and Interaction is more advantage of multimedia.

Disadvantages

- It requires more technical support from the software personnel, and it is more complex in the software programmes.

- When students are creating or using multimedia (interactive) they are not conforming to the traditional factory model.

4.11 COMPUTER ASSISTED INSTRUCTION (CAI)

Uses the computer as a self-contained teaching machine to present individual lessons. The advantages and disadvantages as under:

Advantages

- Computer assisted instruction (CAI) is relatively easy and inexpensive to produce. The CAI produces clear and demonstrable results. Individual students can learn at their own pace through CAI.
- CAI provides to teachers can spend their time working one-on-one with students. An important activity that is almost impossible in typical presentation and discussion classrooms.
- CAI can turn practice in to an entertaining game it motivates students to practice arithmetic, spelling, touch typing, piano playing and other skills that might otherwise be tedious to learn.
- CAI can help timid children become comfortable with computers as well as with the subject matter being taught. A well-designed programme is infinitely patient, and it allows students to make mistakes in private.

Disadvantages

- Not all computer assisted instruction [CAI] software deserves praise. CAI software is flawed because it gives in appropriate feedback, allows a student to practice mistakes.
- CAI discourages students to moving in to new material. CAI can work only with tightly defined subjects, in whom every question cab has a single, clear, unambiguous answer.
- CAI presents information in the form of facts, leaving no room for questioning, creativity or cooperation. Computer networks are costly to develop.

4.12 COMPUTER-MANAGED INSTRUCTION

Uses the computer to organize instruction to track student records and progress. The instruction itself need not be delivered via computer, although CAI is often combined with CMI. The advantages and disadvantages as under:

Advantages

- The computer managed instructions (CMI) helps to administer testing, record keeping etc. The CMI gives the tests and grades to the student regarding the results.
- The CMI can also store the learners responses for the training management team to use this feedback for evaluation and analysis purpose.

Disadvantages

- No need of this programme for higher category of students. A lot of students are not paying interest on this programme, and It is relevant concepts are not enrolled

4.13 EDUSAT

On the fourth of September 2004 the Indian Space Research Organization (ISRO) launched the world's first satellite dedicated to education the EDUSAT. This was a long awaited solution to improve connectivity across the nation for the spread of distance learning. Tele-education is an important step towards improving education standards. And with a dedicated satellite many remote learning initiatives have suddenly sprung up. The advantages and disadvantages as under:

Advantages

- EDUSAT a long awaited solution to improve connectivity across the nation for the spread of distance learning. A satellite has always been known for its very high uptime, reliability, commonality of services, bandwidth sharing, superior network monitoring and troubleshooting services.
- VSAT solutions to take advantage of broadband connectivity at cost effective rates are compared to alternate technologies. VSATs will always be commercially viable for man-to-man applications like corporate training, distance learning, telemedicine and digital cinema.

Disadvantages

- EDUSAT is inadequate availability.

4.14 MANAGEMENT INFORMATION SYSTEM

Management Information System (MIS) may be described as an information system that provides information in the form of standardized reports and displays to managers. MIS is a broad class of information systems that are designed to provide information needed for effective decision-making by managers. MIS emphasizes the management orientation of information processing in business. A major goal of computer based information systems should be the support of management decision-making, not merely the processing of data generated by business operations. The advantages and disadvantages as under:

Advantages

- Management information system (MIS) provides better land record management will lead to less litigation in courts and consequently reduction in violence in the rural areas. MIS provides more efficient natural resource planning will result in optional utilization of water, oil, electricity, coal, etc. there by reduce inter state tension and rivalry.
- MIS helps to better banking and financial services with excellent services to the customers will ensure more efficient management of money. MIS helps to legal delivery system will help a large number of small farmers, small businessman and the common man by way of speedy delivery of justice.

Disadvantages

- It is executive level process but it is not adequate to the all employees, MIS provides information convenience is bar.

4.15 DATA BASE MANAGEMENT SYSTEM

A database is basically a collection of data stored for a particular application so that is available to user for different purpose. Databases contain organized data. Data is organized in such away that a programme or—user was easily store, modify and retrieve the late a set of programme that enables to store, modify and retrieve information from a database is called database management system. The advantages and disadvantages as under:

Advantages

- The Database Management systems (DBMS) provides support language interface used for the definition and manipulation of the data in the database. The database management system provides data catalogs for description of data in the database. The DBMS provides a mechanism for the management of permanent storage of the data.
- The DBMS provides security mechanism for authorized users are

given access to the data in the database. Recovery mechanisms in a DBMS make sure that the database is returned to a consistent state after a transaction aborts.

- The DBMS provides concurrency management for database management activities, i.e. coordination, manipulation, operation and information access. The DBMS provides the transaction processing services for the database operations.

Disadvantages

- In the database management system transaction processing is flexible, The DBMS depending on the access privileges of the users for protection of the data.
- The DBMS create an environment where the users can do their job without worrying about the physical implementation of language interface.

4.16 DECISION SUPPORT SYSTEM

DSS are interactive computer-based information systems that use decision models and specialized databases to assist the decision-making process of managerial and users. They provide managerial and users with information in an interaction session on an *ad-hoc* basis. A DSS provides analytical modeling, data retrieval, and information presentation capabilities that allow manager to generate the information they need to make more unstructured types of decisions in an interaction computer-based process. The advantages and disadvantages as under:

Advantages

- Decision Support Systems (DSS) are interactive software designed to help managers make decisions. The Decision support system provide managerial and users with information in interactive sessions on *ad-hoc* basis.
- A DSS provides analytically modeling, data retrieval, and information presentation capabilities that allow manager to generate the information they need to make more unstructured types of decisions in an interactive, computer-based process.

Disadvantages

- DSS is taking decisions only and It is not allowing in the all Organisations.

4.17. E-COMMERCE

Two Thousand years ago Roman roads brought trade and commerce to Europe in an unprecedented manner. At the dawn of the second millennium, the Internet is making fundamental changes to the lives of every one on the planet changing forever the way business is conducted. Generally there are three kinds of E-Commerce, business to business, business to customer and using digital middleman. The advantages and disadvantages as under:

Advantages

- E-commerce enables consumers to do transactions 24 hours a day from any place in the world. E-Commerce give more liberty and choice to the consumer such that they can choose product from many vendors.
- The market place of E-commerce expends from local market to international market and hence can locate more customers. E-commerce reduces the cost of processing and distributing expenses to the organizations.
- E-commerce provides facilities like delivery of public services such as on line payment of taxes, commodities, healthcare, online education, etc., reduced cost. E-commerce enables rural people from developing countries to enjoy all the facilities that are available to the advanced counties people.

Disadvantages

- E-Commerce has lack of personal privacy and security to individuals. E-Commerce has technical problems due to insufficient communication bandwidth.
- E-Commerce has software problems. Since the cost of E-Commerce software is very high problems may come because of lack of expertise and may results in abnormal delay.

4.18. BUSINESS ANALYSIS SYSTEMS

Managers need solid data from which to extract the information necessary to make good decisions for the business. In the past, these knowledge workers had to relay on their experience and other personal factors to make decisions. A business analysis system provides data that when used with the proper software helps its users better understand the business environment and make more effective decisions. Corporate users routinely use spreadsheets for analyzing cost and benefits and for creating budgets. The advantages and disadvantages as under:

Advantages

- A business analysis system provides data that, when used with the proper software helps its users better understand the business environment and make more effective decisions.
- A business analysis system provides to corporate users routinely use spreadsheets for analyzing cost and benefits and for creating budgets.

Disadvantages

- It provides analyzing attitudes of business; hence they are not achieving goals.

4.19 ONLINE ANALYTICAL PROCESSING

The term OLAP was coined by E.F. Codd in1993 to refer to a type of application that allows a user to interactively analyze data. An OLAP system is often contrasted to an OLTP (on-line transaction processing) system that focuses on transactions such as orders, invoice, general ledger transitions. The advantages and disadvantages as under:

Advantages

- OLAP increases the productivity of business managers developers, and whole organizations. OLAP applications can become more self-sufficient using by the business people.
- OLAP enables managers to model problems that would be impossible using less flexible systems with lengthly and inconsistent response times. OLAP provides more control and more timely access to strategic information equal more effective decision making.
- OLAP system using for software designed for transaction processing. OLAP reduces the applications backlog still further by making business users self-sufficient enough to build their own models.
- It gains more self-sufficient users without relinquishing control over the integrity of the data. It reduces the query drag and network traffic on transaction systems or the data warehouses.
- OLAP enables the organization as a whole to respond more quickly to market demands.

Disadvantages

- OLAP are dependent on data warehouses and transaction processing systems to refresh their source level data.

4.20 TELEMEDICINE

Telemedicine can help in combating tropical diseases, more so in a country like India with poor public health facilities and geographically isolated rural populations. For countries with limited medical expertise and resource, telecommunications has the potential to provide a solution to some of these problems. Telemedicine services have the potential to improve both the quality of and access to healthcare, regardless of geography. The advantages and disadvantages as under:

Advantages

- The telemedicine have made the life of patients easier and enable them to get high quality medical care irrespective of their physical location.
- Telemedicine is the use of electronic information and communications technologies to provide and support healthcare when distance separates the participants. Telemedicine encompasses all of the health care, education, information and administrative services that can be transmitted from are distances by telecommunications technologies.
- Optional character recognition software can translate printed information into computer generated speech or Braille. Telemedicine could serve as a major motivational factor for computer literacy among doctors. Telemedicine can also ensure optimal utilization by the suburban hospitals.

Disadvantages

- It is cost effective and complex process and it needs two or more number of doctors involvement is necessary.

4.21 COMPUTER AIDED DESIGN

There was not any thing at all interactive about the process. With the introduction of computer-aided design software not only are drawing easier to create and store they are much easier to revise, no small advantage since revisions are the main activity in product design. One of the latest innovations is to automatically convert drawings into VRML files so the designer can fly through the product seeing how the components fit together inside the model. The advantages and disadvantages as under:

Advantages

- Computer aided design (CAD) system allow the designer to view a product from different perspectives. The designer can also make proportional changes in scale or change the angle of an are with the click of a computer mouse rather than having to redraw the entire product.

- ❖ CAD system can store the design characteristics of existing products and components. The CAD system determines whether the company is already using an identical of sufficiently similar gear, in which case a new one is unnecessary.
- ❖ One of the most time consuming aspects of design for highly technical products is calculating whether or not product specifications such as strength heat resistance or aerodynamic drag are satisfied. The CAD system reduce the development time and cost.

Disadvantages

- ❖ The CAD system is not used by large automotive and electronic compromise alone.

4.22 COMPUTER AIDED MANUFACTURING (CAM)

It refers to industries automation using computer controlled machines and processes. Some CAM software can take a CAD drawing and create the code for programming a Computer Numerical Control (CNC) machine such as a laser or lathe. Drawing can be used to programme robots the much more versatile machines that are used to assemble. Weld and paint products. The advantages and disadvantages as under:

Advantages

- ❖ Computer Aided Manufacturing (CAM) provides increased effeminacy through work simplification and automation, better production schedule planning and better balancing of production workload to production capacity.
- ❖ CAM can reduce investment in production inventories facilities through work simplification, just-in-time inventory policies, and better planning and control of production and finished goods requirements.
- ❖ CAM can improved utilization of production facilities, higher productivity, and better quality control resulting from continuous monitoring, feedback and control of factory operations, equipment.
- ❖ CAM can improve customer sacrifice by drastically reducing out-of stock situations and producing high quality products that better meet customer requirements.

Disadvantages

- ❖ The CAM systems are not used by large automotive and electronic compromise alone.

4.23 PERSONAL SOFTWARE PROCESS

PSP is an individual level model that helps individual engineers to plan their work, estimate the size, defects, effort and schedule to plan their work and track these while working. According to SEY early experience with the PSP have shown that average test defects rates improve by ten times, and average productivity goes up by 25 percent or more. The advantages and disadvantages as under:

Advantages

- Personnel Software process (PSP) provides better quality of programming. Personnel Software process helps in on-track costs and schedules. PSP reduced cycle times.
- PSP increased productivity and security. PSP provided software engineers with the means to harness their potential to the maximum.

Disadvantages

- Personal software process is only for developing human resources and It is not using for designing and manufacturing.

4.24 E-CONTRACTS (E-LEGAL SERVICE)

The ease and flexibility of communicating across electronic networks allows users to enter into agreements with each other with little, it at all any, difficulty, infact all commercial offerings on the internet could do well to make contract on the internet The proposed contract should be conspicuously displayed and available on the website of the seller company. The seller or distribute goods or services through their websites. Should include draft e-contract to which potential customers must give their unconditional assent. The advantages and disadvantages as under:

Advantages

- E-contracting is a cost effective method of conducting business. E Contracting is that is extremely time-effective. E-Contracting process is also safe since there is no exchange of cash or cheques, and all payments are transmitted electronically.
- Storing documents relating to e-contracts through floppy discs, CD-ROMs is much easier then the conventional paper agreements.

Disadvantages

- E-Contract cans the identity and capacity of all parties to the contract need to be verified beyond doubt.

- The lack of conventional signature on e-contracts exposes the e-contracts to being tampered or repudiated by parties with malaside intentions.
- Lack of appropriate legislations in various countries make e-contracts prone to greater disputes.
- The concept of e-Contracts is relatively new and therefore open to subjective interpretation. E-contracts can it is often physically impossible to store electronic data relating to or evidencing the contract in a manner that prevents alteration.

4.25 HI-TECH TEACHING

It is process of the teaching through the computer and it provides facility of integrated their faculty with other faculties. The advantages and disadvantages as under:

Advantages

- Hi-Tech teaching is learner centered teaching and learning. Hi-tech teaching can adopts new methods of memory management configured in the lines of human brains information processing and learners cognitive styles.
- Hi-tech teaching helps making the students to slowly accustom and interact with computer aided instruction and simulation materials.
- Hi-Tech teaching provides pathfinder for knowledge utility. Hi-Tech teaching selection of students through interests ability and aptitude. Hi-Tech teaching can provide role of the teachers as director, coach and facilitator.
- Teacher should become a software developer for media instruction through Hi-tech teaching. Hi-Tech teaching should create Multi-media instruction.
- Hi-Tech teaching provides teacher taught interaction feedback and control are achieved through mediate interaction using televideo computer conferencing by virtual tale presence of a teacher.
- Hi-Tech teaching provides integrating their faculty with other faculties.
- Hi-Tech teaching can attract international students by making them to understand that quality technical education can be obtained in India at an affordable cost in comparison with other developed countries where the fee can reduce burden on Indian students.
- Hi-Tech teaching provides to act as a coordinator for resource sharing between institutions, R&D organizations & Industries. Hi-Tech teaching provides evaluation of the candidate for a holistic development to achieve large social objectives.
- Hi-Tech teaching can proactive strategic planning to be in tune with the global revolution of IT to produce well rounded persons

with overall development who can be assets to an organized society.

- ❖ From literature survey to active research in dynamically assimilating the fast explosion of knowledge in to teaching methodology using interest through Hi-Tech teaching.

Disadvantages

- ❖ Hi-tech teaching is not teacher centric method. Hence the students neglect teachers.

4.26. VIDEO-BASED TRAINING FOR FARMERS

The emphasis on farmers training continued with the launching of new agricultural strategies during 1960s, beginning with the Intensive Agricultural District Programme (IADP) Farmers Training Centers (FTC s) Block Level Training Programs and later farmers training by the State Agricultural Universities (SAU s), were involved in disseminating messages on new agricultural technologies. A new turn was given to farmers training with the launching of Krishi Vignan Kendras (KVKs) with emphasis on need based skill training.

Advantages

- ❖ Information technology can be used to deliver real time information and customized knowledge to improve farmers decision-making abilities. The Internet provides informing farmers about the current rates of major crops at the local and other recognized auction centres around India.
- ❖ The Internet helps in making copies of land records available. Online registration and down loading of application forms for obtaining income/caste/domicile certificates. Online filing of public grievances. Auction facilities for farmers and villagers for land, agricultural machinery, equipment and other durable commodities via Internet.

4.27. IMPACT ON STUDENTS

The students use the different forms of information technology for developing their human resources. These programmes are e-learning, e-mail, Internet, mobile phone, geographic information system, videoconferencing, teleconferencing, computer conferencing, and computer-based training, computer-based multimedia, computer assisted instruction, computer managed instruction and EDUSAT. Impacts of information technology on students are described as under:

Positive Impact

- Students can network with kids in other parts of the world through the Internet. Students can high school correspondence courses can be completed by modern rather than by mail. Handicapped students can do course work without traveling to central sites. Two-way video links allow visiting experts to talk to students in outlying classrooms and answer their questions in real time. Networked school districts can offer multi school videoconference courses at college level. Students can obtain on line reference materials on web pages; special interest sent news groups and minded modern pals from Internet.
- Information technology enables the students to access large amount of information and knowledge on various subjects and to develop an analytical mind and critical thinking. A computer is a multimedia tool with integrated graphic, print, audio and video capabilities. Computers increase accessibility by local, regional and national networks linked to resources and individuals. Learner could do self-paced learning, which allows slow learners to come at par with others.
- Multimedia technology can make Computer-based Training a pleasant experience. The computer-based assessment can rule out the possibility of any subjectivity in assessment techniques and The computer-based assessment is on line process, the current problem bagging many institutions of delayed exam results can be completely removed.
- One can obtain vast Knowledge through the E-learning programme. E-learning is gives up-to-date information to develop the knowledge and skills. E-mail provides easy communication to the students and saves time.
- Internet provides worldwide information. Hence, one can obtain new concepts in the world and know present attitudes in the society or nation. Chatting through internet is gives capability and knowledge to the students. Internet provides employment opportunities. Hence more people are trying to utilise this programme and it is one of the big source.
- Mobile phone helps to save money as one can get new without cost, and up-to date location identified through mobile phone. So, relevant person where he was called, i.e. known easily through caller identity.
- Different sites are giving different programme details. So, it provides to the students good knowledge and innovative concepts. Internet is essential programme to the students. Because, it gives up to date information in entire the world. So this information is used in Competitive Examinations for getting good results.

- Down load the educational material through the Internet. So money saves to the students, i.e. Internet used cost was Rs. 10 per hour. But which material got it that cost was more then Rs. 10. Therefore, Internet is provides the money saves.
- Video conferencing gives picture and voice to the students. Therefore, it is easily to find out persons emotional feelings for understanding. Computer-based training gives good tool for the students. Because CBT is very useful for developing human resources in the educational field.
- Computer assisted instruction makes individual learning possible. Therefore, there is no for need instruction/teaching of the teacher. Computer managed instruction provides the grades and ranks of the students on the basis of their skills. Hence one can easily find out the mental ability of student. EDUSAT is a innovative programme, it is very successful tool for students in education field, because, it provides students with awareness concepts through with this programme.

Negative Impact

- Not all computer assisted instruction [CAI] software deserves praise. Computer networks are costly to develop. The technology is changing too rapidly. Widespread computer illiteracy still exists. Computer assisted instruction programme do not give broad subjects/contents to the students.
- Students must be highly motivated and proficient in computer operation before they can successfully function in a computer-based distance learning environment Computer-based training is costly therefore, students do no have interest towards this programme.
- Internet gives vulgar cooperation to the students and this makes it difficult for to reach good career.
- Geographic information system is very expensive. So some students do not utilize this programme. GIS gives advance information about the earth quack environment. Therefore, the students are feel inferiority.
- Mobile phone has hearing/voice problem and therefore students are used the mobile phone with in limit. Mobile phone facilitates a lot of money consumption.
- Proper learning is needed for EDUSAT. If there is no proper training the students will face educational inconvenience and it would result in unnecessarily waste of time.

4.28 IMPACT ON EMPLOYEES

The employees use different forms of information technology for developing their human resources. These programmes are e-learning, e-mail, Internet, mobile phone, geographic information system, videoconferencing, teleconferencing, computer conferencing, computer based training, computer-based multimedia, management information system, database management system and decision support system. An impact of information technology on employees is described as under:

Positive Impact

- Network educational institution provided by MIS enables better sharing of resources among large population and the consequent increased access to education for much larger number of aspiring employees. Management Information System helps employees in their operations and Management information system provides to the manager in the organization, they are taken information to their employees.
- The Database Management systems (DBMS) provides support language interface used for the definition and manipulation of the data in the database. The database management system provides data catalogs for description of data in the database. Redundancy can be reduced, Inconsistency can be avoided, data can be shared, Security restrictions can be applied Integrity, and conflicting requirements can be balanced through database. Database management system gives data about employees. It also gives entire data about the organization.
- Executive information system (EIS) is easy to operate and understand, provides graphic displays which are used extensively, immediate access to internal and external database is provided. EIS provides information about the current status and projected trends for key factors selected by top executives.
- Employers are getting new organization operations through E-learning. Therefore, organizational efficiency increases with this programme. Employees mostly use computers for easy administration.
- E-mail gives classical and broad information getting with desk top typing is very sufficient to the employees. It provides storage facility the concerned site addresses.
- Employees getting new ideas for training and development through the internet in duty perspective. Computers are most important tool in the organizational scenario. Because, Managers use computers for their decision/operations.
- Mobile phones are highly utilized by the employees because communication of duties and responsibilities through mobile phones take short span of time.
- Employees are mostly using videoconference for their job orientation so, they acquire new knowledge, communication

process. Teleconferencing is more useful to the employees because training and pictorials are done through this programme. Computer conferencing is widely used by the employees for operations hence they reduce the handwork.

- Computer-based training helps in employee training for developing their skills and manpower of the employees. CBT is important tool for developing human resources. Hence employees get promotions after completion of CBT. Computer-based multimedia provides to the employees regenerating pictures, chats and graphs.
- Decision support system is used for employee decisions. Hence result oriented decision can be taken by the manager in the organization for achievement of goals. Managers take decisions through decision support system in the organization.

Negative Impact

- E-learning is not an effective and efficient programme for employee at organizational level, because they have no time for learning. Organisational cooperation is must, but it depends on the top management.
- Computer-based multimedia is a very complex procedure. Computer-based training can prove costly as expensive hardware and software are required.
- Teleconferencing leads to skill requirement, it requires skilled persons with sound knowledge in instructional and educational design as well as computer operations which is always a constrain in India.
- Communication barriers are involved with mobile phone. Literacy is necessary for operation to internet. In the database management system transaction processing is flexible.

4.29 IMPACT ON BUSINESS PEOPLE

The business people utilize the different forms of information technology for developing their human resources these programmes are e-learning, e-mail, Internet, mobile phone, geographic information system, videoconferencing, teleconferencing, computer conferencing, computer based training, computer based multimedia, e-commerce, business analysis systems and online analytical programme. An impact of information technology on business people is described as under:

Positive Impact

- Marketing on the internet may be cheaper and can reach a wider crowd than the normal marketing medium. Increase in customer volume do not need an increase in staff as the sales function is housed in the computer and has virtually unlimited accessibility.

- On line ordering can be automated with checks to ensure that orders are correct before accepting, thus reducing errors and the cost of correcting them. The Website is accessible 24 hours a day, 7 days in a week and reaches a global audience. This is not possible in traditional store front. As customers refer to the website for basic queries the number of customers support staff can be reduced, thus reducing the cost.
- With product information, frequently-asked questions and trouble-shooting information online customers can access them whenever they want without the hassle of phone calls and waiting to get transferred to the correct personnel. Through the internet companies can establish a direct link to customers and critical suppliers of distributors to complete transactions or communicate trade information more easily.
- Companies can use internet to develop and deliver new products and services for new customers. A company could convincingly use the internet to become the dominant player in the electronic channel of a specified industry or segment, by controlling access to customers and setting new business rules.
- Text management systems helps for tasks like writing memos, notes or documents, forms, reports and invoices retrieving and editing etc. Ability to sell and purchase products/services through computer networks. Information technology helps for office automation and quick business transactions.
- Information technology is a tool to improve internal business communication through easy and accurate interaction and information interchange. Information technology can be used in many ways to connect an organization with others, and it leads to higher level of cooperation and ultimately gives a competitive advantage. Information technology when used as a medium for marketing provides two way communications unlike most mass media. Information technology is the immediate acknowledgement and the case of targeting a particular audience.
- An increasing number of customers and potential markets are using and have access to the new digital media. Visual impact immediacy and a lower cost of mass distribution to a targeted audience are the tangible advantage of technology driven media.
- Enterprise resource planning (ERP) to give radio a cutting edge tool that could enable higher productivity and enable faster and more accurate decision-making. Enterprise resource planning system brings in transparency of operations where all data is available on a real time basis. ERP is universality of its applications and the information technology total cost of ownership for solution management. ERP is not a magic that provides a solution for all the

problems in the organization. It is a powerful tool. The ERP solution ensures better under-standing of our needs and faster implementation, resulting in a quicker return on investment.

- Using computerized marketing information system undesirable cost trends are spotted more quickly and corrective action may be taken sooner with the help of more timely computerized reports.
- Executives can ask supplementary questions through computer to help pinpoint reasons for a sales decline and reach an action decision more quickly by the use of flexible on-line retrieval of data by computers. Computer automatically repurchases standard items on the basis of correlation of sales data with programmed decision rules.
- Business people use the E-learning programme and develop their human skills and capability. E-learning provides business sites in the computer desktop. These programmes are very effective to the business people, but they do not need teachers for E-learning programme. Business people are trying to learn the marketing methods through the E-learning programme. Hence, business is to achieve the goals and obtain maximum profits.
- E-mail is effective tool and efficiently used by the business people. Therefore, they feel happy with e-mail programme. It provides the entire information stored in the computer. Whenever they need this information stored in the computer. Whenever, they need this information getting through the particular E-mail addresses. Hence they do not need and writing works.
- Internet helps business people in the business operations. Hence, they are satisfied with this regard the business people highly use the Internet. Marketing activities through internet is very easy. They communicate with others in short time only. Different marketing and production opportunities can be found out through internet, hence, the Business people initiate innovative ideas for developing their business activities and increase their business profits.
- Geographic information system provides to the Business people, about weather and earth particulars. Therefore, Business people can arrange their plans for business activities.
- Video conferencing programme is very effective tool for the Business people. Hence, the business people utilize this programme for easily identifying the product particulars, i.e. size of the product, color of the product, rate of the product, design of the product, effectiveness of the product and packaging of the product. After that the business people make decisions for sale/ purchase.

Negative Impact

- A big short coming of using the technology medium to market is that it can be easily copied. Digital marketing has a limited reach in a country like India. In the interiors and smaller cities of the country marketers still have to fall back upon traditional media. Low quality of communication because of slow connectivity from the users end.

- E-Learning is limited access in and is based on availability of hardware, software connection. E-mail is the distraction and can prevent people from doing any productive work.
- Geographic information system is costly procedure. Hence most of the business people do not pay interest with this regard.
- Video conferencing is lack of availability. So then do not need that it. Teleconferencing is danger of over utilization. Hence the business people are followed with strict process. Computer conferencing results in high cost of production. Therefore the business people do not pay interest to this.
- Computer-based training may induce a sense of isolation as individual work on their own. Computer-based multimedia requires more technical support from the business people. Hence some of the business people arrange this and some of them do not arrange it.
- E-commerce provides lack of personal privacy. Hence the business people are not involved highly in this process. Because, they are concerned about privacy.
- Online analytical processing system depends on data warehouses. Hence business people must first need data warehouses.

4.30. IMPACT ON DOCTORS

The Doctors utilize the different forms information technology for developing their human resources. these programmes are e-learning, e-mail, Internet, mobile phone, geographic information system, videoconferencing, teleconferencing, computer conferencing, computer-based training, computer-based multimedia, telemedicine. An impact of information technology on doctors is described as under:

Positive Impact

- Computers are used for everything from diagnosing illnesses and monitoring patients to controlling movements of robotic surgical assistants. The doctors are obtaining information about the patient, patient history, and the treatment details from the computers. The doctors use computers for the hospital management system.
- The electronic patient records over the paper counterparts is that the electronic documents can be searched for specific key words, can be sent via e-mail to other doctors for second opinions can be stored and retrieved more effectively and so on.

- The computerized systems automate the billing and other administrative processes, thus freeing the doctors and medical staff so that they can spend more time on practicing medicine. The digital and imaging technology have helped in better diagnosis as the images and output produced by the latest equipments are capable of delivering more information.
- The field of biomedical engineering results in the development of laboratory and medical equipments those are better and more accurate. The computer transforms sound into electronic impulses, which are then transmitted to the brain by a device implanted in the inner ear. The teary computers are proving to be valuable diagnostic tools.
- The doctors use magnetic resonance imaging for scanning a patient's body. A computer assembles the information into picture that shows internal organs and diseased tissue. The computers are used in hospitals for automated imaging techniques which produce a fully dimensional picture with much more detail and less risk than the standard x-ray films. Doctors can look in side a person's body and study each organ in detail through the magnetic resonance imaging.
- Videoconferencing involves the patients, along with their healthcare provider and telemedicine coordinator at the rural site interacting with the tele consultant at a metropolitan center. Videoconferencing is used for transferring digital images from one place to another place. Videoconferencing technology plays a sophisticated role in physician training and the dissemination of advanced practices. Videoconferencing involved in healthcare programs enables expert physicians to share advanced knowledge and techniques with counterpart around the country and across the world. Video conferencing technology is playing crucial role in the medicine. Hence the Doctors interact with patients, and they give suggestion or advice to the rural people in the short span of time.
- Local doctors could manage the case only because of timely instruction from specialists via the poly con office solutions.
- The virtue of telemedicine lies not just in diagnosis but in on early diagnosis, without which a case could take fatal turn. Telemedicine can help in combating tropical diseases, more so in a country like India with poor public health facilities and geographically isolated rural populations. Telemedicine services have the potential to improve both the quality of and access to healthcare, regardless of geography.
- Telemedicine is not a great money-spinner, but it is a great way of reaching out to the masses. Telemedicine network gave consultation opportunities to the patient in remote areas. Telemedicine encompasses all the health care, education information and administration services that can be transmitted

from distance by telecommunications technologies. The telemedicine has made the life of patients easier and enable them to get high quality medical care irrespective of their physical location.

- ❖ E-Learning provides very vast knowledge available on numerous topics- something for everyone. Hence the doctors are trying to get knowledge through it and they are paying more interest for his programme.
- ❖ Global communication became easier through E-mail programme. Hence it is interactive with others and shares the knowledge and skills from others through it. Internet eliminates distance between the people. So the doctors at any time, and any where can be connected with other doctors/colleagues to take the medical advice and medical suggestions.
- ❖ Mobile phone helps in the patients relationship for the mutual communication.
- ❖ Teleconferencing improves the learning of doctors in specific skills for medical performance. Computer conferencing programme is to improve the doctor profession performance. So they increase their interest on patients.
- ❖ Computer-based training provide different locations and offer privacy. So the doctors increase their locality environment. Computer-based multimedia is widely used and is enjoyed.

Negative Impact

- ❖ The doctors opined that it is very difficult to diagnose from positron emission tomography. There is a lot of pressure or stress on human eyes at the time of computer operations and Backbone pain and also high strain.
- ❖ Effect of the radiation on legs and other human parts. Repetitive strain injury from the high used computers.
- ❖ Internet leads to isolation tendencies. And Mobile phones are leading to ear problem and health problems. Geographic system is not possible to access by more people.
- ❖ Teleconferencing lacks familiarity and Computer conferencing are over utilized by the doctors and they are dangerous. Hence they have interest ordered.

4.31 IMPACT ON ENGINEERS

The Engineers utilized the different information technology for developing their human resources. These programmes are e-learning, e-mail, Internet, mobile phone, geographic information system, videoconferencing, teleconferencing, computer conferencing, computer-based training, computer-based multimedia, Computer-aided design, computer aided manufacturing and personal software process. Impacts of the information technology on Engineers are described as under:

Positive Impact

- The electronic data interchange offers the computer-to computer exchange of business documents in a standard format.
- One of the time consuming aspects of design for highly technical products is calculating whether the product specifications such as strength heat resistance or aerodynamic drag are satisfied or not.
- Personnel Software process (PSP) provides better quality of programming. Personnel Software process helps in on-track costs and schedules. PSP reduces cycle times. PSP increases productivity and security. PSP provided software engineers with the means to harness their potential to the maximum.
- Electronic Data Interchange (EDI) provides a standardized method for proper trade transactions so that they can be communicated directly from one computer system to another system without the need for printed order and invoices and the delays and errors implicit in paper handling. EDI is extensively used in the large supermarket chains where it is used for transactions with their suppliers. EDI provides information to the customers by straightway giving time for an attractive product to be order or an alternative supplier to be used.
- E- Learning creates a knowledge resource for the nation and any module can be easily shared by only one, anywhere.
- E- Mail is to estimate the data traffic through the Internet which would outstrip the traffic in not-too-distant a future.
- Internet facilitate for visiting websites, send and receive electronic mail, rest and post articles in news groups, down load files to your PC, chat with other user on line.
- Geographic information system helps in the land requisition costs through better analysis.
- Teleconferencing can reduce the cost of training. So the engineers are fed effectively to improve their skills. Teleconferencing provides specialized management systems for tracking trainees progress and location. Computer conferencing programme can reduce time and resource requirements.
- Computer-based training can offer a high level of interaction with immediate feedback. Computer-based multimedia programme, can provide the information very quickly.
- Computer aided design system allow the designer to view a product from different perspectives and it can store the design characteristics of existing products and components.
- Computer aided manufacturing can reduce investment in production inventories facilities through work simplification, just-

in –time inventory policies and better planning and control of production and finished goods requirements. Computer Aided Manufacturing (CAM) provides increased efficiency through work simplification and automation, better production schedule planning and better balancing of production workload to production capacity.

Negative Impact

- Initial investment is needed to the Electronic Data Interchange. Restructuring business process is to fit EDI requirements. Long start up time is required. High EDI operating cost is needed. There are multiple EDI standards. Use of expensive private VAN is necessary; the system is complex to use. There is a need to use a converter to translate business transactions to EDI standards.
- E-learning is a complex process. Hence some of the engineers are not interested on this process. And also E-mail is the individual using the technology that makes communication better or worst.
- Internet gives easy access to adult websites. It will badly effect the engineers and younger people.
- For teleconferencing greater time is needed for preparation of courseware development of instructional packages and requires considerably more time and expertise than an equivalent package required for traditional training.

4.32 IMPACT ON LAWYERS

The Lawyers are utilized the different information technology for developing their human resources these programmes are e-learning, e-mail, Internet, mobile phone, geographic information system, videoconferencing, teleconferencing, computer conferencing, computer-based training, computer-based multimedia and e-legal service. An impact of information technology on Lawyers described as under:

Positive Impact

- The Internet could well become the most important part of a lawyer's practice. Often going through law books, texts, legal reports or judgements is a laborious task. So access to the Internet comes as a great relief to lawyers as they can easily and effectively find the relevant information/counsel through websites, which can be located through such engines like Google, Info space, and Alta Vista.
- The Internet can also provide comprehensive information and authentic materials, which are required by lawyers. The latest judgements, court cases and case laws can be found on the Internet

with various types of options. This helps to save time and effort. So the Internet has a great potential and can be used as an important source of legal reference material.

- The use of computers and the Internet reduces the paperwork of lawyers considerably and enhances their efficiency making them more competent and result oriented. Also a search for relevant materials can be done speedily.
- The strategic use of IT can help build closer client relationships in a number of ways. There is the obvious benefit of being able to provide a faster, more efficient service that responds quickly to the client. But there are additional, value-added possibilities that go much further. To begin with clients themselves are increasingly becoming frequent users of technology. So they expect to deal with their legal advisers in the same way as they deal with other service suppliers-through e-mail, secure online access and even text messaging.
- Legal firms need to plan and deliver traditional services to their clients in the clients preferred format. Examples of such services include the provision of online instructions, financial billing and case progress reports. Beside these there are opportunities to deliver services in new ways and to make relevant use of collaborative working tools, secure information sharing and ultimately re-use of firms knowledge to add value to client solutions.
- A lawyer has to be well versed and prudent in his practice. It is essential that he knows the latest changes in legal matters and thus updating his knowledge is a must. The Internet can play a crucial role as far as obtaining the latest information is concerned. There are several sites on the Internet, which provide updated information in the legal field, particularly the latest information about changes or amendments of laws.
- To ensure the survival and retention of a law practice's knowledge or intellectual capital, an IT system support is crucial in order to Collect, Organise and Exploit legal information. In this way information can be held centrally and made readily available, so that the practice is well protected. Such an approach typically involves a knowledge management system that captures information, organizes it in a structured way and is easy to use while searching or navigating.
- The Internet has created what may in fact be the biggest advent in communications. The invention of electronic mail E-mail has revolutionized the way we as a society communicate, especially the way corporate America communicates. The legal community has embraced e-mail as an efficient tool for both internal and external communication. The internet has defined a common communication interface for firms as well. The popularity of web

browsers and the advent of defined standard communications have made it easier to organize and consolidate internal and external communications.

- The internet has penetrated into a lot of countries that were formerly inaccessible. This connectivity has given rise to E-contracting with people and businessman in the remotest of areas creating cross-border transactions.
- E-learning is effective and efficient programme; it is highly utilized by the lawyers. by developing their skills and knowledge. It provides innovative concepts on desktop of computer. Relevancy is not necessary in the E-learning programme so democracy is enrolled through the programme.
- Computer based training provides development programmes. So the programme is improved their skills, Knowledge and will power. Computer-based multimedia is expensive process; it provides innovative audio, video clips for enjoyable service. So, they improve their knowledge and capability
- Video conferencing is huge process and it improves the abilities and skills for their legal profession. Computer conferencing helps to give expressions of legal attitudes in the legal field. Teleconferencing programme provides specialized computer systems. So they are getting new ideas and concepts through this programme, it increase the human resources.

Negative Impact

- In e-Contract the identity and capacity of all parties to the contract need to be verified beyond doubt and lack of conventional signature on e-contracts exposes the e-contracts to being tampered or repudiated by parties with malaside intentions. Lack of appropriate legislations in various countries make e-contracts prone to greater disputes.
- In E-contracts it is often physically impossible to store electronic data relating to or evidencing the contract in a manner that prevents alteration and Information Technology Act, 2000 not mentioned the term e-contract in its text or Act.
- Mobile phones are increasing the conflict between the people because, wrong number connection is normal.
- Computer conferencing is very expensive as well as teleconferencing and Computer Board Training Programme is complex process. Hence no interest.

4.33 IMPACT ON TEACHERS

The teachers utilize the different information technology for developing their human resources. These programmes are e-learning, e-mail, Internet, mobile phone, geographic information system, videoconferencing, teleconferencing, computer conferencing, computer-based training, computer-based multimedia, hi-tech teaching. Impacts of information technology on teachers are described as under:

Positive Impact

- In the computer technology the material can be customized to meet the needs of the class. Instead of using commercial transparencies and handouts designed for generic classrooms, a teacher can create custom visual aids for specific classes, Instead of being forced to move through videotapes and audio cassettes sequentially. Teachers may become more like guides and mentors along a learning path, its provides the multimedia.
- Multimedia is a sensitive and highly politicized subject among educators, so educational software is often positioned as enriching the learning process. Multimedia can be maximized along term benefit to the teachers.
- Hi-Tech teaching can provide role of the teachers as director, coach and facilitator. Teacher should become a software developer for media instruction through Hi-tech teaching. Hi-Tech teaching should create Multi-media instruction. Hi-Tech teaching provides teacher taught interaction feedback and control is achieved through mediate interaction using televideo computer conferencing by virtual tale presence of a teacher. Hi-Tech teaching provides integrating their faculty with other faculties.
- Hi-Tech teaching can attract international students by making them to understand the quality of technical education that can be obtained in India at an affordable cost in comparison with other developed countries where by the fee burden on Indian students can be reduced. Hi-Tech teaching act as a coordinator for resource sharing between institutions, R&D organizations & Industries.
- Hi-Tech teaching provides evaluation of the candidate for a holistic development to achieve large social objectives. Hi-Tech teachings can proactive strategic planning to be in tune with the global revolution of IT and to produce well rounded persons with overall development who can be assets to an organized society.
- From literature survey to active research in dynamically assimilating the fast explosion of knowledge in to teaching methodology using interest through Hi-Tech teaching.
- Teachers mostly use the E-learning programme because they obtain new teaching concepts and new ideas of teaching through the said programme. The teachers encourage or cooperate to the students to learn the E-learning programme because, reduce their teaching work broadly. E-learning is giving new teaching material and recent information. Hence, the teachers develop their human

resources with this effect. According to the E-learning programme the teacher give the teaching to the students with obtained information through the said programme.

- The teachers utilize the e-mail for easy commutative with others. The teachers store the matters in computer pages. Hence, whenever they need that information the teachers utilize the storage facility through the E-mail.
- Internets give the new material and join the information, so that teachers can improve their teaching attitude and it explains to the students for developing knowledge and skills.
- Teachers are highly utilizing the mobile phone. So they are interacting with students for sharing their knowledge and skills.
- Teleconferencing programme provide consistency of training in terms of quality and quantity of information presented.
- Computer-based training is versatile when it comes to on screen displays of information. Computer-based training can keep student records automatically.
- Hi-tech teaching provides integrating their faculty with other faculties. Hi-tech teaching can proactive strategic planning to be in time with the global evolution of information technology to produce well rounded persons with overall development who can be assets to an organized society.

Negative Impact

- If the Students obtain the E-learning programme, the teachers are not required by the students. Because the students get the information through the E-learning. So they do not need the teacher to teach the class. Importance of the teacher is reduced with effect of the E-learning programme. Teachers must use innovative methods for teaching so that E-Learning becomes an enjoyable experience that sustains the interest and concentration of students.
- Internet need telephone line is must, perhaps no telephone connection not get internet facility.
- Teleconferencing can lack of familiarity of the users with the medium and equipments it requires additional time and resources for training users in understanding the medium and using the equipment.
- Computer -based training does not permit motivational effects of training are forgone. And Computer based multimedia is more complex in the software programme.

4.34 IMPACT ON RURAL PEOPLE

The rural people utilize the different information technology for developing their human resources. These programmes are e-learning, e-mail, Internet, mobile phone, geographic information system, videoconferencing, teleconferencing, computer conferencing, and computer-based training, computer-based multimedia, video-based training for farmers. An impact of information technology on rural people is described as under:

Positive Impact

- Rural people utilize the E-learning programme because the are human and skills are developing through said programme. E-Learning provides innovative educational packages to the educated people at rural areas so they need not travel from one place to other place.
- Rural people utilize the e-mail for getting quick communication with other colleagues.
- Rural people obtain different awareness programmes though the Internet. So they are obtaining new knowledge scenarios in the world. Internet provides to the rural people, i.e. employment opportunities and other job information. Hence they do not need paper work and postal changes. Rural people get the Agricultural information and agricultural recent methods in the cultivation through the internet. Internet provides to the rural people, i.e. electronic service, (payment of electricity bills, payment of house taxes, and payment of land tax assaults). Hence the rural people need not pay the traveling expenditure.
- Rural people feel good responding to the mobile phone. Because, they have no land phone facility hence they are known good communication with together. Rural people are obtaining the operation of mobile phone. So they increase the skill through the mobile phone.
- Geographic Information System provides to the rural people about geographical situations through the computer. Hence, they are obtaining the cultivation production stage and growth timings and seasonal categories.
- Some rural people by video based training are given positive impact regarding programme, i.e. information getting through the said programme. It gives pictorial communication are added advantage. Hence they are easily identified and collect process of new trends in cultivation. Video based training is giving good awareness to the rural people through the operation of completed video conference.
- Computer-based training is excellent method for Rural people because they obtain knowledge through the CBT.
- Information technology can be used to deliver real time information and customized knowledge to improve farmers decision-making abilities.

- The Internet keeps informing farmers about the current rates of major crops at the local and other recognized auction centers around India. The Internet helps in making copies of land records available. Auction facilities for farmers and villagers for land, agricultural machinery, equipment and other durable commodities via Internet.
- Online registration and down loading of application forms for obtaining income/caste/domicile certificates and online filing of public grievances.

Negative Impact

- Lack of facility i.e. current problems, adequate computer centers is not available at rural areas. Hence they are not paying interest for I.T. programmes.
- A Conferencing programme through information technology is not given sufficient knowledge, capability of any skill because they have no teaching facility regarding the conferencing (like video and computer).
- Almost daytime the rural people are spending the time in the agricultural field. So they have no time about learning for Information Technology Programmes.
- Some of the people gave negative opinion on internet because, they student of rural people are obtaining antisocial activities vulgar pictures on the internet, unnecessary time wastage through the internet, making friendship with unknown persons, playing games through the internet in the important situations.
- A video based training programme is not used by almost of all the rural people. Because, some are illiterate, some blind people, some deaf people. Therefore, this programme gives bad opinion to the rural people.

5

Perceptions of Respondents

'Visakhapatnam' the city of destiny is jewel on the east coast of India. It has a population of about 1.7 million. The location of the India's largest colossal integrated Steel Plant, Eastern Naval Command, Natural Port Trust, Hindustan Zinc Limited, Hindustan Shipyard Limited, etc. A panoramic view of the Bay of Bengal and a bird's eye view of the city can be had from the Dolphin's Nose, which is 56 meters above sea level. The city gained strategic importance with the location of the Eastern Naval Command.

Apart from Visakhapatnam city, the district has rich historical and religious background. Simhachalam, the uphill temple of Lord Narasimha, is located at about 23 km. From Visakhapatnam. The journey up the hill and the surroundings present a memorable experience. Connected to Visakhapatnam is the most picturesque 24 km. Long beach road, a scene enchanting the passers by. The natural setting of the Eastern Ghats and the Bay of Bengal looking at each other is Bhemunipatnam. It is unrivaled for its beauty all along the sea-coast since it is the only palm beach in the State. The Araku valley in Paderu Mandal is located in a beautiful valley of Eastern Ghats. It is 1067 meters above the sea level. It is served by the highest broad gauge railway line in Asia with its exciting journey through a number of tunnels. Borra caves, with a million year's legacy, is situated at a distance of five kilometers from the picturesque Ananthagiri Ghats and 88 kms. from Visakhapatnam on road.

The main intention of behind the selection of the Visakhapatnam for this study, because, it is a host of several large, medium and small enterprises, industries, business establishments, professional organizations, different educational institutions and day-by-day it has been improving and it will change to the stage on a metropolitan and also many IT companies are trying to establish their operations and activities at Visakhapatnam to provide employment and financial support to the residents of the city.

These IT Companies are, HSBC have started their business operations this city, Satyam Computers which has planned to establish their operations in the at heart of the city, Infosis is also has been planned for establish their production and functions at this city. Other companies like IBM, TCS, Reliance famous Call Centre organisations were trying to establish their activities and operations at Visakhapatnam.

This chapter intended to cover the research gap through collecting the perceptions of respondents regarding the Role of Information Technology in developing Human Resources with reference to selected sections of society in Visakhapatnam. These selected sections of society are students, employees, business people, doctors, engineers, lawyers, teachers and rural people, who has been residing at urban sub-urban and rural areas of Visakhapatnam. The following are the perceptions of the above sections of society on the different IT programmes, which were helpful to developing human resources.

RESPONDENTS PERSONAL BACKGROUND

The respondents (from different sections of society) personal background relating to age, sex, native place and education background are shown in the following figures with analysis:

FIGURE 5.1

Distribution of Respondents by their Age

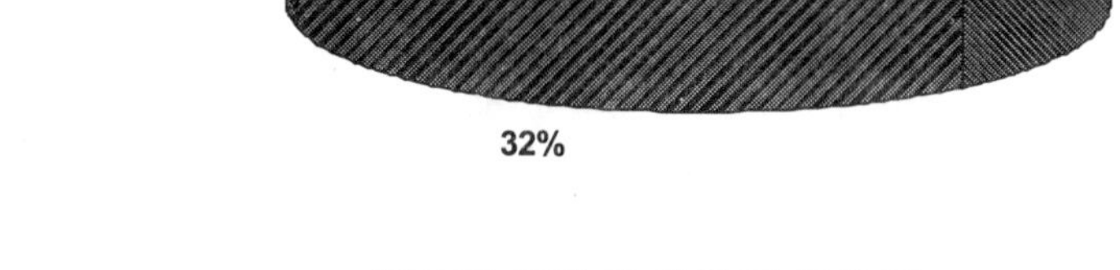

Source : Field Study.

Analysis: The above Figure delineates that distribution of respondents by their age. About 39 percent of the respondents belongs to 21-30 age group, 32 percent of the respondents came under 31-40 age group, while 18 percent of the respondents in the age group of 41-50 and the remaining 11 percent of them belonging to age group 51-60.

FIG. 5.2

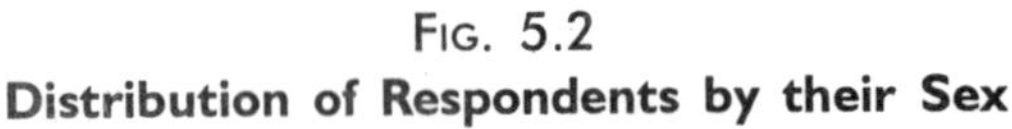

Distribution of Respondents by their Sex

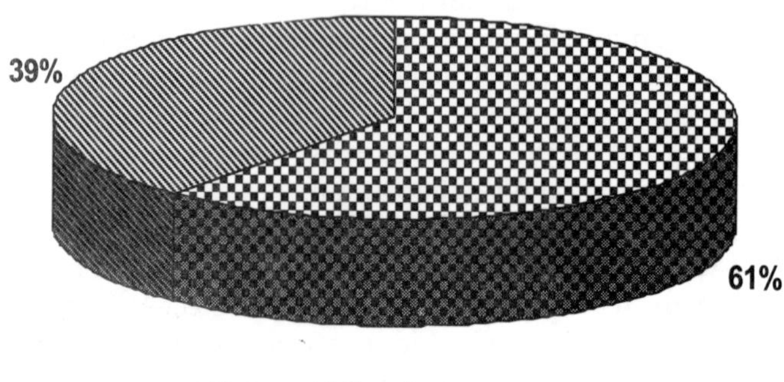

Source : Field Study.

Analysis: The figure shows that distribution of respondents by their sex. About 61 percent of the respondents belong to male group and 39 percent of the respondents females group.

FIG. 5.3

Distribution of Respondents by their Native Place

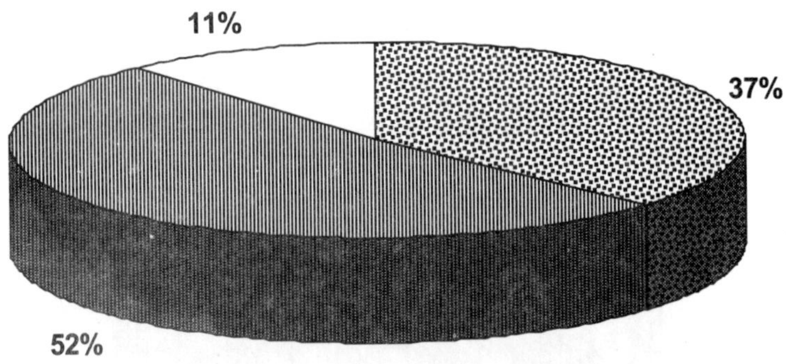

Source : Field Study.

Analysis: As the figure depicts that distribution of respondents by their Native place, about 37 percent of the respondents came from rural area and 52 percent of the respondents coming under urban area. The remaining 11 percent of the respondents belongs to the sub-urban area.

FIG. 5.4

Distribution of Respondents by their Educational Qualifications

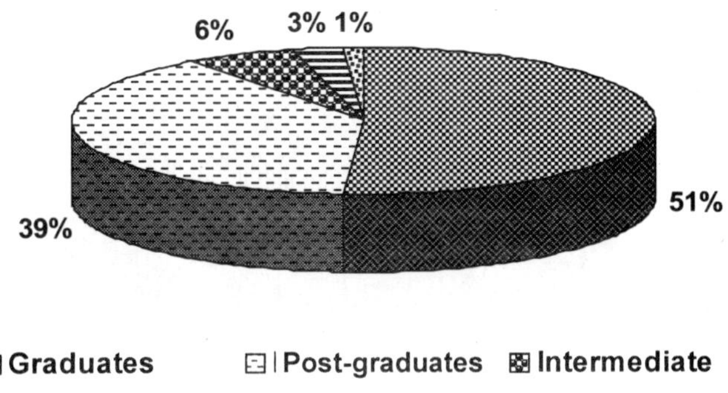

Source : Field Study.

Analysis: The Figure describes that distribution of respondents by their educational qualifications. About 51 percent of the respondents comes under the graduate category, 39 percent of them belong to postgraduates, remaining of the respondents considered as Intermediate, P.G. Diplomas and S.S.C. and they are 6 percent, 3 percent, and 1 percent respectively.

FIG. 5.5

Respondents' Opinion on "Are your living in an Information Age"

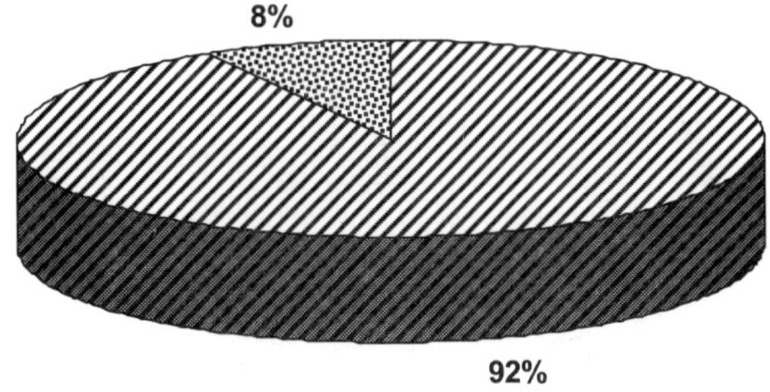

Source : Field Study.

Analysis: The above Figure exhibits respondents view point to the question are your living in an information age? 92 percent of the respondents agreed with living in an information age, i.e. indicated as yes and they remaining 8 percent of the respondents not to be agreed with living in an information age. Because they have no knowledge about the Computers.

FIG. 5.6
Respondents' Response on "from which Period they are being used computers"

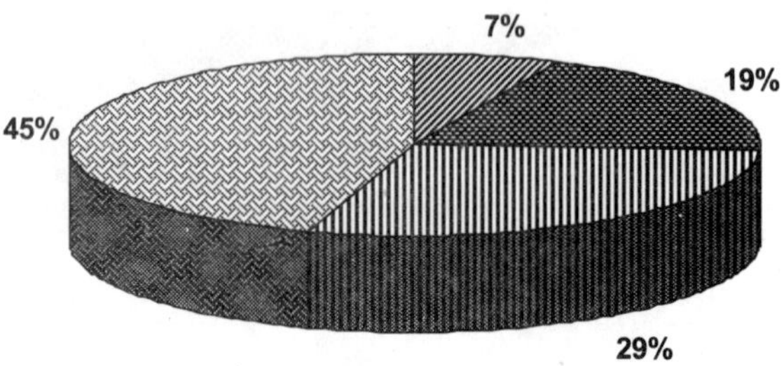

Source : Field Study.

Analysis: The above figure depicts that respondents opinion about from which period of the years they used to start computers. About 7 percent of the respondents using to start computer from the years 1986-90 period. About 19 percent of them using computers from the years 1991-95. Where as 29 percent of the respondents using computer from the period 1996-2000 and 45 percent of them using computers from the period 2001-05.

FIG. 5.7
Response on "From which Institutions, you are Received Training for Information Technology"

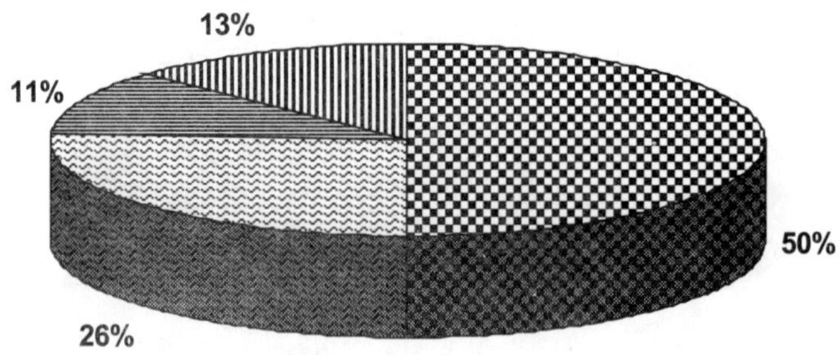

Source : Field Study.

Analysis: From the above Figure we can praises that 50 percent of the respondents took training from the Educational Institutions about the information technology programmes. About 26 percent of them took training from the training centers, 11 percent of the respondents obtaining training from the friends and 13 percent of them trained through self.

FIG. 5.8

Respondents' Opinion about the Facilities in Visakhapatnam with Reference to Information Technology

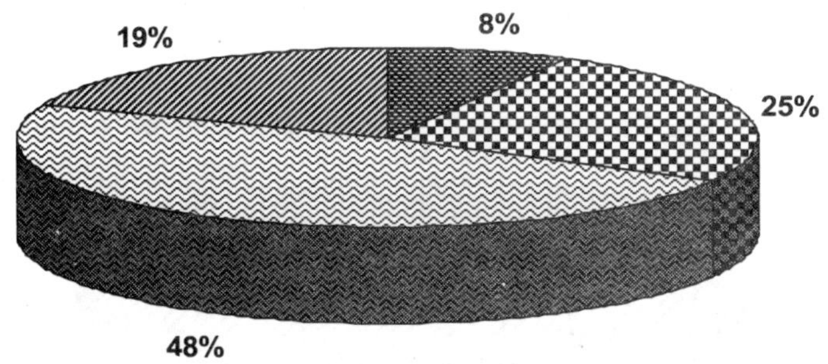

Source : Field Study.

Analysis: From the above Figure depicts that 8 percent of the respondents opined an excellent facilities at Visakhapatnam with reference to Information Technology programmes. About 25 percent of the respondents felt very good, while 48 percent of them felt good and 19 percent of the respondents felt like an average about the facilities at Visakhapatnam with reference to Information Technology programmes.

FIG. 5.9

Opinion of the Respondents about the Attitude of the Presently Available Information Technology Programmes

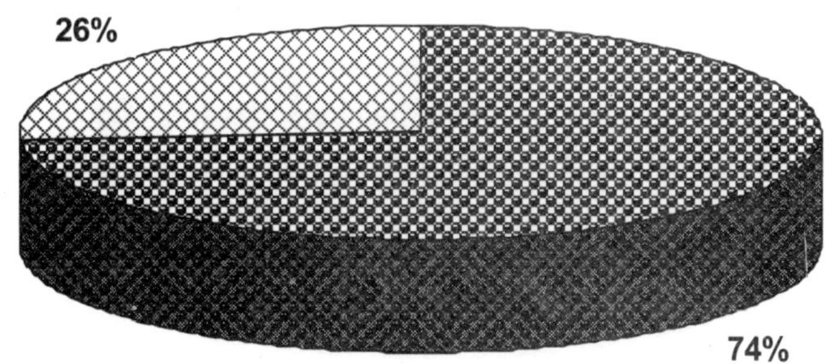

Source : Field Study.

Analysis: The above Figure indicates that the attitude of the respondents relating to presently available Information Technology programmes. About 74 percent of the respondents had as a favourable attitude regarding information technology programmes because of the IT is bringing unprecedented changes in all walks of life and Improvement in quality and variety of recreation is well accepted by the respondents. The remaining 26 percent of the respondents had unfavorable attitude because of the available IT programmes are insufficient.

FIG. 5.10
Opinion of the Respondents Regarding Working on Computer

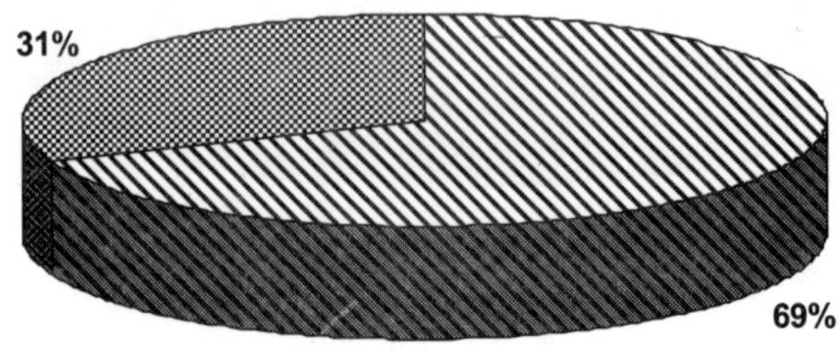

Source : Field Study.

Analysis: The above figure describes that 69 percent of the respondents are satisfied while they are working on computers and 31 percent of them felt unsatisfied because they are suffered with finger pain, strain of eyes, stress on mind and back pains while they are working on computer.

FIG. 5.11
Respondents' Opinions about "IT Programmes are helpful to Develop Human Resources"

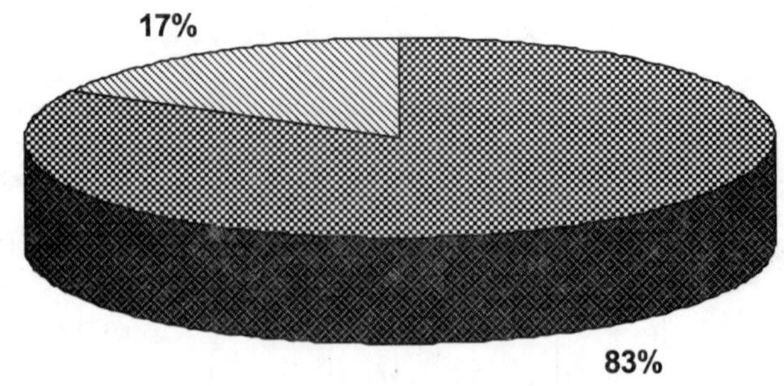

Source : Field Study.

Analysis: The above figure delineates that respondents perception regarding whether the Information Technology programmes are helpful to development of human resources, or not? About 83 percent of the respondents inferred as positively felt that the information technology programmes are useful to develop human resources. And 17 percent of them are felt as negatively. Because lack of facilities, more expensive and lack of training opportunities, etc.

Fig. 5.12

Opinion of the Respondents Regarding "Are you given Importance to Development of Human Resources through Information Technology"?

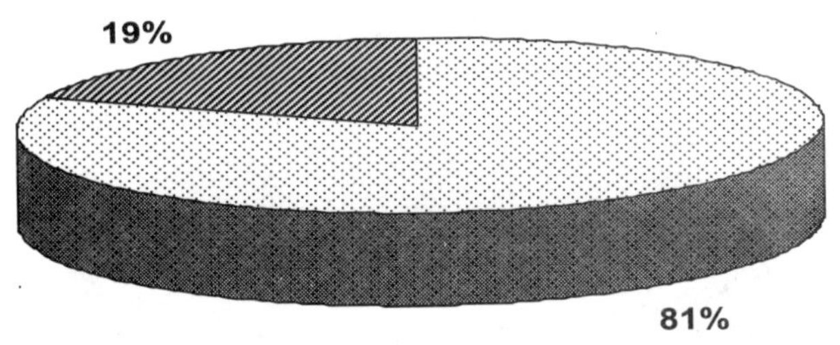

Source : Field Study.

Analysis: The above figure shows the respondents opinion on whether they are given importance to development of human resources through information technology or not? 81 percent of the respondents opined that they are given importance to development of human resources through information technology. And remaining percent of the respondents (i.e. 19 percent) expressed as negative because lack of financial support and family background.

Fig. 5.13

Respondents' Response Regarding "How much time Spend for Development of Human Resources through Information Technology in a Day"?

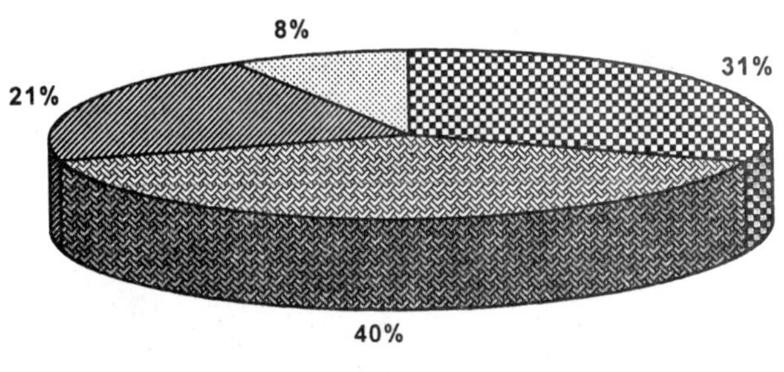

Source : Field Study.

Analysis: The figure depicts that 31 percent of the respondents spending time for development of human resources through different information technology programmes between 1-2 hours in a day. 40 percent of the respondents opined spent time 3-4 hours per day to develop human resources through information technology, while 21 percent of them inferred spending 5-6 hours in a day and 8 percent of the respondents spent 7-8 hours in a day for development of human resources through different information technology programmes.

FIG. 5.14

Opinion of the Respondents about Internet is Important Tool for Developing Human Resources

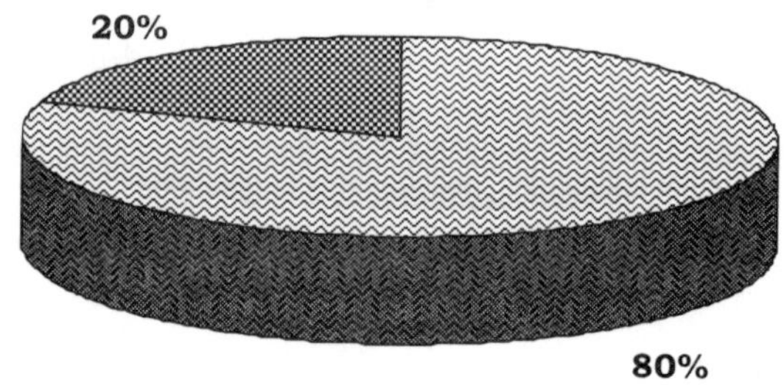

Source : Field Study.

Analysis: The above Figure describes the respondents view point about Internet is one of the important tool for developing human resources. The majority of them are accepted (i.e. 80 percent) because collecting different information, educational material, communication, messages, awareness of various concepts are obtained from the Internet. And 20 percent of the respondents are not accepted because they were expressed that it was lack of availability in villages.

FIG. 5.15

Respondents' Opinion about "Is the Wireless Communication Tools are useful to Develop Human Resources?"

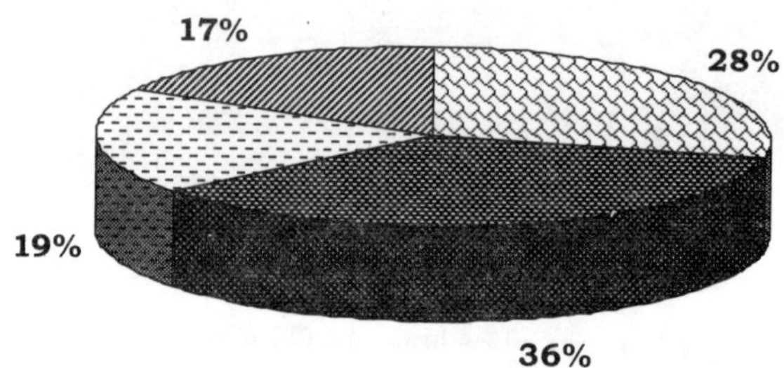

Source : Field Study.

Analysis: The figure exhibits that 28 percent of respondents felt very good opinion regarding usefulness of the wireless communication tools to develop the human recourses. About 36 percent of them felt well and 19 percent of the respondents felt that the usefulness is average. The remaining 17 percent of them expressed that the usefulness of wireless communication tools to develop human resources is low.

Fig. 5.16

Respondents' Opinions on "Human Resource Development through Satellite Communication System

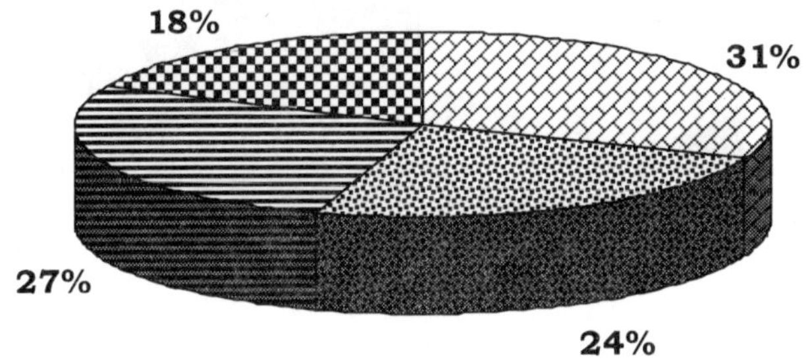

Source : Field Study.

Analysis: The respondents (31 percent) felt that the human resource development through satellite communicate system is excellent. About 24 percent of the respondents opined as very good about the satellite communication system. 27 percent of them expressed that it was good system and 18 percent of the respondents felt that the usefulness of this system is an average for development of human resources.

Fig. 5.17

Opinion of the Respondents about Compact Disk Televisions (CDTV)

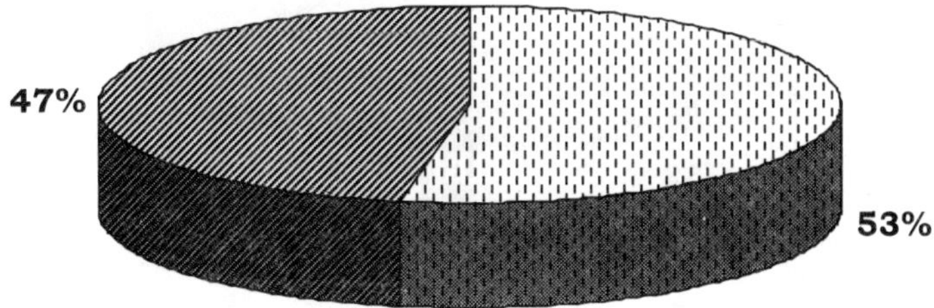

Source : Field Study.

Analysis: The above figure shows that 53 percent of the respondents opined that the Compact Disk Televisions are useful media for development of human resources. And 47 percent of the respondents felt negatively regarding development of human resources through compact Disk Televisions.

FIG. 5.18

Respondents' Perception Regarding Rajiv Internet with Reference to Visakhapatnam People

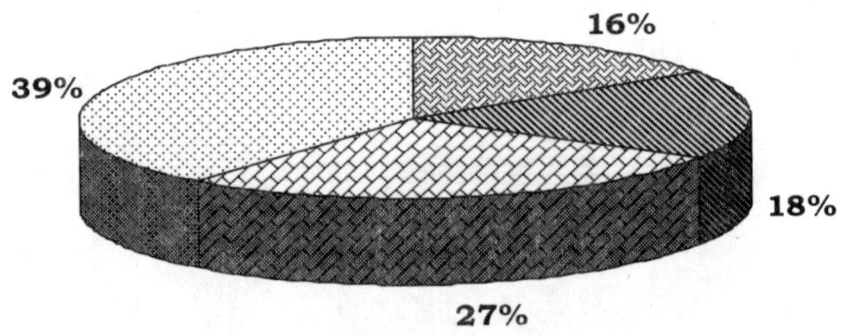

Excellent Very Good Good Average

Source : Field Study.

Analysis: About 16 percent of the respondents opined that the usefulness of Rajiv Internet programme was excellent, while 18 percent of the respondents suggested that the programme was very good. About 27 percent of the respondents felt the Rajiv Internet programme has good. Remaining 39 percent of the respondents felt that usefulness of this programme has an average.

FIG. 5.19

Opinion of the Respondents about Human Resource Development through Jnanadoot Programme

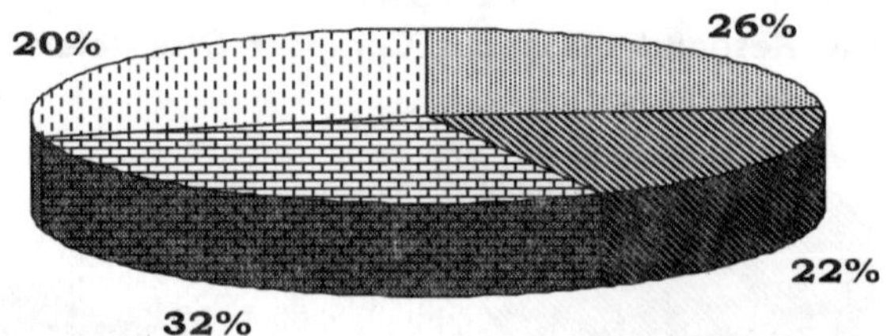

Excellent Very Good Good Average

Source : Field Study.

Analysis: As the figure shows 26 percent of the respondents opined that the utility regarding Human Resource Development through Jnanadoot programme was an excellent. About 22 percent of the respondents felt that the programme has very good. According to 32 percent of the respondents

Jnanadoot programme is good for developing human resources. While the remaining 20 percent of the respondents were inferred that the usefulness of the programme is an average.

FIG. 5.20
Respondents' Opinion Regarding Information Technology Programmes are Over-burdened

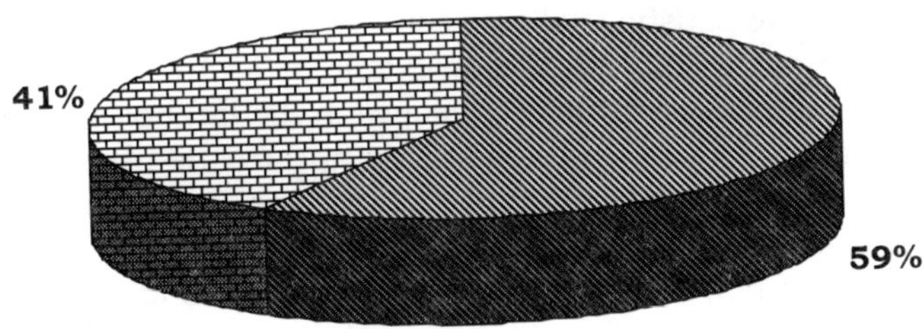

Source : Field Study.

Analysis: The above figure depicts that 59 percent of the respondents felt that Information Technology programmes were over burdened. And 41 percent of the respondents said that the Information Technology programmes are not over burdened.

TABLE 5.1
Opinion of the Respondents on E-learning

Sl. No.	*Respondents*	*No. of Responses*		
		Satisfied	*Dissatisfied*	*Total*
1.	Students	46(77)	14(23)	60(100)
2.	Employees	41(68)	19(32)	60(100)
3.	Business People	43(72)	17(28)	60(100)
4.	Doctors	41(68)	19(32)	60(100)
5.	Engineers	36(60)	24(40)	60(100)
6.	Lawyers	43(72)	17(28)	60(100)
7.	Teachers	41(68)	19(32)	60(100)
8.	Rural People	40(67)	20(33)	60(100)
	Total	331	149	480
	Percentage	69	31	100

Note : Percent of the respondents are indicating in parenthesis.
Source : Field Study.

Analysis: In the opinion of the respondents on E-learning programme, 77 percent of the students are satisfied with the programme and the remaining 23 per cent are not satisfied because of lack of facility in their vicinity. From the category of employees 68 per cent are satisfied because, they are using E-learning whenever they are free, but 32 per cent are dissatisfied.

In the business category 72 per cent of businessmen are felt happy about E-learning programme, as they use this programme for their business purposes. But 28 per cent are not satisfied with E-learning, because of lack of time.

Doctors are also satisfied (68 per cent) about the programme, as they use this programme to the maximum extent to improve their skills and experience and to know about latest changes in the field of medicine. Some of the respondents of doctor's category are not satisfied because they are busy with their duties and have no time to spare on E-learning programme.

Coming to the category of engineers sixty per cent of them are highly satisfied, because it helps them to know the techniques and recent changes in their respective fields. But 40 per cent are not satisfied with this programme, as they cannot spare time on this programme because of tight schedule and since they are busy with technical and domestic work.

Among the lawyers 72 per cent of them really enjoy the E-learning programme and are satisfied fully, because it helps them to know the recent judgments, legal opinions, etc. which in turn helps them to guide their clients and to improve their awareness on legal matters. But 28 per cent of the lawyers are busy with their cases, and they are very old and reputed lawyers, then are not satisfied with E-learning programme.

In the category of teachers 68 per cent are full satisfied with the E-learning programme, as it helps them to know new methods, recent publications on special topics which enable them to improve their standard of teaching and to compete with other teachers in the field of education. But 32 per cent of the teachers are not satisfied as they are working in private schools and govt. schools for whom it is not suitable or advantageous to learn through E-learning.

In the rural areas also awareness is there among the rural people about E-learning. Some educated unemployed in rural areas are interested in E-learning. They use this programme to know about the opportunities available in Cities or in public/private companies. So the 67 per cent of the rural people are satisfied with the E-learning programme as it helps them to know the global changes. But, 33 per cent of the rural people are not satisfied with this programme, as they are out of coverage area. Maximum of the dissatisfied rural people are busy with their cultivation work throughout the year for their survival.

On the whole 69 per cent of the respondents of various sections are satisfied with the E-learning programme and only 31 per cent of them are not satisfied with the programme, which is negligible. They may show interest on this programme at any time irrespective of their personal problem (Table 5.1)

TABLE 5.2

Respondents' Opinion Regarding Utility of E-leaning Programme

Sl. No.	*Respondents*	*No. of Responses*				
		Very High	*High*	*Low*	*Extremely Low*	*Total*
1.	Students	2(3)	45(75)	9(15)	4(7)	60(100)
2.	Employees	8(13)	39(65)	8(13)	5(9)	60(100)
3.	Business People	5(8)	40(67)	11(18)	4(7)	60(100)
4.	Doctors	4(7)	41(68)	9(15)	6(10)	60(100)
5.	Engineers	6(10)	39(65)	10(17)	5(8)	60(100)
6.	Lawyers	7(12)	38(63)	9(15)	6(10)	60(100)
7.	Teachers	9(15)	42(70)	7(12)	2(3)	60(100)
8.	Rural People	4(7)	37(62)	12(20)	7(11)	60(100)
	Total	45	321	75	39	480
	Percentage	9	67	16	8	100

Note : Percent of the respondents are indicating in parenthesis.
Source : Field Study.

Analysis: In the utility of E-learning programme 75 per cent of the students felt that the utility was high and only 3 per cent stated that the utility was very high as they used this programmes regularly for their field of education. Only twenty two percent felt that the utility was not up to the mark.

From the section of employees, 13 per cent felt that the programme utility was very high because they used to depend on E-learning for their regular duties. 65 per cent of the employees stated that the utility was high as it helps them to know the recent changes in their field of work. Only 22 per cent felt that the utility of the programme was low.

Coming to the business people 67 per cent felt that the utility was high, and 8 per cent stated that the utility was very high as it provides necessary and latest information about the products, marketing and distribution of products. Only 15 percent indicated that the utility was low.

Regarding the doctors 68 per cent of the respondents felt that the utility of the E-learning programme was high, because the programme helps them to know the recent innovations, recent drugs, treatment, etc. used by the doctors globally for their patients. Only 7 per cent stated that the utility was very high because they depend on the E-learning programme to the maximum extent for the treatment of patients and to learn recent changes in the field of medicine. 25 percent of the respondents felt the utility was low.

65 per cent of the engineers felt that the utility of the programme was high as it for provides necessary information. 10 per cent of the respondents

stated that the utility was very high and 25 per cent observed that the utility was low. Regarding the lawyers 12 per cent stated that the utility was very high, 63 per cent felt that the utility was high and 24 per cent stated the utility was low.

In the section of teachers 70 per cent stated that the utility was high, as it enables them to know latest information about the recent changes, publications, etc. 15 per cent respondents felt that the utility was very high, and the others stated that it was low. From the rural section, 62 percent of the respondents stated that the utility was high. About 20 percent of them felt that it was low utility, 11 percent stated that the program utility was extremely low, but remaining of them felt it was very high utility.

On the whole 67 percent of the respondents are opined that it was highly utilized. 16 percent said that it was low utility. About 9 percent said that it was very high utilized and 8 percent said that it was extremely low utilized (Table 5.2).

Table 5.2

Response of the Respondents about E-learning Method

Sl. No.	*Respondents*	*No. of Responses*				
		Excellent	*Good*	*Average*	*Poor*	*Total*
1.	Students	20[33]	30(50)	6(10)	4(7)	60(100)
2.	Employees	11(18)	38(64)	5(8)	6(10)	60(100)
3.	Business People	8(13)	37(62)	9(15)	6(10)	60(100)
4.	Doctors	9(15)	36(60)	10(17)	5(8)	60(100)
5.	Engineers	7(12)	37(62)	14(23)	2(3)	60(100)
6.	Lawyers	6(10)	35(58)	12(20)	7(12)	60(100)
7.	Teachers	18(30)	33(55)	6(10)	3(5)	60(100)
8.	Rural People	9(15)	39(65)	7(12)	5(8)	60(100)
	Total	88	285	69	38	480
	Percentage	18	60	14	8	100

Note : Percent of the respondents are indicating in parenthesis.
Source : Field Study.

Analysis: Out of the respondents of students category 50 per cent gave their response as good about the programme and 33 per cent said that it was excellent and the rest stated that it was average and poor.

From the category of employees 18 per cent said that the E-learning method was excellent and 64 per cent stated that it was good. About 8 percent said it was average and poor response about the method of E-learning programme.

The respondents from business section expressed that the E-learning programme was good (62 per cent) because it helps them to adopt new techniques about marketing, distribution etc. 13 per cent of them stated that the programme was excellent as they depend on it to the maximum extent. But 25 per cent responded that the programme was average and low because they are not depending on it for their total requirements.

Out of the respondents of the doctors section 15 per cent expressed that the programme was excellent and 60 per cent opined that the programme was good. 17 per cent stated that the method of the programme was average as they used this method very rarely. But 8 per cent responded that the method of the programme was poor.

Coming to engineers section 12 per cent expressed that the method of the programme was excellent, 62 per cent stated that the method was good and 23 per cent opined that the method of the same was average. But only 3 per cent expressed that the method was poor.

From the lawyers section 10 per cent said that the method was excellent which helps them to know recent amendments, recent judgments in the field of law. 58 per cent expressed good about the programme and 20 per cent said that the programme was average. 12 per cent opined that the method was poor.

Teachers responded (30 per cent) next highest to students about the method and said that the method of the programme was excellent, as it provides necessary and latest information about their field of study, 55 per cent of the teachers felt that the method of the programme was good as it suits their requirements, 10 per cent said that the method was average as they use it very rarely and only 5 per cent said that it was very poor as they are not interested in E-learning programme.

15 per cent of the rural people expressed their opinion as excellent about the method of E-learning programme as they used this programme to the maximum. 65 per cent stated that the method was good as it provides necessary information about the global scenario and it educates them in all aspects. And they expressed that the programme is mode available by the government at the cheaper rates in rural areas through global Internet villages. 12 per cent of respondents felt that the method was average, as they are not acquainted with all the programmes and the use, this program on our average. 8 per cent expressed that the method of the programme was poor because of power failure, lack of experienced persons in the centers and look of centre in few villages.

On the whole 18 per cent said that the programme was excellent, 60 per cent expressed that the programme was good. 14 per cent felt that the said programme was average and only 8 per cent opined that the method was poor. (Table 5.3)

Analysis: 60 per cent of the students section opined that they are satisfied fully with the E-mail programme as they interact through E-mail with their friends, and relatives for sending important messages in detail as the cost is cheaper than post and telegrams. 40 per cent of the respondents were not satisfied about the E-mail programme because of lack of storage facility.

TABLE 5.4
Opinion of the Respondents on E-mail

Sl. No.	Respondents	No. of Responses		
		Satisfied	Dissatisfied	Total
1.	Students	36(60)	24(40)	60(100)
2.	Employees	42(70)	18(30)	60(100)
3.	Business People	48(80)	12(20)	60(100)
4.	Doctors	37(62)	23(38)	60(100)
5.	Engineers	39(65)	21(35)	60(100)
6.	Lawyers	40(67)	20(33)	60(100)
7.	Teachers	38(63)	22(37)	60(100)
8.	Rural People	35(58)	25(42)	60(100)
	Total	315	165	480
	Percentage	66	34	100

Note : Percent of the respondents are indicating in parenthesis.
Source : Field Study.

About 70 per cent of the employees are satisfied with this programme as they used to send the information message to their superiors or subordinates within a short period. About 30 per cent of the employee respondents stated that they were dissatisfied with the E-mail programme.

80 per cent of the business sections are satisfied with the E-mail programme as they use it for sending quotations, enquiries, orders and recent developments. Only 20 per cent are not satisfied with this programme.

62 per cent of the Doctors are satisfied with the programme as they used the E-mail for sending messages to patients and co-doctors and exchange the views with other doctors. But 38 per cent of the respondents are dissatisfied.

The engineers are also satisfied about this programme (65 per cent) which helps them to get latest information and availability of man, material of machines but 35 per cent are not satisfied

Out of the respondents from lawyer section 67 per cent are satisfied with this programme and remaining 33 percent are not satisfied. Regarding the teachers 63 per cent stated that they are satisfied with this programme. But 37 per cent expressed their dissatisfaction. 58 per cent of the Rural people are satisfied, because it is a cheaper method for sending the messages and easily accessible but 42 per cent expressed their dissatisfaction.

On the whole 66 per cent of the respondents are satisfied, but one third are not satisfied because E-mail has created information overload, it can become a distraction and can prevent people from doing any productive work. (Table 5.4)

TABLE 5.5
Opinion of the Respondents about the Utility of E-mail

Sl. No.	*Respondents*	*No. of Responses*				
		Very High	*High*	*Low*	*Extremely Low*	*Total*
1.	Students	5(8)	31(52)	16(27)	8(13)	60(100)
2.	Employees	4(7)	30(50)	18(30)	8(13)	60(100)
3.	Business People	7(12)	36(60)	10(16)	7(12)	60(100)
4.	Doctors	6(10)	34(57)	9(15)	11(18)	60(100)
5.	Engineers	6(10)	35(59)	11(18)	8(13)	60(100)
6.	Lawyers	4(7)	32(53)	19(32)	5(8)	60(100)
7.	Teachers	5(8)	37(62)	10(17)	8(13)	60(100)
8.	Rural People	3(5)	30(50)	14(23)	13(22)	60(100)
	Total	40	265	107	68	480
	Percentage	8	55	23	14	100

Note : Percent of the respondents are indicating in parenthesis.
Source : Field Study.

Analysis: In view of the utility of E-mail programme, the student respondents 52 per cent are expressed that the utility of it was high. Only 8 per cent of the students are opined that it was very high utilised, because E-mail enables to stand out in customer service, competitions and sell products. About 27 per cent of the students are opined said programme utility was low and 13 per cents of them felt that it was extremely low utilised.

From employees section, half percent of the respondents are felt that it was high utilised and 30 per cent of the employees felt that it was low utilised. And remaining of the respondents, i.e. 7 per cent and 13 per cent of the employees, who stated that the utility of e-mail was very high and extremely low respectively. In the opinion of the Business people the utility of Email was high utilized, i.e. 60 per cent and 12 per cent of them, felt that it was very high utilised. However, 16 per cent and 12 per cent of the business people said that the programme utility was low and extremely low respectively.

About 57 per cent of the doctors stated that the utility of E-mail was high and 10 percent of the same section expressed that it was very high utilised. While, the respondents (15 per cent) are opined this programme was low utilised and 18 per cent of the doctors are opined that it was extremely low. From the engineers section 59 per çent of the respondents expressed that the utility of E-mail programme was high. Only 10 per cent of the respondents of engineers are expressed it was very high utilised. However, there are 18 percent and 13 per cent of the engineers, who opined low and extremely low respectively regarding the utility of email programme.

An attempt is made to find out the opinion of the lawyers (53 per cent) on the utility of said programme was high. Only 7 per cent of the lawyers stated that the utility was very high. About 32 per cent of the lawyers expressed that it was low utilised 8 per cent of them felt that the programme was extremely low utilized.

Among the teachers section, 62 per cent of the respondents are opined that the utility of E-mail was high. And 8 per cent of the teachers expressed it was very high utility. However, 17 per cent and 13 per cent of the teachers who are opined said programme was low and extremely low respectively.

From the rural people, half percent of the rural people stated that the utility was high, 5 per cent of the respondents felt it was very high utilized, the low response given by the rural people (23 per cent) about the utility of this programme. About 22 per cent of the respondents are expressed said programme was extremely low utilised.

Whole of the respondent's opinion on the utility of E-mail programme. 55 percent of the respondents are stated that the programme utility was high, only 8 percent of them felt that it was very high because, global communication is easier and it has provide a big blessing for senior citizens and retired persons. But 23 per cent of them are was low and felt that it 14 per cent of the are respondents expressed that it was extremely low because, it has created an information overload and it is that it can become a distraction and can prevent people from doing any productive work (Table 5.5).

TABLE 5.6

Respondents' Opinion Regarding the Method of E-mail Programme

Sl. No.	Respondents	No. of Responses				
		Excellent	Good	Average	Poor	Total
1.	Students	4(7)	48(80)	7(12)	2(1)	60(100)
2.	Employees	9(15)	36(60)	10(17)	5(8)	60(100)
3.	Business People	12(20)	37(62)	8(13)	3(5)	60(100)
4.	Doctors	8(13)	36(60)	9(15)	7(12)	60(100)
5.	Engineers	6(10)	38(63)	10(17)	6(10)	60(100)
6.	Lawyers	7(12)	39(65)	9(15)	5(8)	60(100)
7.	Teachers	5(8)	33(55)	12(20)	10(17)	60(100)
8.	Rural People	4(7)	38(63)	14(23)	4(7)	60(100)
	Total	55	305	79	41	480
	Percentage	12	64	16	8	100

Note : Percent of the respondents are indicating in parenthesis.
Source : Field Study.

Analysis: Regarding the method of E-mail. Out of the student section. 80 per cent of the students have expressed that the method was good and only 7 percent said that it was excellent. But rests of the students are opined that the program was average and poor.

From the employees section, 60 percent of the respondents are opined that it was good method and 15 per cent of the employees are stated that the method was excellent, because, it provides access to the information from any where in the world. But 17 per cent said that it was average and rests of them felt that the method was poor.

Business people (62 per cent) and 20 per cent said that the method was good and excellent respectively. But 13 per cent of the business people are opined said programme was average and 5 per cent of the respondents are stated that the programme was poor.

The doctors (60 per cent) stated that the programme was good and 13 per cent of them are felt that it was excellent because, it is estimated that the data traffic through the internet would out strip the voice traffic in not-too-distant a future. But 15 per cent of the doctors indicated that the programme was average and 12 per cent of them one felt that it was poor.

As can be seen from the table, the engineers (63 per cent) are stated that the programme was good and 10 per cent of them are felt that the method was excellent because, it can enables stand out in customer service, competitions. But 17 per cent of the engineers are opined that it was average and 10 per cent of them felt that the programme was poor because, it is the very existence of electronic communication.

Maximum extent of the lawyers (65 per cent) indicated their opinion on the method of email programme was good, only 12 per cent of the respondents expressed that the programme was excellent. But rest of the respondent are opined that it was average and poor in terms of the e-mail programme.

Teachers (55 percent) expressed that the method was good, 8 per cent said that it was excellent, 20 per cent said that it was average and17 per cent said that the programme was poor about the method of e-mail programme.

Rural people (63 percent) are opined that it was good method, but 23 per cent of them felt that the programme was average; rest of them felt that the method was excellent and poor.

On the whole, majority of the respondents (64 per cent) expressed that the programme was good method, 12 per cent of the respondents opined that it was excellent because, it opened the door for more types of professionals to work at home, because they can still top in to corporate information. But 16 per cent and 8 per cent of the respondents who are opined average and poor respectively, because, it is the individual using the technology that makes the communications better or worst. (Table 5.6)

Analysis: The Table (5.7) exhibits the opinion of the respondents on the Internet programme. 73 per cent of the students are satisfied with the programme because; it can be effectively used to supplement text book

TABLE 5.7
Opinion of the Respondents about Internet Programme

Sl. No.	*Respondents*	*No. of Responses*		
		Satisfied	*Dissatisfied*	*Total*
1.	Students	44(73)	16(27)	60(100)
2.	Employees	45(75)	15(25)	60(100)
3.	Business People	48(80)	12(20)	60(100)
4.	Doctors	43(72)	17(28)	60(100)
5.	Engineers	42(70)	18(30)	60(100)
6.	Lawyers	43(72)	17(28)	60(100)
7.	Teachers	40(67)	20(33)	60(100)
8.	Rural People	38(63)	22(37)	60(100)
	Total	343	137	480
	Percentage	72	28	100

Note : Percent of the respondents are indicating in parenthesis.
Source : Field Study.

learning. But 27 per cent of the students are dissatisfied with the programme because; it gives easy access to adult web sites.

Majority of the employees (75 percent) are satisfied with Internet because, it is foundation pillar for e-governance and public service. But 25 per cent of them dissatisfied because it is a time consuming device. From the business section maximum extent of the respondents (80 per cent) are opined that the satisfaction level is high because it is an ideal marketing medium for companies in the industries. But remaining is dissatisfied because, it requires literacy.

Out of the doctors section 72 per cent of the respondents are satisfied with the programme because, it access online multimedia including radio and video broadcast but 28 per cent of them are not satisfied because, it can lead to isolationist tendencies.

The engineers (70 per cent) are satisfied with this programme because, it offers access to data, graphics, sound, software, text and people through a variety of services and tools for communication and data exchange. But rest of them felt not satisfied because, it can effect leadership qualities.

In the section of lawyers (72 per cent) are opined that the programme was satisfactory because it can provide your own websites. About 28 per cent of them are felt that the programme was not satisfaction because it is a time consuming device

Teachers (67 per cent) are satisfied with this programme because, it can exposes children to a plethora of information and teachers them how to call relevant data. But 33 per cent of the teachers are not satisfied with this regard because it can badly effect the students and younger people.

About 63 per cent of the rural people are satisfied with this programme. But 37 per cent of they are felt dissatisfaction because literacy is necessary for operating Internet. On the whole maximum extents of the respondents (72 per cent) are satisfied with this programme and rest of them are dissatisfied (Table 5.7)

TABLE 5.8

Respondents' Opinion Regarding the Utility of Internet

Sl. No.	*Respondents*	*No. of Responses*				
		Very High	*High*	*Low*	*Extremely Low*	*Total*
1.	Students	9(15)	39(65)	7(12)	5(8)	60(100)
2.	Employees	7(12)	38(63)	10(17)	5(8)	60(100)
3.	Business People	10(17)	39(65)	5(8)	6(10)	60(100)
4.	Doctors	6(10)	35(59)	11(18)	8(13)	60(100)
5.	Engineers	8(13)	34(57)	9(15)	9(15)	60(100)
6.	Lawyers	7(12)	36(60)	12(20)	5(8)	60(100)
7.	Teachers	8(13)	35(58)	7(12)	10(17)	60(100)
8.	Rural People	5(8)	34(57)	14(23)	7(12)	60(100)
	Total	60	290	75	55	480
	Percentage	13	60	16	11	100

Note : Percent of the respondents are indicating in parenthesis.
Source : Field Study

Analysis: Table 5.8 reveals the opinion of the respondents on the utility of Internet programme. From the students section majority of the respondents (65 percent) stated that the utility of the programme was high 15 per cent said that it was very high utilised. But 12 per cent of them felt that the programme was low utility and 8 per cent of the students expressed that it was extremely low. From the employees section 63 per cent of the respondents stated that it was high utilised, 12 per cent of them expressed that the programme was very high utilised. About 17 percent of the respondents of the employees opined the programme was low utilised and only 8 percent of them felt it was extremely low.

Coming to the business people, 65 per cent felt that the utility was high and 17 per cent stated that the utility was very high, because it provides necessary and latest information for the business growth. Only 8 percent indicated that the utility was low and 10 per cent said that the programme was extremely low utilised.

The respondents of the doctors (10 per cent) opined that the utility was very high and 59 per cent stated that the programme was high because they used it for medicine field for immediate treatment. About 18 per cent of the respondents expressed that the programme was low utility and 13 per cent indicated that the programme was extremely low utilised.

The engineers (57 per cent) opined that the utility was high and 13 per cent of the engineers are expressed that the programme was very high. Rest of the engineers felt that the utility was average and poor. Lawyers (60 per cent) indicated that the utility was high. 12 per cent said that the programme was very high utilized. 20 per cent felt that it was low and 8 per cent of them indicated that the programme was extremely low.

About 13 per cent of the teachers expressed that the programme utility was very high and 58 per cent of them felt that it was high utilised. While 17 per cent of the teachers opined that the programme was extremely low utilised and 12 per cent of them felt that it was low utility.

The Rural people (57 per cent) stated that the utility was high, only 8 per cent indicated that the programme was very high, but 23 per cent of the rural people opined that this programme was low and 12 per cent of them felt that it was extremely low because, literacy is necessary for operation of internet and telephone line is must.

Cumulative percentages of the opinion of the respondent's maximum respondents (60 per cent) stated that the programme was high. Because, searching for new information and it facilitates to join in contests. Only 13 per cent said that it was very high utility. About 27 per cent of the respondents felt that the utility was low and extremely low because it effects leadership qualities, and children get used to ready made study material without having to search for it.

TABLE 5.9

Response of the Respondents about the Method of Internet

Sl. No.	*Respondents*	*No. of Responses*				
		Excellent	*Good*	*Average*	*Poor*	*Total*
1.	Students	15(25)	34(57)	5(8)	6(10)	60(100)
2.	Employees	12(20)	36(60)	7(12)	5(8)	60(100)
3.	Business People	16(27)	39(65)	3(5)	2(3)	60(100)
4.	Doctors	12(20)	34(57)	8(13)	6(10)	60(100)
5.	Engineers	13(22)	37(61)	6(10)	4(7)	60(100)
6.	Lawyers	11(18)	35(59)	8(13)	6(10)	60(100)
7.	Teachers	12(20)	34(57)	6(10)	8(13)	60(100)
8.	Rural People	9(15)	33(55)	11(18)	7(12)	60(100)
	Total	100	282	54	44	480
	Percentage	21	59	11	9	100

Note : Percent of the respondents are indicating in parenthesis.
Source : Field Study.

Analysis: In view of the above programme, the respondents of the students (57 per cent) are expressed that the method of Internet was good, 15 per cent said that the method was excellent. But only 8 per cent of them are felt it was average and 10 per cent of them felt that it was poor method. The respondents of the employees (20 per cent) felt that the programme was excellent method. Majority of the employees (60 per cent) said that it was good. About 12 per cent of the Respondents indicated that the method was average. While 8 per cent said it was poor.

From the business section 65 per cent felt that the method was good and 27 per cent said that it was excellent method because, their operation were carried on through the internet, they used it in the marketing, sales and production. But rest of them felt that it was average and poor.

Doctors (57 per cent) opined that the programme was good because they used it in the medicine field for immediate treatment to the patients. 20 per cent of them felt that the method was excellent. About 13 per cent said that it was average and 10 per cent stated that it was poor. As can be seen from the data the engineers (61 per cent) stated that it was good and 22 per cent said that the programme was excellent because, it offers access to date, graphics, sound, software, text and people through a variety of services and tools for communication and date exchange, i.e. remote login, file transfer and hyper text, etc. But rest of them felt that it was average and poor.

About 59 per cent of the lawyers expressed that it was good method and 18 per cent of them felt that the programme was excellent. About 13 per cent of the lawyers opined that the method was average. While 10 percent stated that it was poor.

Out of the teacher's section maximum (57 per cent) of them felt that it was good and 20 per cent said that it was excellent. But rest of the teachers opined that the programme was average and poor.

The rural people (55 per cent) are opined this method was good and 15 per cent of them felt that it was excellent. About 18 per cent of the rural people indicated that it was average and 12 per cent of the respondents felt that the programme was poor.

On the whole 59 per cent of the respondents indicated that the programme was good method and 21 per cent of them felt that it was excellent because, it is the cheapest and fastest. But rests of the respondents are opined that it was average and poor because, Internet gives easy access to adult websites, it will badly effect the students and younger people (Table 5.9).

Analysis: An inquiry into the respondent's opinion on mobile phone. Out of the student section 80 percent of the respondents are satisfied with mobile phone because, they interact through the mobile phone with their friends, relatives, but 20 percent of them were not satisfied with mobile phones because communication barrier are involved in the programme.

From the employee section, 82 per cent of them are satisfied because they use to speak the information, messages to the superiors within short

TABLE 5.10
Opinion of the Respondents about Mobile Phone

Sl. No.	*Respondents*	*No. of Responses*		
		Satisfied	*Dissatisfied*	*Total*
1.	Students	48(80)	12(20)	60(100)
2.	Employees	49(82)	11(18)	60(100)
3.	Business People	51(85)	9(15)	60(100)
4.	Doctors	47(78)	13(22)	60(100)
5.	Engineers	48(80)	12(20)	60(100)
6.	Lawyers	47(78)	13(22)	60(100)
7.	Teachers	49(82)	11(18)	60(100)
8.	Rural People	43(72)	17(28)	60(100)
	Total	382	98	480
	Percentage	80	20	100

Note : Parenthesis values are indicating their percent of the responses.
Source : Field Study.

period. Only 18 per cent of them are dissatisfied because, they are obtaining wrong calls, unnecessary information and lack of need.

In the Business people (85 per cent) are highly satisfied then the other sections of the society, because, they used it for business transactions and recent market particulars and selling models with in time enables the information through mobile phone. But only 15 per cent of the respondents are not satisfied because, customer's requirements are not getting through mobile phone.

Doctors are maximum (72 percent) satisfied with it because they use the mobile phones for interaction with patients and enables the flow of information from the friends or colleagues, but 28 per cent of them are dissatisfied because of the signal problems.

About 80 per cent of the engineers are satisfied and 20 per cent of the engineers are not satisfied with mobile phone. Lawyers (78 per cent) indicate that they are highly satisfied because mobile phones enable immediate interaction with clients to find out the case details. 22 per cent of the lawyers are not satisfied because they often get dangerous warnings through the mobile phone from enemies.

In the Teacher section, 82 per cent of the teachers are satisfied because it enables clarification of doubts from the students. But 18 per cent are not satisfied with the programme.

The rural people (72 per cent) are satisfied with the mobile phone because they use it from the rural areas with convenience and 28 percent of the rural people are not satisfied because some companies have not established their signal towers at rural areas. On the whole 80 per cent of the respondents are satisfied and remaining of the respondents are dissatisfied with mobile phone (Table 5.10).

TABLE 5.11

Opinion of the Respondents Regarding the Utility of Mobile Phone

Sl. No.	Respondents	No. of Responses				
		Very High	High	Low	Extremely low	Total
1.	Students	6(10)	39(65)	10(17)	5(8)	60(100)
2.	Employees	8(13)	38(64)	9(15)	5(8)	60(100)
3.	Business People	12(20)	40(67)	5(8)	3(5)	60(100)
4.	Doctors	11(18)	40(67)	6(10)	3(5)	60(100)
5.	Engineers	10(17)	39(65)	9(15)	2(3)	60(100)
6.	Lawyers	11(18)	39(65)	6(10)	4(7)	60(100)
7.	Teachers	9(15)	37(62)	8(13)	6(10)	60(100)
8.	Rural People	7(12)	33(55)	11(18)	9(15)	60(100)
	Total	74	305	64	37	480
	Percentage	15	64	13	8	100

Note : Percent of the respondents are indicating in parenthesis.
Source : Field Study.

Analysis: Regarding the utility of mobile phone, 65 per cent of the students opined that the programme utility was high. Only 10 per cent of them felt that it was very high utility. 17 per cent of the students observed that it was low utilised and only 8 per cent said that it was extremely low.

From the employees section 64 percent of them felt that the utility was high, 13 percent of the employees stated that the utility was very high. About 15 per cent of them opined that it was low and 8 per cent said that it was extremely low utilised.

Out of the business section 67 per cent highly utilised the mobile phone and 20 per cent of them indicated their response about the utility of mobile phone was very high and rest of them felt that it was low and extremely low utilised.

67 per cent of the doctors opined that it was high utilised and 18 per cent of them felt it was very high. 10 per cent of the doctors felt it was low utilised. Only 5 per cent said that it was extremely low.

The engineers (65 per cent) stated that the mobile phone was highly utilised and 17 per cent said that it was very high utilised. About 10 per cent of the engineers felt it had low utility and rest of them is felt that it was extremely low utility.

About 65 per cent of the lawyers indicated their utility was high, 18 per cent said that the utility was very high remaining of the lawyers opined that it was low and extremely low. From the teachers section 62 per cent of them stated that the mobile phone was highly utilised and 15 per cent of them felt that it was very high utilised. Rest of them felt that the mobile phone was low and extremely low utilised.

About 55 per cent of the rural people opined that the mobile phone was high 12 per cent of them felt that it was very high, 18 per cent stated that it was low utilised 15 per cent said that the utility was extremely low.

On the whole 64 per cent of the respondents expressed that the mobile phone was high utilised and 15 per cent of them felt that it was very high utility. About 13 per cent said that the utility was low and 8 per cent of them felt as extremely low. (Table 5.11)

TABLE 5.12

Respondents' Response Regarding the Method of Mobile Phone

Sl. No.	Respondents	No. of Responses				
		Excellent	*Good*	*Average*	*Poor*	*Total*
1.	Students	11(18)	39(65)	6(10)	4(7)	60(100)
2.	Employees	10(17)	38(63)	7(12)	5(8)	60(100)
3.	Business People	13(22)	39(65)	5(8)	3(5)	60(100)
4.	Doctors	10(17)	35(58)	8(13)	7(12)	60(100)
5.	Engineers	9(15)	37(62)	9(15)	5(8)	60(100)
6.	Lawyers	8(13)	39(65)	7(12)	6(10)	60(100)
7.	Teachers	10(17)	37(61)	9(15)	4(7)	60(100)
8.	Rural People	7(12)	36(60)	12(20)	5(8)	60(100)
	Total	78	300	63	39	480
	Percentage	16	63	13	8	100

Note : Percent of the respondents are indicating in parenthesis.
Source : Field Study.

Analysis: The Table 5.12 depicts the opinion of the respondents on the method of mobile phone. Out of the student section, 65 per cent of the students opined that the method was good and 18 per cent of them are felt that it was excellent. Because it is highly used by the students at present only 17 per cent of the students expressed that it was average and poor responded hereby about the mobile phone.

In the employee section majority of the employees (63 per cent) said that it was good method, 17 per cent stated that the method was excellent. But 12 per cent of the respondents opined that it was average and 8 per cent of them felt that it was poor.

From the business people section, 65 per cent said that it was good and 22 per cent said that the programme was excellent and rest of the respondents felt average and poor.

Out of the doctor section, 58 per cent of the doctors expressed that the method was good, 17 per cent said that the programme was excellent, one fourth per cent of the doctors opined that it was average and poor. The Engineers response (62 per cent) about the method of mobile phone was good. 15 per cent stated that the mobile phone was excellent method, but 15 per cent of the engineers are expressed said it was average and only 8 per cent said it was poor method.

Regarding lawyer section 65 per cent of them felt this method was good, 13 per cent of the respondents expressed that the mobile phone was excellent. But rests of the lawyers are opined that it was average and gave a poor response about the mobile phone. 17 per cent of the teachers expressed that the programme was excellent and 61 per cent said that it was good method. Because, it avoids the communication gap with it. But 15 per cent said it was average and 7 per cent said that the programme was poor because of the misusage of mobile phones by the students. From the rural people section, majority of then (60 per cent) felt that the programme was good method and 12 percent said it was excellent method. But rests of them felt average and poor.

On the whole 63 per cent of the rèspondents stated that the mobile phone was good and 16 per cent of them are felt that it was excellent because, it creates interaction with known persons, it provides convenience and caller identity facility to the users. But 13 per cent said that the method was average and 8 per cent of the respondents opined that it was poor because, barriers of communication are involved, misusages of camera phones, etc.

TABLE 5.13

Opinion on Geographic Information System Programme

Sl. No.	*Respondents*	*No. of Responses*		
		Satisfied	*Dissatisfied*	*Total*
1.	Students	33(55)	27(45)	60(100)
2.	Employees	31(52)	29(48)	60(100)
3.	Business People	35(58)	25(42)	60(100)
4.	Doctors	34(57)	26(43)	60(100)
5.	Engineers	36(60)	24(40)	60(100)
6.	Lawyers	31(52)	29(48)	60(100)
7.	Teachers	32(53)	28(47)	60(100)
8.	Rural People	29(48)	31(52)	60(100)
	Total	261	219	480
	Percentage	54	46	100

Note : Percent of the respondents are indicating in parenthesis.
Source : Field Study.

Analysis: Table 5.13 reveals the opinion of the respondents on geographic Information system programme, 55 per cent of the students are satisfied with this program and remaining of them are dissatisfied because it is more costly procedure. Out of the employees section 52 per cent of the respondents satisfied with the programme and 48 per cent of them felt that it was dissatisfaction. About 58 per cent of 14 business people are indicated their opinion as satisfaction and rest of the business people were dissatisfied.

From the doctors section 57 per cent are satisfied and 43 per cent dissatisfied with this regard. Majority of the engineers (60 per cent) are satisfied with the programme and 40 per cent of them are dissatisfied. Out of the lawyer section, 52 per cent of the respondents are satisfied and rests of them are dissatisfied. The section of teachers (53 per cent) opined that it was satisfied and remaining of them felt as dissatisfied.

Rural people section stated that the satisfaction level was 48 per cent and dissatisfaction level was 52 per cent because, they did not spend more time for this purpose. Hence they are short of awareness on this programme.

On the whole 54 per cent of the respondents are satisfied because, it makes maps on basis of places and it provides database creation. But 46 per cent of the respondents felt that the programme was not satisfied because, it is not accessible by the most of the people.

TABLE 5.14

Response on the Utility of Geographic Information System

Sl. No.	*Respondents*	*No. of Responses*				
		Very High	*High*	*Low*	*Extremely low*	*Total*
1.	Students	3(5)	33(55)	20(33)	4(7)	60(100)
2.	Employees	4(7)	36(60)	11(18)	9(15)	60(100)
3.	Business People	8(13)	39(65)	7(12)	6(10)	60(100)
4.	Doctors	6(10)	36(60)	10(17)	8(13)	60(100)
5.	Engineers	5(8)	37(62)	11(18)	7(12)	60(100)
6.	Lawyers	5(8)	36(60)	12(20)	7(12)	60(100)
7.	Teachers	4(7)	35(58)	13(22)	8(13)	60(100)
8.	Rural People	2(3)	28(47)	17(28)	13(22)	60(100)
	Total	37	280	101	62	480
	Percentage	8	58	21	13	100

Note : Percent of the respondents are indicating in parenthesis.
Source : Field Study.

Analysis: Regarding the utility of geographic information system programme. 5 Percent of the students utilised the programmes very high. 55 percent of the students are opined that the programme was high utilised.

One-third of the students felt that the programme was low utility and only 7 percent expressed that it was extremely low utilised.

From employee section majority of the employees (60 percent) stated that the programme was high, 7 percent said that the programme was very high. But 18 percent said that the programme was low and 15 percent of the employees opined that the programme was extremely low utilised.

In the case of Business people section, 65 percent of them felt that it was high utilised and 13 percent said that it was very high utilised. But 22 percent of the business people expressed that it was low and extremely low utilised. Out of the doctors section 60 percent of the doctors are opined that the programme utility was high. Only 10 percent of them felt that the programme was very high utilised, 17 percent said that the programme was low utilised and 13 percent said that it was extremely low utility.

Coming to the engineer section, 62 percent said that it was high utility and 8 percent observed that it was very high utility. But 18 percent of the respondents opined that the programme was low and 12 percent of them felt that it was extremely low utility. 60 percent of the Lawyers indicated that it was high utilised and 8 percent stated that the was Utility very high, 20 percent said that the utility was low and 12 percent stated that the utility was extremely low. From the teacher section, 65 percent of the respondents expressed that the programme utility was high and very high. But 35 percent of the teachers opined that the programme utility was low and extremely low.

The rural people (47 percent) stated that the programme utility was high and 3 percent said that it was very high, 28 percent said that it was low utility and 22 percent of the rural people stated that it was extremely low utilised.

On the whole 58 percent of the respondents expressed that the programme was high utilised and 8 percent of them felt that it was very high utilized, because, it can improve organisation integration and it helped in the land acquisition costs through better analysis.

But 34 percent of the respondents expressed that the preserve utility was low and extremely low because, it is more costly procedure and it is not possible to access by the more people (Table 5.14).

TABLE 5.15

Opinion on Method of Geographic Information System

Sl. No.	*Respondents*	*No. of Responses*				
		Excellent	*Good*	*Average*	*Poor*	*Total*
(1)	*(2)*	*(3)*	*(4)*	*(5)*	*(6)*	*(7)*
1.	Students	8(14)	29(48)	18(30)	5(8)	60(100)
2.	Employees	7(12)	30(50)	13(21)	10(17)	60(100)
3.	Business People	6(10)	28(46)	19(32)	7(12)	60(100)

(Contd.)

TABLE 5.15 (Contd.)

(1)	(2)	(3)	(4)	(5)	(6)	(7)
4.	Doctors	7(12)	29(48)	13(22)	11(18)	60(100)
5.	Engineers	5(8)	31(52)	18(30)	6(10)	60(100)
6.	Lawyers	6(10)	29(48)	19(32)	6(10)	60(100)
6.	Teachers	3(5)	30(50)	17(28)	10(17)	60(100)
7.	Rural People	4(7)	29(48)	16(27)	11(18)	60(100)
	Total	46	235	133	66	480
	Percentage	9	49	28	14	100

Note : Percent of the respondents are indicating in parenthesis.
Source : Field Study.

Analysis: In view of the geographic information system method, Out of the students section 48 percent of them felt that the programme was good, 14 percent said that it was excellent method. About 30 percent stated that the programme was average and only 8 percent said that it was poor.

An attempt is made to find out the employees opinion, half percent of them felt that the programme was good, nearly 12 percent said that it was excellent method and 21 percent of the employees opined that it was average, about 12 percent of the respondents expressed this programme was poor.

Out of the business section, 46 percent of the respondents opined said that the method was good, 10 percent stated that the programme was excellent, 32 percent said that this method was average and 12 percent of them felt that the programme was poor.

From the doctors section 48 percent said that it was good method, 12 percent of the doctors stated that the programme was excellent, 22 percent of the respondents opined that it was average and 18 percent said that it was poor response.

Engineers (52 percent) opined that the method of geographic information system was good, 8 percent of the respondents are expressed that it was excellent, 30 percent of the respondents of the engineers opined that the method was average and 10 percent said that it was poor.

In the section of lawyers, 48 percent stated that the method was good, 10 percent of the lawyers indicated their response towards the method as excellent. About 32 percent of them felt that it was average and 10 percent said that the programme was poor.

From the teacher section half percent of the respondents felt that the programme was good method only 5 percent stated that the programme was excellent, 28 percent of the respondents are felt that it was average method and 17 percent of them felt it was poor method.

Among the Rural people section 48 percent of the respondents opined that the method was good, only 7 percent of the respondents said that it was excellent, but 27 percent and 18 percent, opined average and poor regarding the method of geographic information system programme.

On the whole 49 percent of the respondents expressed that the programme was good and 9 percent of them felt that it was excellent because, it helped in analyzing data quickly and it presented sufficiently and clearly in the form of a map and accompanying report, allowing decision-makers to focus on the real issues rather than trying to understand the data, because GIS products can be produced quickly, multiple scenario can be evaluated efficiently and effectively. But 28 percent of the respondents opined that it was average and 14 percent said that the programme was poor because it was not possible to access by the more people (Table 5.15).

TABLE 5.16

Opinion of the Respondents about Videoconferencing

Sl. No.	*Respondents*	*No. of Responses*		
		Satisfied	*Dissatisfied*	*Total*
1.	Students	33(55)	27(45)	60(100)
2.	Employees	42(70)	18(30)	60(100)
3.	Business People	40(67)	20(33)	60(100)
4.	Doctors	41(68)	19(32)	60(100)
5.	Engineers	39(65)	21(35)	60(100)
6.	Lawyers	43(72)	17(28)	60(100)
7.	Teachers	38(63)	22(37)	60(100)
8.	Rural People	37(62)	23(38)	60(100)
	Total	313	167	480
	Percentage	65	35	100

Note : Percent of the respondents are indicating in parenthesis.
Source : Field Study.

Analysis: Regarding the opinion of the respondents on video conferencing programme. 55 percent of the students are satisfied with the programme and the remaining (45 percent) are not satisfied. From the employee section maximum extents of the respondents (70 percent) are satisfied and 30 percent have indicated negatively. Regarding the business section majority of business people (67 percent) are satisfied with the programme and one third of them are dissatisfied.

Out of the doctors section 68 percent are satisfied and 32 percent indicates their dissatisfaction. Coming to the engineers section 65 percent of them highly satisfied. But 35 percent are not satisfied with the programme. From the lawyers section 72 percent stated that they are satisfied and 28 percent of the respondents are opined that they are dissatisfied with this programme.

The teachers (63 percent) are satisfied with the programme and 37 percent of the teachers are not satisfied. About 62 percent of the rural people are satisfied with the programme and 38 percent are dissatisfied.

On the whole 65 percent of the respondents are satisfied with video conferencing programme because, it is used for transferring digital images from one location to another location. But 35 percent of the respondents are not satisfied with this programme because, of the danger of over utilization of the equipments. (Table 5.16)

TABLE 5.17

Respondents' Opinion on Utility of Videoconferencing

Sl. No.	*Respondents*	*No. of Responses*				
		Very High	*High*	*Low*	*Extremely low*	*Total*
1.	Students	2(3)	33(55)	19(32)	6(10)	60(100)
2.	Employees	6(10)	37(61)	10(17)	7(12)	60(100)
3.	Business People	11(18)	41(69)	6(10)	2(3)	60(100)
4.	Doctors	9(15)	39(65)	8(13)	4(7)	60(100)
5.	Engineers	7(12)	38(63)	10(17)	5(8)	60(100)
6.	Lawyers	5(8)	37(62)	11(18)	7(12)	60(100)
7.	Teachers	6(10)	39(65)	9(15)	6(10)	60(100)
8.	Rural People	3(5)	34(57)	14(23)	9(15)	60(100)
	Total	49	298	87	46	480
	Percentage	10	62	18	10	100

Note : Percent of the respondents are indicating in parenthesis.
Source : Field Study.

Analysis: From the Table 5.17, opinion of the respondents on the utility of video conferencing programme. From the students section 55 percent of the students are opined that the programme was high utilised. Only 3 percent said that it was very high utilised. About 32 percent said that it was low utility and 10 percent stated that the utility was extremely low.

As can be seen the employees (61 percent) stated that the utility was high about the programme only 10 percent of them felt that it was very high. While 17 percent of the employees are indicated their opinion on the utility of the programme as low rest of them said that the utility was extremely low.

Out of the Business section majority of the respondents (69 percent) are opined that the utility was high and 18 percent of them felt it was very high utilised and rest of them are felt that the utility was low and extremely low.

Doctors (65 percent) stated that the programme was high utility, 15 percent of them opined that it was very high utilized. Only 13 percent are expressed that the programme was low and only 7 percent doctors are opined that the programme utility was extremely low. Majority of the engineers (63 percent) expressed that the utility was high and 12 percent of them are felt that it was very high utilised. One fourth of the engineers felt that the programme was low and extremely low.

About 62 percent of the lawyer's respondents stated that the utility was high. Only 8 percent said that it was very high utility. 18 percent of them felt that the utility of this programme was low and 12 percent of them expressed that it was extremely low.

Out of the rural people section, 57 percent stated that the programme was high utilised and only 5 percent opined that the utility was very high. 23 percent of the rural people expressed that it was low utilised and 15 percent of them felt that it was extremely low utilised.

On the whole 62 percent of the respondents opined that the utility was high and 10 percent of the respondents expressed that the utility was very high because it provides excellent communication to the people. But rest of the respondents felt that it was low and extremely low utilised because it is very expensive process, and it required broad technology to be used.

TABLE 5.18

Opinion of Respondents on Method of Videoconferencing

Sl. No.	Respondents	No. of Responses				
		Excellent	Good	Average	Poor	Total
1.	Students	9(15)	36(60)	9(15)	6(10)	60(100)
2.	Employees	8(13)	40(67)	7(12)	5(8)	60(100)
3.	Business People	12(20)	41(68)	4(7)	3(5)	60(100)
4.	Doctors	10(17)	40(66)	6(10)	4(7)	60(100)
5.	Engineers	11(18)	39(65)	4(7)	6(10)	60(100)
6.	Lawyers	10(17)	38(63)	9(15)	3(5)	60(100)
7.	Teachers	9(15)	39(65)	7(12)	5(8)	60(100)
8.	Rural People	8(13)	38(64)	8(13)	6(10)	60(100)
	Total	77	311	54	38	480
	Percentage	16	65	11	8	100

Note : Percent of the respondents are indicating in parenthesis.
Source : Field Study.

Analysis: Regarding the method of video conferencing programme. In the student section 60 percent said that the method was good. 15 percent of the students stated that it was excellent. About 15 percent of them felt that the programme was average and rest of the respondents are expressed that it was poor method.

From the employees section, 67 percent said that it was good method, 13 percent felt that the programme was excellent. Only 12 percent of the employees indicated their opinion on this programme was average and 8 percent said that it was poor.

Out of the business section majority of the respondents (68 percent) are felt that the programme was good method and 20 percent of the business people opined that it was excellent. However, 7 percent of the business people and 5 percent of the business people indicated the method to be average and poor respectively.

The doctors (66 percent) opined that it was good method, 17 percent stated that the programme was excellent, 10 percent of them felt that it was average and 7 percent indicated the programme was poor.

The respondents of the engineers (65 percent) stated that the programme was good method and 18 percent of the respondents opined that it was excellent. Rest of the respondents are expressed that the programme was average and poor.

From the lawyers section, respondents (63 percent) opined that the video conferencing programme was good and 17 percent of them felt it was excellent method. About 15 percent of the lawyers indicated their opinion on this programme was average and only 5 percent said that it was poor.

The teachers (65 percent) opined that the programme was good and 15 percent said that the programme was excellent method. 12 percent of them felt that it was average and 8 percent indicated their response was poor.

Rural people (64 percent) are indicated that their opinion about the programme was good and 13 percent said that it was excellent and rests of the respondents are felt that it was average and poor.

On the whole 65 percent of the respondents were opined that the programme was good and, 16 percent of them felt that it was excellent because, it is cheaper over the past few years and computer programmes much simpler than before. But 11 percent of the respondents and 8 percent of the respondents, who are opined average and poor respectively about the method of video conferencing programme suggested the reasons such as cost of production and establishments. (Table 5.18)

TABLE 5.19

Opinion of the Respondents about Teleconferencing

Sl. No.	*Respondents*	*No. of Responses*		
		Satisfied	*Dissatisfied*	*Total*
(1)	*(2)*	*(3)*	*(4)*	*(5)*
1.	Students	34(57)	26(43)	60(100)
2.	Employees	38(63)	22(37)	60(100)
3.	Business People	39(65)	21(35)	60(100)

(Contd.)

TABLE 5.19 (*Contd.*)

(1)	*(2)*	*(3)*	*(4)*	*(5)*
4.	Doctors	34(57)	26(43)	60(100)
5.	Engineers	29(48)	31(52)	60(100)
6.	Lawyers	30(50)	30(50)	60(100)
7.	Teachers	31(52)	29(48)	60(100)
8.	Rural People	29(48)	31(52)	60(100)
	Total	264	216	480
	Percentage	55	45	100

Note : Percent of the respondents are indicating in parenthesis.
Source : Field Study.

Analysis: Regarding the teleconference programme 57 percent of the students opined that the were satisfied because it can reduced the cost of training but 43 percent of them are felt that the programme was unsatisfactory because of the high cost of establishment.

From the employee section 63 percent held the opinion that they were satisfied and remaining of the respondents is dissatisfied with the programme. The business people (65 percent) are satisfied with the teleconferencing programme because, it increases access to information tools for decision making. But 35 percent stated that they are dissatisfied with this regard because of the danger of over utilization.

57 percent of the doctors are opined that the satisfaction was high because it is used in the medicine field and 43 percent of the doctors are not satisfied with the programme because it is constantly changing technology.

Engineers are highly dissatisfied with this programme because, of the deficiency of technical expertise to maintain. The system has been poorly maintained as the teleconferencing systems frequently show ghost images, echo effects and voice errors which affect the quality of transmission and reception. 48 per cent of them satisfied with the programme.

Half of the percent of the lawyer respondents opined equally in point of teleconferencing programme satisfaction and dissatisfaction. About 52 percent teachers expressed half of the percent are distributed by the lawyers in their response regarding the opinion of the teleconferencing programme as that they were satisfied and remaining of the respondents are dissatisfied.

From the rural people section 52 percent of them felt that the programme was dissatisfactory because of lack of familiarity of the users with the medium and equipments require additional time but remaining are satisfied.

On the whole 55 percent of the respondents stated that they were satisfied. 45 percent of the people are dissatisfied because, there is a requirement for producing using courseware, the design of multimedia package requires skilled persons with sound knowledge in instructional and educational designs as well as computer operations which is always a constraint in India (Table 5.19).

TABLE 5.20
Respondents' Response Regarding the Utility of Teleconferencing

Sl. No.	*Respondents*	*No. of Responses*				
		Very High	*High*	*Low*	*Extremely low*	*Total*
1.	Students	2(3)	26(44)	18(30)	14(23)	60(100)
2.	Employees	3(5)	29(48)	12(20)	16(27)	60(100)
3.	Business People	8(13)	32(54)	11(18)	9(15)	60(100)
4.	Doctors	5(8)	31(52)	13(22)	11(18)	60(100)
5.	Engineers	4(7)	32(53)	17(28)	7(12)	60(100)
6.	Lawyers	3(5)	28(47)	16(27)	13(21)	60(100)
6.	Teachers	5(8)	30(50)	15(25)	10(17)	60(100
7.	Rural People	1(1)	28(47)	19(32)	12(20)	60(100)
	Total	31	236	121	92	480
	Percentage	7	49	25	19	100

Note : Percent of the respondents are indicating in parenthesis.
Source : Field Study.

Analysis: An inquiry in to the respondent's opinion on the utility of teleconferencing programme. From the student section 44 percent of the respondents felt that the utility of the teleconferencing programme was high, because the programme helps them to know the recent innovations, only 3 percent opined that the utility was very high. But 30 percent opined that the programme was low utilised and 23 percent said that it was extremely low.

From the employee section 48 percent stated that the utility was high and 5 percent felt that utility was very high but 20 percent of the respondents expressed that the programme was low and 27 percent said that it was extremely low utilised.

In the section of business people 54 percent stated that the utility of the programme was high, 13 percent opined that the utility was very high but one third of the respondents are observed that the utility was low and extremely low because greater time needed for preparation of courseware.

Regarding the doctors section 52 percent of them felt that the utility was high and 8 percent stated that the utility was very high. About 22 percent of the doctor respondents felt that the utility was low and 18 percent expressed that it was extremely low.

53 percent of the Engineers opined that the utility was high, only 7 percent stated that the utility was very high. But 28 percent opined that the utility was low and 12 percent of these expressed that it was extremely low.

Out of the lawyers 47 percent stated that the utility was high and only 5 percent of the respondents felt that it was very high utilised. About 27 percent of the lawyers observed that the utility was low and 21 percent opined that the programme utility was extremely low.

Teachers (50 percent) expressed that the programme was high utilised and 8 percent said that the utility was very high. While 25 percent stated that the programme was low and 17 percent opined that it was extremely low.

From the rural people, 47 percent opined that the programme utility was high and one percent stated very high. About 52 percent of the rural people indicated their opinion on the utility of said programme was low and extremely low because of the danger of over utilization and under utilization of the equipments high cost of production, evaluation and distribution of educational multimedia packages.

On the whole 49 percent of the respondents stated that the utility of the programme was high and 7 percent opined that the programme was very high because, training people in general skills broadly affect general performance. It provide enables to training be administered instantly and simultaneously. Only 7 percent of them felt that it was very high utilised. One fourth percent of the respondents felt that it was low utilised and 19 percent opined that the utility was extremely low because confusions and over standards had added to the technofobia created by lack of awareness about the potentials of state of art. (Table 5.20).

TABLE 5.21

Opinion of the Respondents on Method of Teleconferencing

Sl. No.	*Respondents*	*No. of Responses*				
		Excellent	*Good*	*Average*	*Poor*	*Total*
1.	Students	5(8)	32(53)	10(17)	13(22)	60(100)
2.	Employees	6(10)	33(55)	12(20)	9(15)	60(100)
3.	Business People	9(15)	29(48)	13(22)	9(15)	60(100)
4.	Doctors	8(13)	32(54)	12(20)	8(13)	60(100)
5.	Engineers	5(8)	31(52)	20(33)	4(7)	60(100)
6.	Lawyers	6(10)	29(48)	18(30)	7(12)	60(100)
7.	Teachers	5(8)	32(53)	10(17)	13(22)	60(100)
8.	Rural People	3(5)	28(46)	19(32)	10(17)	60(100)
	Total	47	246	114	73	480
	Percentage	10	51	24	15	100

Note : Percent of the respondents are indicating in parenthesis.
Source : Field Study.

Analysis: In view of the students section, 53 percent of the students expressed that the method of the teleconferencing programme was good and 8 percent stated that the method was excellent. But 17 percent opined that it was average and 22 percent observed that the method was poor.

Out of the respondents of employee section 55 percent gave their response as good about the programme and 10 percent said that it was excellent. But 20 percent of the employees are indicating their opinion as average about the programme and rest stated that it was poor.

From the section of business people, 15 percent said that the teleconferencing method was excellent and 48 percent stated that it was good. About 22 percent of the business people opined that the programme was average and 15 percent said it was poor.

An inquiry in to the doctors (54 percent) is indicated that the programme was good, 13 percent said that it was excellent. While 20 percent of the respondents felt that it was average and 13 percent said that the programme was poor response. 52 percent of the engineers felt that the method was good and 8 percent said that it was excellent, but one third of the respondents felt that it was average and only 7 percent said that it was poor.

As can be seen from the lawyer section majority (48 percent) of them felt that the method was good and 10 percent said that it was excellent method. About 30 per cent stated that the method was average and 12 percent of the respondents expressed that it was poor.

As can be seen from the data of teacher section. 53 percent of the teacher respondents opined that the programme was good method only 8 percent said that it was excellent. Average opinion was given by the 17 percent of the respondents and 22 percent stated that it was poor.

From rural people section, 46 percent said that the programme was good, only 5 percent said that the method was excellent, 32 percent said that it was average and 17 percent of the rural people opined that the method was poor.

On the whole 51 percent of the respondents expressed that the method of teleconferencing was good and only 10 percent of them felt that it was excellent because, it reduce the resource persons requirements, it saves teachers time, it reduce and eliminate travel, and the trainees can be trained in the work place. But 24 percent said that it was average and remaining stated that it was poor, because of the lack of familiarities of users, greater time needed and high cost of establishments (Table 5.21).

TABLE 5.22

Opinion of the Respondents on Computer Conferencing

Sl. No.	*Respondents*	*No. of Responses*		
		Satisfied	*Dissatisfied*	*Total*
(1)	*(2)*	*(3)*	*(4)*	*(5)*
1.	Students	38(63)	22(37)	60(100)
2.	Employees	41(68)	19(32)	60(100)

(Contd.)

TABLE 5.22 (Contd.)

(1)	(2)	(3)	(4)	(5)
3.	Business People	39(65)	21(35)	60(100)
4.	Doctors	37(62)	23(38)	60(100)
5.	Engineers	43(72)	17(28)	60(100)
6.	Lawyers	33(55)	7(45)	60(100)
7.	Teachers	40(67)	20(33)	60(100)
8.	Rural People	29(48)	31(52)	60(100)
	Total	300	180	480
	Percentage	63	37	100

Note : Percent of the respondents are indicating in parenthesis.
Source : Field Study.

Analysis: Table 5.22 reveals the opinion of the respondents on the computer conferencing programme. Majority of the students (63 percent) are satisfied with this programme and remaining of them are unsatisfied. From the employees section 68 percent are highly satisfied and 32 percent of them felt that it was dissatisfaction. The respondents of the business people are opined with satisfaction (65 percent) and 35 percent of the business people opined with dissatisfaction. An over whelming majority of the doctors (62 percent) are satisfied with this programme but 38 percent are dissatisfied.

Regarding the engineers section 72 percent are satisfied with this programme and 28 percent are dissatisfied. From the section of the lawyers, 55 percent are satisfied and remaining people are dissatisfied. Regarding the engineer section 72 percent of the respondents are satisfied with this programme and 28 percent are dissatisfied.

From the section of the lawyers, 55 percent are satisfied and remaining people are dissatisfied. About 67 percent of the teachers indicated their opinion on the computer conferencing programme as satisfactory but 33 percent are dissatisfied. Rural people are also satisfied (48 percent) about the programme and remaining respondents are not satisfied.

On the whole 63 percent of the respondents are satisfied with the programme because, it reduces time and resource requirements, trainers have increased control over the training. But 37 percent of the respondents indicated their opinions as unsatisfactory because it needs more cost of production investment.

Analysis: Regarding utility of computer conferencing programme. 48 percent of the students felt that the utility was high and only 5 percent stated that utility was very high as they used this programme. But 32 percent of them felt that the utility was low and 15 percent of the students stated that the programme was extremely low.

Table 5.23
Response of the Respondents on Utility of Computer Conferencing

Sl. No.	Respondents	No. of Responses				
		Very High	High	Low	Extremely low	Total
1.	Students	3(5)	29(48)	19(32)	9(15)	60(100)
2.	Employees	5(8)	31(52)	13(22)	11(18)	60(100)
3.	Business People	9(15)	33(55)	11(18)	7(12)	60(100)
4.	Doctors	6(10)	29(48)	16(27)	9(15)	60(100)
5.	Engineers	5(8)	32(53)	10(17)	13(22)	60(100)
6.	Lawyers	4(7)	32(53)	9(15)	15(25)	60(100)
7.	Teachers	6(10)	28(46)	13(22)	13(22)	60(100)
8.	Rural People	3(5)	27(45)	16(27)	14(23)	60(100)
	Total	41	241	107	91	480
	Percentage	8	50	23	19	100

Note : Percent of the respondents are indicating in parenthesis.
Source : Field Study.

From the business section 55 percent of them felt that the it was high utilised and 15 percent stated that the utility was very high. But remaining of the business people (30 percent) opined that utility was low and extremely low.

The Doctors (48 percent) stated that the utility was high, 10 percent stated it was very high utilised. But 27 percent of the doctors stated that the utility was low and 15 percent of them felt that it was extremely low utilized. Coming to the engineers, 53 percent felt that the utility was high, 8 percent stated that the utility was low and 22 percent stated that the programme was extremely low.

53 percent of lawyers stated that the utility was high, only 7 percent of them indicated that the utility was very high but 40 percent of the lawyers expressed that it was low and extremely low.

According to teacher section, 46 percent stated, that the utility was high and 10 percent opined that it was very high utilised. But 22 percent of the teachers expressed the programme utility was low and 22 percent of indicated that the utility was extremely low.

The rural people (45 percent) opined that the programme utility was high and only 5 percent felt that the programme was very high utilized. Remaining of the rural people, i.e. 27 percent and 23 percent indicated low and extremely low respectively about the utility of computer confirming programme.

On the whole half percent of the respondents stated that the utility was high and only 8 percent of the respondents opined that it was very high utilised because it is important for a user to choose the configuration according to their needs and conditions. But 23 percent stated that utility was low and 19 percent opined it was extremely low utilised, because, of the danger of over utilization and under utilization of the equipments and it needs more cost of production and investment. (Table 5.23)

TABLE 5.24
Opinion on Method of Computer Conferencing Programme

Sl. No.	*Respondents*	*No. of Responses*				
		Excellent	*Good*	*Average*	*Poor*	*Total*
1.	Students	11(18)	33(55)	9(15)	7(12)	60(100)
2.	Employees	7(12)	29(48)	10(17)	14(23)	60(100)
3.	Business People	11(18)	34(57)	9(15)	6(10)	60(100)
4.	Doctors	9(15)	33(55)	10(17)	8(13)	60(100)
5.	Engineers	10(17)	34(56)	9(15)	7(12)	60(100)
6.	Lawyers	9(15)	29(49)	17(28)	5(8)	60(100)
7.	Teachers	10(17)	31(51)	9(15)	10(17)	60(100)
8.	Rural People	4(7)	28(47)	19(31)	9(15)	60(100)
	Total	71	251	92	66	480
	Percentage	15	52	19	14	100

Note : Percent of the respondents are indicating in parenthesis.
Source : Field Study.

Analysis: Opinion of the respondents regarding the method of Computer Conferencing Programme. The respondents of the students (55 percent) stated that the method was good, 18 percent opined that it was excellent. But 15 percent of them felt that it was average and 12 percent of the students felt that it was poor.

Coming to the employees section 12 percent of the employees stated that the method was excellent, 48 percent opined that the method was good, 17 percent felt that it was average method and 12 percent expressed that it was poor method.

From the Business section 57 percent stated that the method was good, 18 percent expressed that it was excellent because, it provides more configuration to the business people. But 15 percent said that it was average and 10 percent said that it was poor response, as it was not cheaper cost.

Out of the Doctors 55 percent of them felt that the method was good, 15 percent said that it was excellent, 17 percent of the doctors opined that it was average and 13 percent said it was poor.

Among the engineers 17 percent opined that the method was excellent, 56 percent of the said people are expressed it is a good method because it helps in the engineering fields for improve the skills. About 15 percent of them felt that it was average and 12 percent said that it was poor.

From the lawyer section 49 percent of the lawyers stated that it was good method, 15 percent said that itwas excellent. But 28 percent of the lawyers felt that the programme was average and 8 percent said that it was poor.

In the section of teachers 51 percent stated that the programme was good, 17 percent felt that this program was excellent. While 17 percent of them felt this method was poor and 15 percent said it was average.

47 percent of the rural people opined that the programme was good, 7 percent felt that it was excellent, 31 percent stated that the method was average and remaining of them felt that it was excellent, 31 percent stated that the method was Average and remaining of them felt that it was poor.

On the whole 52 percent of the respondents are opined that the programme was good and 15 percent of them felt that it was excellent because, it enables in participating in the various programmes i.e. bulletin boards, e-groups, mailing lists, real time chat and email and it is capable of evolving unique instructional strategy for each educational task. But 19 percent of the respondents agreed that the programme was average and 14 percent of them, are opined that it was poor because, it needs more cost of production and investment and the danger of over utilization and under utilization of the equipments (Table 5.24).

TABLE 5.25

Opinion of the Respondents about Computer-based Training

Sl. No.	*Respondents*	*No. of Responses*		
		Satisfied	*Dissatisfied*	*Total*
1.	Students	41(68)	19(32)	60(100)
2.	Employees	43(72)	17(28)	60(100)
3.	Business People	39(65)	21(35)	60(100)
4.	Doctors	40(67)	20(33)	60(100)
5.	Engineers	38(63)	22(37)	60(100)
6.	Lawyers	39(65)	21(35)	60(100)
7.	Teachers	40(67)	20(33)	60(100)
8.	Rural People	37(62)	23(38)	60(100)
	Total	317(529)	163(271)	480(800)
	Percentage	66	34	100

Note : Percent of the respondents are indicating in parenthesis.
Source : Field Study.

Analysis: In view of the above programme majority of the students (68 percent) found that pay to be satisfying with computer-based training programme because, it enables learners to study at time of their own choice. About 32 percent of the students felt that they were dissatisfied. Maximum extent of the employees stated that the satisfaction level was highly (72 percent) and remaining of them are dissatisfied with this required programme.

From the business section 65 percent of the respondents are satisfied with this programme and only 35 percent of them are dissatisfied because, it can prove costly and expensive hardware and software are required.

Doctors are also satisfied (67 percent) about the programme, as they use for developing their skills. Rest of the respondents of the doctors are not satisfied, because they lack of time. Regarding engineers section 63 percent of them felt happy because they use this programme for their professional purpose, But 37 percent are not satisfied with this programme, because they have no flexibility.

An enquiry in to the lawyer's opinion on this programme reveals that majority of the lawyers (65 percent) are satisfied and remaining of them dissatisfied. From the teachers section, the respondents (67 percent) expressed that the programme was satisfied and one-third percent of the respondents are dissatisfied with this programme.

The Rural people (62 percent) stated that they were highly satisfied with this programme. But 38 percent of them indicated their opinion on this as dissatisfaction. On the whole 66 percent of the respondents are stated that the programme was highly satisfactory because it is available vehicle for learning technical skills, particularly where large numbers of persons are to be trained and it makes the medium sophisticated training tools. But 34 percent of the respondents are not satisfied because it may induce a sense of isolation, and the individuals work on their own. (Table 5.25)

TABLE 5.26

Response on the Utility of Computer-based Training

Sl. No.	*Respondents*	*No. of Responses*				
		Very High	*High*	*Low*	*Extremely low*	*Total*
1.	Students	6(10)	35(58)	11(18)	8(14)	60(100)
2.	Employees	11(18)	37(62)	9(15)	3(5)	60(100)
3.	Business People	10(17)	36(60)	8(13)	6(10)	60(100)
4.	Doctors	9(15)	35(58)	9(15)	7(12)	60(100)
5.	Engineers	5(8)	34(57)	12(20)	9(15)	60(100)
6.	Lawyers	7(12)	29(48)	18(30)	6(10)	60(100)
7.	Teachers	9(15)	32(53)	12(20)	7(12)	60(100)
8.	Rural People	5(8)	30(50)	19(32)	6(10)	60(100)
	Total	62	268	98	52	480
	Percentage	13	56	20	11	100

Note : Percent of the respondents are indicating in parenthesis.
Source : Field Study.

Analysis: Regarding the utility of computer-based training programme. 58 percent of the students stated that the utility was high and 10 percent of the students expressed that it was very high utilised remaining of the student respondents are opined that it was low utilised because, it requires a greater self-discipline and commitment by the learner.

An over whelming majority of employees (62 percent) stated that the utility was high and 18 percent of them felt that it was very high utilised. About 15 percent of the employees opined that the utility of the programme was low and only 5 percent of the employees indicated their utility was extremely low because it is relatively inflexible.

From the business section maximum respondents (60 percent) utilised this programme for their business activities and improving their skills, 17 percent of them felt that it was very high utilised. While 13 percent and 10 percent of the respondents, opined that it was low and extremely low respectively.

Doctors (58 percent) stated that the utility of this programme was high and 15 percent of them felt that it was very high utilised. Remaining of the doctors are expressed that it was low and extremely low utilised.

The section of engineers (57 percent) felt that the programme utility was high because they used to depend on this programme for improving their skills. Only 8 percent of them are felt the programme was very high utilised. Nearly 20 percent of the engineers expressed that it was low utilised and 15 percent of them felt that the programme was extremely low utilised.

Coming to the lawyers section 48 percent of the lawyers opined that the utility was high and 12 percent of them felt that it was very high utilised, because they were getting legal transaction ideas through this training. About 40 percent of the lawyers opined that the utility of this programme was low and extremely low (30 percent and 10 percent) because they have no time and busy work schedule.

Inquiries in to the teachers (53 percent) stated that the utility was high, 15 percent of the teachers expressed that it was very high utilized, because their teaching capability and skills were developed through the programme. Remaining of the teachers indicated that the utility was low and extremely low, i.e. 20 percent and 12 percent respectively about the computer-based training programme because, the teachers are over confident regarding this programme.

Half percent of the rural people opined that the utility was high only 8 percent of the rural people expressed that the programme utility was very high because they have interest for training and they have need about this training. But 32 percent of the rural people felt it was low and 10 percent stated that it was extremely low utilised because facilities are required.

On the whole 56 percent of the respondents that the utility was high and 13 percent of the respondents stated that it was very high utilized. Because it is user choice of control and routing through the programme that make the medium of sophisticated training poor. It can keep student record automatically and it can offer a high level of interaction with immediate feed back. Remaining of the respondents indicated that the utility of said programme was low and extremely low because it does not permit direct personal reinforcement, and effects of training are forgone. (Table 5.26).

TABLE 5.27

Opinion on Method of Computer-based Training Programme

Sl. No.	*Respondents*	*No. of Responses*				
		Excellent	*Good*	*Average*	*Poor*	*Total*
1.	Students	8(13)	31(52)	14(23)	7(12)	60(100)
2.	Employees	7(12)	33(55)	11(18)	9(15)	60(100)
3.	Business People	10(17)	29(48)	12(20)	9(15)	60(100)
4.	Doctors	11(18)	34(57)	7(12)	8(13)	60(100)
5.	Engineers	9(15)	28(47)	16(26)	7(12)	60(100)
6.	Lawyers	8(13)	32(53)	14(24)	6(10)	60(100)
7.	Teachers	9(15)	31(52)	15(25)	5(8)	60(100)
8.	Rural People	6(10)	29(48)	21(35)	4(7)	60(100)
	Total	68	247	110	55	480
	Percentage	14	51	23	12	100

Note : Percent of the respondents are indicating in parenthesis.
Source : Field Study.

Analysis: It can be seen from the (Table 5.27) that in the opinion of the students on computer-based training method, as many as 52 percent stated that the methods was good and 13 percent of the students felt that the programme was excellent method. But 23 percent and 12 percent of the respondents opined that the method of the programme was average and poor respectively.

From the employees section 55 percent expressed that the programme was excellent and 12 percent opined that the programme was good. About 18 percent of them stated that the method of the programme was average as they used this method very rarely. But 15 percent responded that the method of the programme was poor.

Coming to business section 48 percent of them felt that the method of the programme was good, 17 percent stated that the method excellent and 20 percent of the respondents opined that the method of the same was average. But only 15 percent of the respondents are expressed that the method was poor.

From the doctor section 57 percent said that the method was good, because it helps them to know recent treatments in the field of medicine, 18 percent stated that the method was excellent and 12 percent opined that the method of the same was average. But 13 percent expressed that the method was poor.

Engineers (47 percent) said that the method of the programme was good because it provides necessary and latest information about their field of engineering, 15 percent of the engineers felt that the method was excellent, 26 percent said that it was poor. 53 percent of the lawyers opined that the programme was good and 13 percent expressed that the method was excellent remaining of the lawyers said that the method was average and poor.

From the teachers section 15 percent of the teachers stated that the programme was excellent and 52 percent opined that the method was good, 25 percent of the teachers expressed it was average method and 8 percent said that the method was poor.

Rural people (48 percent) said that the method was good and 10 percent of them are felt that it was excellent. But many (42 percent) expressed that it was average and poor.

On the whole 51 percent of the respondents are opined that the method was good and 14 percent of them expressed that it was excellent method because, it can be cost effective depending on the circumstances and it can be made available at different locations and offer privacy. About 23 percent of the respondents said that it was average method and 12 percent responded it as a poor method because, it can prove to be costly as expensive hardware and software are required.

Table 5.28

Opinion of the Respondents about Computer-based Multimedia

Sl. No.	*Respondents*	*No. of Responses*		
		Satisfied	*Dissatisfied*	*Total*
1.	Students	34(57)	26(43)	60(100)
2.	Employees	39(65)	21(35)	60(100)
3.	Business People	40(67)	20(33)	60(100)
4.	Doctors	38(63)	22(37)	60(100)
5.	Engineers	37(62)	23(38)	60(100)
6.	Lawyers	40(67)	20(33)	60(100)
7.	Teachers	39(65)	21(35)	60(100)
8.	Rural People	34(57)	26(43)	60(100)
	Total	301	179	480
	Percentage	63	37	100

Note : Percent of the respondents are indicating in parenthesis.
Source : Field Study.

Analysis: Regarding the opinion of the respondents on computer-based multimedia programme, 57 percent of the students are satisfied with the programme and the remaining (43 percent) is not satisfied because they have no interest in their vicinity.

From the employee section 65 percent are satisfied because they are using computer-based multimedia, whenever they are free, but 35 percent are dissatisfied. Maximum extents of the business people (67 percent) are full happy about this programme, as they use this programme for their business purpose. But one-third of the business people are not satisfied because they have lack of time. Doctors (63 percent) are satisfied about the programme and remaining of the Doctors respondents (37 percent) opined that they are dissatisfied.

The section of Engineers (62 Percent) highly satisfied. But 38 percent of the engineer respondents are not satisfied with the programme. Majority of the lawyers (67 percent) opined that they are satisfied with the programme and remaining (33 percent) of them felt dissatisfied.

About 65 percent of the teachers are expressed that the satisfaction level is high. But 35 percent indicated their dissatisfaction. While 57 percent of the rural people stated that they are satisfied and 43 percent of the rural people opined said their dissatisfaction.

On the whole 63 percent of the respondents of various sections are satisfied with the computer-based multimedia programme and 37 percent of them are not satisfied with the programme because of lack of time, bring in the professional field and lack of inconvenience (Table 5.28).

Table 5.29

Response on Utility of Computer-based Multimedia

Sl. No.	*Respondents*	*No. of Responses*				
		Very High	*High*	*Low*	*Extremely low*	*Total*
1.	Students	5(8)	31(52)	12(20)	12(20)	60(100)
2.	Employees	3(5)	34(57)	9(15)	14(23)	60(100)
3.	Business People	6(10)	41(68)	10(17)	3(5)	60(100)
4.	Doctors	4(7)	42(70)	8(13)	6(10)	60(100)
5.	Engineers	3(5)	39(65)	8(13)	10(17)	60(100)
6.	Lawyers	5(8)	40(67)	11(18)	4(7)	60(100)
7.	Teachers	2(3)	38(63)	14(24)	6(10)	60(100)
8.	Rural People	3(5)	39(65)	7(12)	11(18)	60(100)
	Total	31	304	79	66	480
	Percentage	6	64	16	14	100

Note : Percent of the respondents are indicating in parenthesis.
Source : Field Study.

Analysis: It can be seen from the Table 5.29 the opinion of the various sections on the utility of computer based multimedia programme. From the section of students majority of the students (52 Percent) stated that the utility of the programme was high. Also 8 percent of the students expressed that it was very high utilized. Nearly 40 percent of the students did not utilize it highly because they are busy with their studies.

The employees (57 percent) opined that the utility was high. Only 5 percent of the employees stated that the utility was very high. Remaining of the respondents is indicated their utility was low and extremely low.

Majority of the business people (68 percent) stated that the utility was high, 10 percent of the respondents felt that the programme was very high utilized. About 17 percent of the respondents felt their opinion was low utilized only 5 percent of the business people stated that it was extremely low utilized. Maximum extents of the doctors (70 per cent) stated that it was high utilized. About 13 percent of them felt it was low utilized 7 percent of the doctors indicated their opinion on this regard as very high utilized.

Remaining of the doctors (10 percent) opined said utility was extremely low. From the engineers section 65 percent of them felt that the utility was high, 5 percent of the engineers expressed that it was very high utilized. About 13 percent of them felt that it was low utilised. Only 17 percent of the engineers stated that the programme was extremely low utilized.

About 8 percent of the lawyers opined that the utility was very high. While 67 percent of the lawyers expressed that the utility was high. Nearly 18 percent of the lawyers indicated their opinion on the utility was low. Only 7 per cent of the lawyers are expressed it was extremely low utilized.

In the teacher section, 63 percent of the teachers opined that the said programme utility was high, 24 percent of them felt that it was low utilized. Only 3 percent of the teachers expressed that it was very high utilized. Nearly 10 percent of the teacher respondents stated that the utility was extremely low.

About 65 percent of the rural people expressed that it was high utilized. Only 5 percent of the said people stated that the utility was very high. 30 percent of the rural people expressed that the utility was low and extremely low.

On the whole 64 per cent of the respondents stated that the utility was high because, it is being used in movie-making very extensively and interaction of more advantage of multimedia. Only 6 percent of them felt that the utility was very high. About 16 percent of the respondents expressed that the utility was low, because, it is more complex in the software programmes. And remaining of respondents (14 percent) opined that it was extremely low utilized, because it requires more technical support (Table 5.29).

Analysis: The Table 5.30 depicts the opinion of the respondents on the method of computer based multimedia programme. In view of the students section, 60 percent of them felt that the method was good only 12 percent of the student respondents stated that it was excellent and 15 percent of the respondents of students opined that it was average and remaining of them are expressed that it was poor.

TABLE 5.30

Respondents Opinion on Method of Computer-based Multimedia

Sl. No.	*Respondents*	*No. of Responses*				
		Excellent	*Good*	*Average*	*Poor*	*Total*
1.	Students	7(12)	36(60)	9(15)	8(13)	60(100)
2.	Employees	6(10)	29(48)	18(30)	7(12)	60(100)
3.	Business People	2(3)	28(47)	18(30)	12(20)	60(100)
4.	Doctors	8(13)	40(67)	7(12)	5(8)	60(100)
5.	Engineers	9(15)	41(68)	6(10)	4(7)	60(100)
6.	Lawyers	7(12)	39(65)	8(13)	6(10)	60(100)
7.	Teachers	6(10)	40(67)	6(10)	8(13)	60(100)
8.	Rural People	7(12)	32(53)	12(20)	9(15)	60(100)
	Total	52	285	84	59	480
	Percentage	11	59	18	12	100

Note : Percent of the respondents are indicating in parenthesis.
Source : Field Study.

In the case of employees section 10 percent of them felt it was excellent method. About 48 percent of the employees stated that the method was good, 30 percent of the employees expressed that it was average and 12 percent of them felt that it was poor method.

The business people (47 percent) stated that the method was good and 3 percent of them felt that it was excellent method regarding computer-based multimedia programme. Half percent of the business people indicated their opinion on the method, as it was average and poor. About 13 percent of the doctors expressed that the method was excellent, 67 percent of the doctor respondents opined that it was good method. 12 percent of the doctors stated that it was average method and 8 percent of them felt it was poor method.

In the section of engineers 68 percent stated that the method was good, because it enables them to known latest information 15 percent respondents felt that the method was excellent, and rest of them stated that it was average and poor.

From the lawyer's data 12 percent of them felt that it was excellent method, 65 percent of them stated that the method is good. About 13 per cent of the lawyer indicated their response as average regarding the computer-based multimedia and remaining of them expressed it was poor.

The teachers (67 percent) opined that it was a good method and one 10 percent of the respondents are felt that it was excellent method. Remaining them felt average and gave a poor response regarding the programme.

The rural people (53 percent) are stated that the programme was good and only 12 percent of them are felt it was excellent method regarding the programme. But 20 percent of rural people were expressed it was average and 15 percent of the respondents felt it was poor.

On the whole 59 percent of the respondents are stated that it was good method because, it provides to create presentations quickly and it integrates voice, video and computer technologies in to single delivery system. About 11 percent of the respondents felt that it was excellent method. While 18 per cent and 12 percent of the respondents, opined average and poor respectively regarding the method of this programme because it is more complex in the software programmes, it requires more technical support from the software personnel.

TABLE 5.31

Opinion on Computer Assisted Instruction Programme

Respondents' Opinion		*No. of Responses*	*Percent of Responses*
Opinion	a. Satisfaction	40	67
	b. Dissatisfaction	20	33
	Total	60	100
Utility	a. Very High	7	11
	b. High	33	56
	c. Low	16	27
	d. Extremely Low	4	6
	Total	60	100
Method	a. Excellent	19	32
	b. Good	20	33
	c. Average	14	24
	d. Poor	7	11
	Total	60	100

Source : Field Study.

Analysis: Majority of the students (67 per cent) satisfied with computer-assisted instruction because this programme is relatively easy and inexpensive to produce. But 33 percent of the respondents stated that it was given negatively because it gives inappropriate feed back, allows a student to practice mistakes. Regarding the utility of this, 56 percent of the students expressed that it was high, because it produces clean and demonstrable results. About 11 percent of the students opined that it was very high utilized. The student respondents (33 percent) stated that the utility of this was low and extremely low. About 32 percent of the students opined this method was excellent and the respondents (33 percent) stated that the method of this was good because individual students can learn at their own pace through it. Remaining of the respondents (24 percent) and 11 percent expressed this method was an average and poor because CAI discourages students to move in to new material. (Table 5.31)

TABLE 5.32
Respondents' Opinion on Computer Managed Instruction

Respondents' Opinion		*No. of Responses*	*Percent of Responses*
Opinion	a. Satisfaction	35	59
	b. Dissatisfaction	25	41
	Total	60	100
Utility	a. Very High	7	11
	b. High	26	44
	c. Low	20	33
	d. Extremely Low	7	12
	Total	60	100
Method	a. Excellent	11	18
	b. Good	28	47
	c. Average	19	32
	d. Poor	2	3
	Total	60	100

Source : Field Study.

Analysis: The Table 5.32 depicts the opinion of the students regarding computer managed instruction programme. More than half percent of the students are satisfied with this programme and remaining of them (41 percent) dissatisfied because, the technology is changing too rapidly. About 44 percent of the respondents stated the utility of this programme was high and 11 percent of the opined that it was very high utilized, because it provided for easy communication and learning at instruction level. But one third of the respondents (33 percent) have low utilized this programme because of the widespread existence of computer illiteracy. Only 11 percent of them felt that the utility was extremely low. The respondents (47 percent) stated that the method was good and 18 per cent of the students indicated their opinion as excellent method. Nearly 32 percent of the respondents opined that it was average. Only 3 percent of them felt that it was poor.

TABLE 5.33

Opinion of the Respondents Regarding EDUSAT Programme

Respondents' Opinion		*No. of Responses*	*Percent of Responses*
Opinion	a. Satisfaction	46	76
	b. Dissatisfaction	14	24
	Total	60	100
Utility	a. Very High	11	18
	b. High	36	60
	c. Low	7	12
	d. Extremely Low	6	10
	Total	60	100
Method	a. Excellent	19	32
	b. Good	29	48
	c. Average	9	15
	d. Poor	3	5
	Total	60	100

Source : Field Study.

Analysis: Maximum extent of the students (76 percent) are satisfied with this programme, because, EDUSAT is to improve connections across the nation for the spread of distance learning. But rest of them (24 percent) felt that the programme was not satisfactory, because computer net works are costly to develop. About this programme utility, 60 percent of the students expressed that it was highly utilized and 18 per cent of the said people are opined that it was very high utilized. But 12 percent of the students stated that the utility of the programme was low, and remaining of the students (10 percent) expressed this programme utility was extremely low, because of costly computer networks, connectivity problem. So, students felt low. 48 percent of the respondents felt that method was good and 32 percent of them felt it was excellent method because education through satellite is extremely effective and efficient programme. Only 20 per cent of respondents find this programme to be average and poor. (Table 5.33).

Analysis: An enquiry in to the employee opinion on Management Information System, the employee respondents are highly (72 percent) satisfies with this programme and 28 percent of the employees expressed no satisfaction because, of lack of time spent on this programme. About 52 percent of the respondents felt that it was highly utilized.

Only 8 percent of them stated that the utility of this programme was very high. About 28 per cent responded that the utility was low and only 12 percent of them are opined extremely low utilized. Maximum respondents

TABLE 5.34

Opinion of Employees on Management Information System

Respondents' Opinion		*No. of Responses*	*Percent of Responses*
Opinion	a. Satisfaction	43	72
	b. Dissatisfaction	17	28
	Total	60	100
Utility	a. Very High	5	8
	b. High	31	52
	c. Low	17	28
	d. Extremely Low	7	12
	Total	60	100
Method	a. Excellent	8	13
	b. Good	29	48
	c. Average	16	27
	d. Poor	7	12
	Total	60	100

Source : Field Study.

(48 per cent) indicated their opinion on the method of this programme good. Nearly 13 percent of the employees said that the method was excellent. Rest of the employees opined that it was average and poor. (Table 5.34).

TABLE 5.35

Respondents' Opinion about Database Management Systems

Respondents' Opinion		*No. of Responses*	*Percent of Responses*
Opinion	a. Satisfaction	35	58
	b. Dissatisfaction	25	42
	Total	60	100
Utility	a. Very High	12	20
	b. High	26	43
	c. Low	13	22
	d. Extremely Low	9	15
	Total	60	100
Method	a. Excellent	7	12
	b. Good	29	48
	c. Average	14	23
	d. Poor	10	17
	Total	60	100

Source : Field Study.

Analysis: As can be seen from Table 5.35 the opinion of the respondents regarding the database management system programme. The respondents (58 percent) stated that their opinion on this programme was positive and remaining of the respondents (48 percent) were dissatisfied. Because, they have training facility is needful, the employers (43 percent) said that programme was high utilized and 20 percent responded as very high utilized with this regard. About 22 percent of the employees stated that the utility was low and remaining (15 percent) respondents indicated their opinion as extremely low utilized. The respondents (48 percent) expressed that it was excellent method. Nearly 23 percent of the respondents felt that it was average method and 17 percent of them indicate that the said method was poor.

TABLE 5.36

Response of the about Decision Support Systems Programme

Respondents' Opinion		*No. of Responses*	*Percent of Responses*
Opinion	a. Satisfaction	41	68
	b. Dissatisfaction	19	32
	Total	60	100
Utility	a. Very High	3	5
	b. High	29	48
	c. Low	16	27
	d. Extremely Low	12	20
	Total	60	100
Method	a. Excellent	19	32
	b. Good	26	43
	c. Average	8	13
	d. Poor	7	12
	Total	60	100

Source : Field Study.

Analysis : An over whelming majority of the employees (68 percent) satisfied with decision support system programme. About 32 percent of the respondents as dissatisfied with this effect, because, decisions are taken by the managerial level people only, but not all categories of employees can take the decisions and they have no authority for decisions without prior permissions by top level. The respondents (48 percent) utilized this programme was highly. Only 5 percent of the respondents said that it was very highly utilized. Nearly 27 percent of the people are in the opinion that it was low utilized and 20 percent of them felt that it was extremely low utilized because, decisions basically depends on superiors, but not subordinates. Therefore, subordinates do not utilize this programme. About 43 percent of the employees stated that the method was good and 32 percent of the respondents felt that it was excellent method. Nearly one fourth of them (25 percent) expressed average and poor response because, it was useful for only decision-making but not for operational level. (Table 5.36).

TABLE 5.37

Opinion of the Respondents about E-Commerce Programme

Respondents' Opinion		*No. of Responses*	*Percent of Responses*
Opinion	a. Satisfaction	49	81
	b. Dissatisfaction	11	19
	Total	60	100
Utility	a. Very High	11	19
	b. High	38	64
	c. Low	8	13
	d. Extremely Low	3	4
	Total	60	100
Method	a. Excellent	15	24
	b. Good	38	64
	c. Average	5	9
	d. Poor	2	3
	Total	60	100

Source : Field Study.

Analysis: Maximum extent of the business people (81 percent) satisfied with E-commerce programme, because, E-commerce enables consumers to do transactions 24 hours a day from any place in the world. Only 19 percent of the business people dissatisfied with this regard, because, E-commerce has lack of personal privacy and security to individuals. Regarding the utility of E-commerce programme, majority of the respondents (64 percent) opined that it was highly utilized. About 19 percent of the respondents said that utility was very high. And 13 percent of the business people utilized this programme less because this technique is not needed to them. Only 4 percent of the respondents that felt it was extremely low utilized. Majority of the respondents (64 percent) stated that the method was good. Nearly 24 per cent of the business people said that the method was excellent and remaining (12 percent) of the respondents considered that the method is average and poor.

TABLE 5.38
Responses on Business Analysis Systems Programme

Respondents' Opinion		*No. of Responses*	*Percent of Responses*
Opinion	a. Satisfaction	46	77
	b. Dissatisfaction	14	23
	Total	60	100
Utility	a. Very High	6	10
	b. High	38	63
	c. Low	12	20
	d. Extremely Low	4	7
	Total	60	100
Method	a. Excellent	12	20
	b. Good	38	63
	c. Average	7	12
	d. Poor	3	5
	Total	60	100

Source : Filed Study.

Analysis: In view of the above table (5.38) majority of the business people (77 percent) satisfied with this because, this provides data which when used with the proper software helps its users to understand better the business eminent and make more effective decisions, and remaining of the business people are dissatisfied (23 percent). The respondents (63 percent) stated that the utility was high and 10 percent of the business people expressed this was very highly utilized because, the routinely uses spread sheets for analyzing cost benefits and for creating budgets. About 27 percent of the business people are felt that it was low and extremely low utilized. The reason is that communication analysis always through the computer is impossible, i.e. due to power cuts, barriers of communication. Majority of the respondents (63 percent) are opined that it was good method and 20 percent of them felt that it was excellent method. Only 12 percent of the respondents indicated average and 5 percent of the respondents expressed that it was poor method.

Analysis: Maximum extent of the respondents (72 percent) were satisfied on the online analytical processing system and 28 percent of the business people have anti opinion on it because, it is depends on data ware houses and transaction processing systems refresh their source level data. Majority of the business people (68 percent) opined that the utility of this programme was high. Only three percent of the respondents expressed that it was very highly utilized. Remaining of the business people indicated that it was extremely low. Because, the interiors and smaller cities of the country marketers still have to fall back upon traditional media. Hence only 29

TABLE 5.39

Responses on Online Analytical Processing System

Respondents' Opinion		*No. of Responses*	*Percent of Responses*
Opinion	a. Satisfaction	43	72
	b. Dissatisfaction	17	28
	Total	60	100
Utility	a. Very High	2	3
	b. High	41	68
	c. Low	10	17
	d. Extremely Low	7	12
	Total	60	100
Method	a. Excellent	13	22
	b. Good	38	63
	c. Average	6	10
	d. Poor	3	5
	Total	60	100

Source : Field Study.

percent of the respondents low utilized this programme less. About 22 percent of the business people stated that the method was excellent. Another (63 percent) of people expressed that it was a good method. Nearly 10 percent opinions on this regard was average and only 5 percent of the respondents felt that it was poor method because it is depends on warehouses (Table 5.39).

TABLE 5.40

Opinion of the Respondents about Telemedicine Programme

Respondents' Opinion		*No. of Responses*	*Percent of Responses*
Opinion	a. Satisfaction	41	68
	b. Dissatisfaction	19	32
	Total	60	100
Utility	a. Very High	10	17
	b. High	28	47
	c. Low	16	26
	d. Extremely Low	6	10
	Total	60	100
Method	a. Excellent	22	37
	b. Good	31	52
	c. Average	5	8
	d. Poor	2	3
	Total	60	100

Source : Field Study.

Analysis: Regarding the telemedicine programme the doctors (68 percent) are highly satisfied with this content because, it is not a great money spinner, but it is a great way of reaching out to the masses. It gives consultation to the patient in the remote areas. Remaining of the respondents (32 percent) stated that the programme was negative, because, repetitive strain injuryoccurring from the high used computers. About 64 percent of the doctors expressed that it was highly utilized in the medicine field. While 26 percent of them said that the programme was low utilized because it is an expensive process. Only 10 percent of the doctors felt that it is extremely low utilized. Telemedicine programme was a good method as said by the respondents (52 percent) because it goes through the network of the patients and doctors. Nearly 37 percent the respondents are opined that it was excellent method. Only 8 percent and 3 percent of them are felt it was and average and poor method, because, the doctors have no time and as they are busy in this medical field. (Table 5.40).

TABLE 5.41

Opinion of the Respondents on Computer Aided Design

Respondents' Opinion		*No. of Responses*	*Percent of Responses*
Opinion	a. Satisfaction	50	83
	b. Dissatisfaction	10	17
	Total	60	100
Utility	a. Very High	21	35
	b. High	33	55
	c. Low	3	5
	d. Extremely Low	3	5
	Total	60	100
Method	a. Excellent	14	23
	b. Good	29	49
	c. Average	10	16
	d. Poor	7	12
	Total	60	100

Source : Field Study.

Analysis: Table 5.41 depicts the opinion of the engineers on computer aided design programme. With reference to data 83 percent of the engineers are satisfied with this programme and only 17 percent of the respondents' opined dissatisfaction. The reason for this is that large automotive and electronic companies do not use CAD system alone. Majority of the respondents (55 percent) opined it was highly utilized. Nearly 35 percent of them felt that the utility of this programme was very high. Very least percent

(10 percent) of the engineers indicated that on the utility of this programme was low and extremely low. About 49 per cent of the respondents expressed that the method was good and 23 percent of them said it was excellent because basically all engineers depended on this programme. Nearly 16 percent of the respondents are felt it was an average method and 12 percent of them, indicated their response as poor.

TABLE 5.42

Response of the Respondents on Computer Aided Manufacturing

Respondents' Opinion		*No. of Responses*	*Percent of Responses*
Opinion	a. Satisfaction	49	82
	b. Dissatisfaction	11	18
	Total	60	100
Utility	a. Very High	17	28
	b. High	34	58
	c. Low	5	8
	d. Extremely Low	4	7
	Total	60	100
Method	a. Excellent	11	18
	b. Good	39	65
	c. Average	3	5
	d. Poor	7	12
	Total	60	100

Source : Field Study.

Analysis: An over whelming majority of the engineers (82 percent) stated satisfaction and 18 percent of the respondents felt unsatisfaction regarding computer aided manufacture programme because this system is not used by large automotive and electronic compromise alone. Maximum extents of the respondents (58 percent) are opined that the utility of this programme was high. Only 28 percent of the engineers stated that the utility was very high. However, 8 percent of the respondents and 7 percent of the respondents opined low and extremely low the utility of this programme. In view of this programme majority of the engineers (65 percent) stated that it was a good method and 18 percent of the engineers said it was excellent method because, this programme need is highly necessary in the manufacturing field. Only 17 percent of the respondents expressed that it was average and poor about the method of CAM (5.42).

TABLE 5.43

Response of the Respondents about Personal Software Process

Respondents' Opinion		*No. of Responses*	*Percent of Responses*
Opinion	a. Satisfaction	34	57
	b. Dissatisfaction	26	43
	Total	60	100
Utility	a. Very High	12	20
	b. High	33	55
	c. Low	5	9
	d. Extremely Low	10	16
	Total	60	100
Method	a. Excellent	2	3
	b. Good	43	72
	c. Average	5	9
	d. Poor	10	16
	Total	60	100

Source : Field Study.

Analysis: It can be seen from the data that as many as 57 percent of the respondents satisfied regarding the personal software process and remaining 43 percent of the respondents expressed dissatisfaction because, a long start up time is required. Out of the engineers (55 percent) stated that the utility of said programme was high, because, it increased productivity and security and it reduced cycle times. About 20 percent of the respondents felt that it was very high utilized because; it provides better quality of programme. Only 9 percent of the engineers said that it was low utilized and 16 percent of them felt it was extremely low utilized. Maximum extent of respondents (72 percent) expressed this programme was good method because; it helps as track costs and schedules. About 16 percent of the engineers are opined that it was poor it is complex to use. Only 3 percent of the engineers stated that the method of PSP is excellent (Table 5.43).

Analysis: Maximum extent of the respondents (70 percent) satisfied with E-legal service because their activities were going though the computer interaction with clients. Remaining of the lawyers (30 percent) was unsatisfied because, all clients have no connectivity through computers. So it is not implementing thoroughly, Nearly 44 percent of the lawyers stated that the utility of E-legal services was high and 28 percent of them felt was very high because it provides easy communication with clients in the short period for the details of the case particulars. However, 12 percent and 16 percent of the respondents have opined low and extremely low utility of E-legal service. Regarding the method of E-legal service, 40 percent of the

TABLE 5.44

Opinion of the Respondents about E-legal Service Programme

Respondents' Opinion		*No. of Responses*	*Percent of Responses*
Opinion	a. Satisfaction	42	70
	b. Dissatisfaction	18	30
	Total	60	100
Utility	a. Very High	17	28
	b. High	26	44
	c. Low	7	12
	d. Extremely Low	10	16
	Total	60	100
Method	a. Excellent	11	18
	b. Good	24	40
	c. Average	19	32
	d. Poor	6	10
	Total	60	100

Source : Field Study.

respondents expressed it as a good method and 18 percent of them felt that the method was excellent. But 32 percent of the respondent stated that the utility of this was average because of the inconvenience and lack of time. Only 10 percent of the lawyers stated it a poor method, because, the concept of E-legal service is relatively new and therefore open to subjective interpretation. Table (5.44).

TABLE 5.45

Respondents' Opinion Regarding Hi-Tech Teaching Programme

Respondents' Opinion		*No. of Responses*	*Percent of Responses*
Opinion	a. Satisfaction	41	68
	b. Dissatisfaction	19	32
	Total	60	100
Utility	a. Very High	13	22
	b. High	38	63
	c. Low	5	8
	d. Extremely Low	4	7
	Total	60	100
Method	a. Excellent	29	48
	b. Good	23	39
	c. Average	3	5
	d. Poor	5	8
	Total	60	100

Source : Field Study.

Analysis: Regarding the Hi-tech teaching programme, the teachers (68 percent) stated satisfaction because, it adopts new methods of memory management configured in the lines of human brains information processing and learners cognitive styles. But 32 percent of the teachers opined negatively because, computer is electronic device and teacher is human body. Hence, computer is not teaching the experimental style. Majority of the teachers (63 percent) expressed that this programme was high utilized. Nearly 22 percent of them felt it was very highly utilised. Only 15 percent of them are indicated that the utility of it was low and extremely low. About 48 percent of the teachers said it was excellent method and 39 percent of the teachers said it was good. However 5 percent of the teachers and 8 percent the teacher opined average and poor respectively regarding the method of Hi-tech teaching programme (Table 5.45).

TABLE 5.46
Opinion on Video-based Training for Farmers' Programme

Respondents' Opinion		*No. of Responses*	*Percent of Responses*
Opinion	a. Satisfaction	37	62
	b. Dissatisfaction	23	38
	Total	60	100
Utility	a. Very High	7	12
	b. High	23	38
	c. Low	13	22
	d. Extremely Low	17	28
	Total	60	100
Method	a. Excellent	22	37
	b. Good	29	48
	c. Average	7	12
	d. Poor	2	3
	Total	60	100

Source : Field Study.

Analysis: Above table (5.46) exhibits the opinion of the rural people on the video based training for farmers programme. The rural people (62 percent) are satisfied with this programme because, it provides pictorial movements and operational methods are explained through it But 38 percent of the rural people are not satisfied with this regard because, they have no adequate facility in rural areas. About 38 percent of the rural people expressed that the utility of said programme was high. Only 12 percent of the respondents are felt that it was very high utilised. Nearly Half percent of them opined extremely low because, electricity problem, communication barriers, awareness programmes were not conducted by the government and maximum time was spent in the cultivation field. While 48 percent of the rural people stated that the programme was good method. And 37 percent of the respondents opined that it was excellent method. However, 12 percent and 3 percent of the rural people opined average and poor respectively regarding the method of video-based training for farmers.

6

Summary and Suggestions

SUMMARY

In the context of global economy and competitive markets, knowledge is a key factor contribution to economic development. Therefore, human resource development through education and training has become a key component within overall strategy for economic restructuring in developing countries. The future of global economy and democratic polity in the 21st century is likely to depend on skilled and educated workers and enlightened citizens. It was the world conference on education for all held in Jomtien (Thailand) in 1990 that high tightened critical importance of addressing the learning needs of all children, youth and adults who have been excluded and unreached by the existing system of formal and informal education, and contributed to building global consensus around the goals of education for All (EFA). In the context of globalization, basic learning skills and competences are necessary not only for children, but also for unschooled and illiterate youth and adults. Who are valuable human resources of every society.

Information Communication Technology (ICT) has become most widely used buzzword of the computer industry. It has affected all walks of life in one-way or another, ICT is the modern science of gathering storing manipulation processing and communicating desired types of information in a specific environment. Computer technology and communication technology are the two main supporting pillars of this technology and the impact of these two in the information storage and dissemination is vital. It is impossible to deny its importance in the educational, cultural, agricultural, scientific and technical disciplines of the world. Information needs are increasing day by day and in the present day society, every person is intending to be information oriented. The definitions of HRD in terms of its components have ranged from the most comprehensive to the narrowest. The most comprehensive has been given by Myrdal who has enumerated eight components, like. 1. Food and nutrition, 2. Clothing, 3. Housing and sanitation, 4. Health facilities, 5. Education, 6. Information media, 7. Energy consumption, and 8. Transport. The narrowest definition is given by the World Bank, which includes only three items—Health, Nutrition and Education. The latter definition has been used most widely. It has also been widely objected to for its narrow scope. Information is the most valuable asset for any organization or institute. The growth of the Internet has greatly influenced the case and speed with which information is shared. Today's challenge is to make the information accessible. A typical information processing cycle consists of five steps namely input, processing, output, storage and retrieval, and distribution and communication. Information Technology is the combination of different fields such as information science, computer technology, communication technology and management science.

Information Technology (IT) is the science and skills of all aspects of computing, data storage and communications. It is a new rapidly growing area that is radically changing the world by making possible new ways of doing business-making entertainment and creating art.

The phrase Information Technology refers to the creation gathering processing storage and delivery of information and the process and devices that make all this possible information technology can do at least three things. Information Technology can process raw data into useful information, information technology can recycle processed information and use it as data in another processing step and information technology can package information in a new form so it is easier to understand, more attractive, or more useful.

As per the foregoing analysis of the review of literature on information technology in developing human resources, the work done by the researchers in the subject was scant in India. Most of the research studies are focused on human resources, training and development, electronic education training, teleconferencing and computer-based training, etc. The research in the area of role of IT in developing human resources has not been given much emphasis by the researchers in India. A comprehensive study on the "Role of Information Technology in Developing Human Resources" in the post-liberalization, globalization and information age was not attempted by any researcher so far.

The present study is intended to cover the research gap in the existing literature on information technology in developing human resources. The study helps for effective and efficient implementation of information technology concepts and the need for development of human resources viz. education, training and development. Information technology improving the standard of knowledge, skill, attitudes and development of living and quality of human will power in rural area and urban area peoples in our country.

The study was carried out following main objectives. 1. to examine and existing methods and techniques of human resource development India. 2. to study the role of information technology in developing human resources in different sections of the society, 3. to assess the impact of information technology on different sections of the society, 4. to analyze perceptions of respondents regarding effectiveness of information technology to develop human resources.

The present study is confined to the selected respondents in the different sections of the society namely students, employees, business people, professional people like doctors, engineers, lawyers, teachers and rural people, which were residing in Visakhapatnam. Visakhapatnam is a host of several large, medium and small enterprises, industries, business establishments' professional organizations, different educational institutions and sub-urban and rural villages.

The data will be collected from both Primary and secondary sources. Primary data will be collected with the help of structured questionnaire. About 480 respondents from different sections of the society will be interviewed. These sections were students, employees, business people, doctors, engineers, lawyers, teachers and rural people. Secondary data will be collected from different text books, journals, magazines, newspapers, records and reports available in different libraries and research centers located at important places in India (Bangalore, Chennai, Hyderabad, Kolkata, Mumbai and Visakhapatnam) are the major sources. The study which presented in six chapters. Introduction, Human Resource Development Methods, Information Technology methods and its role, Impact of Information Technology on Society, Perceptions of Respondents and Summary and Suggestions.

Once the employee has been selected, trained, and motivated he is then appraisal for his performance. Performance appraisal is the step where the management finds out how effective it has been at having and placing employees. Performance appraisal is the process of evaluating an employee performance of a job in terms of its requirements.

In making potential appraisal of managers, levels of talent and ambition have to be clearly identified. Potential typically represents latent qualities in an individual, which manifests in concrete terms while performing various tasks/jobs. Some characteristics representing potential are ability to foresee future opportunities and assess impact of any initiative/decision taken today. Has an institutionalized way of working to ensure continuity and consistency of approach. Ability to identify resource gaps by the use of basic intelligence/subject knowledge/analytical and quantitative skills and further finds ways and means of overcoming these so as to ultimately create higher value. Personal quality to be level-headed and to respond in an effective and measured manner even under conditions of severe stress. Ability to function in varied environments with confidence and deliver high performance. Ability to see the larger picture as well as recognize the need to get into micro-details.

Training is the creation of an environment where employees may acquire or learn specific job-related behaviors, skills, knowledge, abilities, and attitudes. If one wishes to make a distinction between training and development. It would be that training is directed at helping employees perform better on their current jobs, whereas development represents a future-oriented investment in employees. Development is based on the fact that an employee will need an evolving set of knowledge, skills, abilities, (KSAs) to perform well in the succession of positions encountered during his or her career.

The career—a long preparation of an employee for this series of positions is what is meant by employee development. The vast majority of all training carried on is of the job variety. A variety of training aids and techniques can be used in conjunction with on the Job training. Among these are procedure charts, picture manuals, sample problems, demonstrations, oral and written explanations and tape recording.

It suggested that before actual training begins the instructor must get ready to instruct four steps are recommended and these have applicability today in training programmes for unskilled as well as skilled workers.

As development of technologies proceeds at a rapid pace and the cost of computers continuous to decline high-technology training methods are finding increasing use in industry, academia, and the military.

The apprenticeship system is perhaps oldest and most commonly used method for training in industrial crafts, trades, and technical areas this was developed in the middle ages by then so-called trade guilds. The ancient Greek and Roman state rewords go to show that this system of instruction was used to train doctors, dentists, lawyers, architects, teachers, as well as tradesman. In the era that proceeded the industrial revolution there can about further developments in the practices of the system of apprenticeships, which have been made use of advantageously in the training of craftsmen.

An 'understudy' is a person who is under training to assume, at a future time, the full duties and responsibilities of the position currently held by his superior. In this way, it is ensured that a fully trained person is available to replace a manager during his long absence or illness, or on his retirement, transfer or promotion.

Most large companies make use of committees for the training and development of their managerial. These are either regularly constituted or *adhoc* committees entrusted with some special objectives and responsibilities relating to the work of the organization strictly speaking they are not specifically, for training purposes. These membership of these committees is hold by very competent personnel.

There is nothing intrinsically new about visual aids they have been used as a learning device ever since man has been able to draw. But the range variety and sophistication of such devices are increased rapidly over the past twenty years. So much so that there is now a danger of their misuse of relaying too heavily on then with drawing the human element from teaching almost entirely. Visual Aids are of great value in it improving effective communication. Between teacher and student but they should not replace the student teacher relationship.

Off the-job-training mostly commonly called the classroom training–the traditional way of education, places the trainee in a class room, off the job training takes place either in side the organization or at some external selected sites may be institutes universities or professional associations which have no connection with the company.

The Lecture Method a conventional training technique and a traditional form of class room teaching still occupies though a very limited and specific place in the area of training and development because of the advent of a number of other new and improved methods and techniques.

It is a training technique, which indicates the duplication of organizational situations in a learning environment. It is a mock-up of a real thing. This technique has been used for developing technical and inters personal skills. The following procedure is usually adopted.

Programmed instruction involves a sequence of steps, which are often set-up through the central panel of an electronic computer as guides in the performance of a desired operation or series of operations.

The case study method pioneered by the Harvard Business School, Massachusets, U.S.A., was first developed in the 1880's by Christopher langdell at Harvard law school. This is essentially a group-oriented technique, which has been steadily increasing popularity and wide use as a common form of training and a valuable training aid.

J.L. Moreno, a Venetian psychiatrist, developed it. He coined the terms "role playing", "role-reversal", "sociodrama", "psychodrama" and a number of other specialized terms, originally it was developed for group therapy for mentally disturbed people.

This method is mainly concerned with increasing the effectiveness of individuals and meeting the needs of an organization. An individual when he gets opportunity to participate in career. Orientation programmes—specific development assignments of educational activities, he gets varied experiences which help him in the upgrading of his skills, abilities and knowledge. These are designed to enable him to reach his highest potential in the shortest time.

It is a technique whereby juniors are assigned to Board or Committees, by the chief executive. They are asked to participate in deliberations of these Board and Committees. In these sessions, real life actual problems are discussed, different views are debated and decisions are taken. The juniors get an opportunity to share in managerial problems. When Committees are of "*ad hoc*" or temporary nature, they often take a task force activities designed to delve into a particular problem, ascertain alternative solutions, and make a recommendation for implementing a solution.

The on the job training technique of Job rotation is designed to give the trainee knowledge and experience of operations in the various parts of the organization. The trainee while moving through various training positions receives instructions, gains knowledge and experiences in different situations, and is provided with feedback from his superior in each department.

This being association with the Administrative staff college at Honley-on-Thames, U.K. with a group approach was developed and came in vague in 1948.

A syndicate is a form of small group organization various small groups are often designated is syndicate. This method is used as a device not only for the study of specific problems but for other tasks also.

In this method, the participating individuals 'confer' to discuss points of common interest to each other. A conference is basic to most participative group-centered methods of development. It is a formal meeting, conducted in accordance with an organized plan, in which the leader seeks to develop knowledge and understanding by obtaining a considerable amount of oral participation of the trainees. It lays emphasis on small group discussions, on organized subject matter, and on the active participation of the members involved. Learning is facilitated by building upon the ideas contributed by the conferees.

These incidents are brought in use for discussions with the employee trainee for purpose of determining the appropriate training. A superior may also sometimes well develop his own incidents and get at the relevant date-essential to be made use of in the process, through trail. The critical incidents method follows the five steps in the sequence in the process.

Business games are also classroom simulation exercise in which teams of individual compete with one another or against an environment in order to achieve a given obedient. These games designed to be representative of real life situations, under these an atmosphere is created in which the participants play a dynamic role and enrich their skills though involvement and simulated experience manual games was developed in 1956 band described by Andlinger in 1958.

The T-group training is variously termed as sensitivity, L-group (learning group) encounter group or laboratory training. This method is originally developed by Kurthewin and later brought into prominence by the national training laboratories, U.S.A. under T-group training is essentially concerned with real not simulated, problems or situations existing organizations or in some hypothetical settings.

The Bethel group started offering training in group dynamics in many parts of U.S.A. In course of time it came to be recognized as an important technique for training far and wide, outside USA.

Sebastical is the institution or observance of a day of rest, a time of rest, peace, or quit. It is proving a very useful tool for development more particularly in the western industry. It have been quiet popular for many years in the academic world, where professors take a learn top grade their skills and advance their education or research.

T.A. refers to a total system that includes many related branches and ideas. The understanding of behaviour is fundamental to managers success because his personal interactions have increased enormously.

This method developed by Eric Berne, this method commonly known as transactional theory of personality.

O.D. refers to a long range effort to improve an organization problem solving capabilities and its ability to cope with changes in its external environment with the help of external or internal behavioral scientists consultants and change agents they we called as O.D.

The start of quality circles (C) in Japan is generally credited to the Union of Japanese Scientists and Engineers, along with Dr. Kaaru Ishikawa of Tokyo University. In the 1950 s Dr. Edward W. Deming of the United States introduced the concept of statistical quality control in a series of lectures in Japan. A decade later, the idea of involving all employees, not just staff quality control experts and management, was introduced by the union with this total effort, Japan has moved from the little of "Junk Merchants of the World" to one of the world's leaders in quality products.

A part from performance review interviews and discussions between Management and subordinates at the time of completion of employees assessment reports counseling on a regular all-the-year round basis should be regarded as an impartment part of personnel development.

This needs display of sensitivity toward personal behaviour of the members/participants in a group. Making interventions with the objective toad value, adopting open communication on all matters related to group team and display of accountability to the other members in the group/team.

Communication is one of the most basic functions of management, communication forms "a basis for management by objectives, long range strategic goal setting policy formulation, strategic planning, organizational development and organizational effectiveness, control decision-making and allied managerial activities aimed at effective achievement of organizational goals". Communication may be defined, it is a process of transmitting information, thoughts, opinions, facts, ideas or emotions and understanding from one person, place or thing to another person, place or thing, it is called as a communication.

The most widely quoted definition of quality of working life is that formulated by Richard, E. Walton Professor Walton explains it in terms of eight broad condition of employment that constitute a good or desirable quality of working life.

Information Technology stands firmly on two legs hardware and software. The term hardware applied to any of the physical equipment in a system, usually containing electronic components and performing some kind of function in information processing. Hardware includes not only the computer and devices such as screens and printers but also all the elements used to tie information systems together. Software is instructions that guide the hardware in the performance of its duties. There is a slogan button floating around that makes this distinction very clear Hardware the post of the computer that you can kick.

The term hypermedia comprises of a set of ideas although it seems to be understood somewhat differently within different disciplines. The very first person to directly formulate the hypermedia concept was Vannevar Bush. American president Roosewelt appointed him manager of the organization, which coordinated technology research in the USA during World War II. In 1945 published the article "As we may think" in the magazine the Atlantic Monthly addressing some of the problems faced by modern science.

A data warehouse is a collection of computer-based information that is critical to successful execution of enterprise initiatives. A data warehouse is more than an archive for corporate data and more than a new way of accessing corporate data. A data warehouse is a subject-oriented repository designed with enterprise-wide access in mind. It provides tools to satisfy the information needs of the employees at all organizational levels-not just complex data queries, but as a general facility for getting quick accurate and often insightful information. A data warehouse is designed so that its users can organize the information they want and access that information using simple tools.

Two Thousand years ago Roman roads brought trade and commerce to Europe in an unprecedented manner. At the dawn of the second millennium, the Internet is making fundamental changes to the lives of every one on the planet changing forever the way business is conducted. Generally there are three kinds of E-Commerce, business to business, business to customer and using digital middleman.

The term OLAP was coined by E.F. Codd in 1993 to refer to a type of application that allows a user to interactively analyze data. An OLAP system is often contrasted to an OLTP (on-line transaction processing) system that focuses on transactions such as orders, invoice, general ledger transitions.

A GIS is a computer-based tool for mapping and analyzing things that exists and events that happen on earth. GIS technologies integrate common database operations such as query and statistical analysis with the unique visualization and geographic analysis benefits offered by maps. There abilities distinguish GIS from other information systems and make it valuable to wide range of public and private enterprises for explaining events, predicting outcomes, and planning strategies.

In India the government for disseminating information about various development issues has used radio extensively. While meeting some of the information needs of rural communities. However, the potential of a non-visual medium of radio for imparting literacy instructions and training did not happen till the National Literacy Mission (NLM) conducted the Project in Radio Education for Adult Literacy (PREAL) in 1990.

Audio-visual medium of television has been used for distance education at higher levels. In adult education however no systematic efforts were made until 1990 to teach literacy through television. Two experiments in imparting literacy through television show how television can be used for literacy and teaching.

Electronics can counter the lack of interest in learning by bringing excitement and experiences in to the learning process-sights, sounds, games, experiments, simulation anything that can create interest for an individual can be designed into the learning experience. With the aid of electronic device one can learn at one's own pace in one's time. Computers have been found to be very effective in getting school dropouts to go back to studying and learn at their own pace.

Basically teleconferencing is the interactive exchange of information between individuals or groups in two or more locations through an electronic medium. It can bring people who are geographically isolated together to express their viewpoints and share their experiences. In the 1960's the American Telephone and Telegraph Company first introduced the teleconferencing system "Picture Phone" in USA. It has been a common mode of communication in the USA and European countries for many years. There are three basic types commonly available for use. Verbal communication through a telephone with additional capacity for telewriting or telecopying. Exchange of video information and pictures between individuals or groups through specialized equipments. Computer-based meeting involving exchange of voice and pictures between two individuals or groups using special software in a networked environment, e.g. Bulletin boards, e-groups, discussion forums, mailing lists, real time chat and e-mail.

The emphasis on farmers training continued with the launching of new agricultural strategies during 1960s, beginning with the Intensive Agricultural District Program (IADP), Farmers, Training Centers (FTCs) block level training programs and later farmers' training by the State Agricultural Universities (SAUs), were involved in disseminating messages on new agricultural technologies.

Satellite operators are taking advantage of existing space and terrestrial capacity, and new technology to make available flexible solutions that increase network access for customers without requiring significant capital expenditures.

Firms use various media to communicate with their current and potential customers. Marketing communications perform three functions—to inform, to remind and to persuade. The traditional one-to-many marketing communications model has corporations provide contend through a medium, to a mass market of consumers. The first two functions of marketing communications are performed by a traditional communication model. However, the persuasion function necessary to differentiate one brand from another is limited by the unidirectional nature of traditional mass media.

Telemedicine attempts to virtually transport the specialist doctor to a remote patient. Normally doctors rely on all their five senses when treating a patient. In the case of a patient at a remote location, the specialist doctor cannot use his sense of touch. The MBBS doctor present at the telemedicine centre in a remote village will examine the patient, according to the instruction of the specialist and provide feedback related to symptoms. The specialist, in any case, has the patient entire case study before him. Through video conferencing, specialists can see, talk and examine the patient virtually, and all this helps them in making a correct diagnosis. Telemedicine is video conferencing solutions, polycoms reputation for a good sales service, which is critical, especially in remote areas, was the deciding factor.

Distance education covers the various farms in study at all levels which is not bound to continuation and giving lectures in classrooms. This denotes the activity of the student. Thus the distance study can be described as learning supported by those teaching methods in which, because of the physical separateness of learners and teachers, the interactive, as well as the proactive phase of teaching is conducted through print, non-print or electronic devices. Wide ranges of technological options are available to the distance educator. They fall into four major categories, i.e. voice, video, data and print.

One area where governments are interested is in indirect support for the IT sector by boosting the domestic market though its own purchases, of course, purchases sophisticated equipment and software that it is unused in high level bureaucrats offices will have little positive impact. However, there are reasons to be more optimistic about the use of IT for improved government functioning. First, back-office procedures can be made more efficient so that internal record-keeping flows of information and tracking of decisions and performance can be improved. Second, when some basic information is stored in digital form it provides the opportunity for easier access to that information by citizens. More complicated possibilities are checking actual records, such as land ownership or transactions. Still more complicated are cases information is submitted electronically by the citizen. The successful pilot e-governance programmes that have made some of the above actions possible.

MAIN FINDINGS

The study is confined to eight sections of society, viz., students, employees, business people, doctors, engineers, lawyers, teachers and rural people is under which have been implementing the following information technology programmes, these are E-learning, E-mail, Internet, Mobile phone, Geographic information system, Video conferencing, Tele-conferencing, Computer conferencing, computer-based training and computer-based multimedia, computer assisted instruction, computer managed instruction, EDUSAT, Management information system, Database management system, decision support system, E-Commerce, Business analysis System and online analytical processing telemedicine, Computer aided design, computer aided manufacturing and personnel software process, Legal Services, Hi-tech teaching, Video-based training for farmers. The study covers the above information technology programmes. The perception of respondents regarding to develop the human resources through information technology. The main findings of the study were briefly given as under:

I. Findings of the Students

Regarding E-learning programme, 77 percent of the respondents are satisfied because it is an important tool to improve academic quality, effectiveness and efficiency of open and distance education system. But 33 percent of the respondents expressed dissatisfaction because, it is a complex process. Majority of the respondents (75 percent) opined that the utility was high because E-learning is a system that can empower students/teachers and it provides vast knowledge on numerous topics—something for everyone. Only 15 percent of them felt that it was low utilised because, it is an access limited based on availability of hardware, software and Internet connection. Half percent of the respondents opined that the method was good and 33 percent of them felt that it was excellent because knowledge is expanding at lightening speed, students need to learn more, better and faster and limit in the number of students and location of students is irrelevant. But 10 percent said that this method was average because, E-learning may be intimidating to students with low computer skills.

Out of the E-mail programme majority of the respondents (60 percent) are satisfied with this programme because it provides access to the information from anywhere in the world. But 40 percent of them are dissatisfied, because it has created an information overload. About 52 percent said that the utility was high because, it can enable to stand out in student service and competitions. But 27 percent of the students felt that it was low uitlised because, it can become a distraction. Maximum extent of the respondents (80 percent) opined that the method was good because, e-mail ranges from just curious with no computer background to well experience that have a computer at home and a laptop in their travel bag.

From the Internet programme, 73 percent of the respondents are satisfied with this programme because Internet is to eliminate the distance between the people, and country-wise. But 27 percent of them felt dissatisfaction because, it badly effects the students and younger people. Majority of the respondents (65 percent) stated that the utility was high because, it can be effectively used to supplement text book learning. One-fourth percent of the respondent and 57 percent of the respondents opined excellent and good respectively about the method of Internet programme because it facilitates to join in contests, contribute articles, reading materials and also facilitates to do on-line shopping.

About the mobile phone, Maximum of the students (80 percent) are satisfied with mobile phone because making friendship through it is easy but 20 percent of the respondents are not satisfied because, misuse of students in the educational institutions. About 65 percent of them felt that it was high utilised because it helps people and is convenient but 17 percent stated that the utility was low because communication barriers are involved. The respondent (65 percent) stated that the method was good and because it creates interaction with known persons by avoiding the communication gap.

Regarding the geographic information system the students (55 percent) are satisfied with this programme because it helps in analysing data quickly. But remaining of the respondents dissatisfied because, it is more costly programme. About 55 percent of the respondents opined that the utility has high because, it provides database creation and one-third of the respondents stated that it was low utility, it is not possible to access by the more people. While 48 percent of the respondents indicated that the method of the programme was good but 30 percent of them felt that it was average because it is very complex procedure.

About the video conferencing programme, the students (55 percent) are satisfied with this programme because it provides excellent communication to the people but 45 percent of them felt dissatisfaction because lack of availability. Majority of the respondents (55 percent) stated that the utility was high and 32 percent of the students opined that it was low utilised. 60 percent of the respondents opined well about the method of this programme because, it is used for transferring digital images from one location to another location and also plays a large role in the administration.

In the case of teleconferencing programme, 57 percent of the respondents are satisfied with the programme because, it can reduce the cost of training and it reduces the resource persons requirement. But 43 percent of them are not satisfied with this programme because of high cost of establishments and skill requirement for producing using courseware. About 44 percent of the respondents expressed that the programme utility was high because learning transfers well to the real conditions. However, 30 percent of the respondents and 23 percent of the respondent opined low and extremely low respectively because, danger of over-utilization and under-utilization of the equipments, lack of familiarity of the users with the medium, while 53 percent of them felt that it was good method. But 22 percent of the students indicated that it was poor method because, it needs greater time for preparation of courseware development of instructional packages.

As can be seen from the computer conferencing programme. Majority of the respondents opined satisfaction because it reduces time and resource requirements. But 37 percent of the respondents are not satisfied with this programme because it needs cost of production and investment more. The respondents (48 percent) stated that the utility was high. 32 percent of them felt that it was low because, over utilization is danger. About 55 percent of the respondents stated that the programme was good method because it improves the job performance. However, 15 percent of the respondents opined average about the method of computer conferencing programme because, it is costly process and hign investment needed.

In the view of the computer-based training programme, the students (68 percent) are satisfied with this programme, because it enables learners to study at a time of their own choice. Remaining of the respondents are not satisfied with this regard because, it is relatively inflexible, depending on a pre-produced programme. Regarding the utility of this programme, 58 percent of the respondents stated that the utility was high because, it is use choice of control and routing through the programme that makes the medium sophisticated training tool. But 18 percent of them felt that it was low utility because it is expensive. About 52 percent of them stated that the method of the programme was good because it is a valuable vehicle for learning technical skills. While 23 percent of the respondents opined that it was average because it does not permit direct personal reinforcement.

Regarding the computer-based multimedia programme, 57 percent of the respondents are satisfied with the programme because it is widely used in the entertainment and education field. But rests of them were not satisfied because it requires more technical support from the software personnel. About 52 percent said that the utility was high because, it provided very quick presentation. However, 20 percent of them felt that it has low utility and the respondent (20 percent) indicated that the utility was extremely low because it is more complex in the software process. Majority of the respondents (60 percent) expressed that the method was good because, interaction is the advantage of multimedia, and it is being used in movie making very extensively.

Out of the computer assisted instruction programme the students (67 percent) are satisfied with this programme because it produces clear and demonstrable results. It is relatively easy and inexpensive to produce but one-third of them felt dissatisfaction because, widespread computer illiteracy still exists. Computer networks are costly to develop. About 56 percent of the respondents stated that the utility was high because individual students can learn at their own pace through it. While 27 percent of them felt that it has low utility because the technology is changing too rapidly. However, 32 percent of the respondents and 33 percent of the respondents opined excellent and good respectively about the method of the programme, because it can turn practice into an entertaining game, it motivates students to practice arithmetic, Spelling, touch typing, piano playing and other skills. But 24 percent said that it was an average method because it discourages students to move into new material.

An attempt is to be made to find out the programme of computer-managed instruction. The respondent of the students (59 percent) is satisfaction level is high. Because, it gives the tests and grades to the students regarding the results. But rest of them opined dissatisfaction because; it is not necessary for students. 44 percent of them felt that it was high utilised and 33 percent of the respondents are opined that it was low utilised, because it is need too rapidly. While, 47 percent said that it was good method and 32 percent said that it was average method.

In view of the EDUSAT programme, maximum of the respondents (76 percent) are satisfied with this programme because, it is to improve connectivity across the nation for the spread of distance learning. Only 24 percent of them were dissatisfied because, computer networks are costly to develop. Majority of the respondents (60 percent) stated that the utility was high. But only 12 percent said that the utility was low. However, 32 percent of the respondents and 48 percent of the respondents, who are opined excellent and good respectively about the method of EDUSAT programme. But only 15 percent of them felt that it was as average method.

2. Findings of the Employees

Regarding the E-learning programme, the employees (68 percent) are satisfied with this programme because it creates augment employee productivity and empower citizens. But rest of the respondents are not satisfied because, it is not usually associated with formal accreditation. About 65 percent of the respondents stated that the utility was high. Because, it improves customer service and employee morale. While 13 percent of them felt that it was low utilised. Because, it is a complex process. Majority of the employees (64 percent) said that the method was good. The reason is it supports intellectual wealth creation.

Out of the E-mail programme, maximum of the respondents (70 percent) are satisfied with this programme because it provides access to the information from anywhere in the world. Rests of them felt that the programme was not satisfying because it has created an information overload. Half percent of the employees stated that the utility was high, because E-mail ranges from just curious with no computer background to well experience that have a computer at a home and laptop in their travel bag. Nearly 30 percent said that the utility was low because, it can become a distraction. 60 percent of them said that it was good method and 17 percent of the respondents indicated that the method was average.

In view of the Internet programme, majority of the employees are satisfied with this regard because, an early beginning assures that they are computer savvy at a later age. But one-fourth of them opined dissatisfaction. About 63 percent of the respondents stated that the utility was high. Because, it create an E-mail Id and account for us. While 17 percent respondents opined that the utility was low. However, 60 percent of them are opined well regarding the method of internet programme because it covers the globe and includes large international networks as well as many smaller, local area networks.

As can be seen from the data about mobile phone, maximum extent of the employees are satisfied with this regard because it provides easy communication from anywhere to every where. But only 18 percent of them felt that the dissatisfied. About 64 percent of the respondents said that the utility was high because, SMS are very useful to the employees through the

Mobile Phone and 15 percent of the respondents indicated that the utility was low because, communication barriers are involved. Maximum extent of the employees (63 percent) indicated that the method of Mobile phone was good, because it provides interaction with known person. Only 12 percent said that it was average method because signal problems are involved.

An attempt is made to be finding out the programme of geographic information system. The respondents (52 percent) expressed that satisfaction because, it provides data-base creation. But 48 percent of them felt unsatisfied. Because it is more costly process majority of them (60 percent) stated that the utility was high about the programme because it makes maps. 18 percent said that the programme utility was low. Half percent of the employees expressed that the method was good and 21 percent of them felt that it was an average method.

Reveals in the opinion of the employees on the video conferencing programme. 70 percent of them felt satisfaction because it is used for transferring digital images from one location to another location. But 30 percent of the respondents are dissatisfied with this programme because of lack of availability. Majority of the respondents (61 percent) opined that the utility was high and 17 percent said that it was low utility. 67 percent responded that the method was good and 12 percent of them are felt that it was average.

About teleconferencing programme, 63 percent of the respondents are satisfied with the programme, because it provides specialized management systems for tracking trainee's progress and location. But 37 percent of them felt unsatisfied because of high costly of establishments. The respondents (48 percent) stated that the utility was high. 27 percent of them opined extremely low about the utility of video conferencing programme. Because, of lack of familiarity of the users with the medium and equipment it requires additional time and resources for training the user in understanding the medium and using the equipment. About 50 percent of them felt that the method was good because learning transfers well to the real conditions. While 20 percent of the employees stated that the method was average because danger of over utilization.

In the case of computer conferencing programme, the respondents (68 percent) are satisfied with the programme and 32 percent of them are dissatisfied. The employees (52 percent) indicated that the utility was high and 22 percent said that it was low utilised. About 48 percent of the respondents expressed that it was good method and 23 percent of the employers are opined that the programme was poor because; it needs more cost of production and investment.

Regarding computer-based training programme, 72 percent of the respondents expressed satisfaction. Because, it enables learners to study at time of their own choice. But 28 percent said that they are dissatisfied with this regard. Because, it may induce a sense of isolation, as individual work on their own. The respondents (68 percent) indicated that the utility of this programme was high because, it is user choice of control and routing through the programme that make the medium sophisticated training tool. Only 15 percent of them felt that it was low utilised the reason is, it does not permit direct personal reinforcement. About the method of the programme 55 percent of them felt that it was good method. Because it is versatile when it comes to on screen display of information. Only 18 percent of the employees stated that it was average method.

Out of the computer-based multimedia programme, the respondents (65 percent) indicated their satisfaction. But 35 percent said that it was unsatisfying because it is more complex in the software programmes. About 57 percent of the employees opined that the programme utility was high and 23 percent of them felt that it was an extremely low utilized because it requires more technical support. The respondents (48 percent) said that the programme was good method because; it integrates voice, video, and computer technologies in to single delivery systems. But 30 percent said that it was average method because, they are conforming to the traditional factory model.

From the programme of Management information system, majority of the employees are satisfied with this programme because, it provides better land record management and leads to less litigation in courts and consequently reduction in violence in the rural areas. But only 28 percent of them felt that it was unsatisfying. About 52 percent of the respondents are stated that the programme was highly utilized. Because, it helps to better the banking and financial services with excellent services to the customers and it will ensure more efficient management of money. While 28 percent said that it was low utilized because of the lack of facility to all employees. Nearly 48 percent of them felt that the method was good because it provides more efficient natural resources planning which will result in optional utilization of water, oil electrical and coal, etc. But 27 percent of the employees felt that it was an average method.

In view of the database management system programme, 58 percent of them are satisfied with this programme, because it provides support language interface used for the definition and manipulation of the data in the database. But 42 percent of the respondents stated dissatisfaction because DBMS depends on the access privileges of the users for the protection of the data. 43 percent of them opined high about the utility of DBMS. But 22 percent said that it was of low utility. About 48 percent of the respondents indicated that the method of the programme was good because it provides transaction-processing services for the database operations. But 23 percent said that it was average method. Because, it create an environment where the users can do their job without worrying about the physical implementation of language interface.

It can be seen from the data regarding decision support systems programme, majority of the employees (68 percent) satisfied with this programme because it is interactive software designed to help managers make decisions. But 32 percent of the respondents dissatisfied this regard. The respondents (48 percent) stated that the utility was high and 27 percent of them felt that it was of low utility. However, 32 percent of the employees and 43 percent of the employees, opined excellent and good respectively about the method of decision support system programme because, it provides analytical modeling, data retrieval and information presentation capabilities that allow manager to generate the information they need, to make more unstructured types of decisions in any interactive, computer-based process.

3. Findings of the Business People

Regarding E-learning programme 72 percent of the business people satisfied because it creates a knowledge resource for the nation and any module can be easily shared by any one, anywhere. But 28 percent of them felt dissatisfied with the programme because it needs self-discipline. Majority of the respondents (67 percent) stated that the utility was high because it supports intellectual wealth creation. Maximum percent of the business people (62 percent) said that the method was good because, it improve customer service and 15 percent of them felt that it was average method because, it is a complex process.

From the E-mail programme, the business people (60 percent) satisfied with this programme because it enables to stand out in customer service, But 40 percent of the respondents are not satisfied because, it created an information overload. About 60 percent said that it was highly utilized and 16 percent of them said it is low utilized. While 62 percent of the respondents opined that the method was good.

As can be seen from the data of Internet programme maximum extent of the business people are satisfied in this programme. But only 20 percent of the respondents are dissatisfied with this regard. Majority of the respondents (65 percent) indicated that the utility was high because it is ideal marketing medium for companies. However, 27 percent of the business people and 65 percent of the said people expressed that the method of the programme was excellent and good respectively because, it is the cheapest, fastest means to get information, provide information and compile information.

About the mobile phone, 85 percent of the respondents satisfied with the programme because it helps in the mathematical concepts it provides stored messages, provides camera facility. About 67 percent of the Business people stated that the utility was high, because it avoids the communication gap between the people. While 65 percent of them are felt that the method was good, because, it provides easy communication from anywhere to everywhere.

Out of the geographic information system programme the respondents (58 percent) satisfied with this programme because, it helps to reduce costs in stream lining customer service. But 42 percent of the respondents expressed that it was unsatisfying because, more people cannot access it. About 65 percent of them are stated that the utility was high. While 46 percent of them felt that it was good method. But 32 percent of the respondents said that it was an average method because it is a costly process.

In view of the Video conferencing programme, 67 percent said that it was satisfying; rest of them indicated dissatisfaction with this programme. About 69 percent of the respondents stated that the utility was high. But 10 percent of them felt that it was low utility. While 68 percent of the respondents are opined that the method was good because, it provides excellent communication for the people.

The programme of teleconferencing, the respondents (65 percent) satisfied with this programme, because it increases access to information tool for decision-making. But 35 percent of them dissatisfied. The Business people (54 percent) opined that the utility was high, because, it improves training the people in specific skills for specific performance. While 18 percent of them felt that the utility was low, because of the danger of constantly changing technology and the confusions over standards have added to the techno phobia created by lack of awareness about the potentials of state-of-art. Teleconferencing technologies fears over the technology-based learning. 48 percent stated that the method was good and 22 percent said that it was an average method.

From the computer conferencing programme, 65 percent of the respondents and 35 percent of the respondents, expressed satisfaction and dissatisfaction about the programme, 55 percent of the respondents stated that the utility was high, because, it improve the job performance, 18 percent of them felt that it was of low utility because it needs more cost of production and investment. About 57 percent of them felt that it was good method and 15 percent said that it was an average method.

In reference to the computer-based training programme, the respondents (65 percent) satisfied with this programme, because it enables learners to study at their own pace, but 35 percent said that the programme was unsatisfying, because it is relatively inflexible depending on pre-produced programme. 60 percent of the business people stated that the utility was high as it provides opportunity for learners to check their understanding. But the learner feels 13 percent of them that it was low utilized because, it requires a greater self-discipline and commitment. While 48 percent of the respondents are stated that the programme was good method and 20 percent indicated that it was an average method.

As can be seen from data about computer-based multimedia programme, the respondents (67 percent) satisfied with this programme and rests of them dissatisfied. Nearly 68 percent said that it was high utility and 17 percent said that it was low utilized. About 47 percent of them felt that it was a good method. But 30 percent said that it was an average method because, it requires more technical support from the software personnel.

Regarding E-commerce programme, maximum extent of the respondents (81 percent) are satisfied with this programme because, it give more liberty and choice to the consumer so that they can choose product from many vendors. Nearly 19 percent of them felt dissatisfaction because, it has lack of personnel privacy and security to individuals 64 percent of the respondents indicated that the utility was high. Because, it reduces the cost of processing and distributing expenses of the organizations. But 13 percent of the respondents are stated that the programme was of low utility because, it has software problems. However, 64 percent of the respondents opined good about the method of E-Commerce, because it provides facilities like delivery of public series, online payments of taxes, commodities, online education, etc.

Regarding the programme of business analysis system, majority of the respondents (77 percent) satisfied with this programme because it is a process to corporate uses routinely uses spreadsheets for analysis of cost benefits and for creating new jobs. 23 percent of them dissatisfied with this regard because digital marketing has a limited reach in a country like India. About 63 percent said that it was highly utilized. Maximum extents of the business people (63 percent) opined that the method was good.

Out of the programme of online analytical processing programme, the respondents (72 percent) satisfied with the programme because, it increases the productivity of business managers, developers and of the whole organization. 28 percent said that it was unsatisfying because it is depends on data warehouses. 68 percent of them felt that the utility was high because it uses software designed for transaction processing. Only 17 percent of the respondents stated that it was of low utility. The respondents (63 percent) stated that the method was good, because it reduces application backlog and also by making business users self-sufficient enough to build their own models.

4. Findings of the Doctors

Regarding the programme of E-learning majority of the respondents (68 percent) is satisfied because it provides up to date content and testing, timely information. But 32 percent are dissatisfied because; it lacks a seal of human interaction. Maximum of the respondents (68 percent) felt that it was of high utility because it supports intellectual wealth creation. 60 percent said that it was a good method and 17 percent said that it was average.

About E-mail programme, 62 percent of them felt satisfaction, rest of them felt dissatisfaction because; it has created information over load. About 57 percent of the doctors opined that utility was high. 18 percent said that it was of extremely low utility because it can become a distraction. The respondents (60 percent) said that the method was good.

As can be seen from data about Internet programme, 72 percent of them are felt that they are satisfied, because it eliminate the distance between the doctor and patients, rest of them are felt that they are dissatisfied because it leads to isolation tendencies. About 59 percent of the respondents stated that the utility was high, but 18 percent of them felt that it was of low utility. However, 20 percent of the respondents and 57 percent of the respondents expressed that the method was excellent and good respectively because, it is the cheapest and faster means to get information and provide information.

In view of the mobile phone, the doctors (78 percent) were satisfied because it provides easy communication from any where to every where. Majority of the respondents (67 percent) expressed that the mobile phone was highly utilised because it avoids the communication gap between patients and doctor. About 58 percent of the doctors expressed said that the mobile phone was good method because SMS are used through it.

While 57 percent of the respondents expressed that they are satisfied with geographic information system because, it makes maps on basis of places but rest of the respondents not satisfied with the programme because it is a more costly procedure. Maximum of the respondents highly utilised this programme. While 48 percent of the doctors opined that the method of geographic information system was good and 22 percent said that it was an average method because, it is not necessary for medicine field.

An attempt is made to find out the programme of video conferencing, the respondents (68 percent) satisfied with this programme, because, it is used for transferring digitals images from one location to another location. But 32 percent felt dissatisfied because, of lack of availability. 65 percent said that the utility was high and 68 percent of the respondents opined that the method was good because it provides excellent communication to the people.

About teleconferencing programme, 57 percent felt that the programme was satisfying, because it increases access to information tools for decision-making. 43 percent of the doctors not satisfied because, of dangers of over utilisation and under utilisation. About 52 percent of the respondents indicated their utility was high but 22 percent said that the utility was low. 54 percent of them felt that the method was good and 20 percent said that it was average method.

Regarding the programme of computer conferencing, 62 percent of the doctors satisfied with the programme because, it reduces time and resource requirements. But rest of them are not satisfied with this regard because, it needs more cost of production and investment. About 48 percent of the doctors said that the utility was high. But 27 percent said that it was of low utility because over utilization is inconvenient. While 55 percent said that the programme was a good method.

About computer-based training programme, 67 percent of them felt they are satisfied because, it enables learners to study at a time of their own choice. One-third of the respondents expressed that they are dissatisfied because, it is relatively inflexible, depending on a pre-produced programme. The doctors (58 percent) stated that the utility was high because, it uses choice of control and routing through the programme that make the medium sophisticated training tool. The respondents (57 percent) stated that the programme was a good method because; it can be cost effective, depending on the circumstances.

Revealing the opinion of the doctors on computer based multimedia programme, 63 percent of the doctors satisfied with this programme because it integrates voice, video and computer technologies in to single delivery system. But 37 percent of the doctors not satisfied with this programme, because it is more complex in the software programme. The respondents (70 percent) stated that the utility was high because, interaction is of more advantage of multimedia and it provides very quick presentation. 67 percent of the respondents indicated their opinion on the method of the programme was good because it is easier to make a presentation on the computer and it does not need any special skills.

Regarding telemedicine programme, 68 percent of them are satisfied with the programme because, it can ensure optimal utilization by the hospitals and it encompasses all the health care, education, information and administrative services that can be transmitted from distances by telecommunication technologies. But 32 percent said that they are not satisfied because, it does not facilitate to the all of them. About 47 percent of the respondents stated the utility was high because, it network gives consultation to the patient in remote areas. Nearly 26 percent of them felt that it was low utilised because this is an expensive process. However, 37 percent of the doctors and 52 percent of them, who are opined excellent and good respectively about the method of teleconferencing because it can help in combating tropical diseases, more so in a country like India with poor public health facilities and geographically isolated rural populations.

5. Findings of the Engineers

About the E-learning programme majority of the respondents (60 percent) are satisfied with the programme because it provides vast knowledge available on numerous topics—something for every one. But rest of them not satisfied because, it is an access limited based on availability of hardware software and Internet connection. 65 percent said that the utility was high because it increases competitive transparency. About 62 percent of them stated the programme was a good method because, it is lighten administrative load. While 23 percent of the engineers expressed that is an average method, as its needs self-discipline.

Regarding E-mail programme, the engineers are satisfied (65 percent) with this programme, because it is instantaneous with no limitation of timing or location. But 35 percent of them stated that they are dissatisfied because the very existence of electronic communication has perpetuated the myth that it will lead to better communication. But that is not true if you are not a good communicator, with electronic technology you cannot become a good communicator just because you use the technology. The engineers (59 percent) stated that the programme was highly utilised because it enables to stand out in customer service. Only 18 percent of them felt that is of low utility. While 63 percent said that the method was good because it ranges from just curious with no computer background to well experienced who have a computer at home and a laptop in their travel bag.

From the Internet programme 70 percent said that the programme was satisfying because, it helps in creating own web sites and searching for information. But rest of them felt that they are dissatisfied because it discourages the habit of reading as its badly effect by the Internet. About 57 percent of the engineers felt that the utility was high because it offers access to data and it facilitate for websites. 61 percent of the respondents opined good about the method of Internet programme because in its early beginning it assures that they are computer savvy at a later age.

Out of the mobile phone, maximum extents of the respondents (80 percent) are satisfied with mobile phone because, it helps in the mathematical concepts, it provides and stores the messages provides camera facility and video facility, is expensive and sufficient to the people. Nearly 65 percent of the engineers opined that the utility was high because it provides communication with others, 62 percent of the respondents indicated that the method of the programme was good, because it helps to people and is convenient.

Regarding the opinions on the geographic information system programme, majority of the engineers (60 percent) opined satisfaction. But remaining of them felt that they are dissatisfied because it is complex process and it is not accessible by more people. While 62 percent felt that the utility was high, about 52 percent said that the method was good. But 30 percent said that this method was average because, it is a difficult process.

Exhibits the opinion of the engineers on the video conferencing programme, 65 percent said that they are satisfied with the programme because it provides excellent communication to the people. And 35 percent of them felt that it was not satisfying because lack of availability of the said programme. Nearly 63 percent of them felt that the utility was high because, it is used for digital images from one location to another location. The engineers (65 percent) stated that programme was good method because it is cheaper over the past few years, and computer programmes are much simpler than before.

In view of the teleconferencing programme, 48 percent said that the programme was satisfied by the engineers and rest of them (52 percent) dissatisfied because, of high cost of establishments, production and designing. About 53 percent of the respondents indicated their opinion on the utility of the programme was high. But 28 percent of them felt that the utility was low because of danger of over utilization. The respondents (52 percent) stated the programme was good method because training can be administered instantly and simultaneously. One-third of the respondents opined that the method was average because, it needed long time.

As can be seen from data about the computer conferencing programme, 72 percent of the respondents opined that they are satisfied because, it is capable of evolving unique instructional strategy for each educational task. Only 28 percent are dissatisfied with the programme as it needs more cost of production. About 53 percent of the respondents felt that it was highly utilised and 22 percent of them stated that the utility was extremely low. Majority of the engineers (56 percent) opined that it was good method.

About computer-based training programme, 63 percent of them felt satisfied, because it is versatile when it comes to on-screen display of information. Nearly 37 percent of them felt that they are not satisfied because, it depends on a pre-produced programme. Majority of the respondents (57 percent) expressed that the utility was high because it is a valuable vehicle for learners. 47 percent of the respondents felt good about the method of this programme. But 26 percent of them felt that it was average method because, it does not permit direct personal reinforcement.

Out of the computer-based multimedia programme satisfaction percent is 62 given by the respondents because interaction is more advantage of this programme. But 38 percent said that they are dissatisfied with the programme because, it requires more technical support from the software personnel. Maximum of the respondents (65 percent) stated that the utility was high because, it referred to a room having slide projectors, tape decks and movie projectors. Majority of the respondents indicated that the programme was good because, it is being used in movie making very extensively.

Regarding computer aided design programme, 83 percent of them are satisfied with the programme, because it allow the designer to view a product from different perspectives, the designer can also make proportional changes in scale or change the angle with the check of computer mouse rather than having to redraw the entire product. However, 35 percent of the respondents and 55 percent of the respondents, opined that the utility of this programme was very high and high respectively because, it can store the design characteristics of existing products and components, it can also reduce the development time and cost. About 49 percent of the respondents expressed that the method was good because, it determines whether the company is already using an identical or sufficiently similar gear, in which area new one is unnecessary. But 16 percent of them felt that it was an average method because, large automotive companies do not use it alone.

About the programme of computer aided manufacturing, the respondents (82 percent) satisfied with this programme, because, it can reduce investment in production inventories, facilities through work simplification, just in time inventory policies, and better planning and control of production and finished goods requirements. But 18 percent said that it was unsatisfied because it is complex to use. About 58 percent of them felt that the utility was high and 65 percent of the engineer expressed that the method was good because, it can improve customer service by drastically reducing out of stock situations and producing high quality products that will meet customer requirements better.

As can be seen from the data of personal software process the respondents (57 percent) indicated they are satisfied because it increased productivity and security but 43 percent of them stated that the dissatisfaction because, it requires long start up time. Nearly 55 percent said utility was high because it provides software engineers a means to harness their potential to maximum. But 16 percent of them indicated that utility was extremely low. Maximum of the respondents (72 percent) opined this programme was good because it provides better qualities of programming, it helps in on track costs and schedules it reduced cycles times.

6. Findings of the Lawyers

In view of the e-learning programme, majority of the respondents (72 percent) are satisfied with this programme because it gives knowledge and it expands at lightening speed and it is self-paced learning. But rest of them are dissatisfied, the reason is a complex process. Nearly 63 percent indicated that the utility was high and 58 percent said that the method was good because, it finds immediate feedback. About 20 percent of the lawyers expressed that it was an average method, because it is not usually associated with the formal accreditation.

About the programme of E-mail the lawyers (67 percent) are satisfied with the programme because global communication is easier. But 33 percent said that they are not satisfied because, it can become a distraction and can prevent people from doing any productive work. About 53 percent said that the utility was high. But 32 percent felt it was of low utility because, it is the very existence of electronic communication. While 65 percent said that the programme was a good method.

About the Internet programme, 72 percent said that they are satisfied with this programme because, it covers the globe and includes large international networks as well as many smaller, local area networks. But 28 percent of them felt that they are not satisfied because it can affect leadership qualities. 60 percent of them felt it was highly utilised and 20 percent said that it was low utilised. About 59 percent of the respondents stated that the programme was a good method because; it posts your resumes on the Internet and creates your own web sites.

As can be seen from data of mobile phone the lawyers (78 percent) are satisfied with the mobile phone because it is easy to communicate with their clients. Only 22 percent said that they are dissatisfied because signals not clear. Majority of the respondents (65 percent) stated that the mobile phone was high utilised because it is very useful to their activities with in short period. While 65 percent said that the method of mobile phone was good because it eliminates communication gap between the lawyer and clients.

From the geographic information system programme, 52 percent of the lawyers opined they are satisfied with the programme. But 48 percent of them felt that they are dissatisfied because it is a more costly procedure. Majority of them are felt that the utility was high, i.e. 60 percent but 20 percent opined that the utilities were low. The respondents (48 percent) indicated that the method was good. About 32 percent said that the method was average, because, it is not accessible by the more people.

Out of the video conferencing programme, the lawyers (72 percent) satisfied with this programme, because, it provides excellent communication to the people. But 28 percent of them felt that it was unsatisfying because of lack of availability. Maximum of the respondent (62 percent) are opined that it was highly utilised. Majority of them (63 percent) felt that the method of the programme was good.

On the opinion of the respondents on the teleconferencing programme, half percent of the respondents are satisfied with the programme because, it provide consistency of training in terms of quality and quantity of information presented. But equal percent of them felt that they are dissatisfied because lack of familiarity of the users with the medium and equipments. It requires additional time and resources for training users in understanding the medium and using the equipment. About 47 percent of the respondents opined that it was highly utilised and 27 percent of them felt that it was of low utility. Majority of the respondents stated that the programme was a good method and 30 percent of the lawyers opined that it was an average method. Because it is a very expensive procedure, and it has a lack of availability.

From the computer conferencing programme, the lawyers (55 percent) satisfied and remaining of them felt unsatisfied. About 53 percent of them felt it was highly utilised. About 25 percent of them felt it was extremely low utilised because it does not permit direct personal reinforcement and hence the motivational effects of training are gone. While 49 percent said that it was a good method. The respondents (28 percent) said that it was an average method because it needs more production and investment.

About the programme of computer-based training, the lawyers (65 percent) opined that they are satisfied with the programme because, it provides opportunity for learners to check their understanding. But 35 percent said that the programme was not satisfying because, it can be cost effective, depending on the circumstances. About 48 percent of them felt that the utility was high because, it offers high level of interaction with immediate feedback. 30 percent said that the utility was low because, it may induce a sense of isolation, as individual work on their own. Majority of the respondents (53 percent) said that the method was good because, it can be made available at different locations and offer privacy. But 24 percent of them felt it was an average method because, it requires a greater self-discipline and commitment by the labour.

Regarding computer-based multimedia programme, 67 percent of the lawyers are satisfied in this regard because it provides very quick presentation. But one-third of them are felt they are dissatisfied because it is more complex in the software programmes. Majority of them (67 percent) felt that it was highly utilized and 65 percent of the lawyer are opined that the method was good

In the view of the E-legal service programme, Maximum extent of the respondents (70 percent) expressed satisfaction and remaining of them is not satisfied. About 44 percent of the respondents stated that the utility was high. While 40 percent said that the method was good and 32 percent said that it was poor method because communication processes always depending on the computer is complex. Because of power cuts and information overload.

7. Findings of the Teachers

In the view of the E-learning programme the teachers (68 percent) said that they are satisfied with the programme and remaining of them are dissatisfied because teachers must use innovative methods for teaching so that leaning becomes enjoy-able experience, that sustains the interest and concentration of students. The teachers (70% percent) highly utilised this programme because of no limit in the number of students and to caution students is irrelevant. However, 55 percent of the respondent who are opined excellent and good respectively about the method of E-learning programme because it improves students' programme it reduces the workload.

About the E-mail programme the teachers (63 percent) stated satisfaction because, it provides access to the information from anywhere in the world but rest of them are dissatisfied with this programme. About 62 percent of the respondents felt that it was high utilised because it has proved a big blessing for senior citizens and retired persons, while 55 percent said that it was a good method because it can enable to stand out in education and competitions. But 20 percent said that it was an average method because, it has created information over load.

Out of the Internet programme, 67 percent of the respondents are satisfied with the programme because it eliminates the distance between people and one-third of them are dissatisfied in this regard because, it is an easy access to adult web sites. Majority of the respondents (58 percent) indicated their utility was high because it is foundation pillar for education and learning, it can expose children to a plethora of information and teaches them how to call relevant data, while 57 percent said that it was a good method.

As can be seen from the data of mobile phone, 82 percent said that they are satisfied with this programme because it avoids the communication gap. Maximum responded (62 percent) that the programme utility was high because it provides easy communication within the world and 61 percent stated that the method was good.

53 percent of the respondents are satisfied with the geographic information system programme because; it helps to reduce costs in streamlining customer service. But 47 percent of them felt that they are unsatisfied because, it is more of a costly programme. Nearly 58 percent of them opined that the geographic information system was high utilized because, it provides database creation and it making maps on basis of places. Only 22 percent said that it was low utilized. Majority of them (50 percent) felt that it was good method, because it helped in analyzing data quickly.

Regarding video-conferencing programme, the respondents (63 percent) expressed satisfaction because it has become cheaper over the past few years and computer programmes much simpler than before. 37 percent of them felt that they are not satisfied with this programme. About 65 percent stated that the utility was high, because it provides excellent communication to the people. While 65 percent of them opined that the method was good.

In view of the teleconferencing programme the respondents (52 percent) stated that they are satisfied with this programme because, training people in general skills broadly effects general performance. About 48 percent said that they are not satisfied with this programme because there is a deficiency of technical expertise to maintain the system. Poorly maintained teleconferencing systems frequently show ghost images, echo effects and voice errors, which effect the quality of transmission and reception. Half percent of the respondents opined that the utility was high because, it helps to identify specific needs. One-fourth of them felt that it was low utilized because of danger of over utilization. While 53 percent of the respondents are expressed that the method was good.

About computer conferencing programme, the respondents are (67 percent) highly satisfied with the programme but one-third of them are dissatisfied about the programme. Nearly 46 percent of them felt that the programme was highly utilized and 51 percent of the respondents said that the programme was a good method because, it participates in the various programmes, i.e. bulletin boards, e-groups, mailing lists, real time, chat and e-mail.

Regarding the programme of computer-based training, majority of the respondents (67 percent) indicated that they are satisfactory, because it can offer high level of interaction with immediate feedback. About 33 percent of them felt that it was not satisfaction because it can prove costly, as expensive hardware and software are required. Nearly 53 percent said that the programme was highly utilized, it can keep student record automatically. While 52 percent of the teachers stated that the method was good because it can be cost effective depending on the circumstances.

An attempt is made to find out the opinion of the respondents, they are highly (65 percent) satisfied in this regard as it refers to a room having slide projectors, tape decks and movie projectors. But 35 percent said that they are dissatisfied, because it requires more technical support from the software personnel. Maximum extents of the respondents (63 percent) stated that the programme utility was high, because, it integrates voice, video and computer technologies into single delivery systems. About 67 percent said that it was a good method because it does not need any special skills.

Out of the Hi-tech programme, the respondents (68 percent) stated that they are satisfied because it acts as a coordinator for resource sharing between institutions. But 32 percent felt that it was dissatisfactory. About 63 percent of the respondents indicated their opinion on the utility of the programme was high because, it should create multimedia instruction and teacher should become a software developer for media instruction through it. However 48 percent of the respondents and 39 percent of the respondents, opined excellent and good respectively about the method because, it provides integrating their faculty with other faculties and it can practice strategic planning to be in time with the global revolution of IT, to produce well rounded persons with overall development who can be assets to an organizational society.

8. FINDINGS OF THE RURAL PEOPLE

Regarding E-learning programme the rural people (67 percent) expressed that the programme was satisfactory in rural areas because it will be a giant step forward towards ensuring quality education for all with cost effectiveness, at the door step of learners. But rests of them felt that they are dissatisfied because it needs lack of real human interaction. Majority of the respondents (62 percent) opined that the utility was high because it provides much freedom to students regarding place and time of learning. This flexibility makes learning an attractive activity particularly for housewives and employed students. About 20 percent of them low utilized the programme because, it is need self-discipline. While 65 percent of the respondents opined that the method was good because knowledge is expanding at lightening speed.

In view of the E-mail programme majority of the respondents (58 percent) opined satisfaction in rural places because it ranges from just curious with no computer background to well experience that have a computer at home and a laptop in their travel bag. But the remaining respondents (42 percent) are dissatisfied because it is the individual using the technology that makes communications better or worst. This programme utility was highly responded by them (50 percent) because it makes global communication easier. The respondents (63 percent) said that the method was good because, it is estimated that the data traffic through the Internet would outstrip the voice traffic in not-too-distant future.

Out of the Internet programme, maximum respondents (63 percent) are satisfied with the programme, because it is the cheapest and fastest means to get information, provide information and compile information. But 37 percent said that they are not satisfied because, literacy is necessary for the operation of Internet. About 57 percent of them felt that the utility was high, because it provides online multimedia including radio and video broadcasts also. While 23 percent stated that the programme utility was low because need telephone lines are necessary. The respondents (55 percent) said that the method was good because, Internet at an early beginning assures that they are computer savvy at a later age.

About the mobile phone, maximum of the respondents (72 percent) are satisfied with the mobile phone in rural areas, because it provides easy communication from rural areas to anywhere and it is very useful to the rural residents for sending SMS. About 28 percent of them felt that they are not satisfied because of financial problems, signal problems and agricultural workload. Nearly 55 percent said that the utility was high because it is convenient to the rural people. Majority of the respondents (60 percent) stated that the method was good because it creates interaction with known persons.

As can be seen from the programme of geographic information system the respondents (48 percent) are satisfied with the programme because it makes maps on basis of places. But highly dissatisfied by respondents (52 percent) say that it is a more costly procedure and it is not accessible by the more people. Nearly 47 percent of them are felt that it was high utilized because it helps in analyzing data quickly. However, 28 percent of the respondents and 22 percent of the respondents opined low and extremely low respectively because it is more costly and complex process. About 48 percent stated that method was good and 27 percent said that it was an average method. Because it is connected with information overload.

An attempt is made to find out the programme of video conferencing. Majority of the respondents (62 percent) are satisfied with the programme and 38 percent are dissatisfied in this regard. About 57 percent stated that the utility was high and 23 percent said that the utility was low. Maximum of the respondents (64 percent) stated that the programme was good method because it is used for transferring digital images from one location to another location and it has become cheaper over the past few years and computer programmes much simpler than before.

Regarding teleconferencing programme, majority of the respondents (52 percent) not satisfied with this programme because of danger of over utilization, high cost of establishments, production and distribution of educational multimedia packages. But only 48 percent said that they are satisfied because it improves the rural people in specific skills for specific performance and it helps to identify specific needs. Nearly 47 percent of the respondents expressed that the utility was high because, it can reduced the cost of training. But 32 percent said that the utility was low because constantly changing technology and confusions over standards have added to the technophobia created by lack of awareness about the potentials of state of art. About 46 percent of the respondents expressed that the method was good because it provide consistency of training in terms of quality and quantity of information presented. Nearly 32 percent of them felt that the method was average because skill is required for producing using courseware.

From the computer conferring programme the respondents (52 percent) dissatisfied because, it needs cost of production and investment more and danger of over utilization. But satisfaction percent is 48 because it reduces time and resource requirements. The respondents (45 percent) are opined that the utility was high because, it is capable of evolving unique instructions strategies for each educational task. However, 27 percent and 23 percent of the respondents opined low and extremely low respectively about the computer conferencing programme because it needs cost of production.

About 47 percent of the respondents expressed that the method was good and 31 percent said that the method was average.

About the computer-based training programme majority of the respondents (62 percent) are satisfied with this programme, because it enables learners to study at a time of their own choice. But 38 percent stated that they are not satisfied because, it is relatively inflexible and it depends on a pre-produced programme. About half percent of them felt that the utility was high because it is user choice of control and routing through the programme that makes the medium sophisticated training tool. While 32 percent said that it was low utilized because it required a grater self-discipline and commitment by the learner. Nearly 48 percent said that the method was good. But 35 percent said that the method was poor because it proves costly, as expensive hardware and software are required.

Out of the computer-based multimedia programme the respondents (57 percent) opined that they are satisfied with the programme. But 43 percent of them are felt that they are not satisfied. Majority of the respondents (65 percent) highly utilized this programme because it is widely used in the entertainment and education fields and it provides very quick presentation. While 53 percent of them felt that the method was good because it referred to a room having slide projector, tape decks and movie projectors, 20 percent said that the method was average.

Regarding video-based training for farmers, 62 percent of the respondents are satisfied with this programme because it can be used to delivery real time information and customized knowledge to improve formers' decision-making abilities. But 38 percent of them felt that they are dissatisfied because of lack of facilities and lack of time. However, 38 percent of the respondents and 22 percent of the respondents opined high and low respectively regarding the utility of this programme. Nearly 48 percent of the respondents and 37 percent of the respondents opined that it was good method and excellent method respectively because it provides informing farmers about the current rates of major crops at the local and other recognized auction centre around India and auction facilities for farmers and villagers for land, agricultural machinery, equipment and other durable commodities, via video.

SUGGESTIONS

- E-learning ensures quality education but cost should be reduced. E-learning needs self-discipline. It is suggested that even though it encourages learner centric personalized education system, to clarify the doubts of the students, teachers must be available. E-learning lacks human interaction. It is suggested that the human interaction must be provided for E-learning also.
- E-mail is that it can become a distraction and can prevent people from doing any productive work. Therefore, there is need clarification for productive work. It is suggested that E-mail should

not disturb the normal productive work. E-mail has created an information over load therefore there is needs exemption from overload of information. It is suggested that the persons should not misuse it and it should not encourage unhealthy atmosphere.

- The telephone connection is must for Internet. So, there is needs facility of telephone. It is suggested that telephone line should be available at cheaper rates. Internet gives easy access to adult web sites. It wills badly effects on the students and younger people. Therefore, some restrictions are needed. It is suggested that students and youngsters should not open the adult websites. For this purpose proper steps are to be taken.
- The mobile phone creates communication barriers. Therefore, proper steps are needed. It is suggested that the communication barriers are to be removed. Otherwise the person may not receive communication on the other hand clearly and signal problems are also to be reduced. The students misuse the mobile phones. So, therefore some steps are needed to avoid it. It is suggested that for students only ordinary mobile phones should be provided.
- Lack of video conferencing facilities in the urban and rural areas. Hence there is need to change the facilities. It suggested that the facilities are to be provided in rural and urban areas, also to keep the system reactable to all types of interested parties. Video conferencing is very expensive process. Therefore, some encourages are required. It is suggested that the government should take necessary steps to reduce the cost, which enables the interested parties to participate or to communicate through it. Lack of availability of video conferencing. Hence some steps for availability is needed. It is suggested that the programme should be made available to all types of categories in the society.
- A number of information technology programmes have been introduced since 1985 in India under the Prime Ministership of Late Sri Rajiv Gandhi. It is observed that wide variations prevail in various information technology programmes. The programmes introduced for development of human resources in different states in the country. It is suggested that it is to be reduced the imbalances between the state variations about information technology development.
- The computer aided design and computer aided manufacturing systems are not used by large automotive and electronic compromise alone. Therefore, there is a need for introducing some changes in both the systems. It is suggested that this technology is to be extended to avoid the lack of utility of the large companies.
- The computer operators are suffering with backbone pain due to the effect of the radiation on legs and other human parts. There is a need for precautions to the computer operators. It is suggested that the computer operator chairs should be adjustable in high and

should have lower-back support and armrests, computers desks should allow adjusting the height of the computers keyboard.

- A lot of pressure is on human eyes at the time of computer operating. Therefore, there is a need for introducing some healthy measures to the computer operators. It is suggested to avoid staring at the computer screen for long periods the position of the monitor between 2 and 2½ feet from operator eyes should be made and sure no bright lights reflect off operator screen.
- The procedure of E-Commerce has software problems and technical problems due to insufficient communication bandwidth. Therefore, there is a need for sufficient communication bandwidth to avoid from the concerned problems. It is suggested that this procedure is to be extended to all technical and software components.
- More than half of the populations in our country are living in the rural areas. They are suffering with lack of facilities, high cost of production of tools, and lack of awareness about the information technology to develop their human resources. Therefore, there is a need for introducing some awareness programme in the rural areas. It is suggested that there should be reduced cost of production tools, providing more facilities like video and teleconferencing, Internet, e-mail in the rural areas.
- As per the provisions of the information technology act, not mentioned the term e-contract in its text or Act. Therefore, there is a need for introducing some changes in the various provisions of the information technology act. It is suggested that this act is to be extended to all the transactions or contracts should be necessary mentioned.
- Deficiency of technical expertise to maintain the system—poorly maintained teleconferencing systems frequently show ghost images echo effects and voice errors, which effect the quality of transmission and reception. It is suggested that the quality of transmission should be improved and technical experts must be available at the time of teleconference to reduce the faults like voice disturbance, etc.
- Constantly changing technology and confusions over standards have added to the techno phobia created by lack of awareness about the potentials of state-of-art teleconferencing technologies and fears over the technology-based learning. Therefore, it is necessary to avoid from this. It is suggested that reducing the confusion over standards should create awareness and giving proper training should reduce techno phobia.
- Teleconferencing is lack of familiarity of the users with the medium and equipments. It requires additional time and resources for training users in understanding the medium and using the equipment. So there needs some changes. It is suggested that

proper training, familiarity in the usage of equipment and medium of communication should be provided to the users and training is must to understand the medium and usage of equipment.

- The E-commerce has lack of personal privacy and security to individuals. Therefore, there is a need for introducing some changes about the E-commerce. It is suggested to develop the software to provide the personal privacy and security to individuals.
- The data base management system transaction processing is flexible. Hence, it needs, fixed transaction processing system. It is suggested that is to be fixed transaction-processing system getting through the data catalogue for description of data in the data base operations is suggested.
- The computer assisted instruction presents information in the form of facts, leaving no room for questioning, creativity or cooperation. So there is need for providing conveniently. It is suggested that it should provide facilities and creativity for information presents in the form of facts.
- Networks of the computers are costly to develop. Hence there is need to reduce the cost of computers networks for development.
- The computer-based multimedia requires more technical support from the software personnel. Therefore, some changes in the system are needed. It is suggested that to develop the software in perspective to avoid from the technical support of personnel. The computer-based multimedia is more complex in the software programmes. It is suggested that developed software is required for easy operations.
- Computer-based training does not permit direct personal reinforcement, and hence the motivational effects of training are forgone. Therefore, it requires some changes in the programme. It is suggested that the software to permit direct personal reinforcement and to avoid from the forgone of motivational effects should be developed.
- The computer-based training can prove costly, as expensive hardware and software are required. Therefore, there needs low cost of production about software and hardware. It is suggested that should be reduced the cost of manufactured the computer hardware tools should be reduced produce the low expensive software programmes. IT industries should also produce the low expensive software programmes.
- According to computer conferencing programme it needs more cost of production and investment. Therefore, a less cost of production and investment is needed. It is suggested that the rate of now material, manufacturing installation charges about the computer conferencing programmes should be reduced.

- Teleconferencing needs greater time for preparation of courseware development of instructional packages. So need less time for preparation of courseware is needed. It is suggested that instructional packages in short span of time should be developed.
- The E-learning is a complex process. Therefore, there is a change needed in this programme. It is suggested that the E-learning programme increases competitiveness, transparency, and efficiency. So the programme should introduce a unique design, which helps the aspirants to learn easily.
- E-learning is an access limited based on availability of hard ware, software and internet connection. Therefore, an extent of the access availability of hardware, software is needed. It is to be suggested that every center should be provided with necessary hardware, software and Internet connection.
- The teachers must use innovative methods for teaching so that learning becomes an enjoyable experience that sustains the interest and concentration of students. Therefore, some steps are needed for this purpose. It is suggested that the innovative methods for teaching should be introduced through E-learning, which provides interest to students and help them to concentrate on it.

Scope for further research: At present, all business establishments, industrial organizations, educational institutions, professional bodies and different enterprises are dynamic. Infect, liberalization, privatization, globalization and changes in the technology made the organizations/ institutions/enterprises further dynamic. Information technology is a recent concept and it includes a number of technology programmes, which are well accepted and adopted by some mentioned organizations/institutions for developing human resources. The new risks and disadvantages of these IT programmes are needed to be studied for better and effective usefulness of these IT programmes to develop the nation.

APPENDIX I

INFORMATION TECHNOLOGY ACT, 2000

India is one of the very few countries in the world to have legislated cyber laws. The United Nations Commission on International Trade Law (UNICITRAL) adopted the Model Law of electronic commerce in 1996. It was followed by the United Nations General Assembly and recommended to all the states, suggesting that they should give favourable consideration to the UNICITRAL model law, when they enact or revise their laws (under its resolution dated 30th January 1997). In discharge of its international responsibilities, Government of India has also recognized the need to legislate and enact a new legislation known as Information Technology Act, 2000. (hereinafter referred to as "the Act").

The main objective of the Act is to provide legal recognition for transactions carried out by means of electronic data interchange and other means of communications commonly referred to as e-commerce, which involve the use of alternatives to paper-based methods of communications and shortage of information to facilitate electronic filing of documents with the Government agencies. The Act, apart from India, has extra-territorial jurisdiction to cover any offence or contravention committed outside India by any person. The Act came into force on 17.10.2000 along with Information Technology (Certifying Authorities) Rules, 2000.

In its present form, the Act, therefore, not only recognizes the usefulness of e-commerce and provides the necessary safeguards for the transactions by creating a necessary legal framework but it also makes consequent amendments in the Indian Penal Code, Indian Evidence Act, Reserve Bank of India Act, and Banker's Book of Evidence Act, so that the offences relating to documents and paper-based transactions are made equal to the offences in respect of the transactions carried out through the electronic funds transfer between the financial institutions and banks, and also to give legal sanctity to books of accounts maintained in the electronic form by the banks.

EXEMPTION

The Act shall not apply to following categories of transactions:

(1) Any negotiable instrument, (2) A power of attorney, (3) A trust,

(4) A will including any other testamentary disposition; (5) Any contract for the sale or conveyance of immovable property; and (6) Any other documents or transactions as any be decided by the Central Government. The Act further provides that no Ministry or Department of Central Government or the State Government or any authority established under any law can insist upon acceptance of document only in the form of electronic record.

CHAPTER I

Section 2 of the Act in Chapter I defines various important words, like "assess", "affixing", "digital signature", "asymmetric crypto system", "computer", "computer networking", "computer system", "data", "digital signature certificate", "electronic form", "electronic record", "private key", "public key", etc.

CHAPTER II
DIGITAL SIGNATURE

Suction 3 provides the conditions subject to which an electronic record any be authenticated by means of affixing digital signature. Any tempering with the contents of the electronic record will immediately invalidate the digital signature. The identity of the person affixing the digital signature is authenticated through the use of a private key which attaches itself to the message digest and which can be verified by anybody who has the public key corresponding to such private key.

CHAPTER III
ELECTRONIC GOVERNANCE

Where any law provides for submission of information in writing or in the typewritten or printed form, form now onwards it will be sufficient compliance of law if the same is sent in electronic form. Further, if any stature provides for affixation of signature in any document, the same can be done by means of digital signature.

Similarly, the filing of any form, application or any other document with the Government authorities and issue or grant of any license, permit, sanction or approval and any receipt acknowledging payment can be done by the Government offices by means of electronic form. From now onwards retention of any documents, records or information as provided in any law, can be done by maintaining electronic records. Any rule, regulation, order, by-law or notification can be published in official Gazette of Electronic Gazette.

The Act, however, provides that no ministry or department of Central or State Government or any authority established under any law can insist upon acceptance of document only in the form of electronic record.

CHAPTER IV
ATTRIBUTION, ACKNOWLEDGEMENT AND DISPATCH OF ELECTRONIC RECORDS

An electronic record can be sent by the addresser himself or by a person acting under his authority. An acknowledgement may be given by any communication by the addressee automatic or otherwise. Even any conduct of the addressee is sufficient to indicate to the addresser that the electronic record has been received, which shall be treated as sufficient acknowledgement.

The dispatch of electronic records occurs when it enters a computer resource outside the control of the originator (i.e., addresser). The time of receipt of electronic record shall be determined when the electronic record enters the digital computer resource or at the time when electronic record is retrieved by the addressee.

An electronic record is deemed to be dispatched at the place where the addresser has place of business and is deemed to be received at the place where the addressee has his place of business.

CHAPTER V
SECURE ELECTRONIC RECORDS AND SECURE DIGITAL SIGNATURES

Under the Act, the Central Government has the powers to prescribe the security procedure in relation to electronic records and digital signatures, considering the nature of the transaction, the level of sophistication of the parties with reference to their technological capacity, the volume of transactions and the procedures in general used for similar types of transactions or communications.

CHAPTER VI
REGULATION OF CERTIFYING AUTHORITIES

The Central Government may appoint a Controller of Certifying Authority who shall exercise supervision over the activities of the certifying authorities.

Certifying authority means a person who has been granted a license to issue a Digital Signature Certificate. The Controller or Certifying Authority shall have powers to lay down rules, regulations, duties, responsibilities and functions of the Certifying Authority issuing Digital Signature Certificates.

The Certifying Authority empowered to issue a Digital Signature Certificate shall have to procure a license from the Controller of Certifying Authority to issue Digital Signature Certificates. The Controller of Certifying Authority has prescribed detailed rules and regulations in the Act, as to the application for license, suspension of license and procedure grunt or rejection of license.

CHAPTER VII
DIGITAL SIGNATURE CERTIFICATES

Section 35 empowers Certifying the Authority to issue Digital Signature Certificates. It empowers the Central Government to prescribe application fees to be paid by persons for getting a Digital Signature Certificate. The Government has the powers to prescribe different fees for different classes of applicants. However, the maximum fee cannot exceed Rs. 25,000. Before granting the Digital Signature Certificate the Certifying Authority should satisfy himself that:

(1) The applicant holds the private key corresponding to the public key to listed in the Digital Signature Certificate.
(2) The applicant holds the private key, which is capable of creating Digital Signature.
(3) The public key to be listed in the certificate can be used to verify a Digital Signature affixed by the key held by the applicant.

The chapter also deals with suspension and revocation of the Digital Signature Certificate.

CHAPTER VIII
DUTIES OF SUBSCRIBERS

A subscriber can publish or authorize the publication of Digital Signature Certificate. Similarly, he can accept such certificate.

It is the responsibility of a subscriber to exercise reasonable care to retain control of the private key corresponding to the public key listed in his Digital Signature Certificate and to take all steps to prevent its disclosure to any unauthorized person.

CHAPTER IX
PENALTIES AND ADJUDICATION

If any person without the permission of the owner accesses the owner's compute, system or computer network or downloads copies or any extract or introduces any computer virus or damages the computer, computer system or computer network, data, etc., he shall be liable to pay damages by way of compensation not exceeding Rupees one crore to the person so affected.

For the purpose of adjudication the Central Government can appoint any officer, not below the rank of a Director to the Government of India or any equivalent officer of any State Government, to be an Adjudicating Officer.

The adjudicating officer, while trying out cases of this nature, shall consider the amount of gain of unfair advantage or the amount of loss that may be suffered by a person.

The aforesaid provisions were not incorporated in the Information Technology Bill, 1999 and the same were suggested by the Select Committee of Parliament. In Delhi, the police on the basis of FIR filed by a retired army officer, whose Internet time has been "stolen" by the accused, has already registered the first case under the Act. However, the City Court has granted acquittal to the accused. Interestingly, although passed by the Parliament, the Act did not come into being until recently and Notification to this effect was made by the Central Government in the Official Gazette on 19.06.2000. This was one of the pleas taken by the accused in the aforesaid case.

CHAPTER X
THE CYBER REGULATION APPELLATE TRIBUNAL

Under the Act, the Central Government has the power to establish the Cyber Regulation Appellate Tribunal.

The Tribunal shall have the power to entertain the cases of any person aggrieved by the Order made by the Controller of Certifying Authority or the Adjudicating Officer.

CHAPTER XI
OFFENCES

Tampering with computer source documents shall be punishable with imprisonment up to three years or fine up to Rs. 2 lakh or with both.

Similarly, hacking with computer system entails punishment with imprisonment up to three years or with fine up to Rs. 2 lakh or with both.

Publishing of information which is obscene in electronic form shall be punishable with imprisonment up to five years or with fine up to Rs. 1 lakh the first time and for the second conviction with imprisonment up to ten years and with fine up to Rs. 2 lakh.

CHAPTER XII
MISCELLANEOUS

Under the Act, any police officer not below the rank of Dy. Superintendent of Police or any other officer of the Central or State Governments, may enter in a public place and search or arrest without warrant any person who is reasonable suspected or having committed or committing or of being about to commit any offence under this Act.

'Public place' includes any hotel, shop or any other place intended for use by or accessible to public.

The above was suggested by the Select Committee of Parliament. This has already raided a hue and cry. Under the Indian Penal Code, even a constable has the foresaid power. However, the power given to the designated police officer is so wide that even on suspicion or on his conviction that an offence is about to be committed, he can conduct search and arrest without any warrant. There is a widespread fear that this may be misused.

CONCLUSION

As indicated earlier, India is one of the few countries to have enacted Information Technology Act. The Act does not cover various other Cyber crimes. It is reported that the Government will being in more specific legislations to combat such crimes once internationally (especially in the US) specific legislations to this effect are evolved. In the absence of the Indian Act, any Cyber crime as mentioned in the Act, would have gone un-punished.

APPENDIX II

Prime Minister's National Task Force on Information Technology and Software Development: Extract of Action Plan Relevant to Electronic Commerce

INFO-INFRASTRUCTURE DRIVE

1. INTERNET access nodes will be opened by Department of Telecommunications and authorized ISPs at all District Headquarters and local charging areas by 26th January, 2000. As an interim measure and till nodes are provided in all local charging areas, access to nearest INTERNET access nodes will be on local call rates with effect from 15th August, 1998. ISPs will be responsible for ensuring that this facility is not misused for telephone traffic.
2. Voice and Data Communication is permitted for IT Software Development and IT Services on dedicated or leased circuits, but no telephone traffic is permitted. Surcharge on 64 Kbps and higher capacity circuits for vice-*cum*-data applications is withdrawn with effect from 15th August, 1998.
3. Doubling of the lease rental charged by DoT for high-speed data circuits leased by Closed User Group (CUG), licensees of Basic Service, Cellular Service and other Value Added Services and users shall be reduced to single normal lease rental charge.
4. For setting up ISP Operations by companies, there shall be no license fee for the first five years and after five years a nominal license fee of one rupee will be charged.
5. The monopoly of the VSNL on International Gateway for INTERNET shall be withdrawn and authorized public/ government organizations will be allowed to provide INTERNET Gateway access directly without going through VSNL Gateways. Private ISPs are allowed to provide such Gateways after obtaining Defence clearance. Suitable monitoring mechanisms will be put in place to take care of security considerations.
6. The Railways, Defence, State Electricity Boards, National Power Grid Corporation as organizations like ONGC, GAIL and SAIL who have rights of way shall be allowed to host a fibreoptic

backbone. These organizations shall be allowed to provide service to the public based on this backbone by having an interface with the existing or new public networks, but without necessarily having to go through DoT network.

7. Networks such as NICNET, STPs, as well as private networks shall be allowed inter-connectivity without necessarily having to go through the DoTs INET network.
8. Providing access to INTERNET through authorized Cable TV shall be permitted to any service provider without additional licensing.
9. The 'last mile' linkages shall be freely permitted either by fibreoptic or radio communication for IT application enterprises. IT promotional organizations and ISP. In case of radio linkages, coordination by the Wireless Adviser will be observed to avoid frequency interference.
10. The radio frequency band in the range of 2.4-2.483 MHz shall be open as 'public wireless' for any Government organization or PSU or Private Sector company to set Spread Spectrum-based non-interference type Wireless data/multimedia communication equipment subject to a maximum of 4 Watt EIRP, WPC will periodically issue a district-wise directory of two or three selected sub-bands of 10 MHz each for each of the districts on the criteria of least congestion and reserve these sub-bands maximally for the exclusive use of Spread Spectrum Communication as above. The use for he and will be on the basis of non-interference, non-protection and non-exclusiveness. Private sector, public sector and Government operators shall bilaterally obtain Defense Clearance for location, the area covered and the frequency sub-band. The Private Sector Units will be required to obtain MHA clearance directly; the security agencies shall convey their decision within 30 days of application failing which the application would be deemed to have been cleared from the security angle; if cleared, the Private and Public Sector operators shall be required to obtain a registration and automatic license directly form WPC by producing the copies of security clearances; the Government operators will directly register with WPC; WPC will be empowered to monitors the violation of the above conditions and impose penalties on defaulters in three stages; Written warning, monetary penalty and debarring for two years. A public Wireless Technical Audit Unit comprising a representative each form the Defense, DoT, NIC and from NASSCOM for the limited purpose of representing private user interests, shall monitor the implementation of the above policy.
11. Data communication requirements for Electronic Commerce (EC/EDI) shall be met by DoT in a liberal framework by assigning the highest priority under their priority classification if the EC/EDI

requirement is certified by authorities in Government authorized by the Ministry of Commerce.

12. Public TeleInfo Centres (PYIC) having multimedia capability specially ISDN Services, Remote Database Access, Government and Community Information system, Market Information, Desk Top video-conferencing, TeleInfo and INTERNET/Web Access Services shall be permitted and encouraged by the Government. DoT and other Basic Service Providers, Value Added Service Providers and authorized IT promotional organizations shall be permitted to promote these services on non-exclusive basis. No license fee will be charged for operating these services and the usual tariff, where applicable, will be payable by the PTIC Service providers/franchisees. Efforts will be made by DoT and other Service Providers to upgrade STD/ISD PCOs to convert them into these powerful PTICs for which ISDN or other digital facilities shall be provided on priority without necessarily having to make additional investment on this account.
13. DoT shall take suitable action to delicense multimedia services, including FAX, provided by PCOs.
14. To enhance the pace of PC and INTERNET penetration in remote and far-flung areas in the country, the Defense Services shall enable provisions of connectivity for civilian applications to their communication backbone.
15. 'Mega websites' shall be created on INTERNET for promoting marketing and encourage Indian software products and packages under multiple initiatives. Creation and hosting of websites on servers located in India will be encouraged.
16. The Government shall take necessary measures to develop, product vise and use, in domestic and global markets, indigenous technologies in wireless telecommunication such as CorDECT, remote access switch, etc. to achieve the national objective of rapid, low cost expansion of telephone and internet connectivity in rural and remote areas. Similarly, promotional measures shall be taken to encourage technologies that bring IT and Internet to the masses through the vast network of Cable TV houses.
17. For promoting electronic commerce in a time-bound manner, a strict directive shall be given to Sea Ports, Airports Authority of India, DGFT, Banks, Container Services, Customs and Indian Railways in accordance with the programme approved in the tenth Export Promotion Board meeting.
18. Bar Coding of every item sold in the country shall be made compulsory within a five-year period.
19. A National Institute of Smart Government shall be set-up to focus on all issues concerning IT-supported governance.

20. A National Computerized Records Security Document shall be prepared within three months for enforcing security requirements by consulting similar documents prepared by SAG, JCB, SESEE, etc.
21. An Information Security Agency shall be set-up at the national level to play the role of Cyber Cop.
22. A National Policy on Information Security, Privacy and Data Protection Act for handling of computerized data shall be framed by the Government within six months.
23. Cyber infractions shall be addressed within the legal framework by the Ministry of Law, Justice and Company Affairs.
24. The cryptology and Cyber Security knowledge and experience developed by the Defense establishments shall be suitably transferred to the civilian information security agencies for wider dissemination in the country to increase information security, network security and bring about a greater degree of secure use of EFT, Digital Signature, etc.
25. The procedure of keeping records in paper form in public and private STPs shall be restricted to maximum duration of two months after which the records shall be kept only in the Electronic/Magnetic/Optical media.
26. The Indian Telegraph Act of 1885, the Indian Post Office Act of 1888 and the Indian Wireless Telegraphy Act of 1993 shall be suitably modified in the light if the growing predominance of IT in day-to-day life. Suitable changes will also be made in other Laws/Acts, wherever necessary.
27. The draft set of Cyber Laws prepared by the Cyber Law Committee set-up by the Committee of Secretaries, shall be approved by the Government with suitable modifications and implemented as a first step, within six months.

Bibliography

Text Books

Abrol, D., Jain, A., Introduction of Information Technologies in India, New Delhi, Wiley Eastern Ltd., 1990, 51 p.

Akhilesh, K.B., Nagaraj, D.R., HRM 2000, Indian Perspectives, New Delhi, Wiley Eastern Ltd., 1990, 295 p.

Alvarez, J.L., The Diffusion and Consumption of Business Knowledge Houndmills, Mcmillan Press Ltd., 1998, xii, 318 p.

Anthony, W.P. and Others, Strategic Human Resource Management, NY, Dryden Press, 1993, xix, 791 p.

Asian Productivity Organisation, National IT Strategies and Economic Development, Tokyo, Apo, 1996, 451 p.

Ball, M.J. and Others, Eds, Strategies and Technologies For Health Care Information-theory Into Practice, New York, Springer, 1999, xvii, 216 p.

Beerel, A., Expert Systems in Business-real World Applications, Ellis Horwood, 1993, 267 p.

Bernardin, H.J., Russell, J.E.A., Human Resource Management—An Experiential Approach, NY, McGraw Hill, 1993, xiv, 722 p.

Bhatnagar, S.C., Bjorn-Andersen, N. Eds., Information Technology in Developing Countries, Andersen Eds., North-Holland, 1990, 283 p.

Biddiscombe, R., Training for I.T., London, Library Association Pub., 1997, 71 p.

Billimoria, R.P., Singh, N.K., Human Resource Development: A Study of the Airlines in Asian Countries, Delhi, Vikas, 1985, X, 128 p.

Blattberg, R.C. and Others The Marketing Information Revolution, Massachusetts, Harvard Business School Press, 1994, viii, 373 p.

Blyton, P., Turnbull, P., Reassessing Human Resource Management, London, Sage, 1992, X, 270 p.

Boar, B.H., Strategic Thinking For Information Technology, NY, Wiley, 1997, xv, 270 p.

Bock, W., Getting On the Information Superhighway, California, Crisp, 1996, viii, 133 p.

Boisot, M.H., Information Space, A Framework For Learning in Organizations, Institutions and Culture, London, Routledge, 1995, xiii, 550 p.

Borghoff, U, W, Pareschi, R., Eds., Information Technology for Knowledge Management,

Bowen, D.E. and Others, Service Management Effectiveness, Sanfrancisco, Jossey Bass Pub., 1990, xxviii, 414p.

Branscomb, L.M., Empowering Technology Implementing A U.S. Strategy, Cambridge, MIT, 1993, 315p.

Bratton, J., Gold, J., Human Resource Management, Houndmills, Mcmillan, 1994, Xvi, 342p.

Carr, J.G, Information Technology and Accountant—Summary & Conclusions. Aldershot Gower, 1985, xii, 103p.

Cassidy, A., A Practical Guide To Information Systems Strategic Planning, Boca Raton, St. Lucie Press, 1998, xvi, 282 p.

Ciborra, C., Jelassi, T., Strategic Information Systems, NY, Wiley, 1994, xx, 242.

Clark, J., Human Resource Management and Technical Change, London, Sage, 1993, xiii, 240p.

Conference Board, Information Technology—Some Critical Implications for Decision-makers, NY, the Board, 1972 vii, 240 p.

Conlan, J., Principles of Management in Export, Oxford, Blackwell, 1994, xxi, 325 p.

Cornish, E., Exploring Your Future Living Learning and Working in the Information Age, Maryland, World Future Society, 1996, 160 p.

Cortada, J.W, TQM for Information Systems Management Quality Practices for Development Continuous Improvement, NY, McGraw Hill, 1995, xvii, 301p.

Curtin, D.P. and Others, Information Technology—the Breaking Wave (Hihm), New Delhi, Tata Mcgraw-Hill, 1999, xx, 300p.

Davenport, Process Innovation, Boston, Harvard Business School Press, 1993, X, 337 p.

Donaldson, I., Scannel, E.E., Human Resource Development—The New Trainers' Guide, Reading, Addison Wesley, 1978, xvii, 151 p.

Donovan, J.J., Business Reengineering With Information Technology, NJ, PTR, Prentice Hall, 1994, xix, 189 p.

Duysters, G., The Dynamics of Technical Innovation, Cheltenham, Edward Elgar, 1996, 259 p.

Earl, M.J, Information Management, New York, Oxford University Press, 1998, xvii, 514 p.

Eimicke, V.W., Klimley, L.E., Managing Human Resources, Oxford, Pergammon Press, 1988, 220 p.

Estabooks, M., Electronic Technology Corporate Strategy and World Transformation, London, Quorum Books, 1995, x, 269 p.

Ettinger, J.E., Information Technology For Development, Washington, World Bank, 1994, xxi, 121 p.

Forester, T., Silicon Samurai, Cambridge, Blackwell, 1993, X, 230 p.

Fransman, M., Market and Beyond Cooperation and Competition in Information Technology Development in the Japanese System, Cambridge University Press, 1990, 333 p.

Galier, S.R.D., Bates, W.R.J., Information Technology and Organizational Transformation Innovation For the 21st Century Organization, NY, Wiley 1998, xix, 298 p.

Gallimore, A., Developing an IT Strategy for Your Library, London Library Association Pub., 1997, 192 p.

Gokak, A.V., Telecommunications, Delhi, B.R. Pub. Corpn, 1999, iv, 118 p.

Hammer, M. and Champy, J., Reengineering the Corporation, A Manifesto For Business Revolution, London, Nicholas Brealey Pub., 1993, 223 p.

Han, C., K. Walsham, G., Government Information Technology : In Policies and Systems, London, Common Wealth Secretariat, 1993, ix, 157 p.

Hanna, N.K., The Information Technology Revolution and Economic Development, Washington, World Bank, 1991, 57 p.

Heller, R., Spenley, P., Riding the Revolution, London, Harpercollins 2000, X, 288 p.

Hogbin, G., Thomas, D.V., Investing in Information Technology, NY, McGraw Hill, 1994, xv, 254 p.

Hope, J., Hope, T., Competing in the Third Wave: The Ten Key Management Issues of the Information Age, Boston, Harvard Business School Press, 1997, vii, 25 3p.

James, J., Globalisation Information Technology and Development, Hampshire, Macmillan, 1999, xii, 163 p.

Japan Information Seravice Industry Association, Information Service Industry in Japan, 1999, Tokyo, 1999, 74 p.

Joseph, J., Strategic Industrial Relations Management, New Delhi, Global Business Press, 1991, 527.

Kanungo, S., Making Information Technology Work, New Delhi, Sage, 1999, 430 p.

Kaul, M., From Problem to Solution Commonwealth Strategies for Reform, London, Commonwealth Secretariat, 1996, ix, 69 p.

Kendall, K.E. Ed., Emerging Information Technologies, Thousand Oaks, Sage, 1999, X, 373 p.

Keyes, J., Technology Trendlines, NY, Van Nostrand Reinhold, 1995, 394 p.

Kim, S.H., Essence of Creativity, NY, Oxford, 1990, 134 p.

Kirchmer, M., Business Process Oriented Implementation of Standard Software, 2nd Ed., Berlin, Springer, 1999, xii, 233 p.

Kissinger, K.; Borchardt, S., Information Technology for Integrated Health Systems. NY, Wiley, 1996, 252 p.

Laudon, K.C.; Turner, J., Information Technology and Management Strategy, NJ, Prentice Hall, 1981, 147 p.

Legge, K., Human Resource Management, Houndmills, Mcmillan Press, 1995, xiii, 385 p.

Leonard-barton, D., Wellsprings of Knowledge, Boston, Harvard Business School Press, 1995, 334p.

Locksley, G., Single European Market and the Information and Communication Technologies, London, Belhaven Press, 1990 291 p.

Lubbe, S., IT Investment in Developing Countries : An Assessment and Practical Guideline, London, Idea Group Pub, 1998, 226 p.

Lucas, H.C., the T-form Organization-using Technology to Design Organization For the 21st Century, San Francisco, Jossey-bass Pub., 1996, xv, 249 p.

Luftman, J.N., Competing in the Information Age Strategic Alignment in Practice, NY, OUP, 1996, xvii, 414p.

Mahajan, Y.S., Human Resource Development in Public Enterprises, Delhi, Centre for Public Sector Studies, 1988, 307 p.

Maitra, A.K., Building A Corporate Internet Strategy, New York, Van Nostrand Reinhold, 1996, Xix, 236p.

Malone, S.A., How to Set Up and Manage a Corporate Learning Center, Aldershot, Gower, 1997, xiv.

Mankin, D. and Others, Teams and Technology Fulfilling the Promise of the New Organization, Boston, Harvard Business School Press, 1996, xv, 284p.

Martin, E.W. and Others, Managing Information Technology : What Managers Need to Know, NY, Macmillan, 1994, 755p.

Mc Donald, S., Information For Innovation, Oxford, Oxford University Press 1998, xiii, 290p.

Mcgowan, W.G., Revolution in Real Time—Managing Information Technology in the 1990s, Boston, *Harvard Business Review*, 1991, 276 p.

Mckenney, Waves of Change, Boston, Harvard Business School, Xiv, 230 p.

Mclaughlin, J. and Others, Valuing Technology, London, Routledge, 1999, Diff. Pages.

Mitter, S. and Rowbotham, S., Women Encounter Technology, London, Routledge, 1995, 356 p.

Mondy, R.W., Noe, R.M., Human Resource Management, Boston, Allyn and Bacon, 1993, xiv, 744 p.

Moneta, J., Ed., Information Technology: Proceedings of the 3rd Jerusalem Conference On Information Technology (JCIT), Jerusulem, August 6-9, 1978, Amsterdam, North Holland Publishing Co., 1978 xxi, 804 p.

Morrison, I., Schmid, G., Future Tense the Business Realities of the Next Ten Years, NY, William Morrow and Co. 1994, 304 p.

Moschella, D.C., Waves of Power : The Dynamics of Global Technology Leadership, 1964-2010, NY, Amacom, 1997, xx, 300 p.

Niehaus, R.J, Price, K.F., Human Resource Strategies For Organizations and Transition, NY, Plenumpress, 1990, viii, 335 p.

Noam, E., Nishuilleabhain, A., Eds., Private Networks Public Objectives, Amsterdam, Elsevier, 1996, xxv, 439p.

Odedra, M.; Madon, S., Information Policies and Applications in the Commonwealth Development Countries, London, Commonwealth Secretariat, 1993, 203 p.

Organisation for Economic Cooperation and Development, Information Technology Outlook 1997, Paris, 1997, 234 p.

Owen, T., Success at the Enquiry Desk, London, Library Association Pub., 1996, 82 p.

Peterson, B.L., Cargo, D. Ed., Cyberwar 2.0 Myths, Mysteries and Reality, Virginia, Afcea International Press, 1998, vi, 403 p.

Pitroda, S., Exploding Freedom—Roots in Technology, New Delhi, Allied, 1993, 192 p.

Poppel, H.L., Goldstein, B., Information Technology : The Trillion Dollar Opportunity, NY, McGraw Hill, 1987, xx, 207 p.

Prietula, M.J. and Others, Simulating Organisations, Menlopark, Aai Press, 1998, xix, 248 p.

Rao, M.K., Sharma, P.P., Human Resource Development for Rural Development, Bombay, Himalaya, 1989, 294 p.

Rao, N.P., HRD in Management and Administrations, Delhi, B.R. Pub., 1986, viii, 122 p.

Rao, P.S., Rao, V.S.P., Personnel Resource Management : Text Cases and Games, New Delhi, Konark Pub., 1990, 507 p.

Rao, R., P. Das R., Thakore, D.K., Human Resource Management in Municipalities, New Delhi, Discovery Pub. House, 1990, 414 p.

Ravisankar, S. and Others, Human Resource Development in a Changing Environment, Bombay, Dhruv and Deep Books, 1988, 233 p.

Reddy, Y.R.K., Strategic Approaches To Human Resource Management, New Delhi, Wiley Eastern Ltd., 1990, 102 p.

Reddy, M.T., Securities Operations : A Guide to Operations and Information Systems in the Securities Industry, NY, New York Institute of Finance, 1995, 626 p.

Russeft, E., and Others, Human Resource Development—Research and Implications, New Delhi, Sage, 1997, xviii, 425 p.

Sadler, T., Human Resource Management, London, Kogan Page, 1995, 208 p.

Sah, S.L., Information Technology, New Delhi, Gyan Pub. House, 1999, 348 p.

Salaman, G. and Others, Human Resources Strategies, London, Sage, 1992, ix, 350 p.

Shankar, R., Jaiswal, S., Enterprise Resource Planning, New Delhi, Galgotia, 1999, 298 p.

Shankaraiah, A. and Others, Eds., Human Resource Management—Cases Games and Exercises, New Delhi, Discovery Pub. House, 1992, ix, 306 p.

Sharma, R.D., Human Resource Development and Environment, New Delhi, Commonwealth Pub., 1991, 328 p.

Sifonis, J.G., Goloberg, B., Corporation on a Tightrope Balancing Leadership, Governance and Technology in an Age of Complexity, Oxford University Press, 1996, xiv, 315 p.

Silk, D.J., Planning it, Oxford Butterworth, Heinemann, 1991, X, 161 p.

Singh, N.K., Human Resource Development in Indian Public Sector, Delhi, A Scope Pub., 1987, 74 p.

Singhal, A., Rogers, E.M., India's Information Revolution, Delhi, Sage, 1989, 244 p.

Soni, P., Ed., Energy and Environmental Challenges in Central Asia and the Caucasus, New Delhi, Tata Energy Research Institute, 1996, xiv, 264 p.

Straub, M.O. and Others, Information Technology and Globalisation Implications For Developing Countries, London, Common Wealth Secretariat, 1995, vi, 168 p.

Tapscott, D., Caston, A Paradigm Shif—The New Promise of Information Technology, NY, McGraw Hill, 1993 xvii , 337 p.

Techno Management R&D, Information Technology Applications, Experiences and Impact, Chennai, Techno. Managt., 1998, viii 174 p.

Tiffin, J., Rajasingham, I., In Search of the Virtual Class Education in an Information Society, London, Routledge, 1995, 204 p.

Tseng, G. and Others, The Library and Information Professionals Guide To the Internet, London, Library Association Pub., 1996, 199 p.

Turban, E., Mclean, E., Wetherbe, J., Information Technology For Management, 2nd Ed., New York, Wiley, 1999.

U.S. Congress Office of Technology Assessment, Information Technology Research and Development, NY, Pergamon Press, 1985, 342 p.

Venkataraman, N., Henderson, J. Research in Strategic Management and Information Technology, Vols. 1&2, Connecticut, Jai Press, 1994-99, X, 184 p.

Venkataratnam, C.S., Human Resource Development For Adjustments at the Enterprises Level, 2 Vols., Geneva, ILO, 1999, Diff. pages.

Verma, M.M., Human Resource Development, Delhi, Gitanjali Pub. House, 1988, xxii.

Vickerstaff, S., Human Resource Management in Europe : Text and Cases, London, Champan and Hall, 1993, xv, 258 p.

W.T.O, Electronic Commerce and the Role of the WTO, Geneva, WTO Organisation, 1998, 73 p.

Wang, C.B., Techno Vision II, New York, McGraw Hill, 1997, xx, 285 p.

Weill, P., Broadbent, M., Leveraging the New Infrastructure, Boston, Harvard Business School Press, 1998, xv, 294 p.

Weitzen, H.S., and Parkhill, Infopreneurs Online and Global, NY, Wiley, 1996, 225 p.

Willcocks, L.P., Lester, S., Eds., Beyond the IT Productivity Paradox, Chichester, Wiley, 1999 Xii, 417 p.

Wise, J.M., Exploring Technology and Social Space, London, Sage, 1997, xvii, 213 p.

Wodaski, R., Virtual Reality Madness (with Floppy), New Delhi, Sams Pub., 1993, 554 p.

Wodaski, R., Virtual Reality Madness, New Delhi, Sams Pub., 1993, 554 p.

Zack, M.H., IT Knowledge and Strategy, Boston, Butterworth, Heinemann, 1999 xii, 312 p.

Articles

Aarti Gupta, Captain Speck A New Form of Computing Can Change the Face of IT, *Business India*, June 23, July 6, 2003, p. 93.

Abrol Sunil, Km., Brand New Hr Tool, *Management Review*, April-June 2001, pp. 3-4.

Ahuja Sobhya, Creating Corporate Advantage Through Human Resource Development, *Vision*, January–June 2002, pp. 73-86.

Ajay Kumar Singh, Human Dimensions in the Information Age, *The Indian Journal of Commerce*, April-September, 2003, pp. 60-69.

Anjali Dhingra, Rural Informatics Network For E-governance in Rural Development Sector, *Journal of Rural Development*, October-December, 2001, pp. 711-20.

Arjun Chauhan, Managing Human Capital in Information Technology Companies, *The Indian Journal of Commerce*, October-December 2000, pp. 93-99.

Asthana, M.K. and Panda, D.M.R., Technology Convergence : The Human Perspective, *Delhi Business Review*, January-June 2002, pp. 1-18.

Athreya, Mrityunjay, HRD For Improving Indias Telecomgovernance, *Delhi Business Review*, January–June 2001, pp. 19-20.

B. Chalvarai, Design and Development of Information Centres for DICS *Small Enterprises Development Management Extension*, September 1984, pp. 39-50.

B.K. Singh, Redesigning Corporate Horizon via HRD, *Personnel Today*, January-March, 2000, pp. 27-34.

B.M. Kapoor, HRD Should be part of Business Strategy, *Indian Management* January 2001, pp. .59-63.

B.S. Bhatia and Gurcharan Singh, E-commerce Skirting Issues, *The Indian Journal of Commerce*, January-June 2002, pp. 51-57.

Berner Colette, Transformation of work and New model of Qualification/ Training, *Industrial Relations*, Winter 1999, pp. 51-79.

Bhagavan Prasad, Technology Management : A few imperatives, *Small Enterprises Development Management and Extension*, March 2003, pp. 9-15.

Bhanu Pant, Measuring Investment Payoffs in Information Technology, *Productivity*, April-June 2003, pp. 281-88.

Bharat Wakhlu, Effective Approaches for Training and Development, Personnel Today, April-June 1997, pp. 17-19.

Bhunia, C.T., Upadhyaya, N., Technical Education and Training for the Information age, *Productivity*, January-March 1999, pp. 579-87.

Billimoria, R.P., HRD Strategies for Globalisation, *Productivity*, October-December, 1997, pp. 362-70.

Brishtij Guha, IT-Deconstructing the Bust that followed the Boom, *Economic Political Weekly*, June 2003, pp. 2368-70.

C. Apparao, A.P. Guptha, Training for Excellence at RINL (VSP), *Indian Journal of Training & Development*, January-June 2003, pp. 79-84.

C. Ramachandra Prabhu, Invasion of Information Technology on Technical Education, *University News*, May 28-June 3, 2001, pp. 5-10.

C. Ramachandra Prabhu, Impact of Information Technology in Widening the Rich-Poor Divide? *University News*, 41(15), April 14-20, 2003. pp. 13-14.

C.S. Chaintanya, Electronic Credit Card, *Indian Journal of Training* and *Development*, August 2002, pp. 7-9.

C.S. Venkataratnam, HRD for adjustments, *Personnel Today*, July-September 2000, pp. 10-16.

Chandra, Gunawardena, Using Technology for quality Improvement of Teacher Education in OVSL, *Indian Journal of Open Learning*, January 1999, pp. 73-78.

Chauhan, Daisy and Chauhan, S.P., Future directions of HRD Aligning the HR functions to organizational goal, *Management & Change*, Summer 2002, pp. 295-308.

Chittaranjan, N. Daftuar, Allam Vijay Guptha, People Technology Interface: Issues Experiences, Challenges for HRD in the New Millennium, *Indian Journal of Training & Development*, October-December 2000, pp. 15-23.

Chung-Jen Chen and Bou-Wen Lin, A Resource-Based view of I.T. Outsourcing, *Asia Pacific Management Review*, June 2001, pp. 149-73.

Col. D.P. Dimri, Role of Counseling and Mentoring in HRD, *Indian Journal of Training & Development*, April-June 2000, pp. 19-31.

Currie, Graeme and Procter Stephen, Impact of MIS/IT upon middle managers, some evidence from NHS, *New Technology Work and Employment*, July 2002, pp. 102-18.

D.D. Arora, Business Process Reengineering, *The Indian Journal of Commerce*, October-December, pp. 88-92.

D.K. Mitra, G.S. Bhatia, R. Panneraelvam, Mary H. Powell, Training Methodologies and Inputs for micro, small medium scale enterprises in UK, *Small Enterprises Development Management and Extension*, June 1997, pp. 29-49.

D. Mukhopadhyaya, Information Technology for Quality Education of Learning Society, *University News*, November 4-10, 2002, pp. 11-16.

D. Venkateswarlu, Information Communication Technology for the Differently-abled, *University News*, November 25-December 1, 2002, pp. 9-10.

Das, Krishna Shekhar Lal, Workers hit by tech slum of 2001, *Labour File*, December 2001-March 2002, pp. 46-51.

David, W. Bracken, Lynn Summers, Hi-Tech 360, *Executive Capsule*, May-June 1999, pp. 19-22.

Deepak Halan, Special Technology for Special People, *Information Technology*, March 2004, pp. 42-44.

Devashis Rath, Outsourcing HR Activities a decision matrix, *Personnel Today*, April-June 2003, pp. 37-40.

Dharam Kumar and Pardeep Rai, Education; Use of Computers and Problem of Copyright, *Library Herald*, July 2002, pp. 119-30.

Dr. (Mrs.) Savita Rastogi, Executive Training and Development, *Indian Journal of Training & Development*, July-September 2002, pp. 86-94.

Dr. Rajeswari Narendran and Dr. V. Narendran, IT Revolution: Challenges for HRD, *Indian Jol. of Training and Development*, April-June 2001, pp. 22-35.

Dr. Uday Sankar Singh and Ram Sagar Singh, Managing HRD Challenges of the 21st century through self-Managed teams: An HRD Technique, *The Indian Journal of Commerce*, October-December 1998, pp. 206-11.

Dr. Usha Mujoo-Munshi and Dr. Inder Vir Malhan, Information Technology: Concerns and Issues in Developing countries with Special Reference to India, *Library Herald*, July-September 1998, pp. 68-79.

Dr. V.B. Dudeja, Info Tech : Challenges and Opportunities in new Millennium, *Indian Management*, August 1999, pp. 21-24.

Dr. Zillur Rahman & Md. Nishat Faisal, IT and Business: The Strategic Advanatage, *Indian Management*, October 1999, pp. 51-55.

Dr. A.P.J. Abdul Kalam, India Millennium Missions 2020 Challenges, *University News*, July 30 to August 5, 2001, pp. 13-16.

Dr. Ajay Kumar Singh, HRD Perspectives in 21st century, *The Indian Journal of Commerce*, October-December 1998, pp. 167-76.

Dr. C.S. Rayudu, Information Technology Applications, *Indian Journal of Training and Development*, May 2000, pp. 41-43, June 2000, pp. 36-37.

Dr. M.P. Gupta, Electronic Education and Training, *Indian Management*, September 1998, pp. 45-50.

Dr. Nawal Kishore, Electronic Commerce—Potential and Challenges : An Indian Perspective, *The Indian Journal of Commerce*, January-June 2001, pp. 28-39.

Dr. Neelu Rohmetra, Achieving Excellence through HRD, *The Indian Journal of Commerce*, December 1995, pp. 60-66.

Dr. Pathak, R.D., S.K. Tripathi, Zafar Hussain and Dr. Sushil, Harnessing Information Technology trends, *Indian Management*, April 1998, pp. 32-43.

Dr. Rabinarayan Mishra, Strategies of Knowledge Management in Information Technology Age, *Library Herald* March 2002, pp. 36-42.

Dr. T.R. Borse, Information and Information Technology, *Iaslie Bulletin*, June 2001, pp. 79-82.

G. Mulini Darshan, Human Resources availability in the Software Industry, *Personnel Today*, January-March 2002, pp. 9-15.

G.P. Pandey, Role of Information Technology in Higher Education in The 21st Century, *University News*, February 25-March 3, 2002, pp. 11-14.

Ganesh Sharman, The Shared Service Center Approach to HR, *Indian Management*, pp. 72-74.

Gopalakrishna, H.N., Training and Development, *Indian Journal of Training and Development*, Jan.-June 2003, pp. 85-88.

Gupta, M.P., Electronic Education and Training, *Productivity*, January-March 1999, pp. 541-48.

H.K. Shee, K. Momaya and D.K. Banwet, Competitive of Indian Software Industry : An Empirical Study, *The Indian Journal of Commerce*, January-June 2002, pp. 75-92.

H.V. Deshpande, Information Technology and Higher Education: Towards a just Perspective, *University News*, June 4-10, 2001, pp. 9-12.

Hinasidhu, Trade Liberalisation and Indian IT industry, *Productivity*, April-June 2002, pp. 149-55.

HR and Technology, *Human Capital*, May 2003, pp. 28-31.

Hrish Kumar and Alpana Mishra, Role of IT in Leveraging HR, *Personnel Today*, July-September 2000, pp. 17-20

Ila Patel, The challenge of Illiteracy: Can Information Technology Help? *Indian Journal of Adult Education*, July-December 2003, pp. 5-13.

Ilapatel, Information and Communication Technology and Distance Literacy Education in India, *Indian Journal of Open Learning*, May 2002, pp. 255-68.

Indranilnath, Information Technology Ethics, *Information Studies*, Jan. 2000, pp. 1-4.

Ishwal Dayal, Measuring Training effectiveness, *Indian Journal of Industrial Relations*, January 2001, pp. 339-44.

J.C Prasad and Kiran Kumar Varma, IT-Human and Managerial Facts, *The Indian Journal of Commerce*, April-September 2003, p. 83.

Jack Fiori to and William Bass, The use of Information Technology By National Unions : An Exploratory Analysis, *Industrial Relations*, January 2002, pp. 34-47.

Jacob Real, The Employee Training and Development Function and Diffuse Innovation : Some thoughts and Proposals, *Industrial Relations*, Summer 1999, pp. 472-88.

Jayant, Krishna, On-line Governance Made Easy, *Indian Management*, November 2000, pp. 66-68.

John, G. Burch, Garry Grudnitski, Information Systems (Theory and Practice), Fifth Edition, pp. 367-95 (Text Book).

Joi Luiz Antonio, Information Technology as a Strategic Tool for Workers Retaining in Brazil, *Productivity*, January-March 1999, pp. 556-66.

Jyotsna Bhatnagar and Anuradha Sharma, Strategic HR roles in India: A rehetoric or reality, *The Indian Journal of Industrial Relations*, April 2003, pp. 409-23.

K.G. Tyagi, Information Support for Development Studies, *Defence Research Development Organization Bulletin*, July 1998, p. 58.

K. Raghavendra Rao, Automating Employee Interactions, *Indian Management*, June 2003, p. 58.

K.V. Rangarao, Information Technology Act, 2000, An Understanding, *Small Enterprises Development Management and Extension*, March 2001, pp. 67-74.

Kapoor Gitika, Collaborative Framework for HRD Need, Issue and Interventions, *Vision*, July-December 1998, pp. 23-28.

Keki, B. Dadiseth, The Y2k and urgent challenges for Indian Business, *Indian Management*, July 1998, pp. 24-28.

Kerrin Maire and Hone Kate, Job seekers perceptions of Teleworking : A cognitive mapping approach, *New Technology work and Employment*, July 2001, pp. 130-43.

Kumar, Nagesh, Small Information Technology service Employment Entrepreneurship Development : Some Explorations in to Indian Experience, *Indian Journal of Labour Economics*, October-December 2000, pp. 935-48.

Kumtageeta, A., Shah Mitul, D., Capability Maturity Model A Human Perspective, *Delhi Business Review*, January-June 2002, pp. 47-60.

Kundu, S.C. and Punia, B.K., Management Challenges and HRD Intervention for future orgonisations, *Prestage Journal of Management and Research*, Vol. 6, Nos. 1-2, April-October 2002, pp. 82-90.

Lal, Jauhari, Managing change through HR, *Delhi Business Review*, July-December 2001, pp. 5-8.

Lt. Col. S.K. Tripathi and Dr. Pathak, Information Technology Management in Indian Army, *Indian Management*, November, 1999, pp. 60-68.

M. Narayanaswamy, A study on computer uses among teacher Educators in Teacher Training Institutions in Tamil Nadu, *Indian Journal of Open Learning*, January 2001, pp. 60-67.

M. Natarajan, Selection and Evaluation Criteria for e-resources, *Iaslie Bulletin*, January-March 2003, pp. 15-18.

M.P. Gupta, Electronic payments services in India, *Management Dynamics*, March, 2002, p. 23.

M.P. Srivastava, HRD Strategy to Balance people firm needs, *Indian Management*, January 2001, pp. 52-55.

M. Sulochana, Challenges of Corporate Sector in the Digital Era, *The Indian Journal of Commerce*, January-June 2000, pp. 78-91.

Maj. M.D. Apte: Place of Meditiation in Training and Development, *Indian Journal of Training and Development*, January-Mar. 2002, pp. 110-20.

Manoj Killedar, Distance Education Through Internet Based E-Learning, *Indian Journal of Open Learning*, January 2001, pp. 68-79.

Manoj Modak, IT-enabled Services: The Growth Engine of the Indian IT Industry, *The Management Accountant*, June 2002, pp. 405-09, 413-14.

Mary, C. Lacity, IT Outsourcing Maximize Flexibility and Control, *Harward Business Review*, May-June 1995, pp. 84-102

Md. Nishat Faisal and Md. Naved Khan, PCs are out—WAP is in, *Indian Management*, July 2000, pp. 76-80.

Mohan, R.K. Nimmaggdda, Role of Knowledge Internets in R&D, *Productivity*, April-June 2003, pp. 50-54.

Morin Fernand, New Technology and Employee Telesubordination, *Industrial Relations*, Autumn 2000, pp. 746-69.

Mukesh Dhunna, Anil Khurana and Neelam Dhunna, Recruitment and Retention Challenges in the DOTCOM World, *The Indian Journal of Commerce*, April-September 2003, p. 77.

N. Vittal, Moving forward of software, *Indian Management*, Feb. 1995, pp. 19-25.

N.M. Agarwal, HRD in Public Enterprises, *Indian Journal of Training & Development*, July-August 1989, pp. 4-9.

N.Upadhyaya, Information Technology : A Tool for Decision-making, *Personnel Today*, January-March 1992, pp. 27-38.

N. Upadhyaya and R.M. Panth, An aid to HRD and I.T. in 21st Century, *The Indian Journal of Commerce*, October-December 1998, p. 226.

Nasir Zamir Qureshi and M. Ashraf Ali, Measures for Improving Training & Development Programmes more effective and efficient for better Utilisation of Human Resources in I.T. Sector, *The Indian Journal of Commerce*, April-September, 2003, p. 77.

Nirupam Bajapai, Navi Radjou, Raising Global Competitiveness of Tamil Nadu's IT Industry, *Economic and Political Weekly*, Febraury 2000, pp. 449-65.

Nitin, V. Patil, Computer Based Training and Perspective, *Indian Journal of Training & Development*, October-December 2002, pp. 36-43.

P.C. Panda, Mentoring an Effective HRD tool for Career Development, *Personnel Today*, October-December 1995, pp. 23-24.

P.K. Chatterjee, IT Revolution and HRD Issues and Challenges, *Personnel Today*, January-March 2001, pp. 19-22.

P.L. Rao, National HRD strategy for The New Millennium, *Personnel Today*, January-March 2000, pp. 35-38.

P.N. Singh, HRD Perspectives for Next Millennium, *Indian Journal of Commerce*, October-December 1998, pp. 213-15.

P.N. Shah, HRD Concepts and Context : An Introspection, *Indian Journal of Training and Development*, pp. 23-37.

P. Radhakrishna, Applications of Information Technology, *Information Technology and Methods*, pp. 4-7.

P.S. Yadapadithaya, Strategic Human Resource Development : A Key to Competitive Advantage, *The Indian Journal of Commerce*, 1998, pp. 195-203.

P.S. Hari Haran, Globalisation of Indian Corporate Sector : Requirements for HRD, *Indian Journal of Training and Development*, January-Mar. 2001, pp. 3-20.

P. Seethuraman Sivakumar, Teleconferencing : A New Technology for Extension Training in India, *Indian Journal of Training and Development*, October-December 2002, pp. 55-62.

P.T. Joseph and Sachin Kuchchal, Internet—Opportunities for Business in India—(2nd), *Management & Labour Studies*, July 1998, pp. 410-19.

P.T. Joseph, Sachin Kuchchal, Internet Opportunities for Business in India : A Study, *Management and Labour Studies*, April 1998, pp. 342-55.

Padma Ramanth, HR Outsourcing Moves up the Value Chain, *Business India*, September 29-October 12, 2003, pp. 156-57.

Palaniswamy Kamraj and Sushil, Empirically Testing the Relationship between user Involvement, Information Waste MIS Success, *Journal of Service Research*, April-September 2001, pp. 73-106.

Pantel, Niki, Dawson, Patrick, Video Conferencing Meetings Change Patterns of Business Communication, *New Technology Work and Employment*, July 2001, pp. 88-99.

Parasuraman Balakrishnan, An Information Technology and Teleworking in Malaysia : A Study, *Management and Change*, Winter 2001, pp. 263-76.

Pathak, R.D., Tripathi, S.K.L., Impact of Information Technology and HRD In the Indian Army, *Productivity*, July–September 1998, pp. 291-98.

Patnayak, B., HR Perspeitive in Sustainable Competitive Development—A Proposed Model, *Indian Journal of Industrial Relations*, January 2003, pp. 335-43.

Peretto, P. and Smulders, S., "Technological Distance, Growth, and Scale Effects", *Economic Journal, Journal of Royal Economic Society*, July 2002, pp. 603-24.

Peter, F. Drucker, Next Information Revolution, *Executive Capsule*, May-June 1999, pp. 5-8.

Prasanna Jackson T., R. Venkatapathy, Human Resource Development Attitude and Climate : An Empirical Verification with Reference to Various Types of Organizations, *Small Enterprises Development Management Extension*, March 2000, pp. 47-55.

Praveen Agarwal, Role of IT in HR Management, *The Indian Journal of Commerce*, April-September 2003, p. 79.

Prof. Harish Suryavanshi, The impact of IT on legal Practice, *Information Technology*, April 2004, pp. 84-85.

Prof. K. Rama Krishnan, Greasy hands HRD or, HRD as if workers mattered, *Indian Management*, October 1999, pp. 44-47.

Prof. M.G.K Murthy, Globalisation and HRD, *The Indian Journal of Commerce*, October-December, 1998, pp. 179-86.

Prof. Thomas Fernandez, Training and Development for the New Realities, *Indian Management*, August 1999, pp. 65-67.

Prof. V.D. Dudeja, HR Challenges of IT, *Indian Management*, February 2001, pp. 20-27.

R.G. Desai, Information Technology at Regional level, *Productivity*, April-June 2003, pp. 55-62.

R.L. Bhatia, Training and Development, Management Issues for the New Decade, *Personnel Today*, July–September 1992, pp. 37-38.

R. Nageswara Rao, Human Resource Management Practices in India, *Indian Management*, August 1999, pp. 68-71.

R.P. Saxena, Information Technology as a Strategic Tool for Attaining Success in Global Environment, *Paradigm*, July-December 1999, pp. 95-103.

R. Seeregarajan, Role of Information Technology in Textile Industries—Some Issues, *The Management Accountant*, September 2002, pp. 670-673.

R.V.R. Chandrasekhar Rao, Learning in Information Society, *Indian Journal of Open Learning*, January 2001, pp. 1-18.

Rachid Zeffane, Inter-Organizational Alliance and Networking : The Enabling Role of IT, *Asia Journal of Management*, September 1995, pp. 6-10.

Rahman Zillur, Information Technology Impact Management Awareness *Pranjana the Journal of Social Awareness*, January 1998, pp. 69-82.

Rainer Ommerborn and Rudolf Schuemer, Using computers in Distance Study: Results of a Survey amongst Disabled Distance Students, *Indian Journal of Open Learning*, January 2002, 51-72.

Reema Khurana, Information Technology and Education delivery, *Paradigm*, July-December, 1999, pp. 75-80.

Robert, M. Corderoy and Paul Cooper, The Development of an online Problem-based Learning Environment to support the development of Engineering professional practice skills; *Indian Journal of Open Learning*, September 2000, pp. 339-50.

Rohit Jain, Outsourcing, New I.T. Engine, *Indian Management*, September 1999, pp. 18-30.

Roy, Soumya Sankar, Role of the system Manager in Implementation of Computer-based Information System in Business—A Practitioners Approach." *Survey (Kolkata)* Vol. 41, No. 3-4, 2001, pp. 12-15.

Rozhan Othman, Antecedents and Outcome of I.T. Use: How does HRM fit in, *Asia Pasific Management Review*, Mar 2001, pp. 91-103.

S. Balakrishnan, HRD initiatives in SAIL, *Personnel Today*, pp. 48-52.

S.C. Bhatnagar and H.S. Vegneshwar, Improving-Literacy: Is there a Role for Information Technology, *NIRNAY*, September 1993, pp. 14-26.

S. Datta, A Decision Support System for Facility Location, *Paradigm*, July-December 1999, pp. 12-17.

S.K. Saxena, Mrs. Chanchal Mehra, A model for developing curriculam in Emerging Technology, *Indian Journal of Training & Development*, October-December 2000, pp. 24-31.

S.L. Mahajan, Information Communication Technology in Distance Education in India: A challenge, *Indian Journal of Open Learning*, May 2002, pp. 269-77.

S.P. Gupta and Pithadia, HRD by way of I.T., *The Indian Journal of Commerce*, April-September 2003, p. 84.

S.P. Saha and Diwakar Panjiyar, Civic Education and Information Systems, *The Indian Journal of Commerce*, April-September 2003, p. 84.

S.S. Sree Kumar, Distance Education and Human Resource Development, *Indian Journal of Open Learning*, May 2000, pp. 169-78.

S.S. Thette, B.V. Pawar and R.H. Guptha, E-commerce in India : A Perspective, *The Indian Journal : Commerce*, January-June 2003, pp. 108-14.

S. Umadevi, Globalisation, Information Technology and Asian Indian Woman in US, *Economic Political Weekly*, October 26, 2002, pp. 4421-28.

Sadagopan, S., Information Technology Redefining Boundaries, *Management Review*, June 1999, pp. 237-61.

Sahu, Partha Pratim, Education and Skill Development of Workers Engaged in Small and Tiny Enterprises, *Indian Journal of Labour Economics*, October-December 2002, pp. 1195-1208.

Sami, A. Khan, What HR Manager need to know in The New Millennium, *Paradigm*, July-December 1999, pp. 81-93.

Samoff, Joel and Stromquist Nelly, P., Managing Knowledge and Storing Wisdom, New forms of foreign aid, *Development and Change*, September 2001, pp. 631-56.

Sapna Poti and Nisha Sasidharan, E-HR, *Human Capital*, September 2003, pp. 42-47.

Sarita Singh and Jai B.P. Sinha, Human Resource Development in an Indian Cultural Perspective, *Management and Lobour Studies*, July 1998, pp. 389-99.

Sasi Bhushan Rath, Human Resource Strategy for the Next Millennium, *Indian Management*, July 1998, pp. 73-76.

Saurav Mitra, Information Technology The Hidden Cost, *Paradigm*, July-December 1999, pp. 65-74.

Sayeed Omarbin, Understanding HRD System : A Critical Appraisal of HRD Practices and Facilitator, *VISION (MDI)*, July-December 2002, pp. 87-98.

Seema, S. Singha and D. Singha, HRD Perspectives in the 21st century, *The Indian Journal of Commerce*, October-December 1998, p. 226.

Senguptha, Anil, K., Human Resource Development in 2000 AD, *Samridhi*, Vol. 1, 1998, pp. 1-5.

Sheela, Singh, HRD in Public Sector Undertakings, New Directions, *Management Labour Studies*, February 2003, pp. 37-46.

Singh, Saritha and Sinha, Jai B.P., HRD in an Indian Cultural Perspective, *Management and Labour Studies*, July 1998, pp. 389-99.

Singh, S.P., Technical Education in India Some Emerging Issues, *Indian Journal of Labour Economics*, October-December 2002, pp. 1149-62.

Singh, Surjit, Education Skills and Training : Some Perceptions, *Indian Journal of Labour Economics*, October-December 2002, pp. 1079-94.

Singh, Ajay Kr., Goel. K.K., Moral Values in the Cyber Age : An Empirical Study of the Impact of High moral Values on Efficiency and Effectiveness of 21st Century Managers of different Age Groups in India, *Pranjana*, Vol. 4, 2001, pp. 13-29.

Singh, V.K., Knowledge Management : A Necessity in new Millennium, *Delhi Business Review*, July-December 2001, pp. 91-94.

Singhal and Dange and Pravin, E-manafacturing : New Paradigm for Design and Supply Chains, *Pranjana (AIMT)*, January-June 2002, pp. 15-37.

Sruti Chaganti, Information Technology Act, *Economic and Political Weekly*, August 2003, pp. 3587-95.

Sujit Sen and Sailendra Saxena, Positive Self-regard as an Instrument of HRD, *Personnel Today*, July-September 1996, pp. 20-24.

T. Raju and Sangeetha Mohandas, T., Knowledge Management—Sowing the New Seeds of Technology, *Indian Journal of Training and Development*, October-December 2002, pp. 22-29.

T. Beckmuratov, Akodirov and B.O. Ismailov, Choice of Information Systems for Rural Geographical Database, *Small Enterprises, Development Management and Extension*, June 1999, pp. 101-06.

T.V. Rao, HRD needs for Employment-oriented Education, *Indian Journal of Training and Development*, July-August 1989, pp. 16-22.

Talloo, T.J., Contemporary issues in Information Technology, *Pranjana (IAMT)*, January-June 2002, pp. 39-49.

Tanuja Agarwal, HRM: Emerging Trends, *Indian Journal of Industrial Relations*, January 2002, pp. 315-31.

Teena Gomes, IT Education for the rich and the poor, *Information Technology*, February 2004, pp. 28-32.

Teo Thomon, S.H., Impact of Information Technology on Management Control, *Productivity*, January-March 1999, pp. 567-74.

Tomohiro Ohashi, Electronic government in Japan for better public service, *Productivity*, April-June 2000, pp. 38-45.

Tridib Chottopadhyaya and Chandra Lekha Mohante, Virtual Reality: A future Progency of Information Technology, *Indian Library Association Bulletin*, June-September 2003, pp. 28-32.

Unni Jeemed Rani, Uma, Globalisation Information Technology Revolution and Services Sector in India, *Indian Journal of Labour Economics*, October-December 2000, pp. 803-28.

Usha Mujoo-Munshi, Manju Kanth, "Information Seeking in Electronic Environments", *Libray Herald*, October 1996-March 1997, pp. 100-10.

V.K. Singh, Seema Pandey and Sujoy Bhattacharya, Human Dimensions in Information Age, *The Indian Journal of Commerce*, April-September 2003, p. 86.

Varsha Mehta, Management Education in 21st Century : An Information Technology Perspective, *The Indian Journal of Commerce*, January-March 1999.

Vikrant Saxena and T.B. Bhat, e-commerce; Implications for India, *The Indian Journal of Commerce*, October-December 2000, pp. 70-87.

Vimmy Sahay, Information Technology Society, *Executive Capsule*, May, pp. 36-39.

Vira Komarraju, The New breed IT Professional, *Human Capital*, September 2003, pp. 48-52.

Vishal, Rajan and Kumar, Rajesh, IT-Revolution in Rural India Researched, *The Business Economist Annual, 2003*, pp. 82-85.

Vittal, N., Human, Dimensions in the Information Age; *Delhi Business Review*, January-June 2001, pp. 640-74.

Wegenberger, Mag Josef, Potential Appraisal and Development Seminar : A Challenges for HRD In Future, *Prestige Journal of Management and Research*, April 1998, pp. 62-63.

Wu Steven Hung-chi, IT applications in SMEs Impact of e-commerce and corresponding solutions, *Productivity*, July-September 2001, pp. 256-64.

Y.V.S.S. Prasada Rao, K. Ravindranath, Technology—Some Issues, *UDYOGA PRAGATI*, July-September 2002. pp. 18-22.

Index